georges joubert

SKIING

AN ART...   A TECHNIQUE

Poudre Publishing Company
LaPorte, Colorado   80535

Original title: *Le Ski: Un Art...   Une Technique*
Copyright © Georges Joubert, 1978
              35 Chemin de Halage
              38000 Grenoble, France

First United States Edition

T6/80

English translation by JAMES MAJOR
                       SIM THOMAS
                       DOUG SMITH

All photographs, photomontages and illustrations by
Georges Joubert.
Cover design by MACPIE GRENOBLE.
Cover photographs by DEL MULKEY, ERIC VODINH, IFOT,
DIATEC Agency, Grenoble.

Library of Congress Cataloging in Publication Data

Georges, Joubert
   Skiing: An Art...   A Technique

   1. Skis and Skiing.   2. Ski Instruction.
Library of Congress Catalog Card No.: 79-90394
ISBN 0-935240-01-2

Printed in the United States of America

Poudre

Poudre Publishing Company
LaPorte, Colorado   80535

by

Georges JOUBERT

President of the Grenoble University Club
Technical Director of the Grenoble University Club
Professor of the Scientific and Medical University of Grenoble

In collaboration with

The coaches of the Grenoble University Club

ALIX BERTHET • ROGER BUSSMANN • DENIS FUMEX
FRANCOIS MEZEI • DESIRE ROSSI • PASCAL VANAKER

English translation by

James Major • Sim Thomas • Doug Smith

other titles by Georges Joubert:

SKI TECHNIQUE MODERNE — 1956
SKI ABC TECHNIQUE MODERNE — 1958
SKI MODERNE — 1960
VICTOIRE OLYMPIQUE — 1961
SAVOIR SKIER — 1963
HOW TO SKI THE NEW FRENCH WAY — 1967
TEACH YOURSELF TO SKI — 1971

CONTENTS

Part 2
LEARN TO SKI EFFECTIVELY
OFF THE TRAIL AND IN COMPETITION

Part 3
DO YOU WANT TO BE AN INSTRUCTOR ?

Part 4
TECHNICAL DOCUMENTS FOR SPECIALISTS

        • A few biomechanical considerations (285) • Movements in the fore-aft plane. The modern flexion. The forward thrust of the feet (288) • Vertical movements. Unweighting and compression (290) • The muscle mechanisms that pivot the skis (294).

INTRODUCTION

In 1957, Georges Joubert coauthored a revolutionary new book, Ski Technique Moderne, *with the French ski racer Juan Vuarnet who later became an Olympic Gold Medalist and directed the Italian National Ski Team to international dominance in alpine skiing.* Ski Technique Moderne *launched Joubert's career as the world's foremost ski teacher and technician. In the following years he authored 6 more books, which have been translated into 13 languages, plus countless technical articles which have appeared in nearly all of the major ski magazines of the world.*

In this, his eighth and most comprehensive book to date, Joubert has delivered the most monumental treatise on skiing ever published. It is inconceivable that anyone other than Joubert, with his extensive experience as a teacher, coach and technician, could duplicate this effort.

Joubert has done it all. He has established himself as one of the world's most successful coaches, graduating several skiers to the French National Ski Team, including world champions Patrick Russel and Perrine Pelen. But like all of the best coaches, Joubert remains first and foremost a student of the sport. Every season he can be found alongside the race courses of all the major international ski competitions with motorized camera and notebook in hand.

SKIING: AN ART... A TECHNIQUE *is more a product, however, of Joubert's years of training ski coaches and instructors at the University of Grenoble where he is a Professor of Physical Education and where, among other duties, he directs what is likely the world's largest ski school through the Grenoble University Club. It's in this exceptional environment where he has been able to reduce the latest technical innovations of the champions in international ski competition to elements which can be systematically taught to all skiers to make them more effective on all terrain and in all conditions. The result, which comprises the bulk of this text, is the most progressive ski teaching system ever devised; yet, through extensive field testing at Grenoble University, it is a system with proven effectiveness.*

Joubert has consistently been the most innovative ski teacher and technician in the world and, as such, his ideas have often been ahead of their time. Nevertheless, history has invariably proven him to be correct with the result that the techniques first described by Joubert, and the names that he gave to them, have been integrated into the official ski teaching systems of all the major skiing nations of the world.

Translating the original French text of this monumental work into English has been a joint effort which took place on 3 continents. Two remarkable American ski coaches, James Major and Sim Thomas, worked with me on this project. Both raced in Europe and trained and studied under Professor Joubert at the University of Grenoble. James went on to direct the European factory racing service department of the world's largest ski manufacturer and became the only American ever to coach a foreign national ski team. In recent years, he has authored numerous technical articles which have appeared in ski magazines both in the United States and in Europe and he recently co-authored a new book, World Cup Ski Technique: Learn and Improve (Poudre, 1979) which has already been published in 5 languages.

Since graduating from the University of Grenoble, where he was captain of the Grenoble University Club Ski Team, Sim Thomas has established himself as one of America's foremost ski coaches. Racing programs that he has directed have graduated several skiers to the United States and Canadian National Ski Teams and, since Sim translated the only Joubert books to have been published in English editions, How To Ski The New French Way (1967) and Teach Yourself To Ski (1971), he was uniquely qualified to assist in this project.

Insofar as possible, we have attempted to use terminology that is consistent with that used in the American Teaching Method of the Professional Ski Instructors of America. Nevertheless, since we are principally ski coaches, rather than instructors, it is doubtful that we have always succeeded in selecting terms that are in most common usage in American ski schools. Occasionally we have coined new terms to describe techniques and concepts which have never been fully defined in English and, in some instances, we have opted to retain the original French terms used by Joubert with the thought that they may find their way into the American ski jargon, just as other terms introduced by Joubert, such as avalement, vissage and braquage, have.

Likewise, we have attempted to retain, as much as possible, the terminology used in the English language editions of Joubert's last two books. Due to the tremendous technical evolution that skiing has experienced since they were published, however, we often found ourselves trying to describe concepts which have never been articulated in English. In all cases, we have attempted to capture the true meaning of the original text rather than limit ourselves to leteral translations.

Doug Smith
Former Director of Racer Development
United States Alpine Ski Team

FOREWORD

In 1956, Emile Allais, the brilliant innovator in ski instruction, agreed to write the preface for a revolutionary but very intricate new book which I had just finished writing with my friend Juan Vuarnet. At the time, Vuarnet was a member of the French National Ski Team.

In 1960, Jean and I wrote a 3rd work intended for the general public and made possible by the publicity surrounding his Olympic victory at Squaw Valley. Our readership already included people from all over the world, as our previous works had been published in five different languages and extracts had appeared in most of the foreign ski magazines.

Two new and equally succesful books followed in 1963 and 1966.

In 1968, Jean Vuarnet temporarily set aside his work with the Avoriaz ski resort, which he had founded, in order to assume the directorship of the Italian National Ski Team. His exceptional success in that position is well known.

As for myself, I continued to coach the racers of the Grenoble University Club who competed successfully against the strongest ski area racing programs in France.

It was in 1970, after having developed four skiers named simultaneously to the French National Ski Team, that I decided to write a new book, probably even more revolutionary than our work published in 1956. In this work, entitled Teach Yourself To Ski, *I already included the basic principles of avalement which I had presented and named in 1966 in my book* How To Ski The New French Way, *whereas no other ski technician had even noticed the movement at that time. Three years later, avalement had become a part of the national ski teaching methods throughout the world, except in France.*

Published in 13 different languages and gratified by the success of Patrick Russel, who became the top slalom racer in the world in 1970 and 1971, and by the vctories of my Grenoble University students at the University World Championships, I thought that I might take some time to catch my breath.

It was at this time that Maurice Martel, president of the French Ski Federation, and Jean Vuarnet, recently returned from Italy, induced me to accept the directorship of the French national teams. Though appearing healthy, the men's team was already in very poor shape. The decline had begun as early as 1968. At that time, our men's team dominated all other nations in slalom and giant slalom. Among the top 75 racers in the world, we had 15 ranked in slalom and 12 in giant slalom. The Austrians had 13 and 9, the Swiss 10 and 10 and Italy 7 and 8. In downhill we were very close to the Swiss and ahead of the Austrians and Italians. By 1972, the situation had reversed entirely. We had moved into last place in downhill and giant slalom. In slalom, the Swiss and Austrians were catching us and the Italians had already overtaken us. In all 3 alpine disciplines — slalom, giant slalom and downhill — French racers ranked among the top 75 numbered only 30 compared to 41 in 1968, while the Austrians numbered 46 compared to 34, the Italians 39 compared to 22, and the Swiss 36. At the time, a very poor relationship existed between the racers and the directors of our teams. On two different occasions, the racers had "fired" their team director. Given the French Ski Federations incompetence, it was foolish to believe that the national program could be straightened out at that time. As a matter of fact, I had made this very statement in a television interview just a few weeks before.

I do not regret having had the experience. In two seasons, I succeeded in gathering together a group of very competent managers and coaches. We had the support of the majority of the members of the team. Their improvement was spectacular. I do regret, however, that open warfare, declared by a few stars of the team against the coaches and team officials, led to extreme decisions which prompted certain "politicians" of the ski federation to reduce our already meager budget by 20%.

Lacking the minimum funding to meet my responsibilities, I resigned. The same politicians then engineered the removal from their positions with the French Ski Federation of my colleagues in the administration of the national team program, Maurice Martel, Juan Vuarnet and Roger Chastagnol.

However, the door to international ski competition had been opened to me and made it considerably easier to continue my research in ski technique and coaching. In particular, I was able to observe at close hand the development of the brilliant Italian team as well as the rise of the super champion Ingemar Stenmark.

Upon my return to the University in 1974, I was given the responsibility of instructing the first students to become professors of physical education specialized in skiing. I worked within the School of Medicine and Science of the University of Grenoble and was able to launch a program of research in ski technique and teaching method which led to the writing of this new book.

At the same time, young coaches who I had developed in collaboration with Roger Bussmann, Technical Director of the Grenoble University Club junior racing program, succeeded brilliantly in preparing young Perrine Pelen who, at the age of 16 and 17 years and 7 years after Patrick Russel, became the number one slalom skier in the world.

This success, which followed that of Fabienne Serrat in 1974, could not, however, prevent the decline of the French National Ski Team. This decline, which began in 1968 for the men and in 1974 for the women, was caused essentially by incompetence and self-satisfaction among the direcotors of the French Ski Federation, the coaches of the teams and the officials responsible for ski instruction in France.

Certainly the current "pholosophy" of youngsters in France is not conducive to the sacrifices required in top international competition, especially when accompanied by the intolerable paternalism of sports officials today. I believe, nevertheless, that these youngsters have pride and are capable of real accomplishments if given a true basic sports education so that they can then accept the responsibility for themselves.

A sport is a personal thing, as much for the beginner as for the champion and, even though this book is directed very little toward champions, I hope that the approach can benefit them as much as any other skier.

May this book contribute to the re-emergence of French competitive skiing !

Georges JOUBERT

What is new in skiing ?

Almost without having to learn, people seem to know how to ski !

Beginners are no longer viewed as objects for derision.

It would seem that skiing has become a new mores, that our children are born knowing how to ski.

In the past, people learned to swim by being suspended at the surface of the water and practicing their strokes to the count of the swimming instructor, often seated on a stool in the shade. Today beginners glide over the water, swim underwater, then, without further effort, swim like you and me while beginning swimmers of the past spent months "swimming in place". What has happened ?

There is no doubt that a barrier has been broken down.

A psychological barrier ? Perhaps. The primary difficulties of any undertaking are those which we impose on ourselves. Why did a one night bivouac exhaust mountain climbers 40 years ago when now they remain in good shape after 6 or 7 nights ? Within a group of skiing friends, the person who started skiing the latest quickly catches up to his comrades. Being able to ski has become natural, just like driving or swimming. Can one accept to remain unnatural ? The time is past when knowing how to ski was something special. One should know how to ski. Learning is just a formality.

Isn't it likely that a technical or instructional barrier existed ? This fact becomes obvious to one who can remember, for example, that in France as late as 1956 ski school participants were not allowed to plant their poles and were told to "get forward" and to throw their arms in large movements. No one protested. Everybody suffered while a beginner, and if you didn't like it you taught yourself to ski, often more rapidly and more efficiently but in an unacceptable fashion, until you finally returned to the fold in your attempts to ski like those demi-Gods, the ski instructors.

Sports instruction has changed

I would have preferred the title "skiing instruction has changed". I couldn't use it, however, because only a small minority of ski instructors have passed beyond the level of the swimming instructors whom I described in the previous section. Only a few have become sports educators. For many, the desire to teach stereotyped movements is more important than teaching the client to ski effectively. The national technique, that is to say the chosen target movement, and the national teaching method, a rigid progression of exercises leading to the target movement, are considered more important than the personality of the learning skier, the initiative of the instructor, and even the profound nature of skiing. The instructor becomes the preacher of a false religion. The technician and ski technique researcher becomes the heretic.

The French government even named a great leader of the inquisition, the protector of French ski instruction. I was declared a heretic as early as 1952 ! Today, the world is full of heretics.

The so-called GLM, or graduated length method of instruction developed in the United States and employing skis of gradually increasing length, did a great deal to free French instructors from their subservience to the official technique. It was actually possible to learn to ski in another manner and to learn more quickly. The considerable success of compact skis carried on from this point. It was very easy to pivot the skis and even to wedel after just a few days experience. Using a whole series of exercises is no longer considered indispensable. It is enough to convince the learner to dare, and then expose him to a wide enough variety of conditions to discover those movements which are essential to skiing.

Next, it was discovered that this approach does not necessarily require the use of compact skis. With slightly longer and more stable skis the learner is easily able to develop more speed and thus perform the movements just as easily as could be done with short skis.

Thus, the skier learns almost without instruction. How does one help learning

14

skiers and respect their individual approaches at the same time ? That, today, is the real problem for the technician and instructor.

A problem of communication between the instructor and the learner.

Any intelligent instructor has always known that in a private lesson it is best to address the learner directly, to put himself or herself in the learner's shoes through a complete understanding of the difficulties of learning to ski and to give the learner common sense tips rather than comments only from the approved method. In a class situation, however, it is almost impossible to instruct in this manner if one must respect the approved technique to the letter.

As early as 1963, in our book Savoir Skier, *Juan Vuarnet and I decided to break with the tradition of describing skiing movements as seen from the outside. We described only the feelings which the skier must sense in order to perform the movement. The difference between these two approaches is considerable. For example, instead of asking the learner to perform a down-up motion, one asks him or her to push his feet against the snow "as if to jump into the air".*

The learner is given a mental image an image made up of feellings which is much more liable to result in a correct performance of the movement.

This new language between instructors and learners is being used more and more.

If it creates a new logic in the linking of the suggestions which the instructor makes to the student, it is an internal logic for the learner and not the rigid reasoning of the creators of the approved method.

A new goal: help the learner through his own personal experience

How does one really learn to ski, to avoid falling, to turn, to wedel, to improve beyond a few rudimentary movements to the full potential of the marvelous machine which is the human body, or more exactly man ?

This is the essential problem which we have approached over the last few years. The systematic collection of data based on thousands of observations and the precise analysis of the results of hundreds of teaching experiments have permitted us to derive a concept, an understanding of the process of learning naturally to ski through experience. The process is not linear, but involves a thousand variations corresponding perfectly to the variety among human individuals and their behavior.

This new concept has not disturbed our approach to instruction which remains above all "experimental". But the concept has helped to emphasize the essential character of our approach. It has also permitted a greater unity in our instruction; whether beginner, intermediate or advanced, the learner discovers a certain number of similar movements which gradually increase in complexity. The importance of such a discovery should be obvious.

Skiing is more an art than a technique

For half the people who ski, the sport is an artistic expression like figure skating or dancing. For others, it is utilitarian or a search for efficiency.

There is a very fine distinction between an artistic expression and art.

The distinction remains because the concept of ski technique remained too mechanical to be applied to an art.

Today all that is changed.

The skier's talent will permit him to develop his technique just as the musician, the painter or the dancer does.

This does not diminish the importance of technique. No one criticizes the musician who practices for hours in order to refine his ability to play his instrument. Technique is fundamental, but it is only a means to an end.

From the moment of your very first attempts, I am going to try to awaken this inspiration in you which can turn you into a great skier, or at least greatly increase the pleasure you derive from skiing.

The great champions are artists

What skier was able to contain his admiration a few years ago, while watching Gustavo Thoeni, or is able to do so today while watching Ingemar Stenmark play with the difficulties in a slalom which the other competitors wildly attack like savages ? Who wasn't aware of the touch of genius in some of Franz Klammer's downhill runs ?

Like other geniuses in painting, music and sculpture, these artists make ski technique evolve. Some perfect the technique of their predecessors to a supreme degree. Others innovate and leave their personal imprint on a new age.

It is not high treason to analyze the technique of these masters. Certainly it is inspiration that makes them artists, but without a means of expression, that is without technique, how would they express their inspiration ?

The same is true for you.

Give yourself the means to express the joy, harmony and communion with nature which you feel on the snow just as does the bird in the air.

If I succeed in helping you in this discovery, I will have attained my goal.

TECHNIQUE, ELEGANCE AND SECURITY.

Ski technique should not be reserved for those who are obsessed with efficiency, for speed fanatics or for ski racers, for whom one hundredth of a second can be critical.

Technique can also emphasize the charm of a figure; and bring safety when skiing the snows of a glacier where even a minor fall can be very serious.

TECHNIQUE AND PURITY OF MOVEMENT.

These two photos of Olympic Champion Piero Gros show how an efficient gesture can also be elegant; even during the wild combat of Olympic competition. Memorize the silhouette of this great champion: it is perfectly representative of modern skiing.

I DISCOVER
AND CULTIVATE
THE ART OF SKIING WELL

BECOME A SKIER QUICKLY

It's easy to become a skier.

What is your first problem ? It is to keep your balance on your skis. To solve this problem, venture into this new world where the ground flees under your feet: the world of sliding.

Your problem will be less one of learning new movements than of conditioning your behavior in a new manner. This is why, with simple trial and error and without any outside help, you can begin to ski.

However, what you learn should, over the long run, form a homogeneous whole. You should be effective now, but also properly prepared for later improvement. You must avoid the obstacles which prevent 30% of all intermediate skiers from improving further. If you follow my suggestions, the elements you acquire will fit together like the pieces of a puzzle.

This puzzle with gradually increase in complexity as you pursue each piece, that is each element, more deeply.

Let me suggest the following objectives:

• On very flat slopes: slide with suppleness; wind your way down the slope in wide turns.

• On difficult slopes, learn to check or brake your speed by turning quickly out of the fall line.

On moderate slopes, check your speed, then turn. Use the bumps.

Once you have attained these goals, you will be able to ski any slope you like.

A few preliminary suggestions to get you started right.

Have you selected an appropriate ski area ?

Not all ski areas satisfy the needs of beginning skiers. Does the area you have selected provide sufficiently long and flat slopes ? Are the lifts appropriate for beginners ? Are they properly maintained ? Are they within easy access of hotels or the day lodge and not stuck off on some distant summit ? Are they lighted by the sun for a good portion of the day ? Is the snow generally packed powder ? With this last point in mind, high altitude ski areas are usually superior. Is the terrain in the area generally demanding or is it easier, allowing the beginning skier to remain more confident and relaxed ?

These are some of the questions you should ask your friends or other advisors before taking off on your adventure in learning to ski.

Select appropriate equipment.

Skis: If you're aggressive, athletic and not afraid of speed, choose normal or intermediate length skis.

If you are cautious, choose intermediate or compact length skis.

If you're not at all athletic, use compacts.

The shorter your skis, the more manueverable they will be, but you will not feel confident on them at higher speeds. Note, however, that speed facilitates most manuevers on skis.

This idea is the basis of the graduated length methods of learning to ski. The necessity of becoming accustomed to a new pair of skis at each level is the only inconvenience. In my opinion, the improvement of a beginning skier today can be very rapid if the problems of balancing are avoided. Thus, I recommend intermediate length skis which are flexible at the ends but of normal stiffness through the mid-body. Such skis are equal to the height of the skier plus 10 to 15 centimeters. In any case, the skis should be in perfect condition. The bases must be perfectly smooth and flat so that they can be easily manuevered on the surface of the snow.

Boots: Don't buy racing boots. They're too stiff for you. Buy the most modern plastic boots but be sure they are flexible and comfortable. Before purchasing them, put them on and walk around in the store for as long as possible.

Then wear them around the house as much as you can to get used to them. Once you start on snow, the boots won't seem so cumbersome and you will be able to concentrate better on your first attempts at skiing.

Bindings: Don't try to save money on the purchase of bindings. Buy the best. Have your shop adjust them at the loosest possible setting for your weight and ask how to tighten the adjustment if the ski falls off too easily during your first on-snow experiences.

Are you in adequate physical condition ?

You mustn't count on skiing to get back in shape. You would only be risking injury. On the contrary, you should improve your physical condition before going skiing. If you are, or if you have been athletic, go back to your favorite sport; tennis, bicycling, volley ball, calisthenics or jogging. If you've never been athletic, take some vigorous walks every chance you get. If you don't have much time, use your imagination. You'll find other solutions. My own approach to the problem is to try to beat the elevator up and down the 13 floors of my apartment building.

Should you take lessons ?

If you're athletic and aggressive, and prefer to act on your own, my answer to you would be a resounding no !

If you're enthusiastic and confident and tend to succeed in most undertakings you could start without the help of this book. You could always refer back to the book if you run into difficulty.

Otherwise, follow my suggestions to the letter.

If you like to be directed, advised and encouraged, take a lesson or seek the help of a good friend. But don't be mistaken. It is definitely you who must overcome your fears, control your nerves and muscles and even learn from your mistakes.

Before attempting your first downhill runs, walk around on the flats with your skis on.

Little by little, these long planks will become lighter and less cumbersome. You will become accustomed to having your feet held straight ahead rather than being angled slightly outward. You will have adopted the sliding step which results from the fact that your ski boot heels are fixed to the skis. Your ski poles will get in your way to begin with, but you will gradually learn to use them to help maintain your balance. By picking up first one ski and displacing it laterally and then the other, you will learn to change direction. And by pushing off with your poles at the slightest hint of a slope, you will get a taste of the delightful sensation of sliding.

GUIDE TO SKI LENGTH
Choice of ski length as a function of height.

Every skier falls into one of the 3 following categories according to height, body build, ability level and temperament:

1st Category:
— beginning and intermediate skiers and good but timid skiers.
— skiers with light body builds.

2nd Category:
— skiers who fall between the extremes of categories 1 and 3.

3rd Category:
— expert skiers and very aggressive intermediate skiers.
— skiers with heavy body builds.

(ski lengths in cm.)

Skier's height	Traditional skis			Intermediate skis			Compact skis		
	Cat. 1	Cat. 2	Cat. 3	Cat. 1	Cat. 2	Cat. 3	Cat. 1	Cat. 2	Cat. 3
4'11'	175	180	185	165	170	175	150	155	160
5' 1"	180	185	190	165	175	185	155	160	165
5' 3"	185	190	195	170	180	185	160	165	170
5' 5"	190	195	200	175	185	190	165	170	175
5' 7"	195	200	203	180	190	195	170	175	180
5' 9"	200	203	205	185	195	200	175	180	185
5'11" +	203	205	207	190	195	200	180	185	190

Ski pole length.
The poles should extend to ¾ the skier's height plus or minus 1 inch.

Try your first straight runs !

You already know how to walk around on your skis on the flat and how to turn them by stepping around and you have discovered how helpful your arms and poles can be in maintaining your balance. You are now ready to try the slopes; first climbing, and finally descending.

I have already emphasized, and emphasize again, the importance of choosing an appropriate slope for your first attempts at straight running. The slope should be a genuine beginners' trail, and beginners' areas do not exist everywhere. Watch other skiers. Be sure that the slope is not too steep, causing them to gain too much speed. Also be sure that the slope gradually flattens out so that the skier need do nothing other than to ride out onto the flat to stop.

There are 2 methods of hiking up the hill.

Once the slope becomes so steep that you can not walk straight uphill, the simplest and least tiring solution is to sidestep. You stand sideways on the slope and step your skis one after the other up the hill, stepping on the uphill edge of each in order to avoid sliding sideways. The edges of your skis will leave a series of horizontal tracks in the snow.

Another, more tiring manner of climbing up the hill, but one which will help to condition the muscles most often used in skiing, is the herringbone. Facing directly up the hill, you walk with your tips spread to the outside and the heels of your skis close together. The skis thus form a V and you use your inside edges to bite into the snow. By pushing behind you with your ski poles, you decrease the risk of sliding backwards.

Once you have climbed the first half, the first third or even the first 30 feet of the slope, plant your poles down the hill in front of you and gradually step the tails of your skis around until you are facing down the hill, supported by your poles. Check to see that your skis are spread about a foot apart.

This is the moment of truth !

You are going to take off into an unknown world, the world of sliding, which is just as unusual for man as the underwater world or the world of flying. It's not surprising, then, that you feel a bit apprehensive. Nothing I could say to you would help at this moment.

Just let go and let it happen !

Let yourself slide. As you do, you will feel unusual sensations under your feet. You have difficulty maintaining your balance, especially because of the movements of your skis which seem to have a mind of their own. Nevertheless, you have a 90% chance of arriving at the bottom of the slope and feeling your skis gradually slow down and finally stop on the flat.

If you have the misfortune of losing your balance and starting to fall, don't resist and tense your body. On the contrary, you should relax your legs and sit down on the side you are falling. Later, you will learn to intelligently avoid falling without risking injury, but for now, this is not the case. Once seated in the snow, pull your skis around so that they are across the slope below you. Stand up, support yourself with your poles, and take off again.

Now that you have experienced sliding, try again and try to feel more relaxed.

The problem is no longer just psychological, it becomes technical and at this instant you have a choice between a purely instinctive approach characterized by unconscious trial and error and a controlled and conscious approach with which I can help you considerably.

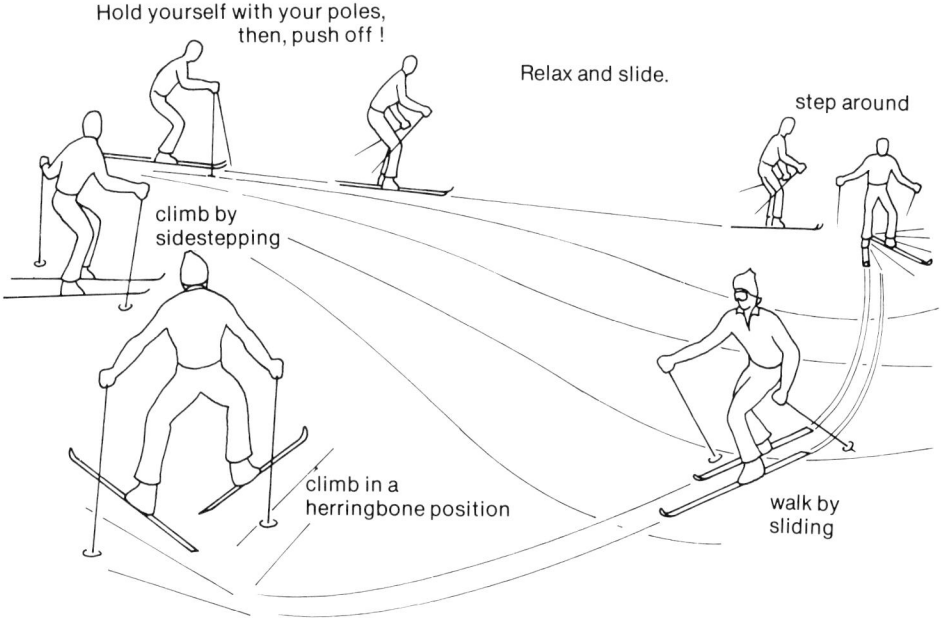

Hold yourself with your poles, then, push off !

Relax and slide.

step around

climb by sidestepping

climb in a herringbone position

walk by sliding

I can perhaps help you more than the instructor whose words, under these circumstances, contribute nothing more than an encouraging background noise, whereas the concentration and analysis required in working from a book results in a more active participation of the learner.

I am referring here to a partially controlled approach, because while it is possible to avoid some gross errors, it is impossible to directly effect man's intricate balancing system which involves millions of nerve endings and thousands of motor commands per second.

My suggestions are aimed at helping you to acquire the ability to balance as quickly as possible. This ability is the essential skill of all skiers.

Can you expect help from a friend or advisor to be effective ?

If you are naturally very cautious, friendly encouragement could help you to take off down the hill in your straight runs or to get up and take off after a fall. But this kind of help does not always work, and I've seen many attempts at encouragement which have had only negative effects.

As for physical help, that is grabbing the hand of a good skier or some other form of support, do so only after repeated failure or insurmountable fear. Technically, this kind of help is not necessarily ineffective, but since you must, sooner or later, solve the problems yourself, it's just as well to try to overcome them yourself.

Balance, the primary basis of ski technique, is learned through sliding practice. You must slide and slide and slide.

Practice sliding until you are relaxed and comfortable.

Learn to supply control the direction of your skis.

You have almost completely overcome your fears and inhibitions. You are no longer faced with that awesome adventure for any beginner of discovering how to slide. You are somewhat more detached from the problem and ready to improve.

Concentrate on your feet!

Your development as a skier is directly dependent on your ability to use your feet as sensitive feelers and effective motor elements because they are in the most direct contact with your skis.

Try, then, to feel the sliding of your skis with your feet. In order to do so, distribute your weight over the soles of your boots, just as you do when standing upright on the ground. Try to feel precisely this same weight distribution while sliding.

Slight forward and backward oscillations should permit you to identify two pressure zones; one, on the forward part of your foot, underneath the ball, and the second behind, underneath your heel. In order to maintain your balance, you must constantly maintain pressure on both of these zones on both feet. An important point to remember: don't lean on the fronts or backs of your boots; you would develop this bad habit very quickly. In these positions, certain muscles groups are contracted and prevent your development of good balance.

Discover the flexed stance of the skier, muscles ready to react.

Little by little, you should recognize that in order to maintain this balanced distribution of pressure over your feet, your body

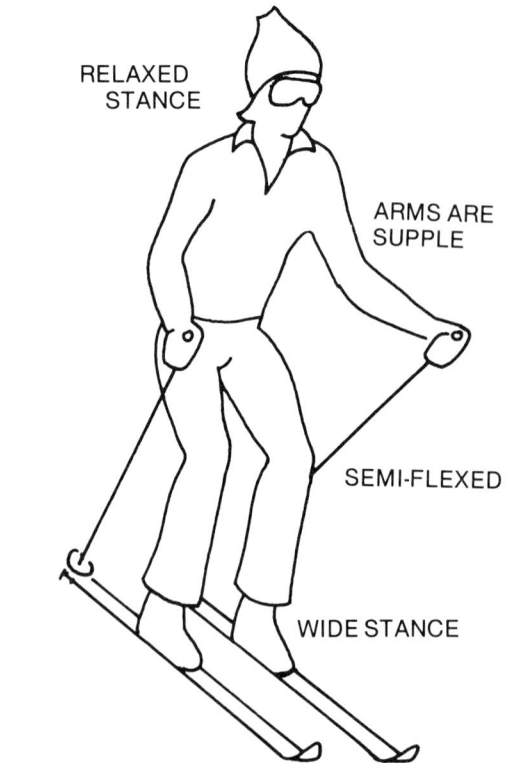

RELAXED STANCE

ARMS ARE SUPPLE

SEMI-FLEXED

WIDE STANCE

must be in a slightly flexed position. You should feel a certain degree of "play" in your ankles, knees and hips.

In order for this play to occur in these joints, your leg muscles must be in an aroused state; a state of very slight contraction and, at the same time, relaxation. Only a slightly flexed position allows this. Be careful, however to avoid two possible extremes. In one, the muscle contraction is excessive and your muscles become stiff. In the second, excessive relaxation forces you to ski in a body position that is too straight and leaves you vulnerable to even the slightest unbalancing force.

At 5 miles per hour, just like the racer at 60, try to relax and feel the two pressure zones on the front and back of your feet over the insole of your boot.

THE KNEES AND
ANKLES ARE
RELAXED

THE SKIS
REMAIN
"FREE"

THE GLIDING
WEDGE

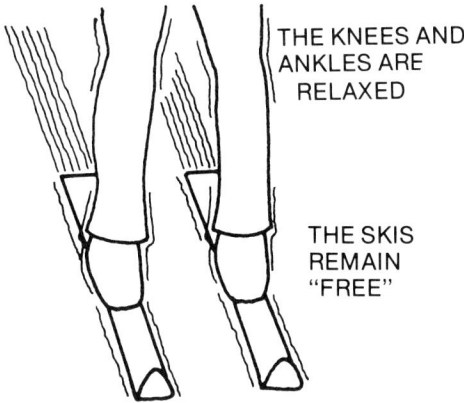

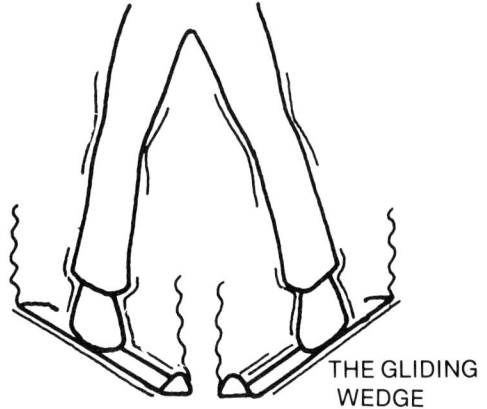

Flexible control of the skis

The proper use of your feet allows you to control the sliding of your skis with suppleness. This type of control contrasts with that in which the skis are held too rigidly and controlled too strictly by the foot of the skier. You should be able to feel your skis reacting to the slightest variations in terrain. You should feel them move laterally and then be pulled back into the line of descent in an elastic fashion by your feet. We refer to this as a supple control of the skis. We emphasize the importance of this use of the feet to supply control the skis, not only for beginners but for skiers of all levels and in particular racers, who are in a constant search for this capacity to slide well, although few of them find it. This very simple idea is absolutely fundamental to learning to ski effectively.

A valuable exercise, the gliding wedge.

In order for you to become aware of this idea of supple control, I suggest that you make long straight runs in a wedged position with your skis held as flat as possible on the snow. You should try to avoid even the slightest braking action. In this manuever, called a "gliding wedge", the oscillations of your skis and the reactions of your feet are amplified. If you have top quality modern boots, which are high and stiff, unfasten the upper 2 or 3 buckles. You will sense the reactions of your feet more easily and improve more quickly.

Try to discover the balancing role of your arms.

Nature has provided you with 2 very effective balancing poles, just like the tight rope walker. Don't hesitate to use them. If you become accustomed to allowing your arms to simply hang at your sides, you will not develop the lateral balancing reflexes for which they, along with your shoulders and even your back, are responsible. Try, therefore, to adopt the rather wide arm position represented in our illustrations.

If you do so, it will be easier for you to learn to use your poles after the next few days. This position also results in that state of muscular arousal which I already mentioned and which will allow you to react more quickly and discover valuable balancing reflexes.

Your skis should not be held firmly in one direction by your feet. They should be free to "float", bases flat on the snow.

Last tip: look for fairly long beginner slopes.

At the beginning of each straight run, you feel an acceleration; and at the end a deceleration. These sensations are a bit bothersome to you, whereas during a straight run down a very flat continuous slope you feel pretty good. Try an experiment. After sliding for 10 or 20 yards, and having attained your terminal speed, try to close your eyes and concentrate on the feelings in your feet, the muscles of your legs and arms, and think of the width of your stance on your skis and the flexible "play" of your skis over the snow.

Discover the drift to the fall line.

You have now spent several hours practicing straight running. You feel fairly relaxed and confident enough to try something new. You're right.

On a fairly wide slope, you're going to begin to slide, not straight downhill but somewhat sideways; to the left, for example. Your goal is to gradually change direction to the right, finally running straight down the hill or, in skiing jargon, straight down the fall line.

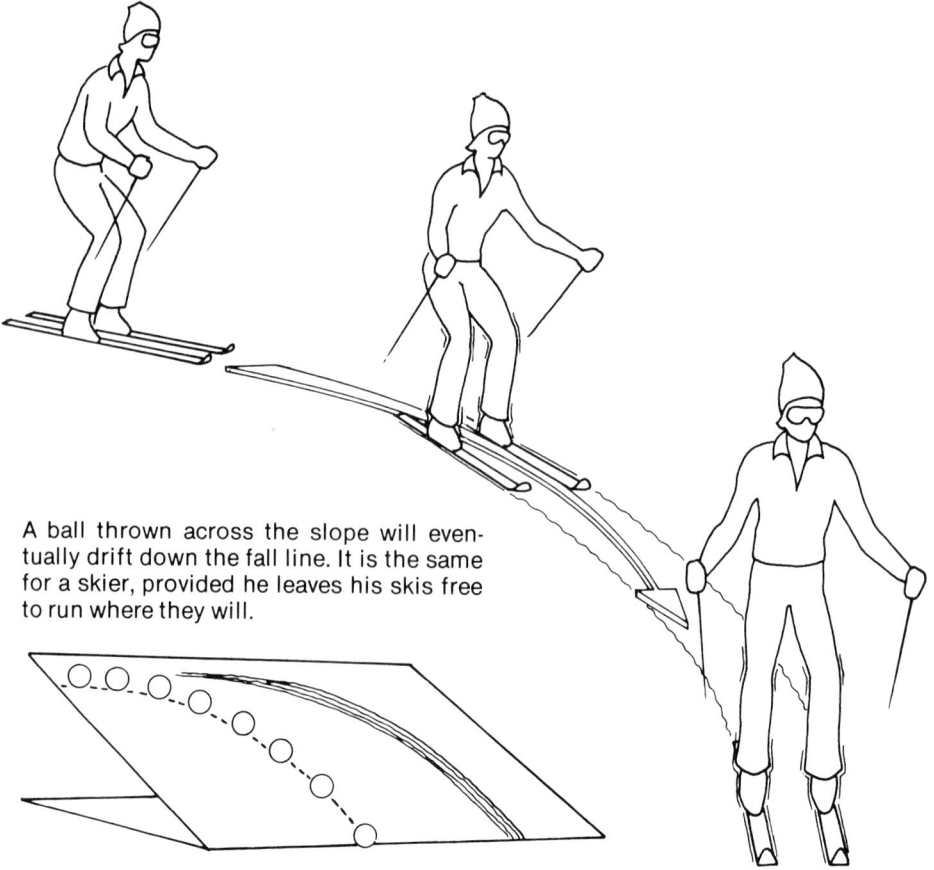

A ball thrown across the slope will eventually drift down the fall line. It is the same for a skier, provided he leaves his skis free to run where they will.

Sliding along a traversing path, relax your legs and feel your skis and body pulled into the fall line.

What do you do to make this happen? Nothing! Simply make sure that your legs are slightly flexed and supple, that your skis are free to follow their own course, *and let it happen!*

You will feel your body and skis gradually change direction down the hill. Just as a ball will gradually seek the fall line if thrown across the hill, you will end up sliding down the line of greatest slope of the hill. Only fear, which would make you tense and stiff, could prevent you from drifting to face downhill. This dive into the fall line is an agreeable, even intoxicating, experience if you just dare to let it happen !

Repeat this exercise many times until you understand how to keep your feet relaxed and your skis flat on the snow. Later, you will run into this downhill plunge again when initiating wide, gliding turns.

Of course, practice these dives to the right as well as to the left, even if you do better on one side than the other. It is normal to do better on one side.

In order to reach the fall line more easily and more rapidly, use the "uphill stem".

Take off across the slope again but this time directed slightly more across the fall line. While remaining relaxed, and with your weight distributed equally over both skis, push the tail of your uphill ski outward but continue to keep it flat on the snow. Then, without changing position and with your weight still distributed over both skis, let it happen. You will progressively drift into the fall line and your skis will return to parallel. By repeating this manuever many times, you will begin to sense that the convergent placement of your uphill ski, in what we call an "uphill stem", exerts a directional effect which enhances the effect of gravity in pulling you into the fall line.

Gradually take off on a straight run further and further from the fall line so that your diving direction change becomes greater and greater. But be sure to maintain the suppleness in your legs and the freedom of your skis to search out their own course. Relaxed legs and a freedom of your skis are an indication of your current, as well as your future, success.

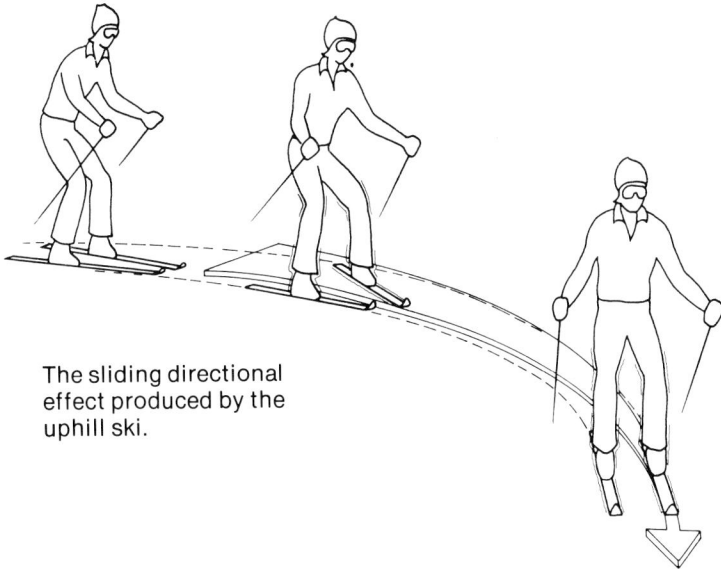

The sliding directional effect produced by the uphill ski.

A slight uphill stem helps the beginning skier, as well as the champion, to dive more smoothly into the fall line.

Learn to turn out of the fall line.

In practicing your straight running down the fall line, you may have already discovered how to change the direction of your slide toward an area which you judge to be more conducive to stopping. If this is the case, I hope you haven't learned to turn your trunk and arms in order to change direction. It is much easier to use your feet.

Before reaching the flat where you come to a stop, you are going to try to exert a light lateral thrust toward the outside on the heel of your right foot. Your weight remains distributed equally over both skis, but this time try to tighten up your right foot a little. As a result, you will feel the direction of your slide begin to change toward the left. Maintaining this firm pressure over the heel of your right ski, which I call the outside ski because it is positioned toward the outside of the curve described by the skis, you will get the feeling of controlling this long turn just as you would control a curve in a sailboat with the rudder. You must first discover this sensation of "rudder pressure over the outside ski" and then you must clearly understand it and finally master it. It requires only a very slight effort with one foot and without any movement or displacement of the mass of your body, thereby without disturbing your balance in the slightest.

As you practice this turn from the fall line, you will gradually learn to describe a tighter and tighter curve. You will begin to feel slightly compressed on your skis due to the effect of centrifugal force and you will observe that the rudder effect is enhanced.

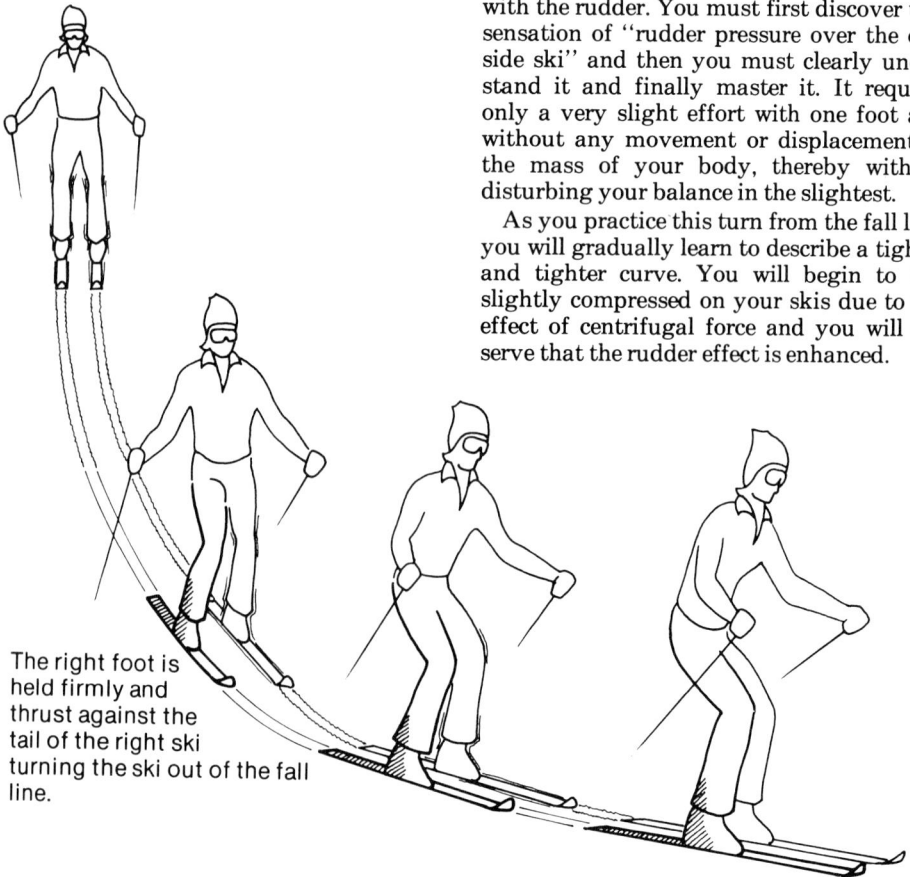

The right foot is held firmly and thrust against the tail of the right ski turning the ski out of the fall line.

In order to turn out of the fall line during a straight run, exert pressure smoothly onto the tail of your ski, much as you would exert pressure on the tiller of a sailboat.

The step turn, a first taste of "independent leg action".

If you succeed in turning out of the fall line as I have described, you are able to do it no matter what your speed. Perhaps you can do it even more easily with greater speed.

However, I would like you to try another method of turning out of the fall line which is effective at lower speeds, the step turn. If you are naturally cautious, you will prefer this second method. However, it could not be substituted for the preceeding approach. Do use both procedures.

The step turn is very easily performed in the elementary manner which I will suggest to you. Sliding at a slow speed, and approaching the flat at the bottom of the hill in a balanced position over both skis, you begin a very rapid left foot... right foot movement from a wide stance. First, pick up one ski for a brief instant and pivot it slightly. Then, do the same with the other so that both skis are parallel or nearly parallel. This, of course, would produce a gradual turn to the left.

Due to the wide base of support that your wide stance provides, you will find it easy to overcome the slight unbalancing disturbances which are created by the rapid displacement of your skis. Having recovered your balance over both feet, you begin again: left foot... right foot, continuing until you come to a complete stop.

Besides the practical application of this movement in changing direction, it also permits you to determine if your legs are relaxed, that each is independent relative to the other and relative to your torso. This independence in your leg action is indispensable to future improvement.

Have you ever noticed how racers work from one ski to the other in slalom ?

The skier absolutely must develop the ability to use independent leg action.

Learn to use ski lifts as soon as possible.

If you have followed my advice, you have chosen a beginners ski area which provides plenty of flat slopes which gradually increase in difficulty. Such areas are often well equipped with ski lifts appropriate to beginning skiers. It's curious to see that often the oldest resorts are those which are most poorly equipped from this point of view, even though a greater effort has been made along these lines over the past few years.

These beginners ski lifts are gold mines for those who take advantage of them. They could be even moreso if instructors adopted the merry-go-round approach to teaching. In this approach, the instructor remains to the side of the slope, or at the foot of the slope, as his clients make repeated runs past him.

It is this kind of skiing, with or without an instructor, which I suggest you discover as quickly as possible in order to increase the mileage of your skiing runs.

How do you ride a surface lift ?

If the lift is actually designed for beginners, with a uniform and relatively flat slope of approximately 5 to 7% and a very slow speed, you won't have any problem. The first time you ride the lift, allow yourself to be pulled by your arms. Maintain a fairly wide stance with your weight distributed over the two forward-backward pressure zones of your feet.

Once you have succeeded in riding the lift by holding on with your arms, move to the next step. If you are riding a platter type lift, place the bar between your legs, or in the case of a T-bar to one side or the other, and as it begins to move, allow yourself to be pulled by the arms for a few meters. Then let the bar slide through your hands until the disk or the bar makes contact with your seat and pulls you upward. Be careful ! Do not try to sit down ! At the end of the lift, a sign will indicate the location at which you are to release the bar. Pull the bar with your arms and clear the disc or bar from your seat in order to let it go at the designated point.

Using the ski lift will not only multiply the number of runs you can take, but gradually you will feel more and more confident as you ride up the slope. At this point, you can begin to practice alternating your skis in short forward-backward displacements, lifting each foot for an instant or making small steps to the right or left. In this manner, you will improve your balance as well as your ability to work your legs independently.

Be careful, however, to avoid moving more than a couple of feet out of the track, or you might risk derailing the cable.

At first, allow yourself to be pulled by your arms...

then by your seat...

and relax your legs.

If the lift available to you has a very abrupt take-off movement, wait to use it until you are very confident of your ability. You can also have a friend take off his skis and duplicate the abrupt action of the lift with his ski pole so that you can learn to cushion the shocks with your arms.

The chair lift

For the time being, you should only consider riding a chair lift which is specially designed for beginners.

These lifts are rare in France and, for the most part, are double chair lifts. In this case, don't ride the lift unless you can find a partner who is a good skier and be sure to take the seat toward the outside of the lift.

Be sure to pay attention to the instructions posted at the loading point; both poles in one hand, your skis placed at exactly the right spot, and your head turned toward the oncoming chair. With one hand you grab the side of the seat, in order to avoid being hit in the calves, and at the same time, you sit down. Once seated, you pull the protecting bar, if it exists, into position in front of you.

If you are truly a beginner, and yet insist on riding a ski lift which is not designed for beginners, don't hesitate to ask for help from your partner. Between sportsmen it is customary to offer a helping hand.

If you must use a more sophisticated lift, however, I would suggest that you consider cable cars or gondolas which shouldn't pose any problems for you; at least during the ride up.

I must emphasize the fact that it will do you no good to attempt to ski terrain which is too difficult for you. You will only learn to check your speed before you learn how to slide. Instead, stay on very flat slopes and practice for miles until you know how to wind down the hill in wide, linked turns and in complete security.

Getting off the chair lift is more difficult. First, lift the protective bar out of the way and take your poles in one hand. Place the other hand on the side of the seat. As soon as your skis touch the snow, stand up and push off of the seat with your hand in order to slide ahead of the chair. A short incline will pull you out of the way of the chair as it swings by.

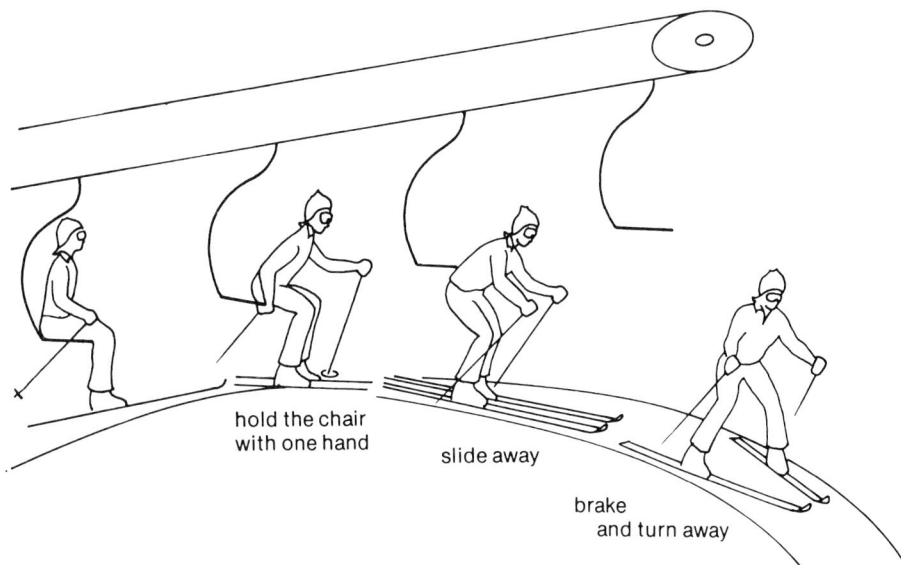

hold the chair with one hand

slide away

brake and turn away

29

Make long serpent turns down the slope.

If you are confident, start right away with your skis parallel.

If you are fortunate enough to have a long, flat slope available to you which you have no fear of sliding straight down, then "schuss", in skiing jargon.

I suggest that you try something that is rare today for beginning skiers, but which can likely be as useful for you as it has been for the majority of our students. It consists of making a very long, drawn out "S" from one side of the fall line to the other with a slight change of direction every 20, 30 or even 40 yards in the beginning.

How to make your first serpents ?

If you have already acquired what I have referred to as a relaxed control of your skis, it is very simple, because, in fact, your skis oscillate constantly on the snow. It suffices for you to make a slight push with your feet for the skis to turn toward the right or left. *Almost only an intention will suffice to make your skis deviate slightly from their trajectory.*

It is very easy for you to understand this if you ski behind a friend who is an accomplished skier and who you have asked to make long serpent turns in front of you down a beginners slope. With supple legs and relaxed feet, and keeping your eyes fixed on your friend from behind, you will make the same serpents that he does. This is exactly the process that takes place when beginning children learn to ski by following behind their parents, provided the latter are wise enough to ski on very easy slopes.

If you are skiing alone, be content to look toward the left, and you will progressively turn to the left; look toward the right, and you turn to the right.

To serpent better.

Flex your legs a little more than usual, widen your stance, and really try to feel the two forward and backward support points of

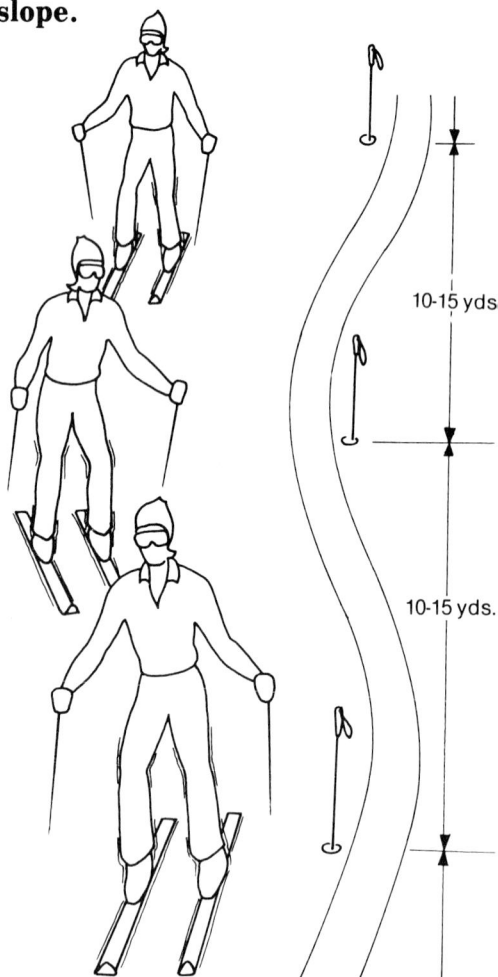

10-15 yds.

10-15 yds.

your feet. While remaining well balanced over both feet, *exert a very slight pivoting push on the soles of your boots.* Do not press too hard, however, or your skis will pivot excessively and turn too far from the fall line.

As soon as you stop this light, pivoting push, you regain a straight, forward sliding that you can continue for several yards while regaining your balance. Then, begin again in the other direction... and then link several turns together.

Be careful, however, to turn neither your body nor your legs. I repeat, you should turn only with your feet.

Steer one ski while in a stem.

You have tried to make a long serpent with parallel skis. Whether you have succeeded or not, you should now attempt a serpent turn while holding your skis in a slightly convergent position — that is to say in a "stem" — but still leaving them very free; very flat on the snow with feet and legs relaxed. This is often referred to as a *"gliding" stem.*

When you slide straight down the slope in this way, you feel that your skis are constantly influenced by slight changes in the snow surface which make the skis oscillate. The smallest push exerted by one of your feet on the sole of the boot suffices to make that ski pivot more than the other and then tend, by itself, to change the direction of your trajectory. If the pressure is applied by the right foot, you turn to the left, while always remaining in balance over the large base of support provided by your stem.

How is this steering of the ski accomplished ?

The slight pivoting push that you exert with your foot on the right ski should be transmitted strictly by contact of the foot against the sole of the boot, and not by a thrust of the leg against the front or back of the cuff of the boot as many beginners do. To avoid this fault, which inhibits the acquisition of a relaxed balance, I often have beginning skiers ski many hours with their boots very loose or even completely unbuckled.

As you push your skis into a pivot, the tail of your ski resists somewhat more than the shovel. You should, therefore, feel that you exert a stronger lateral push with your heel, but without this push tightening your foot.

Don't sway too far from the fall line.

As soon as you feel you are getting too far from the fall line, relax the pressure on your right foot. Then, exert a comparable push with your left foot. Your left ski will pivot slightly and very progressively you will turn toward the right.

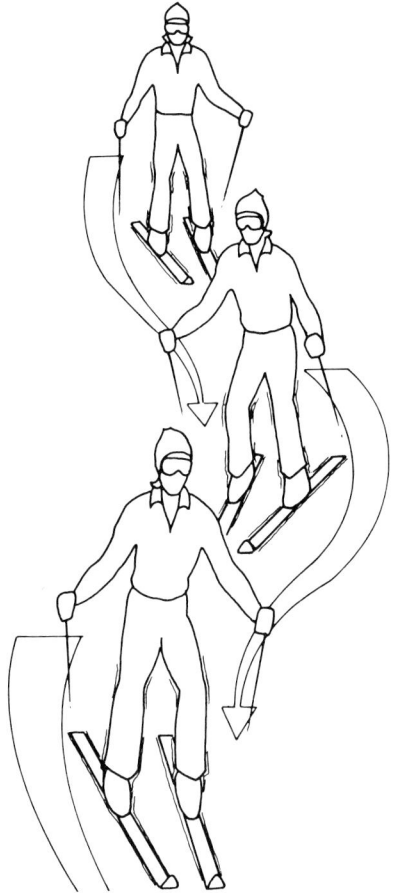

One could say that your ski has produced a *"sliding directional effect"* because the friction between the snow and your ski has modified your trajectory. This sliding directional effect combines with the pull which gravity exerts on you in the direction of the fall line. *Repeat these serpent slidings 100 times.*

Controlling a long serpent turn by "steering" the outside ski is just as easy as turning the steering wheel of a car.

Evolve your long serpents into your first wedel.

With skis parallel

Have you already succeeded in serpenting while keeping your skis parallel ?

If you have not yet been able to discover how a slight push exerted on the soles of your boots can pivot your skis, look for the cause of your failure.

Perhaps you are not relaxed enough to leave your skis "free" on the snow ?

Perhaps you have faulty skis: either with too much camber or too stiff; with concave bases or bases that won't slide ? If so, have them checked by a genuine specialist. Perhaps, on the other hand, your boots are too stiff and block your foot, removing all mobility and feeling. Loosen them up, or even completely unfasten the upper buckles.

Perhaps you're also not sliding sufficiently fast. If this is the case, you have two solutions: either encourage yourself to accept a higher speed, or *use shorter skis* which, at the same speed, pivot more easily. If you have been using long skis, try a compact ski; or short skis (130 cm. or even 100 cm.) if you have been using compacts. After a few days on the shorter skis, return to a little longer length.

If you have already succeeded, accelerate the rhythm.

You should now attempt to exert the same pivoting pressures with both feet, but in a somewhat more pronounced manner. You will feel your skis begin to pivot more distinctly. Immediately stop pressing on the ski and slide in a straight line for several yards. Exert the effort in the other direction, slide, and begin again...

Standing well balanced over both your feet with your skis spread wide enough, you will discover, little by little, that the way in which your feet press on the skis can pivot

the skis more easily and with greater precision. In the jargon of a ski technician, you are in the process of discovering the magical point which we have called the *"pivoting center of the ski"*.

If you are gifted, and especially if you are using compact skis, you should be able to succeed in rapidly linking pivoting turns to the right and to the left and without an intermediate phase. You are already making a first parallel ski wedel !

With a sliding stem.

9 times out of 10, you have been able to succeed in making long serpent turns from a sliding stem after only a few hours of skiing. If not, you owe your failure to one of the three causes which we have just mentioned. Now, enlightened, you will succeed.

While repeating these long serpent turns in a sliding stem, nothing is simpler than to exaggerate slightly the pivoting pressure exerted on the outside ski; called that because it is to the outside of the arc which you make on the snow. Your trajectory is much rounder, but don't overdo it or you will turn too far out of the fall line. Instead, slide straight for a few yards and then pivot the other ski. Little by little, shorten the straight sliding phase between the turns until you have the feeling that you are swinging a little to the right and then a little to the left, while the pivoting pressure alternates from your right ski to your left ski.

Don't let yourself get carried away by this swinging ! Remain properly balanced over both skis with the mass of your body weight centered between your feet. Only in this way will you be able to maintain a stable balance. Be confident and allow your skis to slide supply over the snow with your feet and legs relaxed. I remind you, this is one of the essential conditions for rapid progress.

While linking pivoted turns toward the right and the left, you will notice that they become easier. You are discovering the pivoting center of your skis.

THE GLIDING STEM: A VALUABLE MOVEMENT FOR SKIERS OF ALL LEVELS.

The spreading and placement of the uphill ski in a convergent position increases the base of support, improves balance and gives the beginning skier the confidence needed to plunge into a turn down the fall line.

When used in turns at higher speeds, the centrifugal force automatically balances the skier over the "open" ski, which becomes the outside ski of the new turn. The skier can then link the opening of the stem with a closing of the skis to a parallel position and thus discover an elementary form of leg action under an upper body which remains perfectly stable.

INGEMAR STENMARK
Gold Medalist

PAUL FROMMELT
Bronze Medalist

THE TECHNIQUE AND STYLES OF 3 GREAT CHAMPIONS.

These three series of photomontages show the three medal winners of the slalom event at the last World Championships.

Who would dare to pretend that in skiing technique is individual and not the product of an era? These three champions, each having a very different temperament, display an astounding similarity in their movements; movements which can not be compared to those of the champions ten years ago. Nevertheless, specialists can pick out fine differences in the behaviors of each of the three champions. Each one is recognizable by his style, which is his personal interpretation of the technique of the period; an interpretation which perhaps will open a new era in ski technique tomorrow.

Without fear of becoming a "robot", you should strive to acquire the technique of your time and not that of ten, twenty or thirty years ago.

PIERO GROS
Silver Medalist

A DECISIVE STEP FOR INTERMEDIATE SKIERS: MAKING A PLATFORM.

In the uppermost photomontage, **Perrine PELEN**, the virtuoso skier from the Grenoble University Club, demonstrates that one can be ranked the number one skier in the world and still not be afraid to use a platform with the downhill ski opened into a stem to provide the rebound to then open an uphill stem to initiate a the turn.

In the lower photomontage, **Perrine** uses a classical platform made with skis parallel and then a rebound unweighting to initiate a turn which can not be called "classical" but which is decidedly "feet forward" in a seated position; a technique which **Patrick RUSSEL**, another champion from the Grenoble University Club, and **Gustavo THOENI** introduced to skiing in 1970.

If you are energetic: change your support foot.

With a little aggressiveness and bravery, you can try to skip a few steps, after only a few hours on skis, and try to discover an element of technique which all beginning skiers must eventually master and which constitutes the foundation of the technique of nearly all intermediate skiers.

How to discover this movement ?

Slide straight down the hill in a very wide stance and with your skis parallel or slightly stemmed. Feel the pressure that your feet exert on both skis and concentrate.

Suddenly, lift one foot and, of course, continue to weight the other. The weighted ski then moves laterally in an abrupt manner. Return your weight to both skis, and they will continue to move laterally. Readjust your balance by sliding straight for a few yards and then begin again on the other side. You will notice that when your skis are pushed laterally they pivot, which produces a wedel like movement.

Link these shifts of support foot.

If you have succeeded in these independent movements, try to advance even further. Lift one ski and the other slides out to the side. Immediately place the lifted ski back down and lift the other ski. Link... You can attain a rhythm that is similar to that of a slow walk: left foot... right foot... left foot...

Caution !

You should be careful *not* to move the mass of your body from side to side. What I have proposed to you here is a leg action. Everything happens in the legs; your torso remains immobile. Your arms, spread wide, help you to maintain your balance.

Lifting one ski creates a banking of the body.

The ski, when thrust laterally, pivots by itself.

Beware ! As you accelerate the rhythm, you run the risk of beginning to swing the head, the chest or even the entire body. You must not, for such parasitic movements will hinder your balance and will compromise your later progress.

As soon as you have been able to perform this rudimentary wedel, don't allow yourself to be carried away by it or you will risk, like many other skiers, becoming a slave to this rudimentary movement instead of searching for a more evolved wedel (page 78).

The change of support foot in a wide stance is the most effective way of discovering the wedel. Its efficiency, however, can become a danger...

Make your first large sliding turns.

1st - Open

2nd - Let yourself dive
down the slope.

3rd - pivot your inside ski.

Discover the 3-step stem turn.

If you do not have the kind of slopes available to you that are particularly suitable for the serpentine turn — long, sufficiently flat and served by a surface lift — you can try the 3-step stem turn first. You can then try to serpent on slopes which are not so flat.

The 3-step stem turn is within the reach of all skiers who have acquired a minimum level of balance while sliding after only a few hours on skis. If this is your case, you are assured of success.

Don't start straight down the slope, but slightly across it. Make sure you understand the 3 steps of the turn and mentally count them out as you proceed through the exercise.

"One"! Displace your uphill ski laterally and place it flat on the snow in a stem position. Remain centered over both feet by balancing your body precisely between the two skis.

"Two"! Remain relaxed and just let it happen. You will notice that your uphill ski exerts a directional effect which makes you dive down the slope. Let yourself be pulled down the slope until you are facing straight down the hill.

"Three"! As you face straight down the slope, exert a pivoting push with the foot on

A genuine turn on skis always consists of an initiation, a dive down the fall line, and an end.

the inside ski of the turn to return it to a position parallel with the other. As this happens, you move laterally, more or less sideslipping, and you turn out of the fall line.

In the beginning, and particularly on flat slopes, you can remain in a stem until the end of the turn. Nevertheless, you should try as soon as possible to learn to return your skis to a parallel position and at the most favorable instant; when you are facing straight down the fall line. This movement is not difficult if you remain balanced on both your feet and if you don't move your chest and arms.

Use these turns to cultivate a sliding sideslip.

When should you start the sideslip ?

During your dive down the fall line, and as soon as you are facing straight down the slope, you exert a pivoting push on your inside ski to bring it parallel with the other ski. At the same time, try to exert a pivoting pressure on your outside ski. You will feel both skis begin a lateral sliding or sideslipping morement.

This pivoting push on the outside ski should be applied particularly through the heel of the foot. At this moment, you can flex your legs and better feel the beginning of the sideslip.

How do you control this sideslip ?

As your skis sideslip, you should notice that the push exerted by the heels of your feet has a tendency to increase. Try to establish a new balance position by simultaneously weighting the front and back of the foot. By accentuating the pressure on the heels too much, you run the risk of stiffening your legs.

Your principle problem during this

The skis are pushed into a sideslip.

sideslipping phase is to maintain your balance. You will better succeed if you keep your arms spread wide — and relaxed — so that they can neutralize any beginning of a fall and allow your feet to remain supple.

This sideslip simultaneously represents the learning of new sensations and new reactions for your feet and the acquisition of a new kind of balance for your upper body.

Note: Some of your friends may be surprised to see you perform your first sideslips from a turn whereas some instructors have their students spend a great deal of time sideslipping across the slope from a traverse before teaching a turn. We have noticed that the turn and even serpents facilitate the discovery of sideslipping, making is easier to initiate sideslipping and permit its constant repetition during round-robin training on easy slopes. Then too, probably nothing is more boring than the repetition of simple sideslips from a traverse.

The end of a turn is when it is easiest for you to discover and refine your sliding sideslip with slight heel pressure.

With greater speed, discover the dominant weighting of the outside ski in long turns.

At moderate speed...

...spread the uphill ski...

...then lift the inside ski.

Stem turn while lifting the inside ski several times.

Make hundreds of 3-step stem turns. Try to feel the directional effect of the stemmed uphill ski that makes you dive down the slope. Also, feel that as you cross the fall line at the end of the turn you are compressed onto your outside ski. Accept this compression and absorb it by flexing your legs. Many skiers, by trying to resist this compression, habitually stiffen their outside leg; a very serious fault.

As you gain confidence, you will progressively make more "rounded" turns — that is to say with a shorter radius — and at higher speeds. You will then feel pressure exerted on your outside ski from the beginning of the turn. This pressure is a result of the centrifugal force produced by every turn (207).

It's absolutely necessary that you learn to find your balance, during this compression, with an almost exclusive weighting of the outside ski instead of the equal weighting of both feet you have become accustomed to.

Only one "trick" is effective in helping you to learn this element. Try to lift your inside ski once, twice, then five or six times while your outside ski makes the turn. At first, perhaps you will not succeed in lifting your inside ski until after you have crossed the fall line. It is a beginning, but you must keep on trying.

If your speed is sufficient, you can even manage to lift your inside ski immediately after having opened the uphill ski into a stem. You then place it parallel to the outside ski and, in this way, succeed in making a nearly parallel turn. This is referred to as a *"two-step stem turn"* to differentiate it from the preceeding turn.

The essential condition for making a good turn at moderate speed: balance yourself with dominant weighting over the outside ski.

If you are not so brave

You can, nevertheless, succeed very quickly in making long parallel turns at a slower speed and on flatter slopes if you proceed in the following manner.

Begin with a steeper traverse, directed more down the hill than that used in the previous exercise. Your turns will be intermediate between 3-step stem turns and the serpentine.

Instead of opening an uphill stem, spread your uphill ski but leave it parallel with your downhill ski. Then, try to lift your inside, or downhill, ski while exerting a pivoting push on your outside ski. The turn will begin. Lift your inside ski several times. You will turn with your skis parallel and with dominant weighting of your outside ski. Don't turn too far out of the fall line, however, and begin a turn in the opposite direction.

You may find that the feel of this turn is reminiscent of your first serpent wedeln made with a change of support foot (page 33). This mechanism can help you in the beginning, but don't use it excessively or it may hinder your ability to balance on your outside ski.

Turn with parallel skis by spreading your uphill ski and progressively changing your support foot.

If you are athletic

If you readily accept speed and if you have succeeded in lifting your inside ski for a second or a second and a half while making the preceeding turn, you are already turning with only a slight stem. While progressively increasing your speed, you should spread your uphill ski more parallel than stemmed. You will soon discover, in fact, that as soon as you open your uphill, or outside ski, it is easy to exert a pivoting push on it at the same moment that you lift your inside ski.

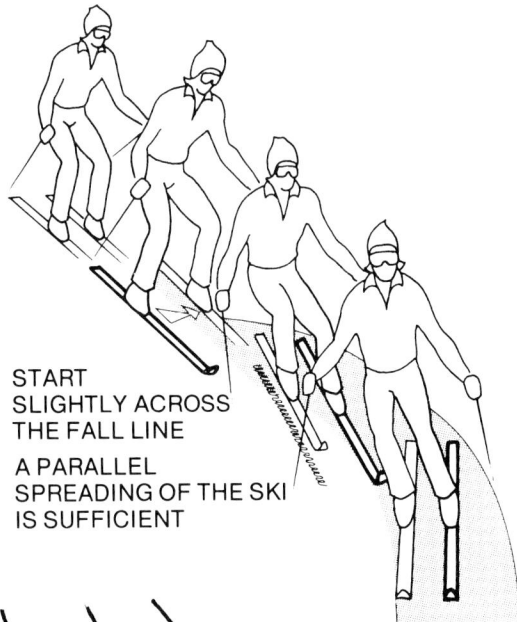

START
SLIGHTLY ACROSS
THE FALL LINE

A PARALLEL
SPREADING OF THE SKI
IS SUFFICIENT

PIVOTING ACTION
OF THE FOOT.

PASSIVE
LATERAL
DISPLACEMENT.

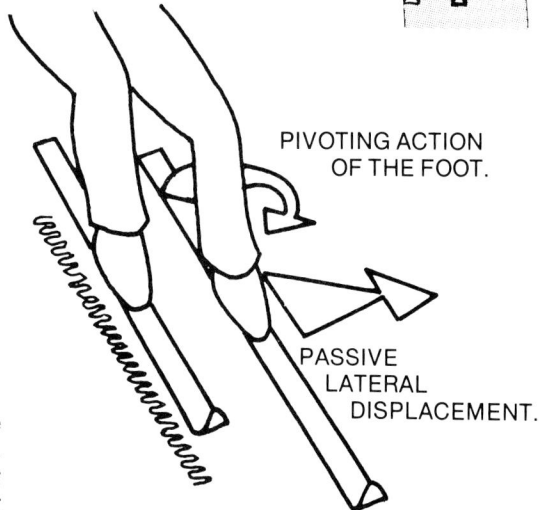

Because of your higher speed, you are able to advance from a stem to a parallel turn initiated by a spreading of your uphill ski and a change of support foot. This turn is more progressive and less brutal than the turn you used for making your first wedeln.

Three elements facilitate the rapid acquisition of parallel turning: speed, a change of support foot and skiing close to the fall line.

Prepare yourself to tackle more difficult slopes !

Use "braquage" to stop yourself quickly with parallel skis.

If you are athletic and aggressive, you can try this stop with normal length skis. After only one or two days on skis, you have a 50% chance of success provided you can use a moderately flat slope and a packed but not icy snow.

With compact skis, your chance for success climbs to 80%, but with very short skis you will be less likely to succeed because you will have difficulty in maintaining your balance.

PIVOT YOUR LEGS IN 1/10th OF A SECOND.

The technique for this stop is very simple because it corresponds to the natural reaction of human beings to being carried away by speed on slippery terrain. It consists of a very quick pivoting of the feet across the direction of sliding and a braking pressure on the edges of the skis.

To succeed in this stop, take four preliminary precautions: 1. Adjust your position to a lower stance than usual. 2. Use a wider stance. 3. Hold your arms firmly in front of your body. 4. Concentrate on pivoting your skis in a fraction of a second to a position perpendicular to your line of travel.

The compression that results aids the pivoting of the skis.

The pivoting effort comes from the hips...

...and the feet.

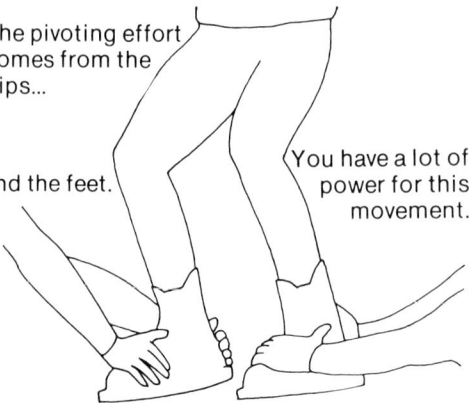

You have a lot of power for this movement.

On the slope, prepare yourself by facing straight down the hill, concentrate, and then push yourself down the fall line. After 10 yards, steer your skis abruptly across the slope with your feet. As soon as this foot steering action has started, you will feel a significant compression under your heels. Resist this pressure and maintain your balance.

Don't give up before 5 or 6 failures: with each attempt you come closer to success. Don't try to analyze or understand this movement; it must be perceived in a global manner. Don't think... act !

The "braquage", a rapid pivoting of the skis in a wide stance, is an indispensable weapon for good skiers. Every beginner with resolve can acquire it after only one day on skis.

With a sliding stem and foot steering.

The *"braquage"* stop presents essentially a psychological problem. You have to be bold ! You must be able to anticipate the movement, slide straight down the slope and then, in a fraction of a second, abruptly pivot your skis across the fall line. It is the fear of this sudden movement that may prevent you from acting as emphatically as you must. If this is your case, the enthusiastic encouragement of a friend or instructor may be decisive.

Of course, it may also help you to understand that you are equipped with extremely powerful muscles for making this almost "natural" pivoting movement from a wide stance. It's practically impossible for you to be limited by a lack of muscular power. But, if you don't succeed in overcoming this psychological barrier, or if you are from the outset too timid to risk a fall, then try the *"braquage"* stop from a sliding stem.

Start by sliding straight down the slope for 10, 15 or 20 yards in a stem, flexed a little lower than usual, and with the mass of your body distributed equally on both skis. Then, rapidly pivot both skis so that within a fraction of a second they are turned across the slope.

The stem will make it easier for you to make a *"braquage"* stop because of the increased stability it provides and because one of your skis is already partially turned in the direction you are going to pivot.

Caution ! The "foot steering" should be performed just as rapidly as for a *"braquage"* stop made from a parallel skis position. A slower steering action will still allow you to produce a stop, but will not prepare you for making a braquage with skis parallel which should be your goal.

Don't try to turn the chest... or the hips.

Everything should happen in the legs... under an immobile upper body.

To slow down, push hard on your downhill foot.

Control your speed by braking with a downhill stem during traverses.

Beginning skiers are often tediously instructed to slide across the slope; to "traverse" in skiing jargon. Considering the very flat or relatively flat slopes which you are now skiing, this is useless. We have noticed that such traverses will pose no problem for you. On the contrary, the first problem that presents itself, as you tackle steeper slopes, will be for you to control your speed while traversing.

You should now look for short, steeper sections on your otherwise flat trails to learn a rudimentary braking manuever using a downhill stem.

How to discover braking with a downhill stem.

Stand in a traverse that is closer to the fall line than to the horizontal and open your downhill ski into a stem, placing it slightly across the direction in which you are going to slide.

Push yourself off. You will immediately feel the metal edge of your downhill ski grate across the snow. As you place more of your weight onto this ski, you slow down. You should feel a dominant weighting of the heel of your downhill foot, which is positioned in front of you and supports most of your weight. Your downhill leg acts as a spring or shock absorber between your body mass and your foot as it presses on the downhill ski.

This movement is both utilitarian and educational.

This braking with a downhill stem is an efficient means of controlling your speed when you must cross a section of a slope that is too steep for you.

It also helps you to develop the habit of weighting your downhill ski, with your torso tilted down the hill in a position which we call "angulation" and which we characteristically use in more advanced turns.

Refine the downhill stem braking technique.

Slide for several yards in a traverse with your skis parallel. Then, while pressing on the heel of your downhill foot, open your downhill ski into a stem and weight your downhill leg with the mass of your body; you will stop within a few yards. Let the downhill ski return to parallel and you continue to traverse. Open your downhill ski and weight it again. This exercise in a traverse is called a *"garland"* because of the tracks drawn on the snow.

Are you having problems ?

If you aren't able to balance the mass of your body out over your downhill foot, you are not weighting your heel enough. At the same time as you open your downhill ski into a stem, you must push your foot in front of you. If you do this, you will have confidence in the support it can give you and will be more confident in placing your weight on it.

More often than not, skiers who are unable to slow down using a stem are those who habitually lean against the front of the shanks of their boots. They must, first of all, rid themselves of this fault.

Brake with a downhill stem, then bring your skis parallel.

You are able to slow down at will with a downhill stem. You have braked, slid, braked... for several miles. Your downhill leg now acts as a good shock absorber between your body mass and your downhill leg. Little by little, you are learning new balance reflexes.

If you have a powerful build, or are particularly athletic, you perhaps have already noticed that as you brake, your uphill ski, which carries very little weight, has a tendency to move down to a position parallel to your downhill ski. Good ! This is the next step to be attained.

Sliding in a traverse, slow down with a downhill stem. Balance yourself with almost exclusive weighting of your downhill ski and bring your uphill ski parallel to it. Continue to sideslip with your skis parallel. It now only remains for you to cultivate new balancing reflexes while moving slowly across the slope in this "braking sideslip".

The essence of the problem is for you to be able to remain in balance while slowing down with your downhill ski. You will not be able to accomplish this unless you press on the heel of your downhill foot, with your downhill leg supply supporting your body weight.

You may have a psychological problem.

The beginner often fears turning his upper body to face down the slope in order to weight his downhill ski. Instead, he often faces up the hill. If this is a problem for you, the solution is simple: use a downhill stem to slow down until you obtain an effective braking. This will give you confidence in the solidity of the support you can obtain with your downhill foot. You will then be less apprehensive about shifting your body weight to this ski.

Another solution: start with a flatter slope.

In order to brake effectively, you must find a support in front of you. The downhill stem is an effective solution.

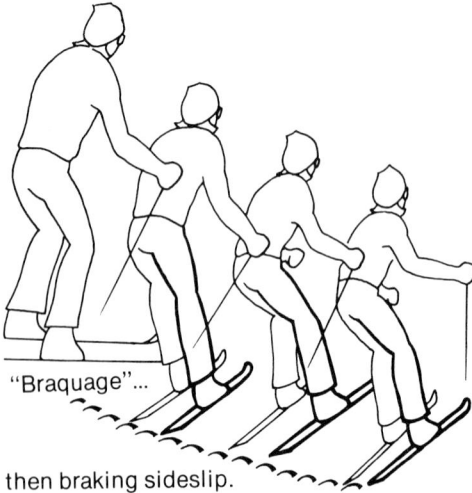

"Braquage"...

then braking sideslip.

better balance. Here again, your chief problem will be to develop appropriate balance reflexes.

Refine your "foot steered sideslip braking".

Try to progressively diminish the foot steering. This will be possible once you have covered long distances in a braking sideslip, which refines your balance and enables you to develop a better sensitivity in your feet. It will then be sufficient for you to weight your heels and apply a mild foot steering in order to start your skis pivoting and then sideslipping.

From a traverse, use foot steering then a braking sideslip.

You have already succeeded in foot steering "braquage" stops with or without a stem while sliding straight down the slope. If you have tried to do this from a traverse, however, you have likely found that it isn't very easy. There are two reasons for this. While traversing, your skis bite the snow with their edges and, therefore, are less free to begin pivoting than when you slide straight down the slope in a schuss. Furthermore, the more emphatic foot steering necessary to start your skis turning tends to push you out of balance to the rear.

Instead, I suggest that you use a less brutal foot steering, while traversing, than you have used to stop while schussing. During this milder foot steering, apply pressure to your heels, but not too much, and you should begin to sideslip much as you did when you brought your skis parallel during the downhill ski stem braking. You can only accomplish this if you have a distinctly dominant weighting of your downhill ski, with your arms spread wide for

Advance from a braking sideslip to a sliding sideslip.

You have now covered several miles, making long turns or making serpent turns down the fall line. If you have tried to supply control your skis, as I have asked you to do, to leave them to slide freely on the snow, then you have been able to feel them slide somewhat laterally at the end of your turns. This is a *"skis-flat sideslipping"* or *"sliding sideslip"* as opposed to the *"braking sideslip"* we have just studied.

It still remains for you, however, to discover all of the intermediate variations between these two types of sideslipping.

Once again, it is a matter of educating your feet!

Only through the repetition of parallel ski braking sideslips will you eventually be able to succeed in eliminating the initial foot steering effort and substitute it for a release of the feet and ankles; a release or relaxation which allows the skis to flatten out and pivot by themselves into a sideslip (134).

Brake...

then sliding sideslip.

If you have concentrated on developing this relaxed freedom of the skis, to which I have attached so much importance, you will be able to prolong your sideslip while keeping yourself in perfect balance. In short, *the sliding sideslip requires a "supple" control of the skis*, possible only when the feet and lower legs are relaxed.

Your upper body should remain "quiet" during the sideslip.

I must emphasize that in both the braking and the sliding sideslip, your upper body should remain quiet. All movement to control the edging and pivoting of the skis is made by the lower body. Your upper body remains relatively immobile. Your head, chest and arms face the direction in which you are sliding and move only slightly to adjust balance. This relaxed body position will play an essential role in your development as a skier.

Discover the biting of the edges while traversing straight forward.

You know that if the need arises, you can reduce your speed with your downhill ski. Now try to traverse confidently across a steep slope with hard packed snow. To keep from sideslipping down the slope, you must set the edge of your downhill ski. You can accomplish this in much the same way as when you brake with your downhill ski. First, transfer your weight to the downhill ski. There should be a dominant weighting of your heel, but this must not be excessive or you will pivot your ski. You must discover the precise point on which you must press so that your skis hold at a maximum.

Your uphill ski, which of course is placed a little higher on the slope than your downhill ski, will naturally be advanced slightly ahead of your downhill ski.

You will easily and naturally discover the correct body position for a traverse if you have made numerous stops and brakings using a downhill stem. This position is commonly referred to as "angulation" and we will refer to it again later.

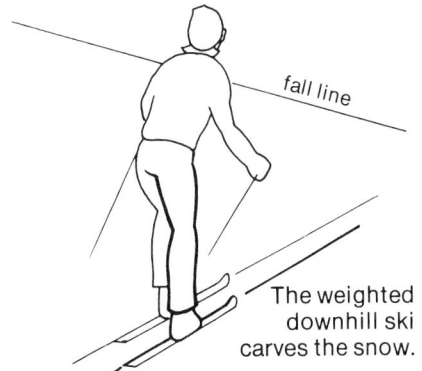

fall line

The weighted downhill ski carves the snow.

While traversing: weighting the heels + foot steering = braking sideslip.
Slight weighting of the heels + relaxed ankles = sliding sideslip.

Use a quick change of direction on difficult slopes.

Make a giant uphill stem, then steer.

I will describe a manuever that can be an effective weapon for you now, but can also be used when you become an accomplished skier and are confronted with a very difficult slope or adverse snow conditions. I don't dare use the word turn, which implies a degree of sliding down the slope, to describe this brutal and inelegant change of direction.

This direction change is made from a flat traverse (almost horizontal across the slope) and at very slow speeds. With your weight balanced over your downhill ski, you open your uphill ski into a very wide stem. If you are tall and limber, you can almost place it down across the fall line, but this is not obligatory. With your uphill foot positioned in front of your body and your uphill ski already largely pivoted into the turn, you abruptly shift your weight to the uphill ski and steer powerfully with both

legs. You should make a genuine "skid" as your skis pivot and finish the direction change with a brief braking sideslip that brings you into a traverse in the opposite direction.

In reality, you have bypassed the fall line phase of the turn and, as I have repeatedly emphasized, a proper turn on skis must include this phase of sliding straight down the slope. Consequently, you shouldn't consider this manuever to be anything more than a utilitarian weapon to be used only when you are in over your head and can't do anything else. On less difficult terrain, of course, you can prolong the final sideslip somewhat by weighting the tails of your skis.

One of the virtues of this manuever is that you can change direction very quickly, finishing it in a relaxed, supple position favorable for sideslipping whereas other turns often tend to stiffen the outside leg at the end of the turn.

At very slow speed,

1st, make a maximum uphill stem.

2nd, Change your support foot and foot steer.

The same techniques can permit both beginners and experts alike to deal with extreme situations. Examples: this rapid direction change with a wide stem and a braking downhill ski stem turn.

Use a smaller stem on the top of bump.

Today, one often sees enormous moguls appear, even on intermediate slopes, as a result of hundreds of turns made in the same place. These bumps will very likely intimidate you. You shouldn't be afraid of them, however, because they can actually facilitate your turns.

Bumps offer two advantages. First, it is easier to pivot your skis on the tops of them and, secondly, it is easier to initiate a sideslip down the steeper backsides of them.

Traversing at a moderate, or even very slow speed, you should aim for the top of a bump. Two yards before reaching the bump, open an uphill ski stem. When you reach the top, shift your weight to change your support foot and pivot your uphill ski. It will immediately pivot into the turn and sideslip down the back of the bump. The sideslipping will brake your speed. As soon as your uphill ski begins to pivot into the turn, bring the other ski parallel. Control your speed by sideslipping, aim for a new bump and turn again...

This is an easy turn to make at very low speed, even over large moguls. If you're afraid of moguls, this turn will allow you to overcome your fear.

Dive down the slope.

Brake

Brake again.

On the crest of a bump,

uphill stem, then foot steer

and braking sideslip.

Use a "downhill stem brake" instead of a "wedge".

In the braking wedge, which is still commonly taught, the skier presses on the skis with both legs and in opposite directions.

If the difficulty of the terrain dictates, you can slow yourself just as effectively by turning with a braking downhill stem, which you have already used and which works only one leg at a time.

Brake yourself with a downhill stem until you nearly stop. Then, weight both skis and, after 1 or 2 yards, they will begin to turn down the slope. Immediately press hard on the outside ski, which has become the downhill ski, and you again brake with a downhill stem. Control your speed and then begin again.

The moment that your skis dive down the slope is critical. If you brake, you risk blocking your hip and this can become a difficult habit to break.

After a prolonged braking...

dive down the
fall line.

On difficult or bumpy terrain, cultivate the "brake then turn" reflex.

You are now equipped to leave the very flat beginners' slopes. You can ski on longer, more varied runs with flats, smooth or bumpy terrain and an occasional steep section down which you can use the extreme weapons which I have just discussed.

You should now concentrate on intermediate slopes on which you can only ski with confidence by mastering simultaneous turning and braking techniques.

Brake with a downhill stem before turning.

A systematic observation of thousands of intermediate skiers has proven to us that nine out of ten intermediate skiers, when skiing on terrain that is, for them, difficult, use a turn as a means of slowing down. The turns of these skiers can not be refined and attain the desired elegance and effectiveness. Furthermore, a braking manuever during a turn is always more unbalancing and more stiffening than a check before the turn.

This is why you must acquire the "brake then turn" reflex. As you know, there are several ways to slow down, but I advise

you to begin by using downhill stem braking, even if you use compact skis and if you already prefer to ski parallel.

Starting from a traverse, first allow yourself to gain a little speed. Then, open the downhill ski into a stem and weight the tail to slow down. Once you have slowed sufficiently, return weight to both skis — by shifting your body mass to a position between both skis — and let yourself dive down the slope. Finally, bring the inside ski parallel to the outside ski and continue the turn in a sideslip.

Repeat this turn 10, 20 or even 30 times and try to feel the contrast between the braking at the beginning of the turn and the acceleration during the dive down the slope.

After having genuinely felt these two phases — braking then accelerating — begin the process again but shorten the duration of the braking. If you braked for 10 yards, reduce it to 8, 6, 4 and even 2 yards. You will discover that by shortening your braking, you can obtain a platform on your downhill ski which then helps you to push your body weight back over both skis to begin the dive down the fall line.

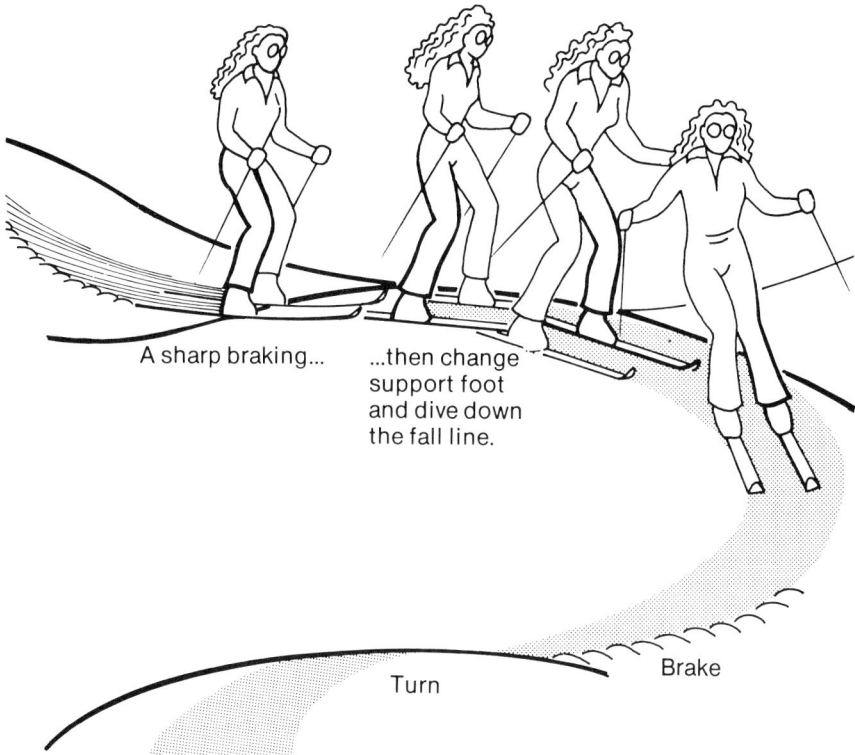

A sharp braking...

...then change support foot and dive down the fall line.

Turn

Brake

Profit from easy bumps to brake then turn with parallel skis.

You have already learned how to use bumps to stem turn at slow speeds (page 45). Therefore, it should be easy for you to brake 10 or 12 feet before a bump at higher speed using either a downhill stem or a sideslip with parallel skis. When you reach the top of the bump, after having checked your speed, change your support foot and pivot your outside ski and your turn will begin as before.

You can discover that moguls, in fact, facilitate the "brake then turn" reflex. As you cross a bump, you undergo a compression on your skis, a compression which can reinforce your braking if done at this precise moment. This compression makes it easier to transform your braking into a platform that launches you into the turn.

By repeating this braking turn a hundred times on moderately mogulled intermediate slopes, you will gradually begin to link braking to a sliding turn. I will return to this point in the following chapter.

The reflex of a mediocre skier is to turn to slow down. That of good skiers and racers, when they must slow down, is to brake first, then turn.

Turn up the hill...

then dive down the fall line.

Another way to reduce your speed: turn up the hill.

You should first attempt this on a slightly mogulled slope. As you slide across the slope, it is easy to direct your trajectory either above a bump 30 to 50 feet in front of you , or below. During several traverses you should systematically aim for a bump situated a little higher than where you normally would ski, and turn on this higher bump. As you climb to the bump, your speed will decrease and you will feel a slight compression on your skis just as you do when braking. This compression likewise facilitates your dive into the turn behind the bump.

This method of skiing is more elegant than using an actual braking.

After you have felt this deceleration and compression during a turn up the hill on slightly bumpy terrain, try the same technique on a smooth slope. As you traverse, direct your trajectory 6 to 10 feet up the slope before you initiate your turn. You will feel a deceleration and compression, although less pronounced than in the previous case but, nevertheless, clearly perceptible. Your turn initiation will not be as easy as over a bump. Therefore, don't hesitate to use a slight uphill stem or simply spread the uphill ski laterally. Shift your weight to the uphill ski and you will dive down the slope.

If you don't like speed, make this turn your basic turn. Always begin a turn with a counter-turn up the hill. This turn can be adapted to all snow conditions and all terrain and can lead you quickly to a very elegant and "modern" skiing. It will also help you to acquire the proper timing for a pole plant at the beginning of the turn.

A good "trick" for a relaxed and elegant reduction of speed before turning: turn up the hill.

THE MECHANISM FOR MAKING A CLASSIC PLATFORM

The classic platform permits a rapid braking or even a complete stop. It can also produce a trampoline effect, throwing the skier into the turn, and can bring precision an dynamism to your turns. It is characterized by a flexing of the legs, an "anticipation" by the torso (that is to say the torso is twisted down the fall line before the skis begin to pivot into the turn), and a pole plant which can be indispensable to maintaining good balance.

The skier's speed compresses him onto his downhill ski at the end of the turn. Once the compression is absorbed, the supporting leg, which acts like a spring or shock absorber, releases its energy by throwing the skier, and particularly the uphill ski, into the coming turn. With a slight pivoting effort on the uphill ski, which is unweighted and rests flat on the snow, the skier places it in the most favorable position for starting the turn.

The shift of weight from a predominant weighting of the downhill ski to a predominant weighting of the uphill ski is called a "change of support foot". Here, it is combined with a platform.

LEARN TO PROFIT FROM MOGULS INSTEAD OF RESISTING THEM

A vertical action is used to absorb bumps. At moderate speeds, the skier should know how to extend or stretch out his body in the troughs and quickly flex as he passes over the crest of bumps to prevent them from becoming a jump which can catapult him into the air. In order to be really effective, these flexions should be "modern", that is they should be executed by lifting the feet up in front of the body and not underneath the body. I call this the "flexion-avalement".

A sliding leg action is used to thread between the bumps. You can absorb the tops of moguls by flexion and then brake by sliding down the back side. Alternatively, and with much greater elegance, you can thread yourself through the troughs which seperate the bumps. We speak of this as skiing "in the ruts". This demands a leg action that is effective and precise; at the same time vertical, lateral and pivoting.

Plant your pole
and pivot.

Plant your pole for greater security on large moguls.

You already have mastered two methods for turning in moguls.

In very difficult mogul fields, you reduce your speed and ski over the tops of the bumps. On the crest of a bump, you either spread your uphill ski into a stem or leave it parallel. You transfer your weight to the uphill ski and then sideslip down the backside of the bump.

On easier, rounder bumps, the tops of which form a small plateau, you first brake, either with parallel skis or a downhill stem, and then change support foot to start sideslipping into the turn.

At this stage in your development, you should concentrate on obtaining an entirely new gesture: the pole plant.

If you have already developed the habit of holding your arms in front of your body and spread wide for balance, you will be able to succeed in your first few attempts. If your arms are properly positioned, it is easy for you to plant your downhill ski pole vertically in the snow precisely in the right place for obtaining a balance support and to do so without moving your hand.

You should try to plant your pole exactly on the top of a bump, immediately after you brake and just before you change your support foot.

Your pole plant will give you better balance as you shift your weight to a new support foot and initiate your turn. And, since it helps you to maintain your balance, it will quickly become a "reflex". Therefore, make 10, 20, or even 100 turns with a pole plant and it will soon become a part of your "technical baggage" and reappear every time you need it.

Your pole plant will become particularly useful, for example, when you initiate turns preceeded by a counter-turn up the hill. The pole plant will help stabilize your body mass at the instant when you change support foot and your skis dive down the fall line.

Caution ! Avoid the common fault of moving the hand forward to plant the pole. This gesture is not only meaningless but detrimental. It tends to provoke a swinging of the torso which compromises your balance.

Skiing in large moguls is the best place for learning to plant the ski pole.

How far have your come ?

Are you comfortable while sliding straight down the slope or traversing at intermediate speed ?

Do you know how to slow down when your speed becomes too high ?

Are you capable of controlling your skis in a stem or in a semi-wide stance to make long turns down the fall line or even across intermediately difficult runs ?

Are you dynamic enough to move from one ski to the other — either in a slight stem or with parallel skis — to ski an elementary wedel down the fall line or to start your turns quicker ?

If you can answer yes, then you are no longer a beginner !

You are already as good as many skiers.

80% of the recreational skiers frequenting the intermediate slopes of ski resorts do not have technical skills better than yours. They have been skiing more hours than you, and perhaps their balance is better, but they have not advanced beyond the stage of using rudimentary skiing mechanisms.

Certainly you see them do a great many things which you don't: move the arm forward to plant the pole, bend the legs, point the buttocks backward or fold at the waist, extend upward, throw the hip, rotate the shoulders, point the elbows out... But almost invariably, these are only affectations ! Beyond these superficial gestures, what is it that actually starts their turns ? A change of support foot, most of the time subconscious; an excessive lateral thrust on the outside ski, and without pivoting or steering; often even a genuine loss of balance to the inside of the turn, crossing the fall line as quickly as possible followed by a poorly controlled sideslip because of inadequate weighting of the outside ski. This is followed by a new traverse with accelerating speed... and a new turn which is, in reality, only a gross change of direction.

Nothing is more instructive than observing a group of students following their instructor; either in France, Austria, the United States, or elsewhere: the instructor is a model of perfection — but the students do whatever they can, and usually something entirely different, to keep up. Their "different" mechanisms, sprinkled with the affectations in vogue in the Ski Schools which purportedly have educated them, are what make them turn.

If you have acquired the "brake then turn" reflex, if you clearly perceive the two forward and backward support points of your foot on the ski while sliding straight forward, if you have felt the slightly dominant pressure on your heels during sideslips and the lateral thrust of your heels that assist the pivoting of the skis into a turn, if you can easily thrust the tails of your skis down the hill in a traverse and then swing them back into the traverse, *if you possess these technical elements, then you are able to use your skis effectively and are better prepared than 80% of all intermediate skiers.* You have acquired the fundamentals which will lead you directly to the ultimate techniques of today's champions.

Their technique is simple. It is the same technique discovered by children from the mountain villages born "with skis on their feet" and who have been fortunate enough to not have been deformed by a technically deficient environment. There is a continuity in this technique from the skiing of the beginner to that of the greatest champions and without interruption.

It has taken more than 20 years of experience and study for us to arrive at this simple fact !

Yet simplicity also means purity. A poorly perceived sensation, a bad habit or the imitation of a poorly chosen gesture can cause the human mechanism of movement to be jammed or falsified or to have its effectiveness diminished. Consequently, I must make you aware of the grossest errors which you could have committed while following our progression... or before availing yourself of our book.

Do you have an unorthodox stance ?

Every skier has a characteristic silhouette which allows one to recognize him on the slope, even though he is in the middle of a hundred moving skiers. This silhouette is linked somewhat to body morphology, but is even more a product of the skier's mechanical behavior on his skis, of his movements, and especially of his basic stance, which is characterized by a few dominant elements and often by one or more of the following affectations.

These faults in stance can effect a skier's technique by making it impossible for him to perform some basic technical manuevers.

• Do you ski too upright, with your arms hanging alongside your body ?

This fault is very much in vogue today and committed by 80% of intermediate skiers. I devote a full chapter to this mistake (page 53).

• Do you ski with your ankles flexed too much, thrusting your knees forward ?

Is the forward position of your knees accentuated as soon as you flex your legs ? If yes, you are probably applying constant pressure to the tips of your skis, a fault which we analyze on page 53.

• Do you ski folded at the waist, with your buttocks thrust backward ?

This position is essentially the opposite of the preceeding one and results in a tendency to excessive backweighting (see page 55), either because of a morphological fault or because of stiffness in the legs which don't flex, thereby resulting in a forward folding at the waist and a backward thrust of the buttocks to counter balance... To correct this fault, you must find a balanced weighting of your feet with relaxed legs and an elastic control of your skis such as I described on pages 22 and 34. Return to easier slopes where you can ski with confidence and where you will more willingly accept higher speeds. You develop suppleness as you gain confidence in yourself.

Folded at the waist.

• Do you ski in a "seated" position.

Perhaps you even press against the backs of your boots ? A stiffness in the muscles of the thighs, back and even arms often accompanies this "sitting back" position (see page 55).

• Do you have poor arm position ?

By now you are aware of what constitutes proper arm position: arms spread wide and placed in front of you. In this position, the arms are alert, ready to react. Your arms can then play an important role as balancing weights and are able to perform a pole plant in 1/10th of a second with minimal hand movement. Every other arm position compromises these two functions and can, among other things, make some skiing movements difficult or impossible.

Most improper arm positions are generally associated with morphological abnormalities which influence the attitude of the back and neck. On the following page, I use drawings to illustrate some of the more frequent arm position faults.

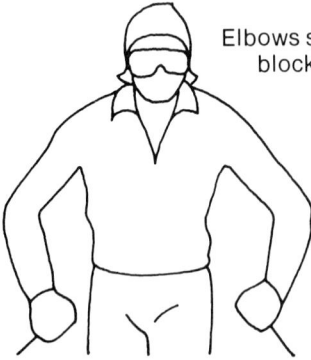

Elbows sticking out;
blocked neck.

Arms too stiff.

Elbows too close
to the body;
back stiff.

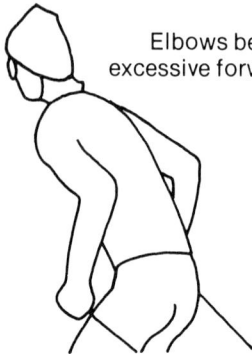

• Do you habitually ski with your head blocked, looking down at your ski tips ?

This error is extremely serious.

First of all, it reduces your field of vision. Instead of a wide and stable view of the snow field, you have a limited and agitated picture of your skis on the snow.

Secondly, skiing with your vision riveted to your tips often results in your body being blocked into a position square over your skis. This blocking prevents you from having the mobility necessary for the acquisition of various skiing skills, in particular pivotement. It also inhibits balancing reactions which often begin in the neck.

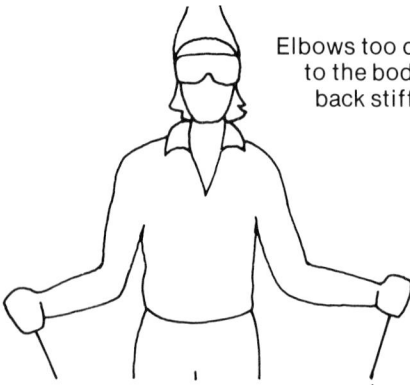

Elbows behind;
excessive forward lean.

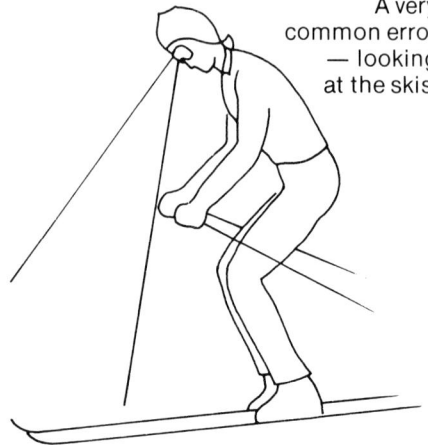

A very
common error
— looking
at the skis.

Do you ski too upright, with your arms hanging alongside your body ?

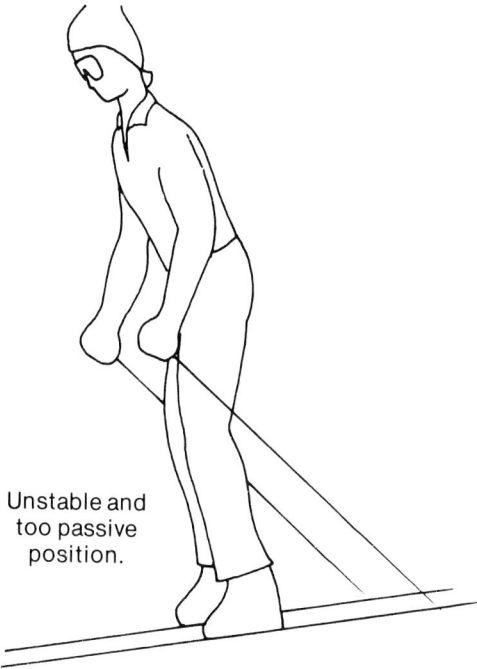

Unstable and too passive position.

This mistake, which particularly in France has become very fashionable, is a very economical and very relaxed way of skiing. At low speed and on intermediate slopes with good snow it is not a serious problem. In fact, it even has a certain virtue, lending itself to a very sliding type of skiing which utilizes fully the directional effects of the skis. In short, it's a skiing of feelings; but not of actions.

It is here where the weakness of the upright position lies: *it does not promote muscular action.*

If you have subconsciously adopted this position, you must correct yourself.

1. Because, in this very upright position your body mass is supported almost exclusively by the skeleton, with very little muscular involvement. The muscles become *too* relaxed and no longer are under the slight tension which would allow them to remain *alert* and ready to contract quickly.

2. Because, in this very upright position you have compromised your ability to very rapidly adjust your balance forward and backward, leading you to be overly cautious and reluctant to confront higher speeds and difficult terrain. Perform the following experiment. Standing still and very upright on your skis, try to slide them forward and backward on the snow underneath you. With difficulty, you can move them a few inches. Simultaneously flex your knees, your ankles and especially your hips and move your arms forward. Now move your skis: you can slide them a foot forward and backward.

3. Finally, because a very upright position makes it very difficult for you to make pivoting-steering movements of your feet at the beginning of turns and during wedeln.

To correct yourself, lower your stance by flexing in the knees and ankles and by tipping your torso slightly forward and spreading your arms wide for balance. At first, you will feel uneasy in this new position. Try to ski at a higher speed, however, and you will discover that you are more stable and more effective. After a few hours, you will adopt this new, flexed position.

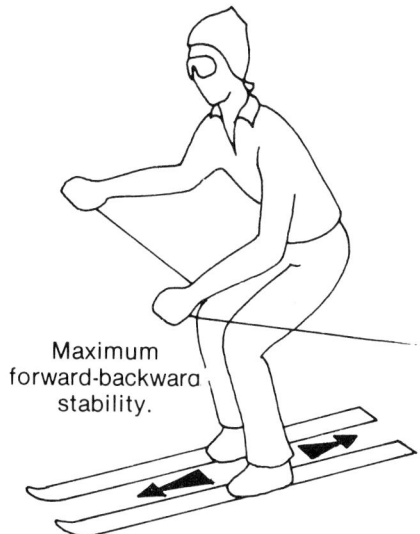

Maximum forward-backward stability.

Do you sideslip with forward weighting and your feet together ?

This fault is much less common today than it was only 5 or 6 years ago. The influence of old techniques, which were characterized by forward weighting and a narrow stance, that is to say dominant pressure on the balls of the feet — and therefore on the front of the skis — to facilitate sideslipping of the tails, has started to disappear, particularly among the younger generation of skiers. There are several reasons for this:

The widespread use of intermediate skis — and in particular the so-called "soft" skis — or compacts has caused skiers to stand more directly over the center of their skis and in a wider stance.

20 years ago, skis were mechanically designed to make forward weighted sideslips. Today, they sideslip easier with slight backweighting. Racers and good skiers no longer use forward weighting and a narrow stance to sideslip. If they do, they do so only to relax while free skiing. Unfortunately, many youngsters imitate these affectations and then are unable to rid themselves of them.

The modern leg action techniques of pivoting the skis with foot steering are not adaptable to a forward weighted position. This results in passive skiing without changes in rhythm or the possibility of quickly reacting to different situations.

A very narrow stance and forward weighting also compromises the ability of a skier to adjust his balance when terrain features disrupt the sliding of the skis. Particularly with compact skis, impacts against the tips become even more disturbing.

How do you know if you are committing this error ?

1. While traversing on an intermediate slope with good snow conditions, very gently initiate a sideslip without pivoting your skis. Try to feel, as best you can, what is happening under your feet. You can even try to close your eyes to better concentrate on your feet.

This position
— once considered elegant —
is now old-fashioned.

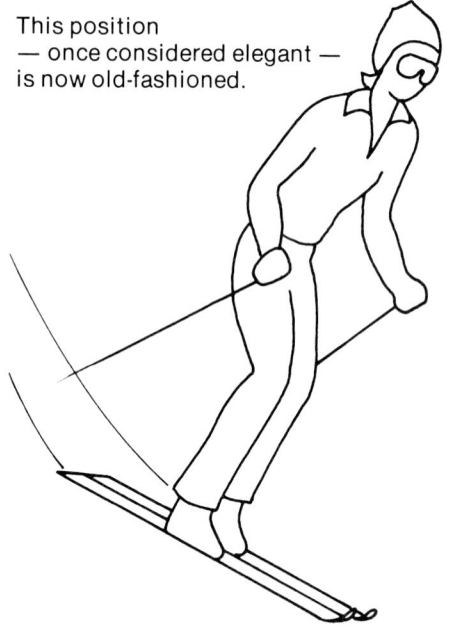

Did you feel that you moved your weight to the balls of your feet ? Or was your weight centered further back ?

2. Begin a long turn on the same slope and, throughout the turn, try to sense whether your weight is centered directly over the middle of your feet or more forward. Again, you can close your eyes to better concentrate on your feet. If your weight is forward, you should feel that your skis grip the snow more firmly in the forebody and that they sideslip around the tips. If you are more properly balanced, with your weight centered over the middle of your feet, you should feel that the center of pivoting of your skis is under your feet, and more precisely in the middle of your feet.

To correct yourself, spread your skis 8 inches and, with moderate speed in a traverse, make frequent brakes with a sideslip and try to sense that this requires you to press harder on the tails of your skis. Then, try to sideslip the skis with more subtle pressure on the tails and essentially without braking.

This requires you to find a new balance while sideslipping. As soon as you have discovered it, even though you don't yet feel at ease, you will notice that you are more successful in adjusting the pivoting of your skis under your body. Your leg action will quickly improve.

Your body enters the turn before your skis.

This error is also a regression to outmoded techniques. Like the preceeding case, it is usually a poor imitation of old rotation techniques, long since abandoned by all ski schools, yet unfortunately still transmitted to learning skiers.

This error is also occasionally made by unskilled skiers who, trying to discover ways to turn their skis, will turn their upper bodies in hopes that their skis will follow. The skis eventually begin to turn, but usually for entirely different reasons. Nevertheless, this reinforces the habit.

Try to analyze your own situation. When you start turns, do you make a movement – even minimal — with your arms or head in

Fault !
the chest is rotated
into the turn.

the skis delay,
then follow

the direction of the turn; a movement which takes place before your skis begin to enter the turn ? If this is your case, don't try to correct yourself by eliminating these gestures; it will be too difficult. Instead, concentrate on developing the independent leg action such as I described on pages 33 and 46. Since it is much easier and more effective to initiate a turn with your legs, once you acquire the necessary reflexes you likely will have corrected yourself. More often than not, this error is associated with a turn initiated with forward weighting and you can correct both faults simultaneously.

Do you lack independent leg action ?

Are you unsuccessful, even on easy slopes, in linking several turns down the fall line in a rapid rhythm ? Perhaps you admire those of your friends who are capable of quickly reacting from one foot to the other to catch themselves when losing their balance ? If so, you haven't yet acquired "independent leg action" !

Your case is common since all of our observations indicate that a deficiency of independent leg action is statistically only exceeded by the error of skiing too upright.

Have you been tenacious enough in following my advice on pages 32 and 33 for evolving long serpent turns into a first wedel down the fall line ?

If you seriously tried and failed, then you are committing another mistake.

— *Perhaps your stance is too narrow ?* In this case you are unable to learn to change your support foot and it is difficult for you to pivot your feet. In fact, pivoting the feet in a narrow stance requires a much more subtle mechanism than that used to pivot your feet in a wide stance (530-550).

— *Perhaps you ski with too much forward pressure and initiate your turn with a rotation of the upper body ?* In this case, your feet and skis are delayed in following your body into the turn and this delay is too slow for a genuine leg action and wedeln.

— *Perhaps you are weighting the tails of your skis excessively ?* Perhaps you are even leaning against the backs of your boots, thereby contracting your leg muscles to the point where rapid leg movement is prohibited ?

Try to correct these faults and return to a study of independent leg action and you will succeed.

Do you ski sitting back, leaning against your boots ?

During the past 5 or 6 years, with the appearance of stiffer and higher plastic boots, children have discovered a new way of skiing. Leaning against the backs of their boots, with their legs extended in front of them, they pivot their skis around the tails. Miraculously, many of them can retain a degree of suppleness and sliding. Yet as they become more muscled and begin to accelerate their leg movements, they gradually correct themselves.

Unfortunately, during the past couple of years we have begun to see a significant percentage of adults, both intermediate and beginning skiers, begin to ski in the same way but without the natural suppleness of children. Leaning against the backs of their boots, they stiffen their legs in front of them, push their buttocks back and their skis bite the snow with little control.

I sincerely hope that you are not committing this serious error, because I have always stressed that you feel that you are weighting the heel and ball of your foot simultaneously (rule of the 2 support points, page 22). In the extreme position described above, you can only weight the tails of your skis.

Perhaps you are committing this error, but minimally; almost imperceptibly ? Perhaps, like many skiers who have learned to change the support foot and abuse it, you utilize a lateral slip of the ski too much by pressing

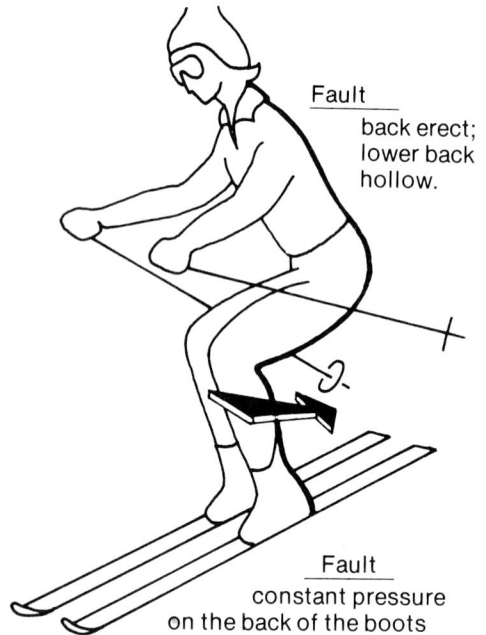

Fault
back erect;
lower back
hollow.

Fault
constant pressure
on the back of the boots

on the heel of your outside foot ? In this case, you almost never genuinely steer your feet into a pivot.

Having gotten into the habit of "sitting back" and weighting the ski behind what we have referred to as the "pivoting center", you are no longer able to pivot your skis and you become content to push them laterally.

If you have difficulty in smoothly pivoting your skis into turns or wedels, carefully analyze your behavior. You may very well be among the 20 or 30% of all intermediate skiers who fall into this category today.

The only remedy is to discover the pivoting center of your skis while ungluing your calves from the backs of your boots (page 32). The moment you do this, you will be able to pivot your skis with half the effort. The correction of this fault is quick, and the result spectacular.

Is the small of your back stiff or hollow ?

This error is often linked to the back-weighted position just mentioned which places excessive pressure on the tails of the skis. The remedy is the same.

But it often is also a consequence of a morphological abnormality of the hip or spinal column and is then generally accompanied by stiffening of the arms. If this is your case, you don't yet have a sufficient mastery of skiing to try to correct yourself.

Instead, be content to use a more erect stance by skiing with less flexion in your knees, hips and ankles. Be particularly careful to flex these joints equally as illustrated in our drawings. You can then ski with greater suppleness and relaxation in your back and arms.

Is your outside leg stiff while turning ?

This fault is statistically situated in third place behind the excessively upright position and the lack of independent leg action.

If you are guilty of committing this fault you are well aware of it because it is easy to recognize it in yourself without the help of film, video or a friend. But to correct it, you must first determine the cause of your fault.

Do you stiffen your outside leg because you are afraid of the slope, and from the middle of the turn do you tend to lean toward the mountain ? If yes, you first must learn to allow yourself to dive freely down the fall line at the beginning of the turn (page 34), even if you must brake to reduce your speed before initiating your turn (page 46). You should also learn that you can brake more effectively while sideslipping, and therefore also while turning, by balancing the mass of your body over your outside ski. Finally, you should perform hundreds of turns on easy slopes while lifting your inside ski several times during the turn to gain confidence in your ability to weight your outside ski (page 36).

Do you stiffen your outside leg while in a backweighted position, because you feel that you must force your ski to pivot into the turn ? This often occurs during a change

A serious fault: stiff outside leg

because you fail to pivot your outside ski

because you lean uphill at the end of the turn

of support foot with excessive lateral thrust on the heel and without a genuine pivoting effort. The remedy consists of using only a very subtle change of support foot and balancing yourself precisely over the pivoting center of your outside ski. It will then pivot to your liking, and perhaps begin to pivot too much !

On the contrary, do you stiffen your outside leg while in a forward weighted position ? Having thrown your body into the turn, do you find yourself "stuck" on your outside ski, weighting its edge so that it can't pivot into the turn ? This error was very frequent only ten years ago, but has since become rare. The remedy consists of ceasing to throw your upper body into the turn (page 54) and ceasing to use forward weighting to control your sideslips and braking (page 53).

Do you occasionally catch your outside edge and fall ?

This consists of a brutal loss of balance at the beginning of a turn which gives you the impression that a force has come out of nowhere to smash you to the ground.

This loss of balance is usually attributable to one of the following causes:

Instead of changing your support foot at the beginning of a turn, you displace your body mass to the outside of the turn.

Some instructors and teaching systems ask their students to shift their body weight from their downhill ski to their uphill ski at the beginning of a turn. If the students understand this to mean a change of support foot, without a lateral displacement of the upper body, they encounter no problems. But those who habitually move the mass of their body toward the outside of the turn at low speed will have problems as soon as their speed increases. On the contrary, they must lean to the inside of the turn at higher speeds to counter-balance centrifugal force. These two movements contradict each other and before they can be modified, they lead to

many faults; in particular a catching of the outside edge.

Many skiers, out of fear of catching their outside edges, will lean toward the inside of the turn and stiffen their outside leg.

In order to avoid this error, and to foster greater confidence in one's balance, we insist that beginning and intermediate skiers ski in a wide stance, with no movement of the torso.

If you have problems with catching your outside edge, return to a wider stance and learn to steer and pivot your ski (pages 32) and change your support foot (page 33).

Have you been unable to progress beyond the wedge turn level ?

Probably your lack of progress is due to your blocking the muscles which control the movements of your legs under your hips and the pivoting of your feet. These muscles play an essential role in skiing.

The only solutions are: 1) On steeper slopes, use a downhill stem brake and turn (page 45). 2) Limit your skiing to flat slopes for a few days. First, evolve your snowplows into sliding wedges (I don't like the expression "sliding snowplow" used in French ski instruction because those two terms seem to me to be contradictory). Then, while sliding close to the fall line, transform your "stem opening" into a simple sliding-pivoting of your outside ski in a wide stance while your skis remain more or less parallel (page 31).

By cultivating a stem opening with the uphill ski placed very flat on the snow — and not on the inside edge — you will discover the sliding directional effect of flat skis, which is quite different from the braking effect produced by the wedge. The discovery of this sliding directional effect may very well be a revelation for you and save you from the wedge.

BECOME A GOOD SKIER

In the first chapter, I endeavored to help the reader discover the basic behaviors of skiing; preserving and preparing the foundation for future evolution.

In this chapter, I begin with the same fundamental concepts, but will attempt to help you discover a more refined, more highly evolved, and often more differentiated behavior.

To use a previously employed analogy of the technique of a skier as a puzzle of special behaviors, I now suggest that we tune, and occasionally fraction, these pieces of your first rudimentary puzzle in order to make a richer unity of them.

In this way, you will be able to reach a new technical plateau, that of the good skier.

If you are beginning your study of this book with this chapter, I will ask you, on several occasions, to refer to earlier pages.

Nevertheless, I hope to help you to discover, in the following chapter, what constitutes the fundamental basics of ski technique, basics just as valid for elementary skiing as for more sophisticated skiing, aiming at a deeper refinement of effectiveness and aesthetics on skis.

I will advise you what to do, you will do it and you will become a good skier. How simple it is !

On the contrary, between the written page and the moment you are able to master a new behavior, there must inevitably be hundreds of miles on skis, repeated references to the pages of this book, multiple attempts and days of unexpected success and momentary failures... But if you have already used your many skiing friends as reference points, you will notice with great satisfaction that your progress is constant.

Many of my former readers write to me or approach me on the slope and ask me for advice concerning various technical problems. I help with pleasure, because each time I am surprised at the technical level and understanding attained by these skiers.

You can be a reader of this book and a passionate skier, not passionate for skiing itself, but for the beauty of the surroundings, the discovery of new horizons or for the unique physical effort required. Technique for you, then is only a means, although an indispensable means, for the satisfaction of your passion. Even if your goal is only to attain the minimum skill level necessary to descend most slopes, you fill glean from these pages precise suggestions that will enable you to overcome whatever difficulties you are having. By returning to the text after many days on skis, perhaps you will find the answers to your questions. And, perhaps, you will eventually gain not only competence but a taste for sports and technical perfection.

And, once having acquired the technical baggage that every good skier possesses, perhaps you will elevate yourself to the search for refinement of your technique; or, as I have called in the following chapters, "the art of skiing" ?

But for the moment, don't aim too high. It is essential that you don't try to progress too fast by leaving out intermediate steps.

I recognize that many skiers, who are capable of comfortably skiing most terrain,

will want to skip the earlier chapters and start with this chapter. Yet many of them have not yet built an adaptive foundation. Perhaps they have been committing the same technical fault for years, a technical fault which has prevented all progress for them. These skiers risk becoming overcome and out of date. In deference to them, I will refer them, throughout this chapter, to the preceeding chapter so that they can build the solid technical foundation without which they can not progress. *In particular, I suggest that these readers refer to the inventory of the most commonly committed technical faults which I presented at the end of the preceeding chapter.*

My advice, throughout this chapter, will be oriented in 4 directions. These should become clearly defined objectives for you:

• A search for comfort in long turns.
• Safety and precision at the beginning of your turns.
• Rapid leg movement.
• Safety in all terrain.

If you are attempting a very systematic approach, I would suggest that you concentrate on not more than one of these objectives in each training unit. Each unit consists of an attentive reading from the book, a personalized program of what you individually will attempt, a session on the snow, and finally a return to the book to define a new program. Perhaps some of you will think this approach too "intellectualized", and rightly so if the on snow session is not physically intense enough, if analysis is substituted for action. I repeat, one learns to ski by skiing. But it is also true that one can ski intensively for ten years without progressing, in reality regressing relative to the norm of skiers which is constantly improving.

Even if you're unwilling to expend the effort I recommend, I still think that by reading this chapter you will generate helpful ideas or better understand your faults or deficiencies and, without much effort, profit from your reading your very next time on skis.

Have courage, and good skiing !

SEARCH FOR EASE AND ELEGANCE IN YOUR TURNS.

Balance on your outside ski.

90% of all skiers who would normally be categorized as "good" control their turns by weighting both skis more or less equally. I didn't include this type of behavior in the listing of faults presented at the end of the preceeding chapter for two overlapping reasons. First of all, I have stressed from the very beginning of this book that the number one problem to be resolved in skiing is to maintain one's balance. This is easier to do when the feet are spread into a wide or semi-wide stance and the weight is distributed fairly equally over both feet. For this reason, we have used this position to introduce beginning skiers to stem openings, independent leg action and the directional effect that the skis can have while keeping the upper body relatively immobile and centered between both skis or, in other words, over the skier's base of support. A more or less equal weighting of both feet is, therefore, desirable up to a point in your evolution as a skier and, according to our statistical studies, is generally adopted by intermediate skiers.

But in becoming a good skier, you must now confront new problems, while turning, which will require you to use a distinctly dominant weighting of the outside ski.

These new problems are: 1. higher speeds; 2. greater centrifugal force; 3. steeper slopes; 4. more difficult snow conditions.

Learn to weight your outside ski by starting your turns with a spreading of your uphill ski.

You should become aware of the cen-trifugal force generated by every turn you make.

To do this, slide in a traverse at moderate speed and in a semi-wide stance. Lift or spread your uphill ski and set it down 8 or 12 inches up the slope. Then simultaneously weight and pivot it; and you will start into a round turn. If you delay bringing your inside ski parallel to your outside ski for 1 or 2 seconds, you will feel that you have almost total weighting of your outside ski as it begins to pivot. You can even lift your inside ski and continue the turn with all of your weight concentrated on your outside ski.

This will enable you to feel: 1. the centrifugal force generated by the turn, 2. that spreading your uphill ski causes you to lean to the inside of the turn to compensate for the centrifugal force, 3. that your outside foot, by controlling your outside ski, allows you to adjust the centrifugal force and the inward lean of your body to develop a new kind of balance which is very different from the balance which you have already acquired by simultaneously weighting both skis.

Caution ! Be careful that you don't bring your inside ski parallel too soon and end up weighting both skis. The centrifugal force will only accentuate your skidding and you will not be able to learn to balance properly on your outside ski.

You can accustom yourself to this new position by hopping back and forth in front of a mirror from the inside of one foot to the inside of the other.

Weighting your outside ski is the first secret to elegance and effectiveness while turning.

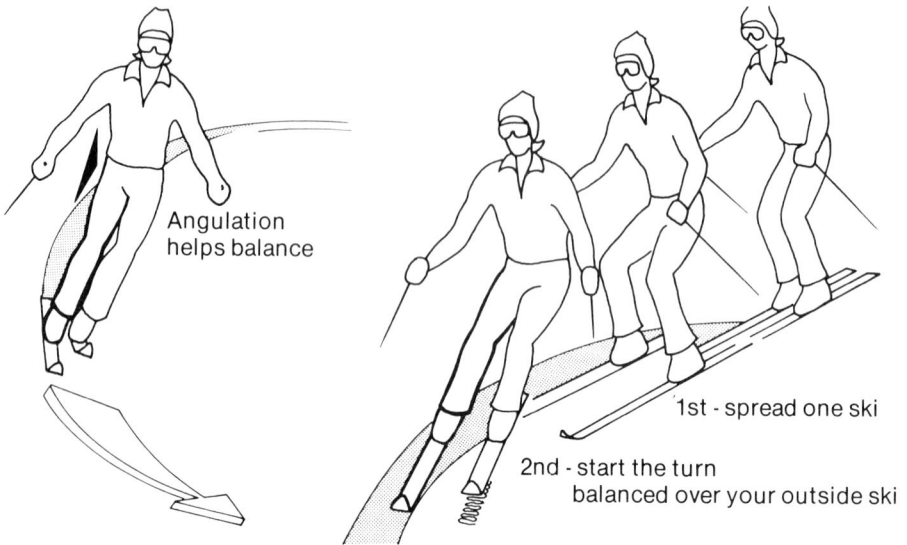

Angulation helps balance

1st - spread one ski

2nd - start the turn
balanced over your outside ski

Discover "balanced angulation" by starting your turns with a spreading of the uphill ski.

The biomechanics of human movement require that when one thrusts off of one foot, for example to hop, a curved body position is assumed, a position called *angulation* in skiing. This position is necessary for balance, hence the term *balance-angulation*. We will discover later that angulation serves another purpose as well.

Do the following experiment in front of a mirror: Hop on one foot in a skiing position; legs slightly flexed and arms spread wide for balance. Hop again, but standing on the inside of the foot, just as you would do while turning on hard or icy snow, you angulate even more.

That this elementary truth should be resisted by some ski schools, is just as absurd as to insist that the earth is not round !

If you have learned to ski with the aid of this book, you have already made movements that place you in an angulated position;

such as braking with a downhill stem and pivoting the legs during serpent turns or to initiate turns. It will be easy for you to understand and use angulation. On the other hand, if you have been skiing for a long time in a narrow stance, always weighting both feet equally, and lack independent leg action, you will have more trouble.

What should angulation feel like in long turns ?

1. A comfortable and relaxed stance with a fair amount of mobility of the upper body in the lateral plane. The arms are spread wider than usual in their role as balancing aids.

2. You should feel that your upper body rests over the head of the femur (thigh bone) of your outside leg, just as the arm of a scale is balanced on its fulcrum.

Your outside leg should be slightly flexed and your weight balanced over the center of your foot or, more precisely, equally distributed between the two support points of your foot (page 22). This double support allows you to better control your skis through the turn.

Dominant weighting of the outside ski in a turn requires a balanced, angulated body position.

The chest is balanced supply on the head of the femur.

Pressure is transmitted to the edge of the ski

Acceleration

Braking

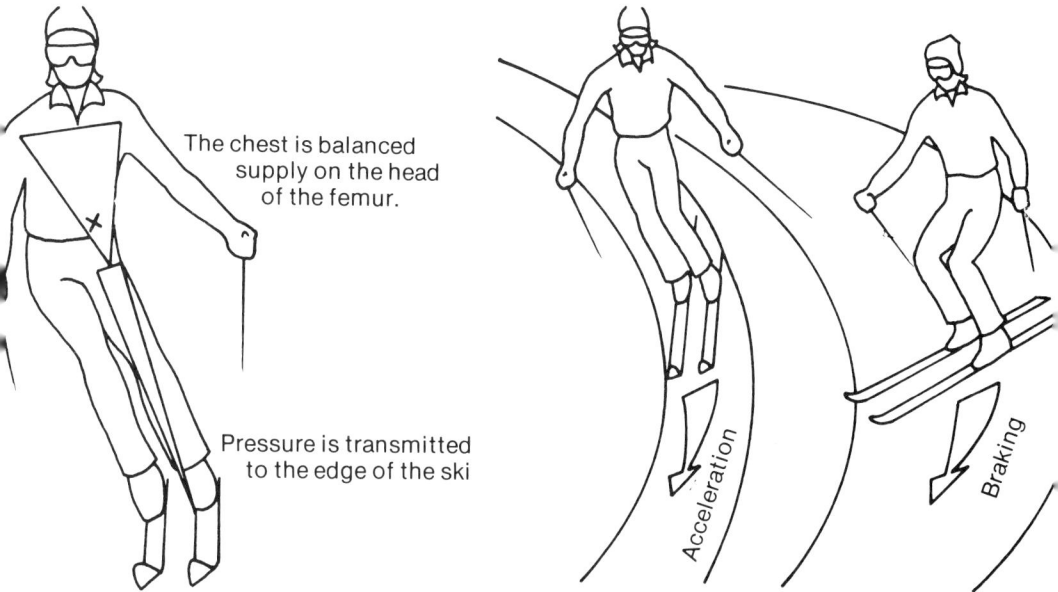

Do you feel that you slide straight down the fall line for a moment in the middle of your turns ?

The most serious fault committed by at least 50% of all good skiers is to confuse turning and braking. I have already discussed this problem (page 46) and will soon return to it. A beautiful turn is a sliding turn during which the skier plays with the slope instead of defending himself against it.

A second secret for discovering the sliding turn is to accept an acceleration as you descend straight down the fall line in the middle of your turns.

Do you feel this acceleration ? Analyze yourself while on snow. All of your turns occur in two phases. During the first phase, you ski into the fall line. Do you, however, you leave the fall line. Do you, however, have the impression that you move as quickly as possible out of the fall line ? Do you pivot your skis so hard that you "refuse" the slope ?

This is more of a psychological problem than a technical problem. In both cases, your average speed can be the same. If you slow down more before starting your turn you can accelerate during the turn and complete it without going any faster than if you swung your skis abruptly across the fall line without first braking your speed. It only requires that you dare, for a brief moment, to let yourself slide straight down the slope. It is the fear of this "dive down the slope" that seriously risks impeding your progress.

You must become accustomed to skiing down the fall line on intermediate or flat slopes: in a schuss, in a serpent or in elongated wedels. This is precisely why I have placed so much emphasis on these manuevers in the preceeding chapter. If you are not familiar with the serpent turn, return to this elementary movement on flat slopes as I described on pages 30 and 32.

You should also be sure to cultivate the "brake then turn" reflex, which is the only way to counter the "turn to brake" reflex (page 46).

A long turn on skis is elegant and effective only if it contains a phase where the skier accelerates in a slide straight down the fall line.

Understand the directional effect of the skis produced during the control of the turn.

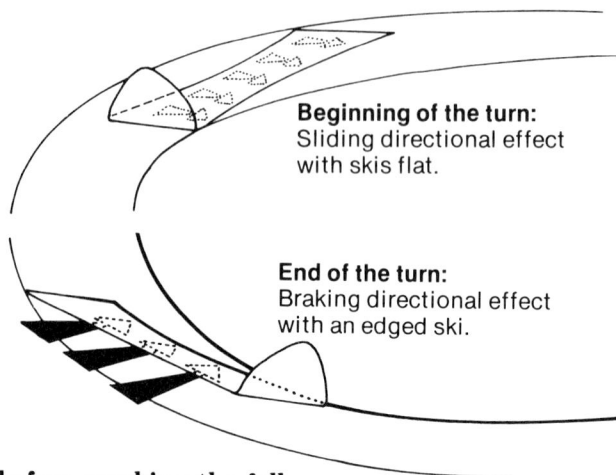

Beginning of the turn:
Sliding directional effect with skis flat.

End of the turn:
Braking directional effect with an edged ski.

With skis flat before reaching the fall line.

If you have not learned to ski with the aid of this book, please refer to pages 24 and 34 to insure that you are aware of two fundamental elements of ski technique which, unfortunately, have seldom been mentioned until now. They consist of:

1. the pull of gravity down the slope which acts on your body and skis to propel them straight down the fall line;

2. the sliding directional effect which causes a ski that is positioned slightly across the direction of travel and lying flat on the snow to move in a curved trajectory.

In every turn down the slope, the skier, upon reaching the fall line, necessarily makes use of these two elements: the pull of gravity and the sliding directional effect of the skis. As shown in our illustration above, one can take advantage of the fact that in the earlier part of the turn, as a consequence of a less pronounced inward lean, the skier has a tendency to hold his skis flat on the snow. It is in this position that the sliding directional effect is the greatest.

Balancing on the edges at the end of the turn.

As the skier leaves the fall line, he gradually turns his skis across it. Even if he maintains an unvarying degree of inward lean, in order to overcome a constant amount of centrifugal force, the angle between the running surface of his skis and the surface of the snow increases. The "edge angle of his skis" is said to increase. In addition, as the skier turns his skis out of the fall line, gravity continues to pull the skier downhill across the direction of his skis and tends to make them sideslip.

The skis continue to turn only as the edges bite into the snow, producing a "directional effect". However, whereas the directional effect of the skis at the beginning of the turn is produced with a very slight edge angle, the increased edge angle toward the end of the turn results in a braking effect. Later, you will learn to decrease this braking action and to use a directional effect of the skis which we call "carving".

Remember that the frictional forces between the skis and the snow are responsible for creating the turns.

PRACTICE TURN CONTROL.

You can make turns with skidding and braking by holding the skis more or less across the path of travel. On the other hand, the art of "good" skiing requires that you hold the skis in the line of the turn as much as possible. To accomplish this, "pilot" the curve of your turn with the foot of your outside leg in a supple, angulated position.

AN EXTENSION FOR ENTERING TURNS WITH GREATER SUPPLENESS

ANDREAS WENZEL executes a classic giant slalom turn. He leaves the preceeding turn in a low, angulated position. Wenzel then extends himself vertically to unweight his skis, allowing them to enter the turn more smoothly. He then flexes again into an angulated position by progressively flexing his legs.

A SPREADING AND CHANGE OF SUPPORT FOOT

We can also observe that as Wenzel extends, he spreads his uphill ski and then shifts his weight to it. We will see this manuever in many of the other photomontages. This movement allows him to place his uphill ski flat on the snow and, therefore, enter the turn with better sliding.

EXITING A TURN WITH PRESSURE ON THE TAIL OF THE OUTSIDE SKI

In these photomontages, **PERRINE PELEN**, the top-ranked slalom racer in the world in 1977 and 1978, and **INGEMAR STENMARK**, the best mens' slalom racer since 1975, use to the extreme the greatest discovery of modern skiers: tail pressure on the edge of the outside ski at the end of the turn to improve holding. Before this evolution in technique, racers, like tourists, finished their turns compressed on their skis, bending too far forward and sliding. In the second photomontage, we can say that Perrine "attacks" the gate with "feet forward". In all three sequences, we sense that the skiers are perfectly stable as they exit the preceeding turns and prepare to start the following turn.

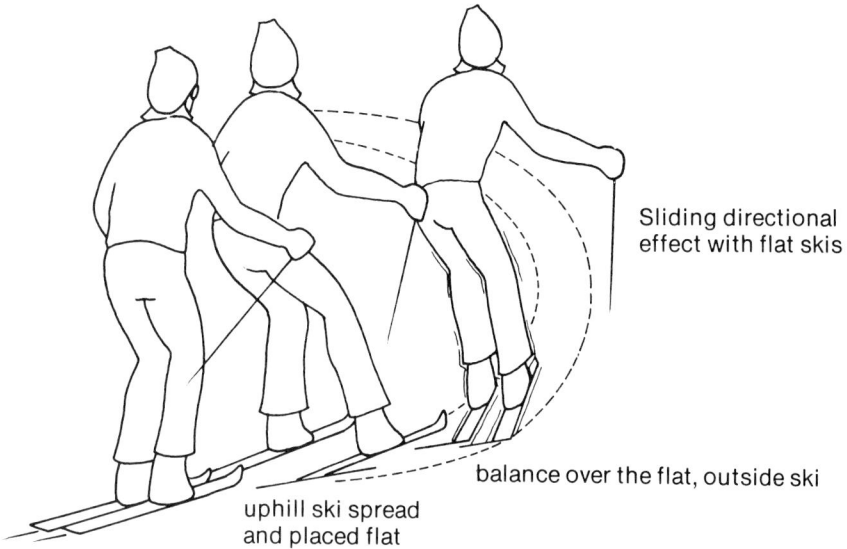

Sliding directional effect with flat skis

balance over the flat, outside ski

uphill ski spread and placed flat

Discover the flat ski directional effect at the beginning of the turn.

Initiate a turn with the help of a slight spreading of the uphill ski, then apply a very light pressure to the skis as you draw them back together. This pressure should be applied more on your heels than on the balls of your feet.

This suggestion will make the old-timers, the fanatic proponents of the "pure christianias" and the "Christiania leger" of the French teaching method shriek. However, current skis have been designed and developed to meet the needs of top skiers and are most effectively controlled at minimum edge angles when pressure is exerted slightly behind the point at which pressure is exerted in a normal straight running stance (117-135). It is in this way that old techniques, in which forward pressure at this point in the turn was advocated, differ with modern techniques.

Try to displace your foot forward a few inches relative to your upper body at the finish of the turn. You will thus discover a new, smoother manner to control the arc of your skis and your feet will remain more relaxed.

Angulate: you will feel more comfortable by again assuming the position which we have called "balance angulation". This angulated position will have developed automatically if you have first stemmed your uphill ski and then drawn the inside ski toward it with a simple movement of your legs and without displacing your upper body in the slightest. By giving you a certain reserve of balance, angulation permits you to more easily remain in balance while your skis pivot automatically and pull you gradually toward the fall line.

Keep your feet, legs and upper body relaxed. The slightest stiffness will result in a braking action of the skis and prevent them from pivoting smoothly.

Discover the flat ski directional effect on soft, packed powder.

If this type of snow is soft enough, you can even use this directional effect after your skis have pivoted through the fall line. On flat and moderate slopes, the flat ski directional effect can be used to make all of your turns in soft snow.

> *The flat ski directional effect is greatest when the skis are pivoted only slightly across their direction of travel through the arc of the turn, when they are held in a reduced edge angle, and when the feet remain as relaxed as possible.*

Discover the directional effect of edged skis at the finish of a turn.

Take off straight down the hill on fairly hard snow and discover the "3 support point rule" and "knee angulation".

Sliding straight down hill in a semi-wide or even wide stance, pivot one ski slightly and tip it on edge. In order to maintain pressure on the edge, feel the support of the front and back part of your foot on the inner sole of your boots. In addition, become conscious of a third source of support, that of your *medial malleolus* against the inside of your upper boot. This combination of feelings is what we call the 3 support point rule.

In order to feel the pressure on these 3 points, you'll become aware that you must displace your knee laterally to the inside. We are referring to "knee angulation" which, paradoxically, is used to a greater degree by champions than by intermediate skiers.

As soon as your right ski is tipped on edge, you feel a change in direction toward the left. At the same time, centrifugal force is generated and compresses you onto the ski and causes you to assume an angulated position somewhat similar to that which I described on page 62. You notice that this compression increases the directional effect exerted by the edge of your outside ski, but at the same time increases its braking action.

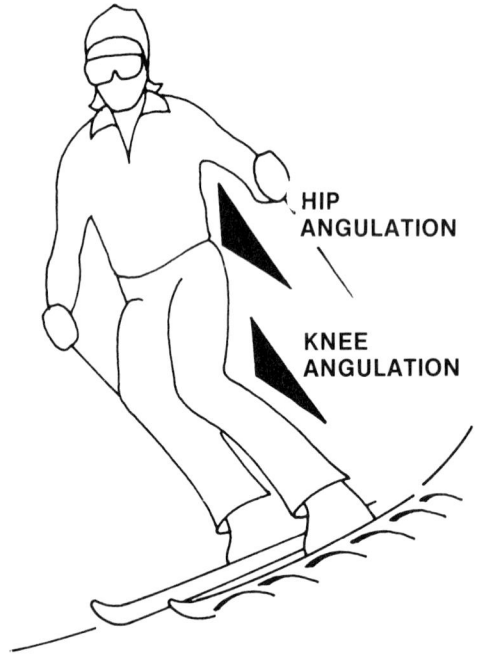

HIP ANGULATION

KNEE ANGULATION

Try to feel that this directional effect increases with a decrease in braking action if you exert pressure slightly more on your heel rather than on the ball of your foot. This result is due to the dimensions and mechanical characteristics of modern skis (120 and 150).

In downhill turns, feel the directional effect of the edge once the ski turns out of the fall line.

If you make a real turn on an intermediate slope, including a phase in which the skis travel down the fall line, you will find it just as easy to create this directional effect of the edge as you did in the preceeding straight run.

On the other hand, if your skis are pivoted excessively in the first half of the turn, if you are standing on both feet, or if your stance is too narrow, you will have difficulty making your edges bite. Begin, therefore, by correcting these errors.

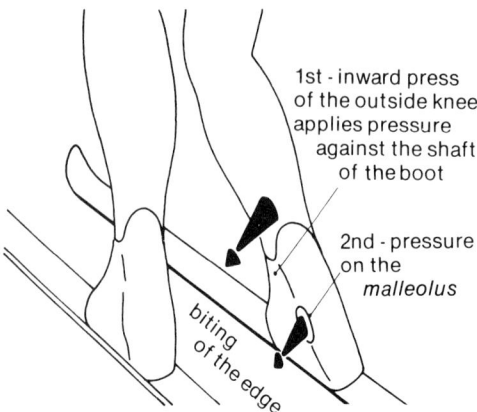

1st - inward press of the outside knee applies pressure against the shaft of the boot

2nd - pressure on the *malleolus*

biting of the edge

In icy conditions on steep hills, use the support of your edge to make your skis "hold" through the arc of the turn.

You have discovered the directional effect produced by exerting pressire on the edge of your outside ski. This directional effect is rather easily obtained on less hard snows on which the edge of the ski can hold reasonably well and in moderately long turns. In these circumstances, you experience relatively little sideslipping and little braking action.

On the other hand, on very hard snows, on which the edges hold less effectively, and in shorter radius turns, you sideslip. And sometimes your skis even tend to pivot around your feet without even making a turn. They simply change direction and the directional effect of the edges is reduced, while the braking action is very great. This experience is even more common when the hill is very steep. The skis, under these circumstances, are said to "chatter". They do not carve through the arc of the turn.

In order to carve, you must, above all, hold your skis firmly on edge and prevent them from sideslipping or pivoting excessively. The essential factors are the quality of your skis and your muscle power but also the level of your technique.

You must concentrate on your foot and your hip at the same time.

Apply the "3 support point" rule: you should feel that your foot, the boot and the edge of your ski constitute a very rigid whole laterally. Assume a position very similar to that of angulation described on page 62: feel your upper body relaxed and balanced over the head of your femur. At the same time, however, you should feel your thigh, lower leg and foot muscles contract firmly in the lateral plane. In order to distinquish this type of angulation from that already described ("balance-angulation"), I would

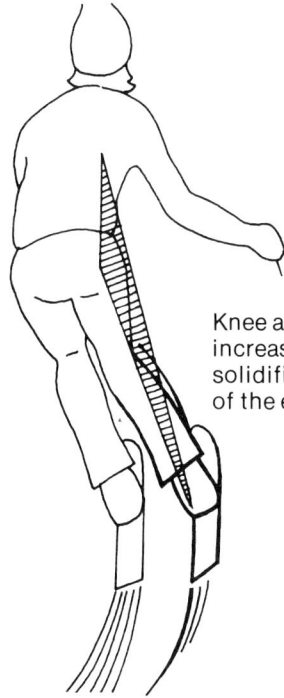

Knee angulation increases and solidifies the hold of the edges.

suggest the expression "edgeset-angulation".

To these two essential technical elements, you can add a slightly greater pressure on the heel of your foot, and therefore over the tails of your ski; especially if you are equipped with the latest competition models. You will thus feel your ski hold even more effectively, possibly even to the point of carving as I will describe later and in which the braking action of the ski is almost completely avoided.

Note: Edgeset-angulation corresponds to a pivoting of the outside ski under the pelvis and relates very closely to the position which you assumed in order to check your speed with the downhill stem or to your first attempts at applying pressure to the ski in a downhill stem (pages 46 and 72). Even in these two manuevers, the desirability of greater pressure on the heel of the foot became noticeable. Thus, eventhough you

---

3 conditions necessary to the directional effect of the ski held on edge are: 1. pressure over the outside ski, 2. a firmly edged ski in the edgeset-angulation position, 3. skis pivoted only slightly across their direction of travel through the arc of the turn.

have reached the "good skier" level, practicing these maneuvers might be well worth your while if you have not yet acquired an effective edgeset angulation.

Maintain a smooth arc through the turn, even in bumpy terrain.

Are you able to make large radius turns through fairly bumpy intermediate terrain ? The problem is double: to avoid being "thrown around" by the bumps, which exert powerful vertical shocks under your feet, and to maintain a fairly smooth arc with a fairly even pressure on your edges so that your skis do not first bite then chatter away laterally.

In order to avoid being thrown vertically, the solution is simple: assume a position similar to that of slalom and giant slalom racers, and which we have named the "modern position" (423). Your ankles are only slightly flexed and your knees and hips are flexed much more. When seen from the side, a simple point of reference, the forward angle of your upper body is greater than the forward angle of your lower legs. Your arms are held somewhat forward. Assume this

position in front of a mirror, bend down and straighten up, learn what the position feels like. Next, assume it while you are skiing. Make some straight runs at moderate speed through bumpy terrain. In this position, you should feel your knees thrown up vertically in front of your body and not underneath it as happens in the traditional straight running position or even moreso in a "forward" position. This type of flexion is sometimes referred to as "avalement-flexion".

In order to maintain the arc of the turn over bumps, you must also use avalement-flexion but in an angulated position with your weight applied almost completely to the outside ski. Try to lift your inside ski while making long radius turns. At first only in the second half of these turns. Try also to lift it during long traverses at high speed through bumpy terrain. You will soon be able to maintain a continuous arc through your turns by sidestepping the bumps and absorbing them instead of smashing into them. At first, this exercise will seem unpleasant and difficult, but *you must emphasize it because there are few exercises as effective in developing a true skier.*

Only the "modern position" allows the skier to maintain a continuous regular arc throughout the turn under all circumstances.

BECOME MORE STABLE AND PRECISE AT THE BEGINNING OF TURNS THROUGH THE USE OF "PLATFORMS".

I described at length the control of the arcs of long radius turns. I emphasized the smooth plunge into the fall line and the need to accept the resulting acceleration in order to describe regular arcs. In order to master these elements, however, you must learn to control your speed and the speed of your skis at the entry into the turn. Without this control, you will rush the initiation of your turns and they will become a series of braking actions.

This control should also permit you to initiate turns with a shorter radius, to link short turns together and finally to learn to perform a true wedeln.

Have you already learned to "check then turn" or have you learned to "turn and brake" ?

I emphasized this point strongly in the preceeding chapter. If you have not read this portion of the book, I would ask you to analyze your skiing carefully. Are you able, while traversing at a moderately high speed, to check your speed quickly and use this check to initiate a turn ? Can you do so on smooth slopes as well as in bumps ? Often the answer is no because this reflex does not develop spontaneously. I should also mention that it is rarely taught because most instructors have their pupils ski at speeds which are too slow for the manuever to be useful.

If you have not already developed the "check then turn" reflex, put in a few hours of practice with the information provided on pages 46 and 47.

First you will learn to slow down over a relatively long distance before turning. Then, to use a shorter period of braking action and, finally, you will learn to check your speed very briefly and feel this check literally propel you into a turn. You will then be able to perfect these checks which result in an increase of pressure on the skis and thus become more effective and more stable at the beginning of your turns. We refer to such checks as platforms.

The advantages of platforms are numerous.

• Platforms permit you to control your speed.

• They permit you to locate the beginning of your turn at a specific point in time as well as at a specific spot on the slope.

• They aid the timing of the pole plant.

• They permit the unweighting of your skis.

• They reduce to a minimum the unbalanced phase which occurs at the initiation of all turns.

• They permit a more precise positioning of the skis at the beginning of the turn which allows the skier to control the arc of the turn more easily.

• After the phase in which the greatest pressure is exerted on the skis, as the

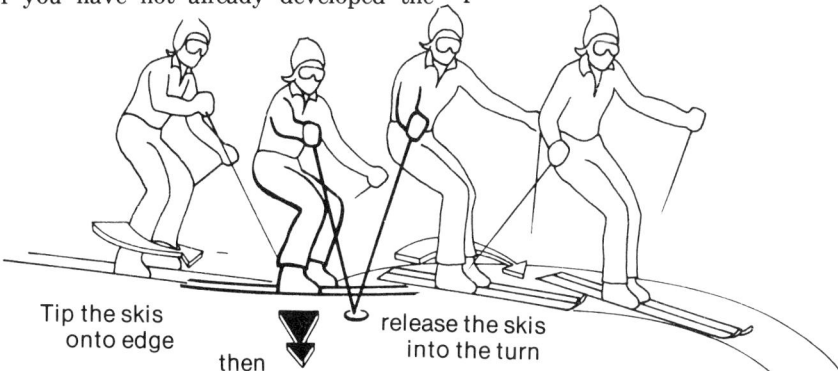

Tip the skis onto edge   then   release the skis into the turn

muscles are contracted and the feet held firm, there is a relaxation phase which favors a balanced and very smooth initiation of the turn of the skis on the snow.

Be sure you understand the four conditions necessary for a good platform before your first attempts.

We are now entering the domain of serious technique which can not be understood without a certain amount of effort and reflection. For this reason, I'm going to try to help you understand the why and how of what you are going to do before guiding your first attempts.

1st condition: displace your skis under your body — "anticipation"

You are traversing the slope with a fair amount of speed. Because your skis are sliding forward, you are unable to exert pressure on the ground other than vertically (211). Thus, you are unable to check your speed and propel yourself into the turn. The only possible solution: displace your skis under your body in order to position them so that you can exert pressure across them onto your edges.

This displacing action is discovered instinctively by talented skiers faced with an obstacle, for example a slalom pole, and thus obligated to check their speed abruptly before turning. It always consists of: an uphill pivoting of the skis so that pressure can be exerted on the edges, a forward displacement of the skis in the direction of the straight run in order to offest the braking action which will result and a slight downhill slide of the skis resulting from the displacements already described.

The first two displacements are absolutely necessary in creating the platform against which the mass of your body, carried along by your initial speed, will be checked and then be made to rebound into the turn.

Note: because the skis have pivoted under the body of the skier, he has assumed a position termed "anticipation". In fact, you will notice that without any conscious effort, once you displace your skis as I have indicated, your upper body will tend to pivot into a position facing downhill, a position of "anticipation" in the direction of the new

turn (531-e).

2nd condition: balance predominantly on your heels.

Your skis, turned slightly across your direction of travel and positioned in front of the mass of your body, create a platform against which you can rebound just like a ball against a wall. This platform permits you to check your speed, or rebound, or both, as is generally the case.

Two elements determine the effectiveness of the platform:

1. The "bite" of the ski. How well the ski holds depends on its quality and on the point at which the skier applies his weight. There is a point a couple of inches behind the normal center point of the ski which is called the "point of maximum hold" (127).

2. The preliminary backward tilt of the upper body. The speed of the entire skier is checked, but the braking action occurs especially at the level of the feet. The upper body tends to tip over the feet as it enters into the turn. It is thus easy to understand that the skier must lean backward preliminarily, balancing predominantly on his heels. Once the movement of his skis is checked, his upper body, carried forward, assumes a balanced position over the middle of his skis (260-270).

If you are accustomed to skiing with a bit of forward lean, this explanation should help you to understand why you have difficulty checking your speed and developing effective platforms. Many skiers developed in French ski schools in the past find themselves in this position.

3rd condition: the movement into and out of a platform is characterized by a distinctive rhythm.

When a platform is used primarily to

1st the skis pivot
and slide forward

3rd a very rapid
rebound

2nd a platform with dominant
weighting of the tails

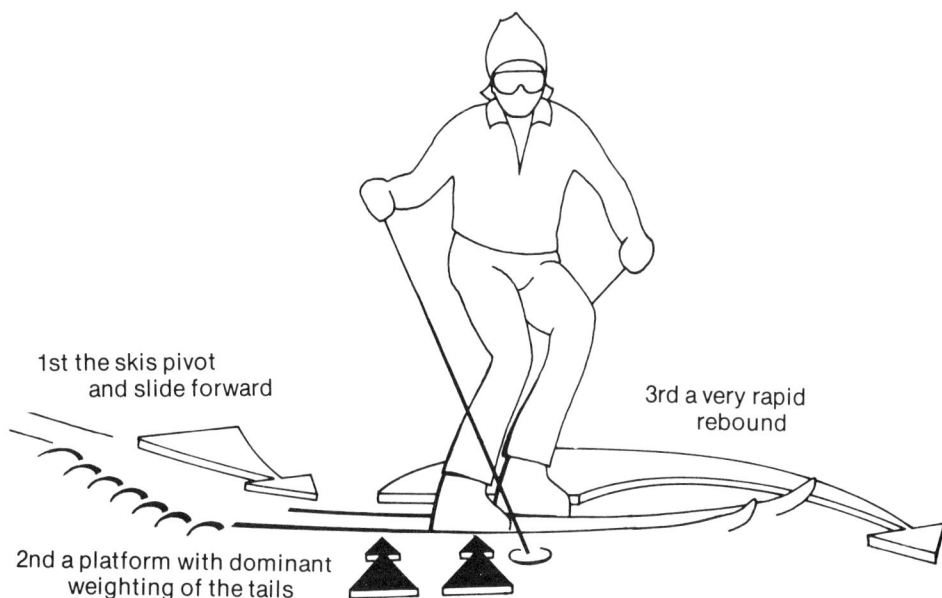

check a skiers speed before the entry into a turn, the checking phase in which the skis hold while the legs flex is dominant. There is an absorption of energy through a braking action and, secondarily, a propulsion into the turn. This rhythm is referred to as a "check platform".

If, on the other hand, the primary goal is to propel the skier into the turn, the braking action lasts an almost imperceptible period of time and seems only to serve to prepare the propulsion into the turn. This is the rhythm of "platform rebound".

All very good skiers are capable of using both of these rhythms, but almost always have a tendency to prefer one or the other. Try to fully understand the difference between these two rhythms so that you can develop them more effectively. Both are indispensable to good skiers and racers.

In my experience, the first rhythm sometimes leads the skier to develop and excessively low stance while the second leads to the adoption of a higher position and to the discovery of "extension" which I will discuss soon.

4th condition: plant your ski pole at the right moment and place.

Slide your skis forward under your body to give yourself a solid support in front of you and, compressed by the speed, "rebound" into the turn. It's easy to understand that this requires very good balance reflexes if you don't make use of the stabilizing support that a pole plant can give.

The pole plant is made precisely as you check your speed but remains in the snow as you start your turn. The pole is planted to the side but the exact location of the pole plant is a function of your speed. If your arms are properly placed, that is spread wide and carried in front of your body, planting your pole doesn't require a gross movement of your arm, only a flick of the wrist to bring the point into contact with the snow. It can, therefore, be made instantaneously.

The pole plant improves the skier's balance considerably during the platform and the following unweighting movement. The skier's base of support is, in fact, tripled. It's easy to understand why skiers who don't know how to use a pole plant effectively are incapable of making solid platforms before beginning their turns. They have an instinctive fear of losing their balance.

71

Two formulas for discovering platforms

First formula: the downhill stem platform.

If you have learned to ski with the aid of this book, you are already very familiar with the downhill stem. If this is not the case, however, I insist that you practice repeatedly the delayed checks with a downhill stem described earlier (page 40) over varied terrain and differing snow conditions.

If this manuever is difficult for you, you must persist, because only serious technical faults can make the execution of this kind of braking difficult. But once you have learned to check your speed with a downhill stem, you have learned to simultaneously utilize: 1. pressure on the heel of your downhill foot. 2. an angulated position to weight your downhill ski. 3. the use of your downhill leg as a "spring" to absorb the compression of your body mass onto your downhill ski.

How do you evolve a braking stem into a platform ?

Abbreviate your checking until you feel that you are merely spreading your downhill

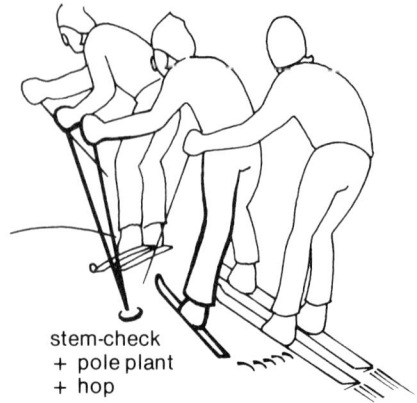

stem-check
+ pole plant
+ hop

A downhill stem facilitates the platform

ski and then immediately thrust against the edged ski with your heel. You will then feel that as you resist the compression that results from this checking with your downhill leg, your body mass is thrown upward. This is known in athletics as a "wind-up - recoil" movement.

You must insist on holding your downhill ski on the edges to prevent sideslipping. Your forward movement then accentuates the overloading of your downhill ski and the recoil increases until your skis literally are catapulted, pivoting into the turn. But just as your feet must hold the skis firmly on edge during the check, they must then be supple as your skis start to slide freely into the turn.

This is the moment to try to plant your ski pole.

Your arms should be carried normally, spread wide for balance. Open your downhill ski into a stem and then, at this precise instant, check vigorously with your downhill ski and plant your downhill pole. These two movements compliment each other perfectly; one facilitating the other.

The downhill stem platform is an effective way to combine angulation, tail-pressure, the pole plant and the catapulting rebound of your skis into the turn.

Flex and plant...   then rebound.

Second Formula: a pivoting hop into the turn

First make a platform with parallel skis without hopping

If you have succeeded in making a platform with a downhill stem, you should be able to make a platform with parallel skis after a few tries from a wide stance. You begin from a sideslip and then rapidly pivot your skis and apply your weight to the heel of your downhill foot to make the edges bite. You balance yourself by simultaneously planting your downhill pole. This manuever will compress you onto your downhill ski just as the platform from a downhill stem did and as you resist this compression with your downhill leg you will be catapulted into the turn.

You can make the turn initiation sharper by immediately shifting your weight from your downhill ski to your other ski as you rebound from your platform and thereby enter the turn more dynamically. A turn initiated in this way simultaneously uses two technical elements: the platform, a very evolved manuever, and a change of support foot, a more rudimentary element which you were first introduced to on page 34.

A platform and pivoting hop at the beginning of the turn

This is a way of refining your platforms — until the time when you can eliminate the change of support foot — and make possible the use of a narrower stance with your feet held closer together through the manuever.

The execution of this movement is easy. Begin with a sideslip then pivot your skis and create a platform by weighting your heels to make the edges bite. Use a pole plant as you did before but in a narrower stance. Check more abruptly and you will literally hop into the turn, balanced on your ski pole. You will notice that your skis automatically start to pivot into the turn.

As you hop into the turn, your upper body is stabilized by your ski pole which allows you to remain in balance. You should land supply on your skis with your ankles relaxed and start the next turn.

This manuever will help you to make short radius turns.

Caution ! You will find that your skis pivot so easily that you risk overturning them and this will result in a sideslipping-braking turn. Your pivoted hop should bring you into the fall line but under no circumstances should you jump completely across the fall line.

A platform followed by a pivoting hop into the turn is the best way to discover the genuine rhythm of platforms.

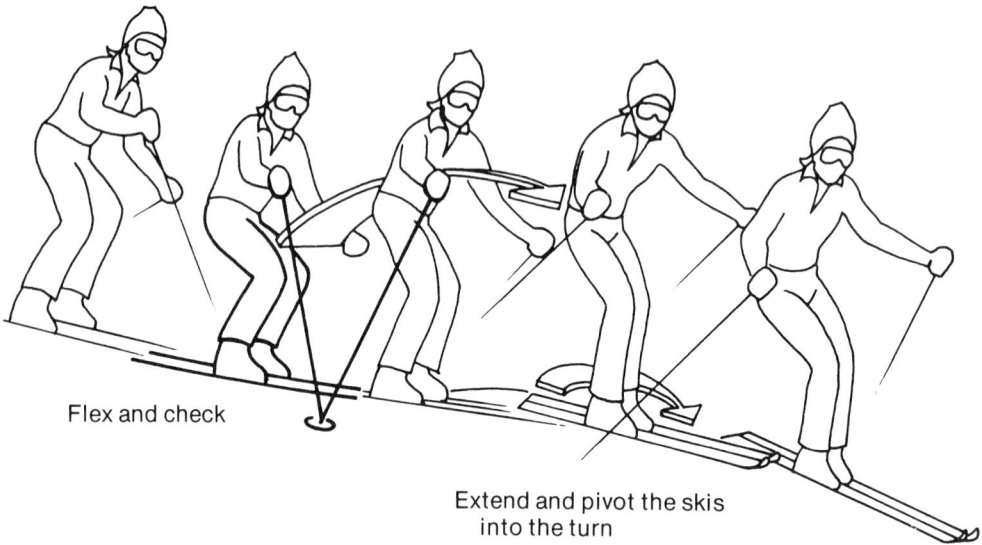

Flex and check

Extend and pivot the skis
into the turn

Delay your platforms: unweighting, flexion-extension and extension

You have already discovered the link between a platform and unweighting

In learning to use a brief checking with either a downhill stem or a parallel skis sideslipping to initiate your turn, you have unknowingly used an unweighting action of your skis. Every downward thrust of the feet is followed by an unweighting of the feet. This can be verified by standing on a bathroom scale.

It can be psychologically unsettling for a beginning skier to feel himself lifted away from the support of the ground but he soon learns to become accustomed to it. By now, you should have arrived at a stage in your progression where you enjoy the sensation of unweighting and therefore have found pleasure in cultivating the preceeding turn with a pivoting hop.

Evolve the pivoting hop into a flexion-extension

To make your first pivoting hops, you flexed your legs slightly and then extended upwards, straightening your legs. Now try to progressively flex faster so that the check becomes more dynamic and is followed by a genuine upward rebound movement. This rebound justifies the unity that is implied in the contraction "flexion-extension". This movement is, in fact, simple and is exactly the same as you experience when you jump rope. Your muscles are elastic like the rubber wall of a tennis ball which rebounds against the ground.

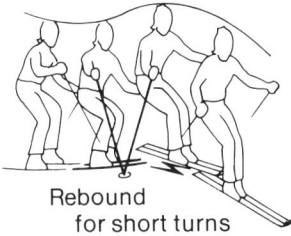

Flexion-Extension
for long turns

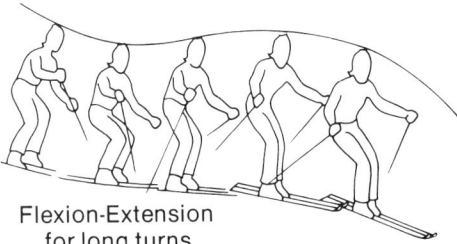

Rebound
for short turns

An extension can coincide with a stemming or lateral spreading of your skis or a change of support foot

Having discovered that an extension following a platform permits your skis to enter a turn more smoothly, you will now be able to include an extension in most of your turn initiation techniques. An extension can be used in turns initiated with a stemming or lateral spreading of your uphill ski or a shifting of weight (change of support foot) from the downhill to the uphill ski in a wide or semi-wide stance.

But be careful! Don't extend and throw your entire body, hip or even arms into the turn. Such movements, known as *projection circulaire*, have been abandoned by all the ski schools of the world because they are diametrically opposed to the use of leg action which is a major theme in modern techniques. These movements will always be part of the "suit of armor" of very good skiers, but are only used well and in moderation.

Gradually prolong your flexion-extension

As you make a pivoting hop at the beginning of a turn with the kind of rebound I just described, you extend very little yet your skis are thrown off the snow. They then tend to slam hard as they land. You should try to prolong your unweighting by extending your body during the unweighting phase. *This will enable you to be more elegant and your skis will land more softly on the snow.* Eventually, you will be able to pivot and slide your unweighted skis into the turn while maintaining contact with the snow.

A FAULT !

Only differences in rhythm distinguish rebound platforms and flexion-extension and extension unweighting.

A judicious choice of line and terrain facilitates the platform

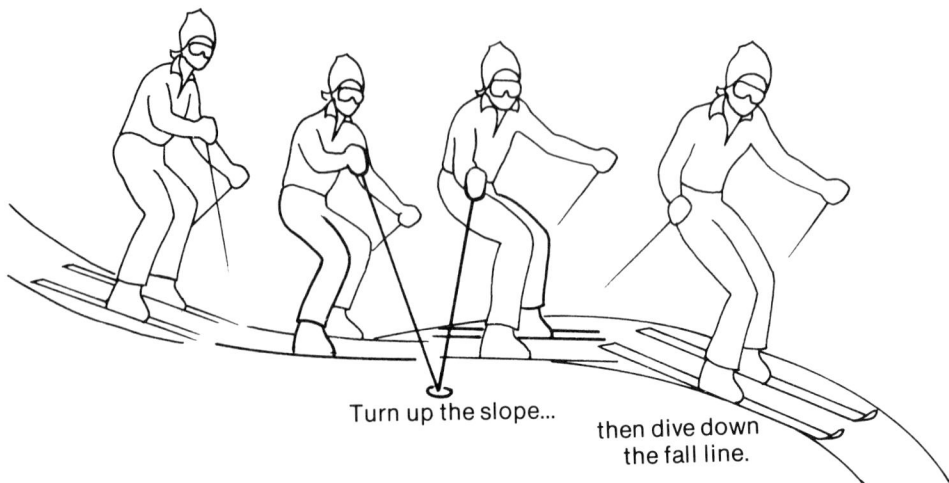

Turn up the slope...
then dive down the fall line.

Use bumps

If you have difficulties making a platform at the beginning of a turn, try them in moguls. When you are obliged to check quickly and decisively before a bump, you will feel yourself more compressed, then more distinctly thrust upward and your skis pivot easily over the bump. You risk, in fact, being compressed too much and rebounding excessively !

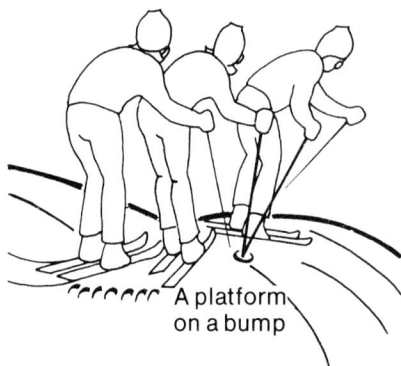

A platform on a bump

A platform becomes twice as effective if made on the top of a bump.

Pivot slightly uphill before making your platform

Try an experiment. Slide in a traverse at moderate speed on a smooth slope. Pivot your skis uphill for one or two meters then make your platform. You will feel a greater compression and will notice that your skis pivot smoothly into the turn.

Your pole plant, made at the instant you set your edges, will be very useful in this turn to stabilize your upper body and improve your balance as your skis start into the turn.

This turn will become even easier if you change your support foot by shifting your weight from your downhill ski to your uphill ski (which becomes your outside ski as you enter the turn) at the end of your counter turn up the hill.

Once refined, this gesture is the so-called 'S' counter turn of very good skiers.

Beginning a turn with a counter turn up the slope permits a smoother, more effective and more elegant platform.

DEVELOP YOUR LEG ACTION BY WEDELN

You should strive to master two distinctly different kinds of leg action

You have already developed a kind of "independent leg action" if you are capable of rapidly reacting from one ski to the other to prevent a fall. You have also used leg action to rapidly pivot your skis under your body when you are surprised by a turn or obliged to rapidly link several short turns.

If you feel you are deficient in this area, refer to pages 32 and 46 in the preceeding chapter. You can also use "compact" or short skis, particularly if you don't like speed.

If you have already developed the rudiments of leg action, you can try to refine them by simultaneously evolving two nearly opposite kinds of movements:
• toward a pivoting leg action with flat skis
• toward a leg action to make platforms with edge sets.

I have noticed that very good skiers, and even racers, tend to specialize in one kind of leg action, in relation to their temperament, and are deficient in the other. Try to become a complete skier.

To start with, understand the distinction between these two types of leg action.

Flat ski pivoting on soft snow

The pivoting of flat skis on the snow is propelled by muscular action which pivots the feet under the torso (500). This pivoting can be prolonged by a passive action of the frictional forces between the skis and the snow (134-155). The faster the leg action, the more important becomes the muscular work relative to the passive pivoting. The feet and skis pivot distinctly more than the knees, which may not even pivot at all (534).

This kind of leg action is generally made

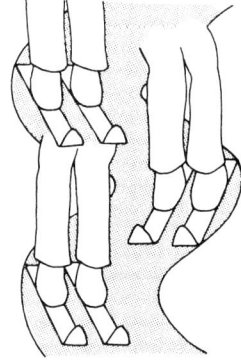

with both skis more or less equally weighted.

Edge-set platform and recoil pivoting on hard snow

During an edge-set platform at the beginning of a turn, there is a lateral displacement of the skis, a biting of the edges, a compression and a recoil into the turn. After this quick muscular phase, the skis can continue to pivot passively due to the frictional forces between the skis and the snow.

In this kind of a movement, the knees pivot as much as the feet and the skis because the position of the knees plays a major role in making edge-set platforms.

At the precise instant that the edges bite, there is a dominant weighting of the outside ski.

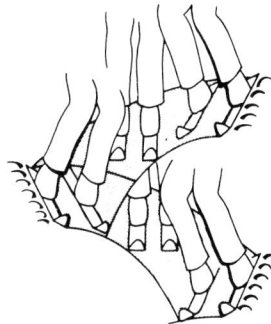

Leg action is balance, the freedom to improvise and quickness; it is the youth of a skier.

How to discover and refine the pivoting of flat skis on easier slopes

Parallel skis

With your skis spread one foot apart and your weight equally distributed over the front and back of your feet, place your hands on your knee caps and schuss down a relatively flat slope.

Once you have attained a fairly high speed, simultaneously pivot both feet, controlling your knees with your hands so that they move very little, if at all. Pivot your feet to the left, then immediately to the right, then to the left again, then to the right, etc... You will discover that your skis pivot very poorly and tend to catch edges. Don't try to turn your body. It should remain fairly immobile, facing down the fall line and weighting both feet; only the feet and calves should be involved in this movement. Repeat this manuever during long schusses. Eventually, you will feel that your skis pivot more easily and you will discover that by weighting a very specific point on the ski, the *"pivoting center of the skis"*, you can enhance the pivoting almost without muscular effort (135).

You can experiment with this pivoting action in your stocking feet on a slippery floor in your living room

Stand with your hands on your knees, your feet spread one foot apart and flexed deeply in the knees but only slightly in the ankles. You are in the stance of the modern skier.

Pivot your feet. You should see your toes and heels pivot simultaneously but in opposite directions although the toes are displaced further. You will notice that it is easy to link such pivoting movements in opposite directions: each movement seems to flow into the next. This is called a "wind-up" movement in sports.

This exercise is much easier to do with compact skis. Particularly for skiers who are reluctant to ski fast enough. It is likewise made more difficult if the bases of your skis

Only the feet pivot

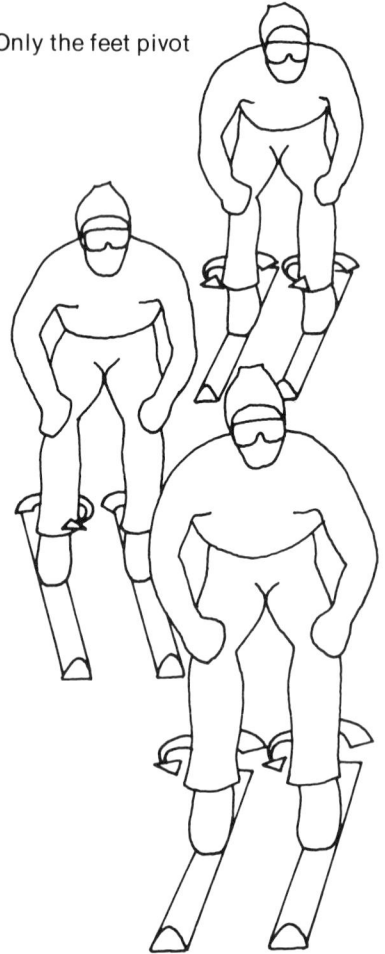

are hollow or concave or if they have scratches (138).

By repeating this kind of leg action manuever 100 times, you will be able to accelerate it and eventually will be able to do it with parallel skis in a narrower stance. This only requires a slight desynchronization of the pivoting of the two skis which is often preferable for your continued progress.

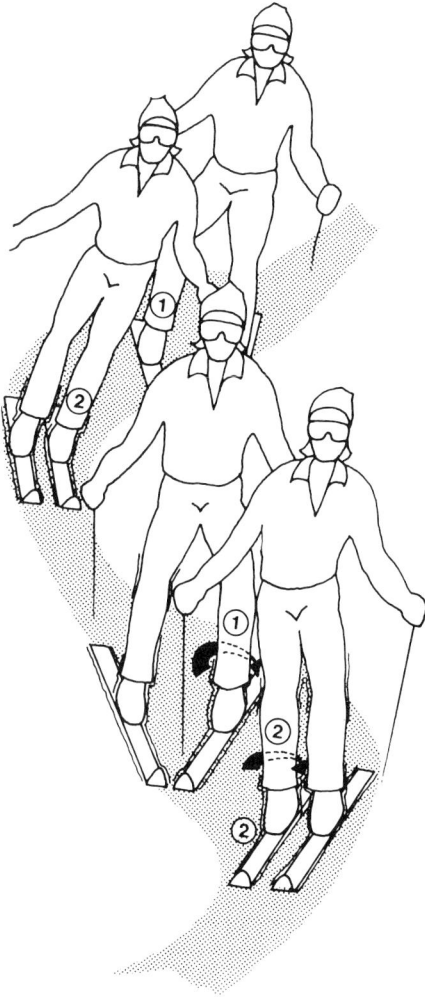

it. Your skis will begin to sideslip immediately but don't let them pivot too far. Immediately spread your inside ski into a stem and again bring your skis parallel. Continue. Try to find a "one-two" rhythm on one side, then a "one-two" rhythm on the other and link them together. "One" - open a flat ski stem. "Two" - bring the skis parallel together again but still flat. "One" - open a stem on the opposite side, etc... All of this should be accomplished without rotating your chest and with your poles held in front of you.

The legs pivot under a stable upper body

With a two-step stem

If you don't succeed in the wedeln by pivoting your skis when parallel and with your hands on your knees, try another approach. Hold your ski poles in front of you with both hands. Flex your legs more than usual and, standing in a wide stance and well balanced over both feet, slide straight down the slope. Once you attain sufficient speed and can feel your skis sliding "freely" on the snow, open one ski into a stem and immediately bring the other one parallel to

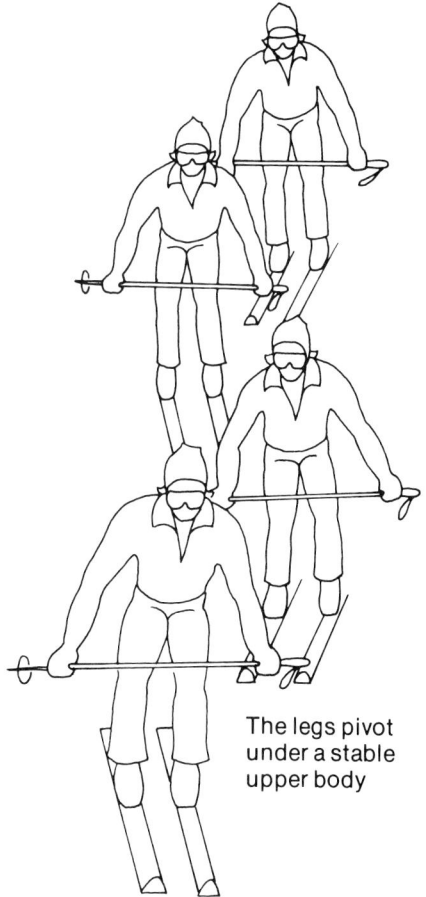

A discovery not to be missed: the central pressure point on the ski allowing the skis to pivot when flat.

79

A "trick" to accelerate your leg action: a change of support foot and a lateral slipping of the ski

I've already spoken a great deal of the change of support foot. It is a rudimentary mechanism whereas leg action is more evolved. Nevertheless, a change of support foot is almost always involved to a greater or lesser extent in the quick leg actions of very good skiers and racers. Why deprive yourself of this worthwhile tool? If you have used this book to introduce yourself to your first leg actions you have already assimilated a change of support foot. If not, refer to page 33 and discover it.

Change of support foot

An inward lean and passive slipping of the flat skis

Now try to combine a change of support foot with the flat ski leg action you have just discovered

Slide straight down a flat slope, preferably on soft snow, in a low position and in a wide stance. After you have gained sufficient speed, try to simultaneously lift one ski and thrust on the other while pivoting it. You will notice that it pivots more readily as it slips laterally. Immediately put the ski back down, lift the other and apply a lateral thrust and pivoting action to your support ski. It pivots and slips laterally. Continue the exercise and link the manuevers. Gradually limit the lifting of a ski and the movement becomes more effective.

Careful! You will experience a bit of swinging from one ski to the other and this swinging is both enjoyable and will seem to help you. Effectively it does help but be careful not to exaggerate it or you will not be able to rid yourself of this change of support foot and this will make you far less effective in deep and soft snow where it becomes necessary to weight both feet simultaneously.

You can combine this movement with edging

In this case your skis will move laterally only with difficulty. You will quickly discover that a thrust of the support foot and an extension will initiate the lateral movement, but don't abuse this gesture as it leads to brutal, inelegant skiing.

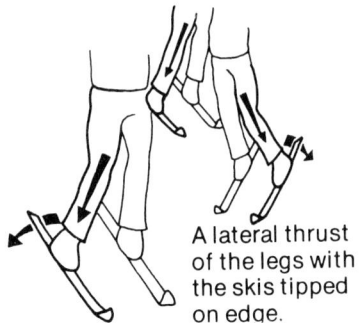

A lateral thrust of the legs with the skis tipped on edge.

A change of support foot is a part of good leg action, but only one element.

How to discover wedeln with platforms

First, use a downhill stem on intermediate slopes

In order to use a platform in a wedeln, you must have first mastered its use at the beginning of a turn (page 72). Therefore, I will assume that you already know how to make a short check and use this manuever to start your turns.

Slide straight down an intermediate slope in a low position and with your legs supple and the skis sliding freely. The slope should be steep enough that you feel a need to control your speed.

With determination, but without brutality, open your right ski into a stem and press on your heel to make the edge bite and slow yourself down. By keeping your leg rigid to resist the compression that results from this edging, you will be thrown laterally to your other ski. Immediately open this ski into a stem and again, while pressing hard on the edge with your heel, brake and feel yourself thrown laterally.

Continue until you distinctly feel that a platform on one ski propels your skis laterally and not the mass of your body. Your upper body should remain stable with your arms spread wide and chest facing down the fall line and centered between your two skis.

A wedeln involves a "lateral action" and an "alternating pivoting action" of the legs under the body

At first, you may feel that without wanting to do so, you tend to use a change of support foot more than the lateral rebound from your platform to initiate your turns. This is normal, but if you continue to use these elementary mechanisms you risk blocking your progress. Persevere in your search for an effective checking and particularly for a more distinct rebound and in a refinement of the rhythm which con-

stitutes the essence of this movement.

Repeat this movement with stem platforms 100 times. This is the most instructive of all leg action movements. If you attempt to execute it while well balanced over your outside ski during each platform, you will subconsciously progress from a stemmed leg action to a parallel ski leg action in a wide stance. But by using only the parallel ski leg action, you run the risk of not discovering genuine platforms, but merely a slipping of the edges.

The pole plant

If you have already learned to plant your pole during platforms made with a downhill stem at the beginning of your turns (page 72), you can try to plant your pole during this wedeln. But don't insist if you don't succeed because it is far better to not plant your pole at all than to plant it improperly.

A stem platform, during a wedeln, is as useful for the intermediate skier as it is for the slalom specialist on difficult or hard snow.

With parallel skis and a pole plant on steeper slopes

Even though you have mastered the flat ski pivoting leg action on flatter slopes, you can not utilize this technique on steep slopes without losing control. You need to learn a genuine wedeln with braking and platforms in order to be able to ski down an intermediate slope with your skis parallel making linked short radius turns and controlling your speed. Many skiers who mistakenly consider themselves to be "good" are incapable of performing this manuever.

Even though more complex, this wedeln is within your reach if you have already mastered the following three technical elements: 1. A rapid pivoting of your skis under your body by what I have called "braquage" (page 38). 2. A downhill stem platform and rebound (page 72) or parallel ski platform and rebound (page 73) at the beginning of the turn. 3. A pole plant to assure balance at the beginning of your turns (page 72).

It is in precisely this manner, through the assembly of the pieces of a puzzle, that the technique of a skier is built. A completed puzzle presents ease, elegance and efficiency in every circumstance. A puzzle with holes presents a technique that *appears* to be sound, but suddenly disintegrate in certain situations.

How to execute this wedeln.

Slide straight down an intermediate slope in a wide stance and low position. Shift your weight to your heels and pivot your skis under your body but keep your torso facing down the slope. As soon as your skis begin to sideslip, apply pressure to the tail of your outside ski, making the edge bite, and plant your pole. Your upper body should continue to face down the slope. You can then use the compression generated on your outside leg to rebound your skis and pivot them into the turn. This rebound will not be sufficient to pivot your skis past the fall line, so you must also apply a steering action of both legs under your body to complete the turn. Then, weight the heel of your downhill foot to set your edge, plant your downhill pole and rebound off of your downhill ski to turn again in the opposite direction with your upper body continuing to face down the fall line.

A wedeler or slalom specialist who fails to use a pole plant during his platforms is a seriously handicapped skier.

The essential ingredient of this wedeln is the linking of the platform-rebound action with a pivoting of both legs. You should clearly feel the two "steps": 1. platform-rebound with a pole plant, 2. pivot, 1. ... etc. The first step is brief and dynamic and the second more flowing. Once you have totally mastered the pole plant, it becomes so effective that you can no longer perform this wedel without it. Therefore, make sure that you learn to use it correctly and you will have acquired once and for all the synchronization of the edge-set platform and the pole plant.

Learn to wedel securely on even steeper slopes

If you have easily succeeded in wedeln on intermediate slopes, don't hesitate to confront steeper slopes. You only need to exaggerate your gestures to succeed.

First of all, start with a wider stance and a lower position. Don't start from a straight run down the slope but from a lateral sideslip with your chest already twisted, facing down the hill and your arms spread wide for balance.

Suddenly "check" your sideslip with a thrust of your heels on the edge of your downhill ski and plant your downhill pole. Let your self be compressed enough to give a dynamic rebound and pivot your skis down the fall line. You can assist this pivoting with a foot steering action and will end up in a braking-sideslip on the other side of the fall line. Control this sideslip by shifting weight to your heels while remaining in a low, very wide stance with your upper body turned to face down the fall line. You are now in a position to check by applying pressure to the edge of your downhill ski and begin again.

Only my most athletic and gifted readers will be able to succeed immediately in this manuever. The others should not become discouraged, however, because this is one of the summits of ski technique. I will present it again later as the number one weapon at the disposal of a very good skier for confronting the problems of extreme skiing. You aren't there yet !

A wide stance, total weighting of the tail of the downhill ski, a pole plant with the chest facing down the fall line; these are the essential elements of wedeln on steep slopes.

Cultivate the aesthetic "classic wedeln"

This paragraph doesn't concern you unless you have already more or less acquired: 1. a genuine leg action — that is to say an ability to smoothly pivot your legs under an immobile torso; 2. an ability to utilize the directional effects of your skis — that is to say their capacity for turning by themselves; 3. a platform-rebound mechanism combined with a pole plant.

It now remains for you to melt these elements into a sober and harmonious unity combining both elegance and efficiency.

It is extremely difficult to make a perfect wedel; even for a very good skier. You should, therefore, begin to prepare yourself without feeling self-conscious.

How to execute it

My first important counsel: begin by sliding straight down the slope — and *not* in a traverse — in a high and narrow stance with your legs relaxed and your skis sliding freely.

By applying greater weight to your heels, make your skis pivot slightly and immediately set your edges by angulating and plant your outside pole while your chest continues to face down the fall line. Your platform creates a rebound, unweighting your skis and allowing them to pivot toward the fall line.

By tipping your skis on edge and weighting them, they will continue to turn by themselves. Your legs should be supple and follow your skis, but your torso continues to face down the slope with your arms open for balance.

Once again, weight your heels and angulate to make your edges bite. Plant your pole, with your chest continuing to face down the slope, and your skis will rebound again.

In conclusion, you stand relaxed, with your chest facing down the slope during the wedel except during the brief instant of the pole plant and platform. The supple movement of your legs under your torso, the sliding curve that your skis make by themselves and the precise change of rhythm of the edge-set is elegant, along with the cleanness of your line, the position of your arms and the placement of your pole in an oblique direction forward and to the inside. You are entering the realm of "classical" skiing which I will describe later.

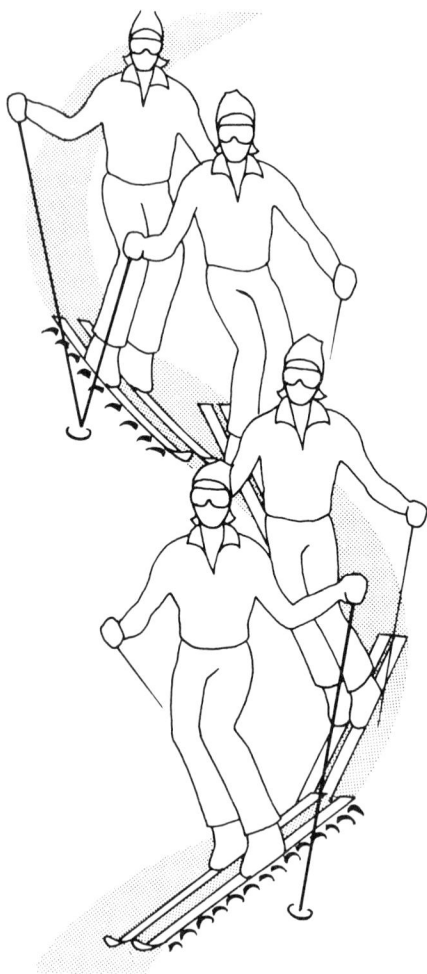

The classic wedel is characterized by its elegance and two step rhythm: the first, lively, is a platform; the slower second step, a sliding movement.

LEARN TO MASTER ALL TERRAIN

Perhaps this title is ambitious. It still is not possible for you to perform the manuevers which I describe later in the chapters devoted to extreme skiing and to the latest technical innovations on the most difficult slopes.

What you should acquire, as soon as possible, is the technical repertoire that will prevent you from being afraid of terrain which you might mistakenly judge to be too difficult for you.

We have already studied a form of wedel which can permit you to ski with security on steep slopes (page 83). We will now examine the difficulties imposed by mogulled slopes and difficult and deep snow.

Ski moguls with confidence

At lower speeds, down steep slopes and in difficult bumps: brake then flex and foot steer.

You already have developed a means of skiing in bumps. If you have learned to ski with the help of this book, you know how to pivot your skis in a wide stance on the tops of moguls by foot steering (page 45). You also know how to check before reaching the top of a mogul, then change support foot and sideslip down the back side (page 47). You also have developed the habit of planting your pole on the tops of bumps (page 48). But all of these techniques are only useful at low speeds. If you are skiing faster, or if you don't have time to check your speed before reaching them, the moguls become jumps that catapult you down the slope at the precise moment when you want to brake your speed with a sideslip.

You must learn to swallow the tops of the bumps so that they don't become jumps. The first formula for doing this is to check earlier and more briefly than you normally do. Then, as your tips begin to ascend the

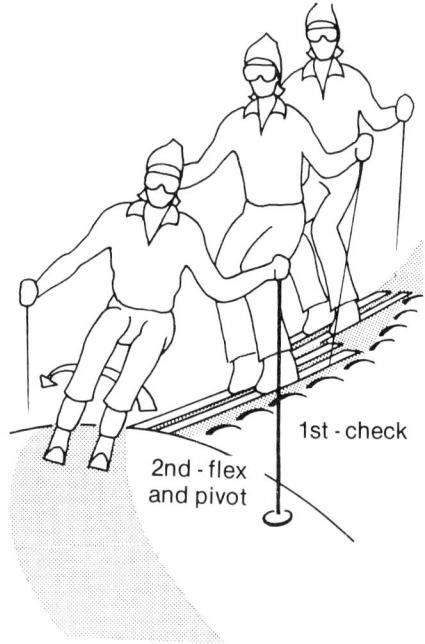

1st - check

2nd - flex and pivot

bump, plant your pole and flex your body by letting your legs rise in front of you. You will arrive at the top of the bump in a very low position where you use foot steering to rapidly pivot your legs. Continue to pivot as your legs extend on the back side of the bump to maintain contact with the snow. You can check your speed by sideslipping down the back of the bump with your weight balanced over your outside ski. Aim for another bump, brake, plant your pole. While your chest continues to face down the fall line, flex again so that you arrive at the top of the bump in a low position. Continue.

The first elementary reflex you should develop to turn in moguls: 1. brake in the ruts while anticipating and plant your pole; 2. flex while pivoting on the top of the bump.

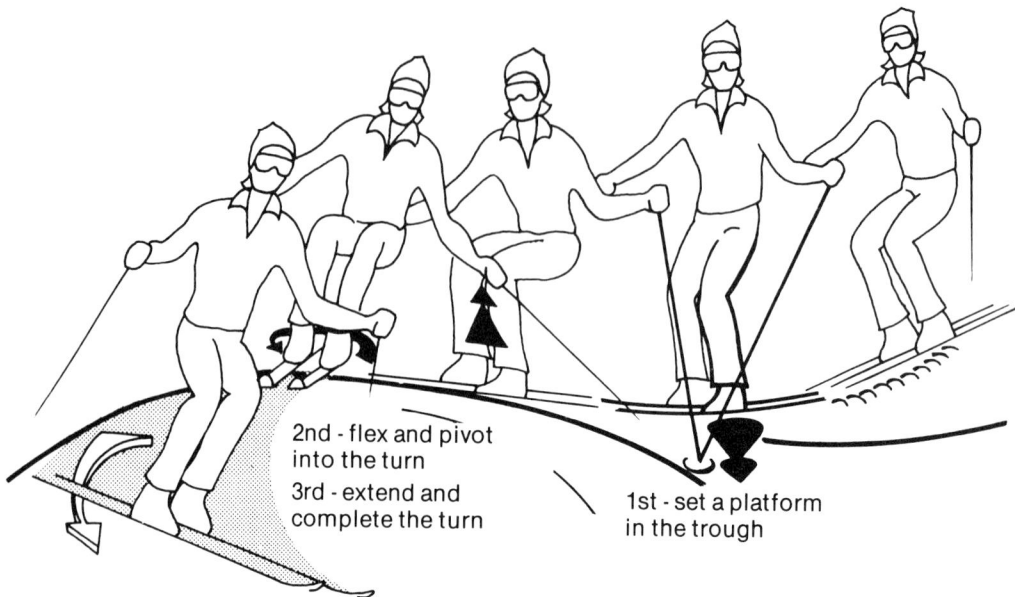

2nd - flex and pivot
into the turn

3rd - extend and
complete the turn

1st - set a platform
in the trough

At intermediate speeds, on mogulled slopes, make a platform in the ruts and absorb the bumps.

If you are naturally athletic and if you have experienced no difficulty in learning to make platforms, then you likely have had problems in acquiring the "brake then flex and foot steer" reflex. You will certainly succeed, however, with the type of turn which I am going to propose here and which consists of absorbing bumps after making genuine platforms. You should then return to the "brake then flex and foot steer" type of turn because it leads more directly to the modern techniques of avalement, the most effective in extreme conditions.

How do you learn the "platform, then absorb the bump" reflex ?

As you approach a bump with your skis in the trough 1 or 2 yards before the crest of the bump, pivot them slightly uphill and make a platform

As you approach the bump, and when your skis are still in the trough 1 or 2 meters before the crest of the bump, pivot your skis slightly uphill, plant your pole and make a platform while your upper body twists down the slope. The terrain will exaggerate the compression of your platform and as you rebound, you only need to retract your feet up under your body for your skis to slide smoothly over the crest of the mogul and pivot into the turn. You can then check your speed on the backside of the mogul and aim for another bump.

This *"platform - retract the legs - brake"* movement is very enjoyable, even exhilarating, but it can also be a very precarious way of turning in bumps. If you delay only slightly in setting your platform, you will be launched into the air... unless you have already learned the "brake then flex" manuever described on the preceeding page.

This is precisely why it is necessary for you to acquire both techniques in order to avoid being "overcome" by moguls.

A more advanced manuever for turning in moguls: 1. platform; 2. retract the legs; 3. pivot and extend.

Wedel down the fall line at high speed while absorbing the bumps.

Select a slope of intermediate steepness. Since your speed is going to accelerate during this exercise, which is designed to develop "flexion-extension" reflexes, the slope should be short and finish with a flat.

Begin in an upright position and head straight down the slope. As you arrive at the first mogul, flex rapidly, plant your ski pole on the top of the mogul and pivot your skis. This rapid flexion will allow you to absorb the compression as your skis slide over the mogul. As soon as your feet pass over the top of the bump, however, you must extend your legs to maintain contact with the snow and let your skis drift back into the fall line. Arriving at the next bump: "flex - pole plant - pivot your skis" then immediately extend your legs and continue this vertical movement through the mogul field; flex, extend, flex, extend, etc.

Nothing is more effective than this gymnastic exercise for developing the reflexes to absorb bumps as soon as your ski tips contact them.

When you try this wedel you will notice that the flat area on top of the bumps is always less icy than the sides of the moguls. This is because the snow scraped away by skiers sideslipping down the sides of the bumps is deposited on top of the bumps below.

You will also notice that this wedel is only possible if your upper body constantly faces down the fall line. This is necessary to pull your skis back into the fall line at the end of each turn.

The fact that your skis twist back into the fall line following each compression-braking is a result of the release of pivoting force that is stored in the muscles of the lower torso and legs during the flexion. This twisting of the skis back into the same direction as the upper body is called "vissage recoil" or "de-angulation" (531e and 533e) and returns the legs and skis to a more or less normal position under the torso during the un-weighting phase and the extension which follows the compression. It is an automatic reaction to the flexion and, therefore, can be very rapid. It is popular among freestyle skiers who can use it to link several very quick turns.

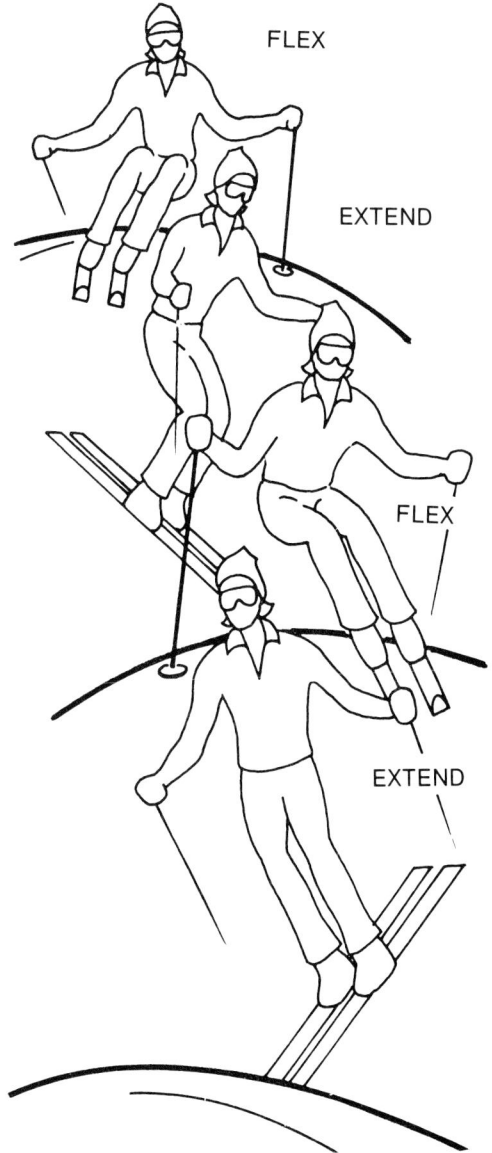

FLEX

EXTEND

FLEX

EXTEND

It is the lack of a vertical flexion-extension movement to absorb bumps which limits the speed at which a skier can tackle bumpy terrain, either in a schuss or wedeln.

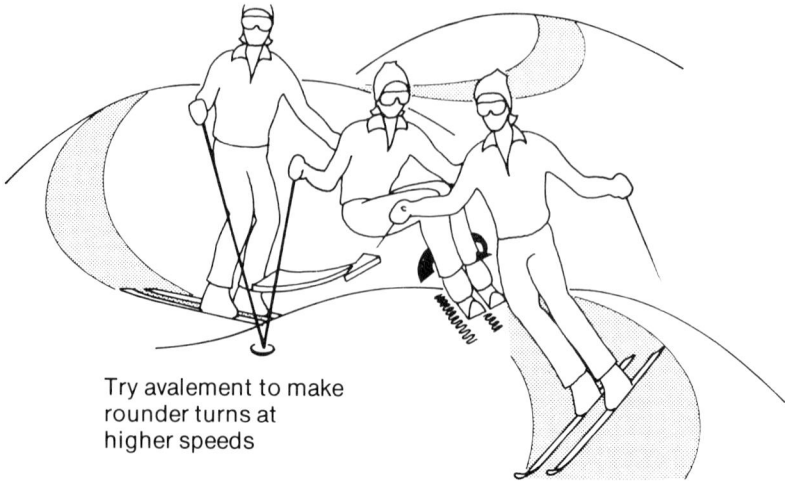

Try avalement to make rounder turns at higher speeds

Try to turn rounder as you "swallow" the bumps

I now propose that you attempt something that is perhaps a little too difficult. Nevertheless, some skiers who have easily mastered the "brake - flex - foot steer" technique should be able, even now, to successfully attempt this highly evolved turn with "*avalement*".

At moderate speed, make relatively short turns down a slope with fairly smooth and symmetrical moguls. You should make your turns significantly rounder, continuing them to the point that you are actually turning uphill such as I suggested on pages 48 and 76. You should feel a distinct compression as your skis climb uphill approaching a mogul. During this compression phase you should plant your pole, twist your upper body to face down the fall line and flex by retracting your legs upward in front of you and lifting your skis over the bump. As your skis reach the crest of the bump they will pivot in front of you down the fall line. You must then extend your legs to maintain contact with the snow as your skis pass over the mogul and sideslip down the back side. You will accelerate in the traverses between turns but can reduce your speed in the counter-turn up the slope in preparation for turning over another mogul.

You should strive for a global movement that makes use of your stomach muscles.

As soon as you make a genuine avalement, you should clearly perceive the involvement of the abdominal muscles.

But at intermediate speed, you can first attempt what we call a "*passive avalement*" and which uses the bump itself to lift your feet in front of your body.

At higher speeds, it becomes necessary for you to actually lift your legs up in front of your chest in order to cushion the thrust of the bump and prevent you from losing your balance. You can then better and more precisely control the placement and pivoting of your skis.

Note: The pivoting of your skis into a turn with avalement is largely propelled by the anticipated position of your upper body at the time of the pole plant although you can always enhance or continue this pivoting of the skis by steering of your outside foot and leg (540).

You will have acquired the "avalement" of the champions when you can absorb a bump by pulling your legs up in front of you with your abdominal muscles.

Handle all snow conditions with confidence.

If you are afraid of difficult snow, return to a wide stance and stem turn with foot steering.

A great many skiers who have become accustomed to skiing with their feet close together use unweighting and occasionally even wedel are still uneasy in difficult snow conditions which "grab" their skis and hinder their movements. These skiers have lost the first requisite of a skier: the ability to adapt to the snow.

When heavy, unpacked snow makes it difficult for you to pivot your skis into a turn, you can choose one of two solutions. First, you can force your skis to pivot by using the powerful muscle movement in what I have called "braquage" (page 38) but this requires a sideslipping of your skis and this is difficult because they are blocked by the heavy snow which they have to push to the side. This technique is more effective for making a short wedeln that requires relatively little sideslipping.

The other alternative is to use an uphill stem and then the sideslipping directional effect and pull of gravity to pull you down the fall line. It is then relatively easy to accentuate the pressure on the tails of your skis and use a progressive foot steering of both skis to finish the turn with a sideslip. It is this second solution, discussed in greater detail on page 34, which I recommend that you use.

Even though you have never used a stem, try one now!

Leave the packed runs and use a stem to tackle slopes which you wouldn't dare to attempt otherwise. If you don't see immediate success, you have major technical deficiencies. Often this is because you have become accustomed to turning suddenly to avoid the

1st - stem your uphill ski

2nd - drift into the fall line

3rd - brake your speed

fall line, even though every good turn includes a dive down the fall line followed by a turn out of the fall line (pages 34 and 63). If this is your case, nothing can be more educational for you than to return to the 3-step stem turn (1. stem; 2. dive down the slope; 3. turn out of the fall line.)

Try an infallible "trick" in deep snow at low speeds: 1. jump into the fall line; 2. turn out of the fall line with sideslipping.

The term "deep snow" can be very ambiguous. There are, in fact, two kinds of deep snow; those which rest on a harder or packed base that supports the skier as he begins his turns, and the "bottomless" deep snows in which the skier is supported by his speed

In difficult snow, or while touring with a rucksack, return to elementary techniques.

and a sort of "hydroplaning". In this latter case, the traditional platforms are impossible. For the time being, like 90% of all "good" skiers, you can't pretend to be able to ski at ease in these genuinely deep snows. Nevertheless, you can still tackle the first kind of "deep snow" which is far more frequently encountered on and off the marked slopes.

How can you judge the difficulty of deep snow ?

Slide straight down the slope 15, 30 or 50 feet with your weight adjusted slightly to the tails of your skis. Force your skis to pivot with a flexing of your legs and steering. If you succeed in easily starting a sideslip, then this deep snow is within your capabilities. If not, it is beyond your present level of ability and you will have to result to every extreme measure to avoid making kick turns (see page 53).

If you have been greatly influenced by Ski School lessons, or if you have learned to side slip with forward weighting, my test will be useless. You will fail every time. You must first correct yourself; learn to sideslip in a position balanced over the center of your skis or even with a slightly dominant weighting of the tails of your skis and only then can you rejoin us (page 53).

Turn in two steps.

Were you able to turn out of the fall line ? If so, then don't hesitate. Turn from your traverse into the fall line by hopping in a narrow stance. This is easy. Flex your legs, plant your downhill ski pole and twist your upper body down the fall line and rebound: your skis will pivot in the air and land facing down the slope.

You need slide only a few yards straight down the slope before turning out of the fall line. But never jump completely past the fall line under the pretext of making an even shorter turn. Your skis will compress the snow upon landing and won't be able to sideslip.

At slower speeds, on steeper slopes, force

yourself to jump precisely into the fall line and slide at least 2 yards straight down the slope before finishing your turn. At higher speeds, hop and land with your skis not quite in the fall line. They will sideslip a little on landing until they are sliding straight down the slope. On intermediate slopes, by making your landing softer with a flexing of your legs and progressively evolving your hop to a flexion-extension, you will eventually execute a more "classic" turn.

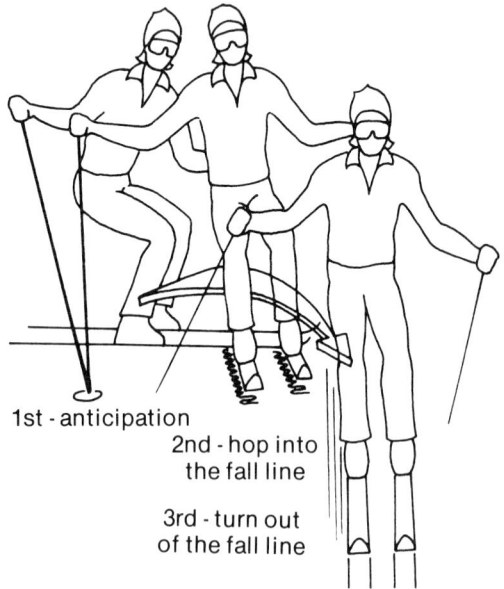

1st - anticipation
2nd - hop into the fall line
3rd - turn out of the fall line

Use "hip projection" to turn in light snow at higher speeds.

Opening a stem or hopping into the fall line is perhaps effective, but it isn't very elegant; and every good skier aspires to starting his turns in a more supple, more sophisticated manner, particularly if a light powder snow covers a denser base which provides the skis with a reassuring support.

What to do ?

You have to find a way to start your skis to pivot at the initiation of the turn

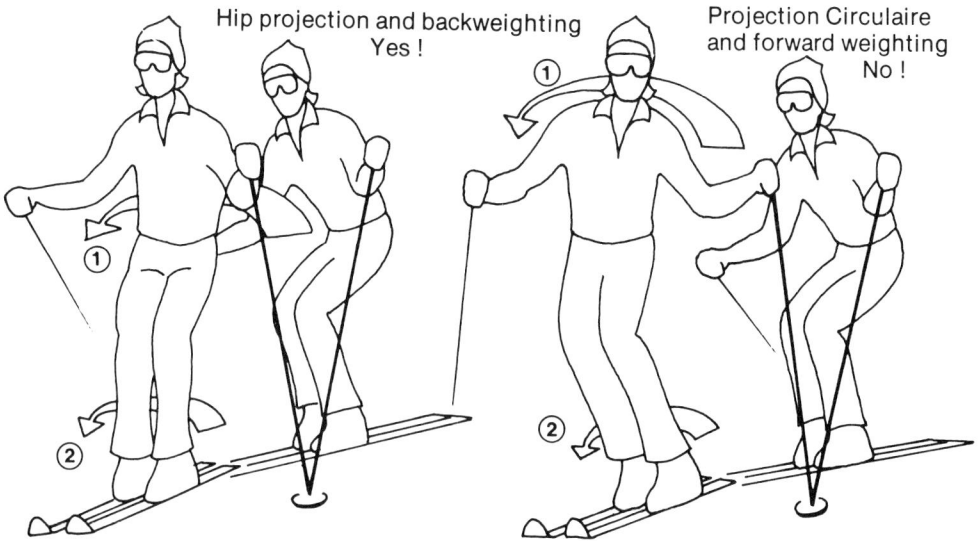

Hip projection and backweighting
Yes !

Projection Circulaire
and forward weighting
No !

while keeping them flat so that they literally slice through the snow sideways until they have reached the fall line. If they are tipped onto edge, the bases of the skis will pack the snow underneath them and the increased resistance will prevent the skis from pivoting and "block" the turn.

A technique which is now within your capabilities is the following. From a traverse, and in a narrow stance, flex your legs while twisting your upper body to face down the slope and thrust vertically on the tails of your skis while planting your ski pole. In contrast with the platforms described previously, *don't* pivot your skis up the hill to weight the edges. Weight your skis as they rest flat on the snow and without displacing them and with a less dynamic movement than you used during edge-set platforms. As you extend upward, project your hip into the turn. Your skis will close and the thrust of your hip will cause your

skis to pivot laterally through the snow while held flat to provide the least possible resistance. Once again, a pole plant provides stability and balance.

You may discover this hip projection independently while making shorter, linked turns, or even a wedeln which alternately repeats this movement to the right and to the left. You can then try to prolong the hip projection through longer radius turns.

If you have diligently heeded our advice throughout this book to allow your feet to be as "free" and relaxed as possible, then you will develop the subtle foot control and finesse which skiing in deep powder demands. Eventually you will ski powder more with your feet and with less hip projection and ultimately approach the most modern of techniques of the deep snow specialists which I have baptised the "surf technique".

Don't confuse a "hip projection" turn with flat skis in powder snows and a "projection circulaire" of the chest which often leads to forward weighting.

To conquer "rotten" snow, return to the most rudimentary direction changes: the "tournant".

Earlier in this book, in order to equip beginners with a means of dealing with snow and terrain that is too difficult for them, I proposed techniques for changing direction which I have been reluctant to call turns. I will henceforth refer to them as "tournants" as suggested by one of my colleagues (page 44).

The problems posed when you confront "rotten" snows, which are very difficult to ski in, are exactly the same. Therefore you should use the same techniques.

A "tournant" that is far more effective and less laborious that the wedge turn (see page 45).

1. Slow down with a downhill stem by pressing very hard on the tail of your downhill ski. 2. Lean down the slope and your skis will climb to the surface of the snow and turn into the fall line. 3. Brake again with a downhill stem while forcing the tail of the downhill ski to pivot.

This "tournant" produces a great deal of pressure on the downhill leg but not on both legs simultaneously and therefore avoids the blocking of the hip that is common in the wedge turn.

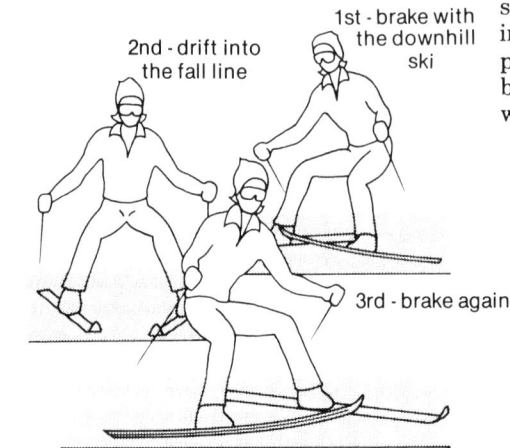

1st - open an uphill stem to maximum

2nd - weight the uphill ski and steer through the tu▮

Note: You can combine a foot steering with a weighting of the tails of your skis to the third step, then a sideslipping.

The hopped turn.

From a traverse at very slow speed: 1. twist your upper body down the fall line and flex while planting your downhill pole. 2. Hop with both feet and rotate your body down the slope and pivot your skis as much as possible. If the support under your skis is poor, begin to jump and then quickly "retract" your skis up under your body. 3. Land in a traverse in the opposite direction and use your ski poles to help maintain your balance.

The foot-steered uphill stem (see page 44).

At low speed in a traverse: 1. open the widest possible uphill stem. 2. Weight both skis in order to free the downhill ski and immediately foot steer. 3. Try to use the pivoting momentum of your skis produced by the foot steering to attempt a sideslip while flexing your legs.

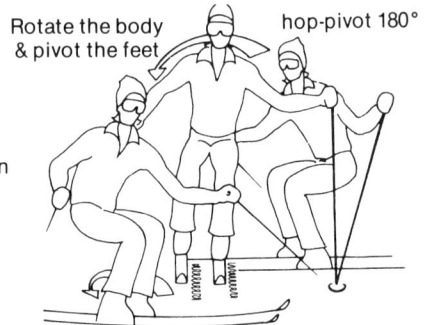

2nd - drift into the fall line

1st - brake with the downhill ski

3rd - brake again

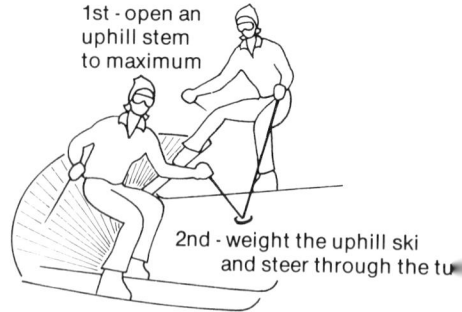

Rotate the body & pivot the feet

hop-pivot 180°

This pivoting momentum can be used to help you avoid leaving the turn with a stiff outside leg, which is often the origin of ligament strains and leg fractures in very heavy snows.

TAKE ADVANTAGE OF EVERY OPPORTUNITY TO SCHUSS

It is curious to note that one sees fewer and fewer skiers take advantage of those sections of steep slopes that end with long flats to "schuss", gain "maximum speed" and feel the wind whistle in their ears as they cross the flats.

This is unfortunate. First because nothing is more exhilarating than speed on skis, speed that can be experienced almost without risk if you are in a wide stance with your legs flexed and balanced properly over your feet with your arms spread wide for stability. Secondly, because a familiarization with speed gives every skier confidence.

Do you know what your terminal velocity is ?

Terminal velocity is a "speed plateau" which is quickly reached in a schuss and where the friction of the air and the snow is equivalent to the accelerating pull of gravity. The result is no more acceleration, that is down a constant slope of even pitch, while maintaining the same position, you will reach a speed, your "terminal velocity" at which you no longer accelerate. Discovering this fundamental principle will give you greater confidence.

Have you already experienced reaching terminal velocity ? If not, first try on intermediate slopes and then progressively steeper slopes. Standing upright, with your arms held in front of you, this terminal velocity will decrease. Flexed low, crouched into the aerodynamic "egg" position, it will be higher. Experiment with these positions.

You should be fully aware that by occasionally skiing at speeds of 40, 50 or even 60 miles per hour you will be much more relaxed making turns at 20, 25 or 30 miles per hour.

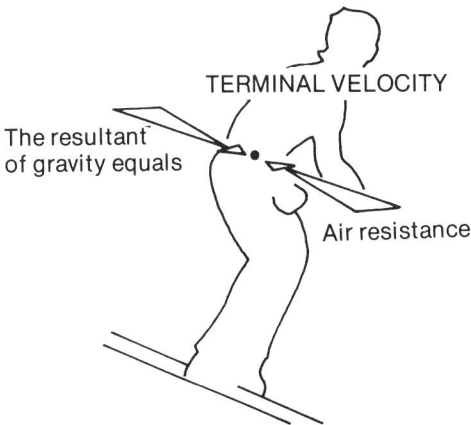

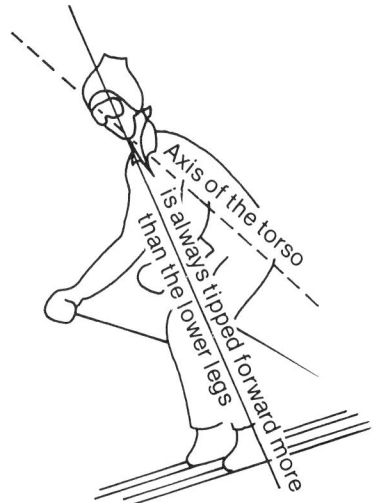

TERMINAL VELOCITY

The resultant of gravity equals

Air resistance

Axis of the torso is always tipped forward more than the lower legs

Supple legs, the modern stance and flexion-avalement are the three essential weapons for schussing over all terrain.

93

Passive flexion-avalement

the more rapid
active flexion-avalement

Upward thrust
of a bump

retraction
of the legs

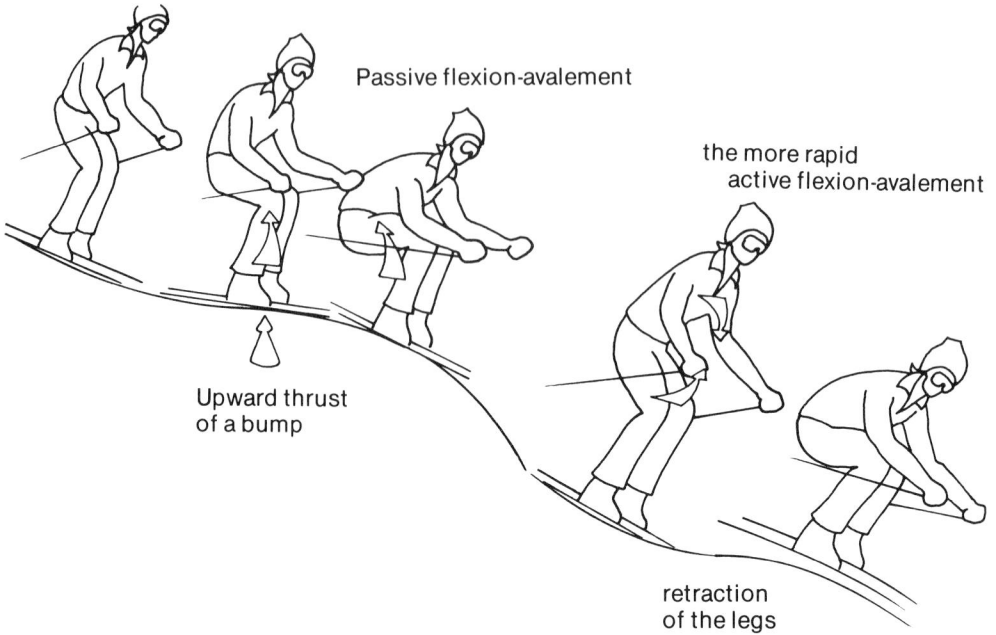

Absorb the bumps with your "feet forward" while schussing.

What I told you regarding absorbing bumps during long turns (page 68) or even during the initiation of turns (pages 85 and 88) is even truer during a schuss.

9 out of 10 skiers are so "thrown" when passing over bumps in a schuss that they must ask themselves if there isn't a secret that they aren't aware of. In fact, there are many.

• First secret: *"the modern stance"* with ankles straighter, the upper body tilted forward more than the lower legs, arms spread wide and in front, legs supple and feet relaxed.

• Second secret: *Let the bumps lift your feet vertically in front of you.* We call this *"passive flexion-avalement"* because it is related to the movement at the initiation of turns with avalement.

• Third secret: if the bump is more pronounced, you must not be content to let the bump lift your feet. You must use the abdominal muscles to pull them upward and literally swallow the bump. We call this "flexion-avalement" and this gesture has become so commonplace in downhill racing that it has modified the aerodynamic tuck position of the downhiller. Downhill racers no longer use the "egg" position which I first described in 1956 with my friend Jean Vuarnet, but the "round" position which I describe in the Downhill chapter.

Profit from long flats and bumpy catwalks to schuss in an exaggerated "modern stance" and notice the play of your feet which, thrust upward by the bumps and ripples, lift upward *in front of you.* But watch out ! This in no way means that you should adopt a sitting-back stance. You should feel that you are in a perfectly balanced position with both feet supple and relaxed (see the two support points rule on page 22).

HOW FAR HAVE YOU COME ?

Have you learned to balance yourself over your outside ski in long turns ? Are your upper body and arms relaxed and supply balanced over your outside hip in an angulated position ?

Have you discovered, and do you use, the proper attitude and built-in turning characteristics of your skis so that they make turns by themselves with neither excessive sideslipping nor excessive pivoting ?

When you must control your speed, or regain your balance, are you capable of finding a solid point of support from the ground for your skis to begin a turn with greater precision ?

While sliding straight down the slope can you react from one leg to the other, or even use both legs, to link short turns into an effective wedeln. ? Can you do so with solid platforms ?

Are you experienced in skiing fields of moguls, the most difficult of which don't intimidate you and the less difficult of which you can ski without hesitation either straight down the fall line or by making long, round turns ?

If you can answer yes to these questions, you have indisputably become a good skier ! You are far better equipped than the majority of skiers who are capable of skiing all terrain but who have a far less varied technique than you.

If you have not developed a serious fault, you can now strive to become a *very* good skier. To accomplish this, you should ski quite often and simultaneously cultivate both your weaknesses and your strengths. You can even become an *avant-garde* skier if you want to initiate yourself to the latest discoveries of the skiing virtuosos, discoveries which derive directly from the behaviors which I have helped you to acquire. The following chapters can lead you along these two paths.

But perhaps you find yourself blocked, and find it impossible to put one of our suggestions into practice on the slope ?

Perhaps, like the majority of skiers, you suffer from previously acquired faults which slow the acquisition of new behavior ?

I will try to clarify the way for you. This is not as difficult as you might think because the technical flaws which can stop your progression are not very many ! Many days devoted to observing skiers of all levels and in all kinds of ski areas in France and elsewhere have proven to us that 99% of the individual behaviors of all skiers can be reduced to a dozen very characteristic behaviors, each one having its origin in a basic fault.

Several of these faults were mentioned at the end of the first chapter (pages 50-58). We will add a few more which are more characteristically found in good skiers.

If you have not relied on this book to attain your present skiing level you will have greater difficulty in analyzing your behavior and distinguishing your major faults. Perhaps it will be beneficial for you to be helped by a skiing friend who is also an attentive reader of this book. In any case, the time that you devote to a comprehension of skiing movements is not wasted because before you can pretend to correct or modify your behavior it is evident that you must attain a clear vision of what you should do and what you are doing. Not an exterior image, such as a film or videotape will give, but an interior visualization, perceived by your feet, your muscles, your motor nerve system...

Before becoming aware of your faults you should not try to correct everything at once. Every habitual fault, even one that may seem benign, will require hours and miles of skiing before being corrected. *The best way of eliminating a technical fault is not by trying to cancel it, but by trying to substitute another movement for it that is sufficiently different so that there can be no confusion between the two in your nerve centers. (see* Pedagogical and Technical Documents).

It is in this direction that I will advise you in the pages which follow.

Position faults

Have you adopted a poor "intermediate" position ?

At the end of the preceeding chapter, I analyzed a few of these positions which can be found just as frequently among good skiers as intermediate skiers. They consist of:

• *A stance that is too erect with the arms hanging alongside the body.* This position is very fashionable today (page 52).

• *Knees pressed forward with excessive ankle flex.* This fault is a survivor of an-tiquated techniques which have all but disappeared (pages 51 and 53).

• *Chest tilted forward, "broken at the waist", with the seat protruding backward.* This fault is often linked to stiff legs (page 51).

• *A seated position with the lower legs tilted backward.* This position was very popular a few years ago but is now regressing (page 55).

• *Poor arm position,* or useless arm gestures (page 55).

I described these faults in greater detail in the previous chapter and proposed remedies. I won't repeat myself.

Do you have a morphological abnormality ?

I would like to mention four characteristic positions which have their origin in special morphological traits. If you find that one of them pertain to you, you have now attained a level of skiing proficiency which should permit you to correct yourself.

• Bowlegs: feet close together and knees apart.

This silhouette is not only characteristic of skiers who have bowed legs but also those whose legs bow out when they press their knees forward. These latter are more numerous than the former and generally have powerful body builds.

Are you one of them ? are you more comfortable in a narrow stance than in a wider stance ? When making turns on hard snow do you often feel that you weight your inside ski more than your outside ski ? Is it difficult for you to make the edge of your downhill ski bite during edge-sets made with a downhill stem or a wide stance, but easier in a narrow stance ? Do you spread your knees by pushing your inside knee out in a narrow stance to hold an edge-set on ice ?

All of these affectations are due to the fact that the curvature of your legs diminishes the angle of edge-set and therefore the holding of your outside ski, but increases the edging and holding of your inside ski. You are obliged to construct a new balance system using dominant weighting of your inside ski which increases the risk of falling. You are also handicapped when skiing with flat skis in powder snow.

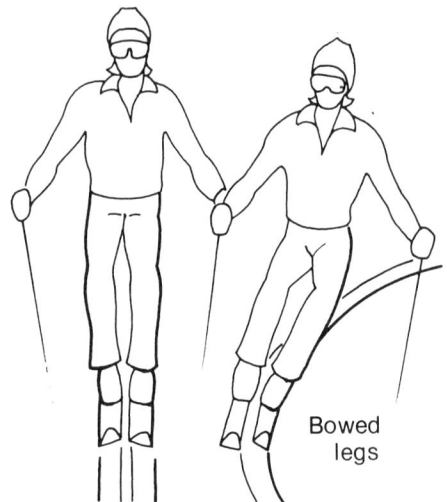

Bowed legs

LATERAL PROJECTION

CINDY NELSON, one of the world's best skiers, uses a movement which I have baptised the "lateral projection". Starting from a solid platform over her outside ski, she moves laterally (or more exactly displaces her uphill ski) to facilitate her entry into the following turn. The uphill ski is placed flat on the snow and then, as shown above, is tipped onto edge to "carve" the turn.

LEG ACTION: ALTERNATING OR SIMULTANEOUS

When two gates of a slalom are very close, or when two turns must be rapidly linked in bumpy terrain, the good skier will work from one leg to the other with his skis very far apart as **INGEMAR STENMARK** does above (left sequence) or by moving both skis through the air as demonstrated by **JAN BACHLEDA**. The Stenmark method is quicker and more efficient and belongs more to the repertoirs of technical baggage of the current champions: anticipation, rapid ski pivoting and the search for ultimate sliding. Bachleda's hop runs the risk of creating a skid and excessive braking.

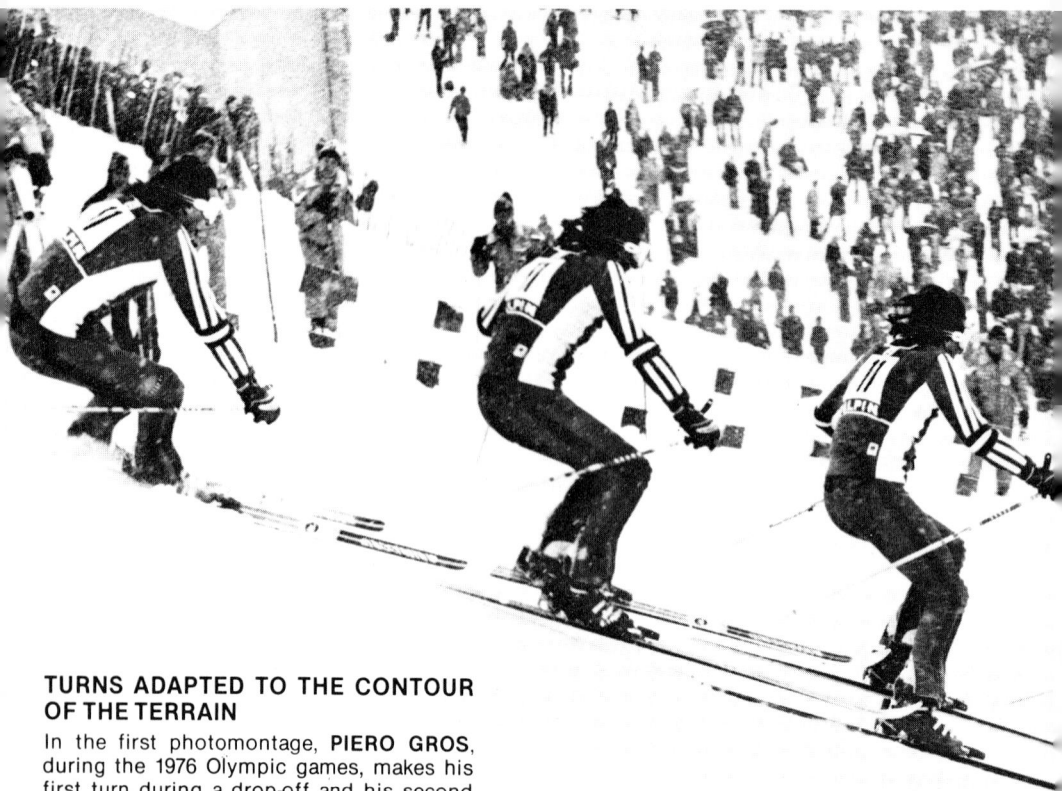

TURNS ADAPTED TO THE CONTOUR OF THE TERRAIN

In the first photomontage, **PIERO GROS**, during the 1976 Olympic games, makes his first turn during a drop-off and his second while he is compressed by a flat. We see him stretch out in the 2nd, 3rd and 4th photos in order to maintain contact with the snow, then flex to absorb the compression produced by the flat in the second turn.

In the 2nd photomontage, **PERRINE PELEN**, makes her first turn in a flexed position as she crosses a bump and extends in her second turn. Note the use of avalement in both sequences.

TO SKI EFFECTIVELY ON STEEP SLOPES: THE CHECK WEDEL

Linking hundreds of tight turns on steep slopes with very hard snow is, for the skier, like playing scales is for the pianist. These turns develop a skier's efficiency by improving his ability to edge check, his capacity to rebound from one turn to the next, the pivoting mobility of his legs under his body and the silidarity of his pole plant made at the instant that he sets his edges.

This drill also can help you to acquire safety and control. It is the door to the outer limits of skiing.

I propose two remedies:

Cant your boots (190).

2. Correct your technique. To do this, you must insist on skiing in a wider stance and with most of your weight on your outside ski. You then must press your outside knee to the inside to increase the angle of edge-set of your outside ski. This requires that you learn to ski with your outside leg always slightly pivoted to the inside of your turns. This in turn means that you must ski in a lower position by flexing your legs more.

This habit takes a long time to acquire. Don't give up.

• Lower back hollow, seat sticking out.

You will only be able to detect this position error, which has a profound effect on your technique, through the attentive observation of another person or by seeing yourself in a photo or on film. This error results from a poor positioning of the pelvis on the heads of the femurs. The pelvis is tilted forward, which in turn presses the stomach forward, thrusts the buttocks backward and exaggerates the curvature of the lower back.

This tipping of the pelvis hinders the skier's ability to make properly balanced

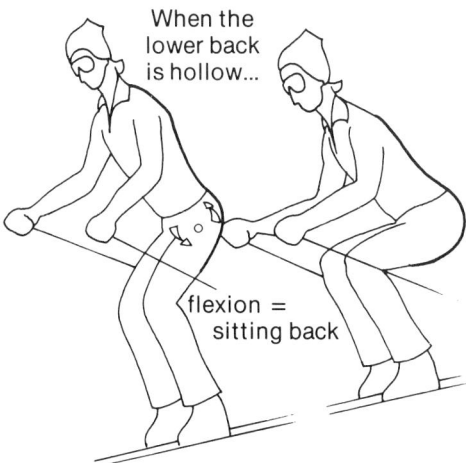

When the lower back is hollow...

flexion = sitting back

flexion-extension movements. He generally tends to ski in a low, seated position which leads to backweighting. To compensate, he often "breaks" at the waist, tilting his upper body forward and, since his lower back is hollow, this frequently results in a stiffening of the back and even the arms and shoulders. Numerous arm position errors are difficult to correct because they have their origin here.

Do you have this problem ? If yes, it is absolutely imperative that you try to correct your posture, both on skis and off, by constantly correcting the tilt of your pelvis. You do this by tucking in your stomach and buttocks and pressing your hips forward. Skiing with your pelvis tilted forward multiplies the risk of your developing lower back pains. Consequently, it is essential that you correct yourself. You should use heel lifts inside your boots and, if necessary, can even use wedges under the heels of your boots to lift them 5 or even 10 millimeters. This should make it easier for you to flex your legs without tilting your pelvis forward and hollowing your lower back.

Also, if you tend to ski in a very low position, try a more upright, intermediate position. When you flex your legs, your lower back should not become hollow, but should be round like the backs of today's top international downhill racers (see Downhill chapter).

It is impossible for you to correct yourself totally within a few days, but you should be able to see progress very quickly if you fully understand how your pelvis *should* be positioned and if you pay the necessary attention to it.

• Back excessively round, buttocks tucked in.

This error is the opposite of that discussed above as it consists of a tipping of the pelvis backward. This error is recognizable by the flat profile of the skier's buttocks; even when flexing down. Flexion movements are made by thrusting the knees forward and flexing the ankles, but with very little dropping of the hips and forward bend at the waist. Occasionally the back even straightens.

When the back
is too round...

flexion =
forward
weighting

Analyze yourself with these few tips. Do you have this problem ?

If so, it will be very difficult for you to correct yourself but you must do so or you will have numerous problems: bumps and rolls in the terrain will throw you forward onto the tips of your skis; you will not be able to angulate effectively and this, in turn, will result in inadequate weighting of your outside ski; you will tend to be out of balance to the rear and will tend to have poor arm position...

I know of only one effective remedy: be aware of what constitutes a proper position and force yourself to use it while schussing in bumpy terrain. Only as you become more effective in this new position will you be able to relax your concentration and the new position become a reflex.

• Knock knees

This is a characteristically "feminine" trait. When found in children with loose joints it is normal and should not be corrected.

In adults it is usually associated with a difficulty in making the edges of the skis bite on hard snow in both traverses and turns. Knock knees are often found in skiers who ski with their lower backs hollow and

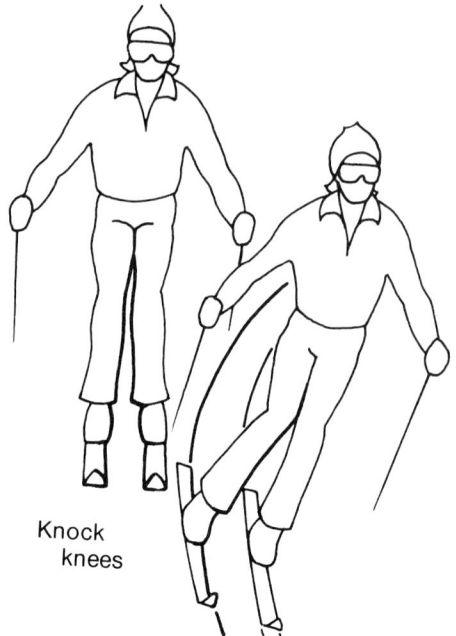

their buttocks sticking out and can then be partially corrected in the same manner.

In general, however, it is necessary to cant the soles or shanks of the boots to reposition the foot directly under the vertical axis of the tibia (190). I sincerely hope that most ski shops will very soon become interested enough in these problems to be able to advise and help their clients. This, unfortunately, is not the case today.

Another recommendation: if you are knock kneed do some physical conditioning before going skiing. Muscle up your legs and tone up your muscles and ligaments and your joints will be stronger, thereby reducing the risk of the tragic knee sprain which is lying in wait for you. Do many repetitions of hopping on both feet, on one foot and deep knee bends or high jumps with both feet. Climb your stairs two at a time, even if you live on the 10th floor. Also, be careful to never let your knees roll to the inside and you will see that your skiing stance improves itself quickly.

Knock
knees

Technical faults

Based on our systematic observations of thousands of good skiers, we can conclude that if you are committing a technical error, it can be placed in one of the following 5 categories:

• **You fail to have sufficient pressure on your outside ski in turns. You have poor turn control.**

90% of the time this error is associated with a very distinct lack of angulation. The upper body — chest and hips — continue to face the skis (are too *square* to the skis) as the turn is initiated. Frequently the outside arm swings out in front of the body, further impeding your ability to angulate.

First, you must determine if you are committing this fault. You can do this by making long turns on hard snow and trying to lift your inside ski. If you are unable to do this, refer to page 60 and approach the problem from the basics. You invariably are committing other errors which are provoking this one. But don't be too concerned. They will soon disappear by themselves once you have established a solid balance while turning with your weight centered over your outside ski.

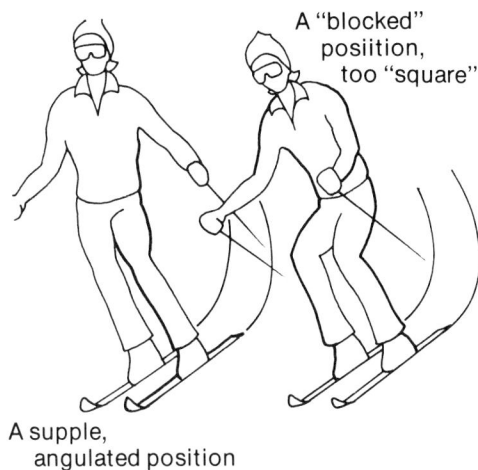

A "blocked" posiition, too "square"

A supple, angulated position

• **You lack leg mobility. You wedel poorly.**

This fault is particularly prominent in France and has become accentuated in recent years as the wedeln has been distinctly regressing, particularly among the youth. One seldom sees skiers link turns down the slopes in a rapid rhythm, even when the snow and terrain are most favorable. This is even more surprising since it is occuring at the same time that the wedeln is enjoying a revival in other countries with the advent of short, and especially compact, skis and the rise of freestyle skiing in other countries.

The technique taught by the French Ski Schools effectively places little emphasis on the development of leg action and wedeln. I believe we have adopted a tendency toward a skiing that is too "relaxed" and insufficiently athletic in our teaching systems.

Is your leg action up to the level of your capability ? If the answer is no, I advise you to not try to over analyze why you have this deficiency but to resolutely attack the various leg action manuevers and platforms which I described for initiating turns (page 70) and for wedeln straight down the slope (page 77). By developing an effective leg action, you will be able to correct yourself without being aware of the faults which have hindered your wedeln.

• **Have you fallen into the trap of banking laterally at the beginning of your turns ?**

This error, a pronounced inclination of the body to the inside at the beginning of a turn, is very much in fashion today, both among tourists and racers.

Among the former, it is made by a global banking of the entire body. It's an economizing of effort at the beginning of the turn. One banks to start the change of edges and a sideslipping of the skis. One then forward weights so that the skis pivot by sideslipping around the tips, then one more or less controls the sideslipping by braking the skis to control the inward fall of the body. I agree this is an easy turn, but it is an

The start of a turn —

2nd - Fault: weighting the inside ski

1st - banking to the inside of the turn

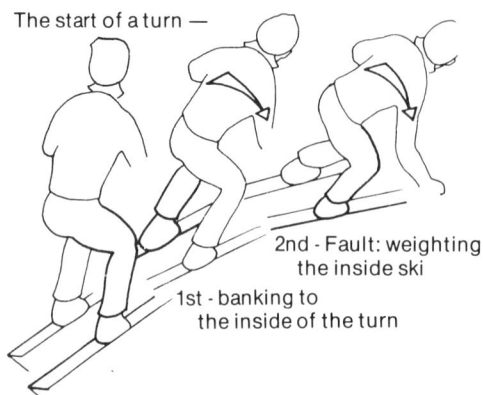

ugly turn and provides no satisfaction other than having saved a little energy.

Among racers, in competition, "banking" consists more of a fall of the hip against the gates. This kind of banking is also an error because it obligatorily leads to a braking of the edges which could have been avoided. While free skiing, racers who bank, and quite often their coaches as well, relax by turning with even more banking than the tourists, but with much greater finesse and less sideslipping. The tourists then try to imitate them...

Do you bank your turns ? If yes, it is imperative that you correct yourself. I suggest you try a technical solution, even if your problem is more psychological and linked to a subconscious desire to "anticipate" your turns.

— In order to prevent banking, you must first try to learn all of the techniques for initiating a turn, dynamic or otherwise, which I have suggested. All of them imply a perfect balance until the instant that the skis start into the turn. Also, always try to use the turn initiation technique which is best adapted to your speed, the snow and the terrain. In this way, you will be able to supplant your banking habits with more proper techniques.

— Another, more radical, solution is to temporarily start all of your turns with a spreading of your uphill ski.

— Be wary of the elementary mechanism which I call the "change of support foot" (page 33). When acquired as a beginner, it can remain the basic turn initiation mechanism for good skiers and be substituted for every other pivoting mechanism. It compliments banking very well and, I think, more often than not is the origin of banking. As I have already told you, use it but don't abuse it.

• Do you hold poorly on ice ?

Are you, like many week-end skiers, incapable of controlling your skis during traverses and turns on very hard or icy snows and particularly on steep slopes ? You doubtless have, by now, purchased quality boots with plastic shells which are very rigid laterally and mold themselves precisely to your heels, your ankle bones and your lower calves. Likewise you have also probably bought quality skis which you regularly "tune" by sharpening the edges and you avoid damaging them by skiing on bare ground or rocks. But in spite of this do you still feel deficient on ice ? I must examine two possibilities with you.

Do you lack the muscle power necessary to block your foot laterally in a traverse — or your outside foot while turning — to assure the lateral rigidity necessary to weight your edges ? If the answer is yes, pay closer attention to the lateral adjustment of your boot to your foot and leg. Consult a specialist to have wedges made to fit inside your boots between the shell and the liner (190). Also, develop the muscle groups that are involved: on skis by making many dynamic platforms and at home by performing multiple repetitions of one foot jumps, deep knee bends, two-legged hops...

On the other hand, perhaps you feel that you are not limited by muscle power ?

An inability to hold on hard snow or ice is usually the consequence of one of the following technical errors:

— Not comprehending the muscular effort required by the foot inside the boot, even though the boot is very stiff. Do you feel the "3 support points" that we spoke of on page 67 ?

— An absence of hip angulation or insufficient hip angulation and a lack of weighting of the outside ski. If you are weighting both skis instead of one, each ski holds less. If both skis hold poorly, you find yourself losing balance to the inside of the turn each time the skis lose their grip and sideslip. This doesn't occur when you are properly balanced with exclusive weighting of your outside ski.

— If you are unsuccessful in making your skis hold during your first attempts at making platforms on your edges, perhaps you don't have sufficient knee angulation at the precise instant of maximum pressure on your skis. In this case, make hundreds of platforms on your downhill ski using a downhill stem (page72). The stem provides you with knee angulation; try to feel this movement.

Also, wedel with stem or wide stance platforms while accentuating the lateral rebound more than the vertical rebound. I have noticed that vertical platforms provide less holding of the edges than lateral platforms.

— Excessive banking at the beginning of turns creates an imbalance to the inside which can only be corrected by sideslipping-braking. This often compromises the holding of your edges without your even knowing it.

— A narrow, forward-weighted stance, and utilization of a passive pivoting of the skis with forward weighting, generally precludes good holding by the edges. The tip of the ski holds but the rest of the ski sideslips under the pressure generated by the turn.

— A turn begun by throwing the upper body or "projection circulaire". The inertia of the upper body hinders the biting of the edges.

— A "seated" position tends to stiffen the legs, hinders angulation and obliges the skier to weight both skis.

In short, good edge holding requires a proper stance, but particularly a perfect balance over the outside ski. One can readily understand the necessity for good lateral balance, but good fore-aft balance is important as well. In fact, *a ski's holding ability is maximum only when the skier weights it in one precise point* on its length. This point, which we call the "center of maximum holding" is situated behind the normal pressure point for schussing and even behind the point considered optimal for the sideslipping and pivoting of the skis. To weight this center of maximum holding, you must press distinctly on the heel of your boot. Instructors rarely insist on this important detail.

• Do you have a genuine repulsion for bad snow ?

Perhaps you have noticed, after numerous attempts, that you are far less successful in skiing bad snow than most of your friends who don't ski better than you on packed slopes. In this case you must be committing one or more technical faults which are incompatible with skiing bad snow. I will discuss the two most commonly encountered technical faults.

— Perhaps you don't have enough respect for the phase of turns down the slope where you accelerate straight down the fall line. Instead, you try to avoid this phase by pivoting your skis excessively at the beginning of the turn (for example by excessive foot steering) or pivot your skis too much as soon as they begin to sideslip (pivoting with forward weighting). As long as you refuse to accept this accelerating, fall line phase of your turns, you will be very handicapped in difficult snow conditions. Refer to page 63.

— Perhaps you use forward weighting at the beginning of your turns to facilitate a pivoting of your skis on smooth slopes. This technique is no longer effective when you encounter difficult snow conditions and your skis are incapable of slicing through the snow laterally.

Perhaps you are simply afraid because you have never really tried to leave the packed runs. If this is the case, ask a friend or group of friends to go with you and help you overcome your apprehension.

Difficult snow conditions require a balanced stance, or even back-weighting, as the skis start into the turn. If you habitually use forward weighting, periodically return to an elementary technique such as the 3-step turn in an uphill stem to develop an appreciation for the dive down the slope, the directional effect of your skis and a slightly dominant weighting of the tails of your skis. You will be amazed when you recognize how effective this elementary turn is in difficult snow. This will then open the door to a technique that is better adapted to these conditions. We have already discussed this on pages 89 and 92.

I would strongly advise you to acquire the skills necessary to face these extreme conditions (pages 44 and 92). Thus prepared, you will readily accept the challenges of the mountain and perhaps amaze your friends...

THE ART OF "CLASSICAL" SKIING
THE JOY AND ESSENCE OF SKIING

This chapter is devoted to good skiers who want, without undergoing the systematic training suggested in the preceeding chapter and while enjoying skiing, to acquire greater ease and more elegance and without pretending to achieve the extreme summit of technical progress.

If you are one of these skiers, if you are searching for "beautiful skiing" as some search for good music, I propose four general principles for improvement.

• Better "gliding", eliminating all unnecessary checking...

With a light touch and flat skis in soft or deep snows.

With vigorous and precise carving on hard snow.

• Substitute vivacity and ease for the brutality or hesitation which often characterizes the first leg actions.

• Discover the harmony of a technique that is adapted to the most mogulled terrain.

• "Attack", as in a race, to be able to ski "relaxed".

You already are a devoted skier.

You no longer are interested in the lessons of a traditional ski school. Some attempts at private lessons, from a wide sampling of instructors, have ultimately convinced you that you can dispense with ski instruction. Certainly you have good friends who are instructors and have enjoyed skiing the untracked slopes off the beaten tracks with them. It is perhaps because you are becoming bored with packed runs that you look for your pleasure elsewhere...

But are you certain you have exhausted the joys of skiing on packed slopes? Does this kind of skiing lack variety? And what kind of variety does the virtuoso pianist find in the keys of the piano? Or the painter in the clean canvas where he is going to place his brush?

The variety and the beauty of skiing is within you. As the pianist expresses himself through his music and the painter through his paintings, the skier expresses himself through his movements on skis. I did not say by the "gestures" of a skier because a certain "feel" for the snow, a kind of aptitude for using the terrain, a certain kind of elegance which emerges from the track left in the snow are added to the movements of the skier and create a harmony that is as complex as that born of the association of the pianist, the piano and the written music that is interpreted.

Perhaps you have perceived this beauty of skiing yourself on blue sky days with beautiful powder snow when you feel marvelously well on your skis and capable of anything. At such a time "technique" is very far from your mind. It is merely a capability that has been laboriously acquired through long learning sessions. And yet doesn't every artist support himself on a technique that has been long and laboriously acquired?

Perhaps because I love skiing, I long ago abandoned this restrictive meaning. Filled with technical knowledge, because my profession demands it, I understand better than others, while skiing, how technical mastery, the infinite variety of possible responses chosen subconsciously as a function of the snow, the slope and the speed, are closely associated with the joy that I feel. And this doesn't happen exclusively under blue skies and in powder snow, on days when I am in form, but in every circumstance. It can be exhilarating to ski at ease in heavy snow or to control to the millimeter the action of one's skis over an icy slope.

Perceiving technique as a certain kind of *quality* in behavior, I have tried since 1963, in my last three books, to no longer present my readers with gestures to be made, but with suggestions as to how they might approach different situations. Although I have succeeded tremendously through the spoken word and with direct contact on the slopes, I am far more modest in evaluating my written attempts through my books. It's true that a diagram or a photo, so indispensable to the comprehension of the text, solidifies the spoken word but poorly distinguishes between the exterior form of a movement and its true essence. Perhaps one day I will try cartoons. A cartoon strip may be a good method of transfering the motor order from the educator to the student provided the latter sufficiently identifies himself with the drawn figure.

This discussion has but one goal: to prepare you for this new chapter in a proper frame of mind.

I ask you, while reading this text, to feel your skis, to relive your sensations and compare them with those that I suggest; I even ask you to try to imagine the sensations that you should perceive while executing ski movements that you haven't yet perfectly mastered.

Later, you will try to regain these sensations on the snow, then return to the book; and by repeatedly going back and forth, I think you will cultivate the art of skiing.

Because culture is within the domain of art, is it not the surest way of making art?

DEVELOP THE ABILITY TO RIDE A FAST SKI

Do you recognize the sensation of riding a fast ski ?

My experience of watching advanced skiers and even racers suggests that you probably do not understand precisely enough what it means to ride a fast ski. I will try to help you to recognize the sensation more easily.

First of all, do you enjoy schussing straight down a moderate slope, or do you prefer to make large turns, allowing your skis to slip sideways, even just a slight amount, in order to control your speed ? In other words, do you enjoy the feeling of pure sliding over that of a slight sideslip through your turns ? It's difficult to believe that you could prefer the latter because the real joy of skiing derives from this feeling of pure sliding. The enjoyment of this sensation increases with increased purity. It's this effect that makes downhill racing so exciting; to the competitor as well as to the spectator.

Perhaps you have come to equate the feeling of riding a fast ski with a feeling of loss of control and risk. This is not at all the case, however, because depending upon the shape of your turn you can ride a fast ski and still remain in perfect control, whereas it is possible to "scream" down the mountain in a sideslip with your skis across your direction of travel.

To ride a fast ski means to eliminate as completely as possible any braking effects exerted between the skis and the snow. It is the ability to most effectively translate the force of gravity, which pulls you straight down, into a force which is exerted along the line of your descent. In skiing, we refer to it as *"gliding"*. It is the very essence, the *raison d'etre* of the marvelous sport of skiing.

Try these 3 tests in order to determine if you've already learned to appreciate riding a fast ski, that you have cultivated the art of gliding:

1st test: You are traversing a slope at moderate speed. The condition of the snow is good and you start a turn down the slope. At this precise instant, do you like to feel your skis accelerate or slow down ?

2nd test: On a moderate slope, and in good snow conditions, you are making a long radius turn. Do you feel a sharp acceleration as you approach the fall line ?

3rd test: Do you enjoy the feeling of accelerating into the traverse at the end of a turn ?

If you answered no to the three questions, you have a wide field of discovery before you. If you answered yes to at least 2 of the questions, you already understand what it means to ride a fast ski, but you can look forward to further improvement.

First you must understand what you must not do ! Then it will be easier for you to apply my suggestions. It is most important to avoid developing a lot of speed in the traverse only to use your turns to slow down by sliding sideways, even linking these slides under the misconception that you are wedeling. In other words, you must avoid constantly fighting gravity and, instead, tame this blind force and use it to propel yourself through elegant arcs.

I am going to mention a few statistics in order to clarify this idea further. Using the broadsliding technique to descend a slope with a vertical drop of approximately 2,000 feet you can, for example, cover about 2 miles at a speed of approximately 20 miles per hour. You would be skiing for ap-

The track of a good skier

The track of a mediocre skier

A braking wedel

A gliding wedel

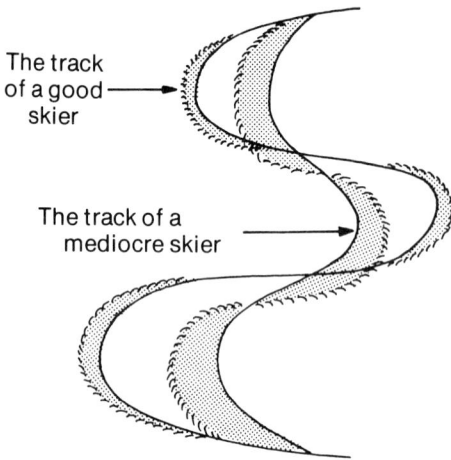

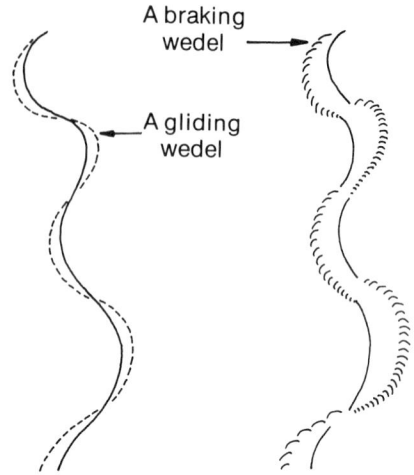

proximately 6 minutes. On this same slope, but riding a fast ski, you could cover a much greater distance, 3 miles for example, at the same average speed (20 mph) and your run would be infinitely smoother and more elegant. You could even carry greater speed and cover a greater distance, for example 2½ miles at 25 miles per hour. This is the reason that a mediocre skier with a broadsliding technique can keep up with a good skier on the same slope. Both reach the bottom of the hill in the same amount of time. One, however, has covered a greater distance at a higher speed in elegant arcs while the other broadslided down the hill, scraping away at the snow in order to control his speed.

Have I convinced you ? If so, I would like to suggest that each time you go skiing, you practice one of the 4 following themes.

During each turn, allow your skis to run straight down the fall line for an instant.

For a few runs, return to flatter or more moderate slopes where you can easily perform large basic turns in a 3-phase rhythm. *1st phase:* from a traverse, start your turn smoothly. *2nd phase:* as you approach the fall line, maintain your balance laterally and slide straight down the fall line without turning, or almost without turning. Your speed will increase. *3rd phase:* Turn out of the fall line and back into a traverse.

Make these three phases last an equal amount of time, because the second phase influences the other two. Little by little you will begin to feel an acceleration, not only upon reaching the fall line, but also as you approach and as you turn out of the fall line. In fact, there will actually be an acceleration during the first two phases, but in the third the feeling of acceleration actually corresponds to an avoidance of braking, a braking that resulted from your habit of pivoting your skis excessively across their line of travel.

Stick with slopes which are well within your ability and spend enough time practicing the manuever to discover the in-

The fall line

1st - the skis pivot
as the edges are released

2nd - ... they then accelerate
as they plunge down the fall line

3rd - the directional effect of the
skis turns them out of the fall line

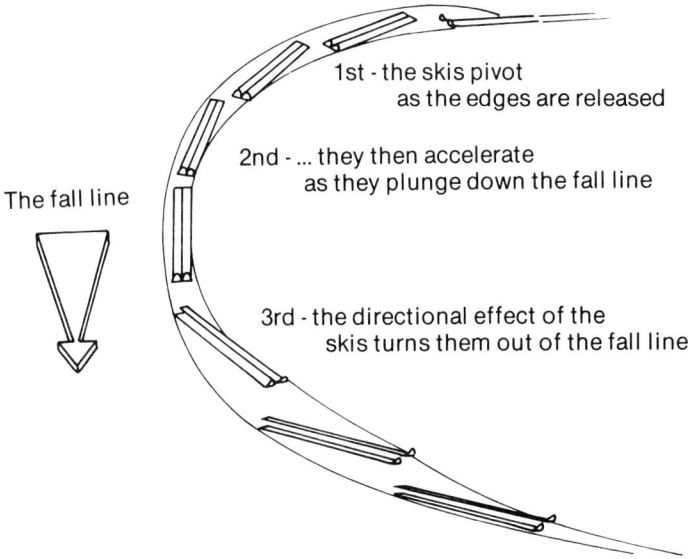

toxicating feeling that results from riding a fast ski and the acceleration which it permits. In order to increase the feeling, you will begin to let yourself go from the very beginning of the turn as you feel the hill pull you downward. Perfectly balanced during the middle of the turn, you will begin to dare to dive into the last part of the arc knowing full well that you can control your speed by turning into as flat a traverse as you like. You can even turn back uphill and slow down before starting the next dive. Take advantage of new-fallen powder and sun softened snows to link hundreds of these 3-phase turns together at a fairly good speed. You will gradually acquire the relaxation which characterizes the advanced skier.

Learn to determine the arc of your turns.

You are a good skier and capable of utilizing the directional effect produced by your skis once the turn has been initiated. But this directional effect is passive. It draws you into an arc which is defined by several elements — the amount your skis have pivoted, their edge angle, their form and the condition of the snow — but you have very little to do with it. This type of skiing isn't dangerous on smooth, wide slopes, and can even be very relaxing, however on more difficult, for example bumpy terrain, or in racing courses, you would need more control. This type of skiing seems too imprecise. The skier must learn to control the path of his skis very precisely. Thus, you must learn to play with the directional effect produced by your skis to increase as well as decrease it. This is what we mean by controlling the arc of your turn and it corresponds to the very fine adjustments that a pilot exerts on the stick of his airplane or that a race car driver exerts on his steering wheel during controlled skids...

107

Would you like to try to pilot your skis better?

To do this, you need to concentrate your attention on your feet, and particularly on the outside foot of the turn. This foot must draw the curve of your turns on the snow much as your hand draws letters on a sheet of paper.

First you must feel that your foot is properly "positioned" on the skis; simultaneously adjust the two pressure points under the heel and ball of your foot (page 22) and the pressure of the inside of the ankle bone against the shank of your boot while skiing on hard snow (page 66). The outside knee should remain "alert", ready to help the movements of the foot. Feel that your thigh is well positioned under your hip and, finally, that your upper body is leaned slightly forward with your arms spread wide for balance and position yourself in a supple, angulated position over your hip (pages 62 and 67).

You have enough time as you control long turns over easy terrain to check point by point the position of your foot, your knee, your hips, your torso and your arms. You can even feel this position by practicing it at home in front of a mirror by holding yourself in balance on the inside of one foot and slightly pivoting this foot under your body to the right and to the left. Eventually you should feel, on snow, that piloting your ski consists of very fine pivoting or counter-pivoting efforts much like the fine adjustments you make with the steering wheel of your car while driving on icy roads. This fine and precise control will seduce you just as it has seduced the greatest international racers once they understood that there is less risk in nibbling away a few hundredths of a second in this way than in assuming extreme risks through the most difficult sections of the course.

You will become even more infatuated once you discover that this piloting is the best way to improve your balance while turning. Because within a margin of a few centimeters, you are able to place your skis precisely where they need to be relative to your body mass and, therefore, can ski with even greater smoothness and acquire the profound relaxation that characterizes the skiing of the virtuoso champions.

Initiate your turns more smoothly

As you slide straight down the slope in the middle of your turns, you can feel the sliding of your skis and the accompanying acceleration. You have learned to pilot your outside ski and to control your turns with great precision. Before refining this piloting by adapting it to soft and hard snows, however, I advise you to concentrate all of your attention on the initiation of your turns.

When you piloted your skis poorly and hadn't yet experienced the dive down the fall line, you perhaps got into the habit of throwing your skis too far into the turn. Perhaps, at the same time, you projected both your body and your skis into the turn and they pivoted excessively resulting in a skid ? Because you now know how to pivot your skis during the turn, and because your only goal at the initiation of a turn is to regain the fall line, now try to start your turns as smoothly and quietly as possible.

Regardless of the turn initiation technique you use, reduce your movements and, consequently, their effect on your skis. With "intelligent" feet, the initiation of a long radius turn on good snow is simple. It suffices to tip the skis on edge and then control them intelligently through the turn.

Naturally, extension can be used to facilitate a soft start, provided you understand the use of this gesture at the start of a turn. But very often the skier associates extension with other useless and even harmful movements. At first, resolve to abandon every gross movement, including extension. Later, you can use it in a more quiet and efficient manner.

For the time being, I recommend that you return to an elementary movement. While traversing, assume a semi-wide stance just prior to the start of your turn. Then, simply shift your weight from your downhill ski to your uphill ski, which you then immediately pilot into the turn. Nothing is simpler, nothing is softer, and nothing more efficient for obtaining a gliding turn initiation. It will fascinate you and open new horizons.

Not until you have really experienced the gliding initiation and piloting of your uphill ski should you return to a slight extension to

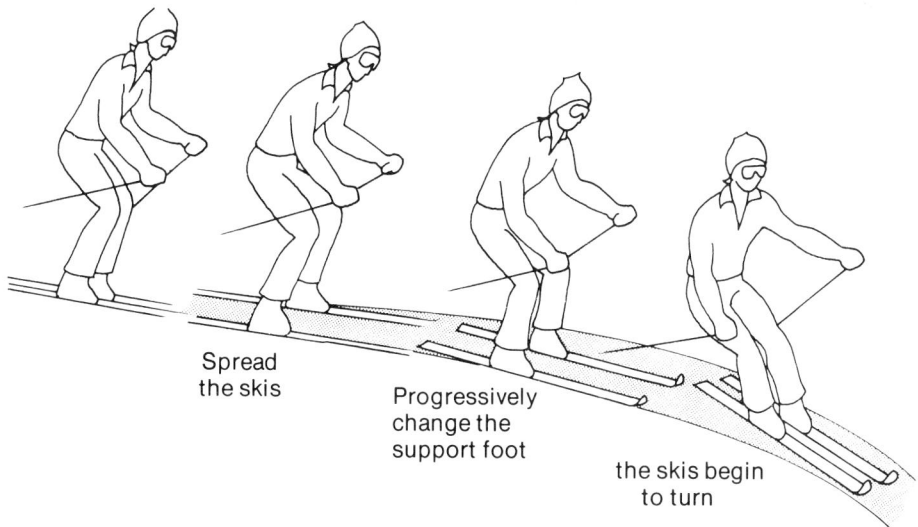

Spread
the skis

Progressively
change the
support foot

the skis begin
to turn

preceed this turn initiation and make it even smoother. First, initiate your turns from a wide stance; then semi-wide and finally with your skis close together but always "free".

Some of you, who have studied this book, may be surprised to recognize numerous concepts that were first explored during the elementary instruction in Chapter 1: the dive down the fall line, the directional effect of the skis, the supple control of the skis with the feet, the change of support foot. This is very natural because each case consists of the skier exploiting the action of his skis on the snow to the greatest possible extent.

"The skier at the service of his skis", could be our motto.

Cultivate harmony in linking turns

Once you have tracked the slope with long, linked and sufficiently round turns, do you feel and elan which propels you from one turn to the next ? Have you recognized that it is much easier to make linked turns than turns that are isolated by interspacing traverses between them ? This isn't only because you profit from a rhythm. You are able to take advantage of your body position and the movements that you exit your turns with and the forces exerted on your skis which considerably facilitate the initiation of the following turn.

Of course you do benefit from a favorable rhythm, but within this rhythm you should feel the entirety of your movements which are linked in several planes.

When you ski from one turn into another, do you feel the weighting and then vertical liberation of your skis ? Without your conscious involvement, your legs are flexed and then extended in a particularly supple extension movement.

Do you feel that this weighting of your skis is, first of all, exerted on your edges with your body inclined toward the inside of the turn and then, as you complete the turn, your body banks forward and down the fall line over your skis ? Do you feel that your skis unweight and then pivot into the coming turn following this movement of your body in the direction of the turn ? This is, in fact, a kind of involuntary anticipation and is particularly exhilarating. Have you developed the reflex of planting your downhill pole during the compression phase of a turn when the pressure on the edges of your skis is maximum and do you use this pole plant to give you support during the unweighted banking which follows and to improve your balance and give you an even smoother leg action ?

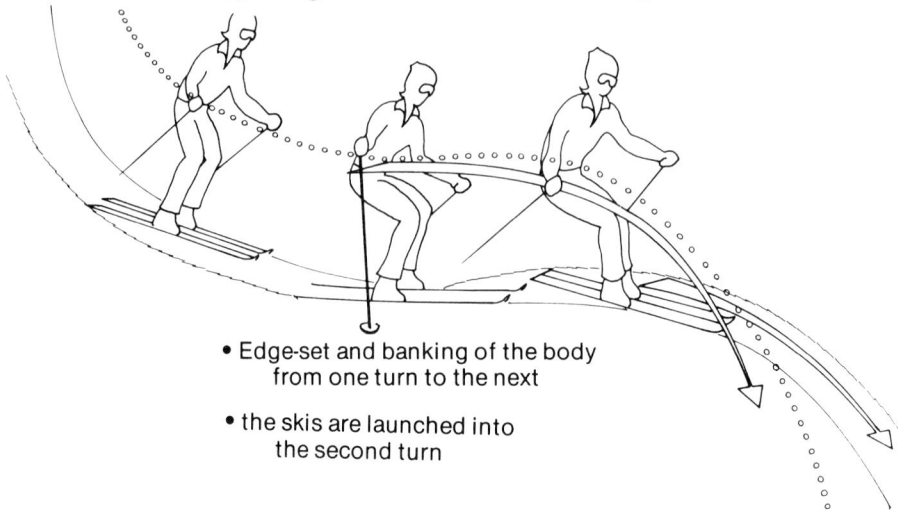

- Edge-set and banking of the body from one turn to the next

- the skis are launched into the second turn

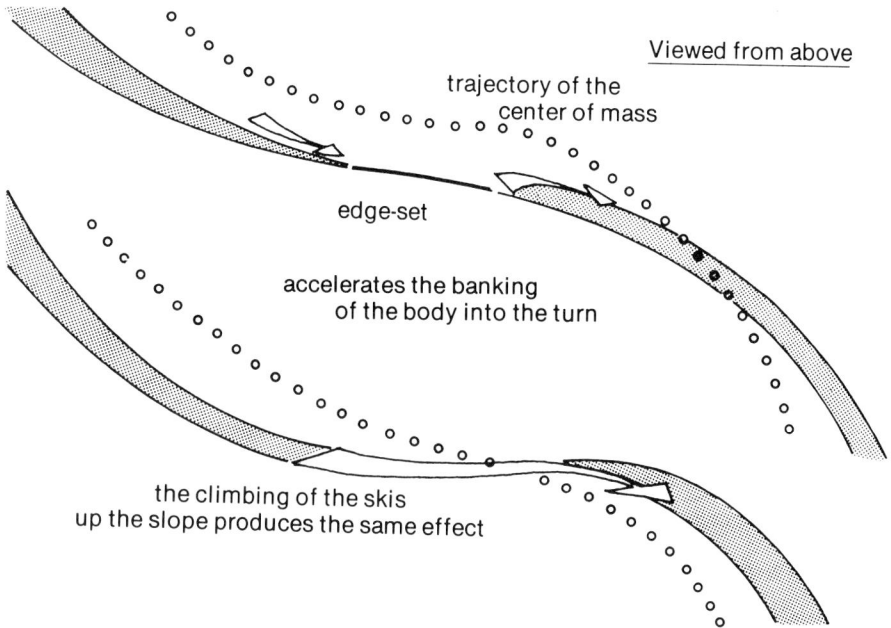

Viewed from above

trajectory of the
center of mass

edge-set

accelerates the banking
of the body into the turn

the climbing of the skis
up the slope produces the same effect

Ski up the slope before turning and you will experience the rhythm of linked turns.

First of all note that the flow from one turn to the next is easier when the turns are rounder. By "rounding out" a turn, that is by continuing the turn until you are practically skiing up the slope, you always establish a better rhythm and more efficient gesture for initiating the next turn. This is due to the more pronounced weighting of your skis at the end of the turn and to the generally more exaggerated twisting of your chest down the fall line at the moment of edge-set. This position, which we call "anticipation" because, in fact, at this precise moment your chest is already positioned for the next turn even while your skis are still climbing up the hill, is the key to a supple and gliding pivoting of your skis into the turn. You should become familiar with this relaxed anticipation and the pivoting motor effect that it produces on your skis once they are unweighted.

Now, start from a fast traverse and counter-turn up the hill and then link this counter-turn to a turn down the fall line. After a few attempts, you should experience this compression on your skis, the banking of your upper body over your skis, the anticipation of the turn by your upper body and in particular the pivoting initiation of the turn by your unweighted skis under a relaxed upper body.

This sensation is so enjoyable that nine chances out of ten, once you have discovered and understood it, you will adopt it. It will allow you to ski with better gliding in numerous conditions as I will have the opportunity to discuss in the following pages.

Another important advantage of this climb up the slope is that it represents an easy way for you to control your speed at the beginning of a turn without having to use a check.

You likely have already felt these elements independently, but I invite you to be more conscious of each one of them so that you can use them with greater precision as a function of your speed, the radius of your turn, the slope, the snow and the terrain. All of these elements impose a thousand nuances in your behavior as we will see in the pages that follow.

111

SEARCH FOR SOFTNESS IN THE CONTACT BETWEEN YOUR SKIS AND POWDER AND DEEP SNOW

Nothing is more enjoyable than skiing in these soft, sliding, silent snows; either freshly fallen or perfectly preserved by the cold. Even when packed, these snows retain their star-shaped crystalline structure and therefore trap a great deal of air. They make a soft and elastic carpet which demands a particularly fine technique of the skier.

Adapt your stance and movements to packed powder.

Even when packed so that the skis don't sink into them, these powder snows will give way to an edged and weighted ski. Consequently, you are obliged to ski with "flat" skis. Excessive pressure on one ski makes it sink further; therefore you are obliged to ski with fairly equal weighting of both skis.

By the same token, a sudden weighting of your skis will make them sink into the snow rather than rebound, thereby requiring you to prolong your platforms.

An equal weighting of both skis held as flat as possible, an extreme softness in the edge-set preceeding your turns and in the loading of the skis during the turn and a delicate touch as you pivot your skis into the turn are the first objectives you should strive for in adapting your technique to the special environment of powder snow.

Also, you should adopt a semi-flexed stance with a balanced weighting of both feet and alert muscles; not for reacting faster and stronger as you would on ice, but to temper your movements, to prolong them. This state of alertness or "attention" of your muscles demands more muscular effort than you might suspect. Don't be surprised if, after a few hours of skiing in deep or powder snow, your reactions are no longer appropriate: your fatigued muscles have stiffened and can no longer "feel" the snow.

Move as if in "slow motion". Do you sense an overloading of your skis ? Absorb it, then act. Have your skis pivoted so far in the turn

Stand with your skis close together and use a very soft flexion-extension as if in slow motion when skiing powder snow.

that they are going to jam harshly against the snow? Flex and release your feet and the shock is absorbed or sufficiently dissipated to lose its effect. You are unable to find a solid contact with your pole? Prolong your pole plant and it will become useful.

Powder snow requires a very special "vertical motion".

If you have learned to ski with a classic extension technique, you must discover a new approach to the vertical extension of your body which preceeds the turn. It should consist less of an upward thrust to move the body mass upward and more of an attempt to gain height so that your legs can flex deeper and more supply at the beginning of your turn. You should feel that your vertical extension is best done with a narrow, feet-together stance which, nevertheless, doesn't hinder the suppleness or independence of the feet and legs.

The "supple suspension" action of your legs is combined with a pivoting action at the beginning of the turn and to a more refined piloting-pivoting control of the turn. It allows the most modern of techniques: avalement, the forward thrust of the feet and the surf technique which I will examine later.

Combine extension and anticipation to initiate your turns.

You already know how to link a flexion and an extension with a pole plant to start your turns. Have you already felt your body wanting to pivot down the fall line during this flexion and extension? I'm not refering here to what we call anticipation, where the chest is twisted down the fall line before the turn is started, but to a global and continuous movement of the body as it pivots down the fall line. If you execute this gesture properly, you should feel your skis, which are held flat on the snow, begin to pivot into the turn at the end of this movement; a pivoting which tends to passively turn your skis into the direction your chest is already facing. What is fascinating about this technique is the delay of the skis into the

turn after the upper body has already started into the turn, although a temporary delay because as soon as the skis begin to pivot into the turn you can accentuate their turning with a pivoting action of your feet.

One often refers to this extension-anticipation as "hip projection" but this implies an image of the movement that is somewhat too dynamic. It is useful for shorter, linked turns, but not for the more progressive, more prolonged and, admittedly, more difficult initiations of long turns. To succeed in this requires a prolonged flexion and a gentle, more progressive weighting of flat skis. But by trying to genuinely feel all of these nuances in soft but easy snow, you prepare yourself for skiing in really deep snow.

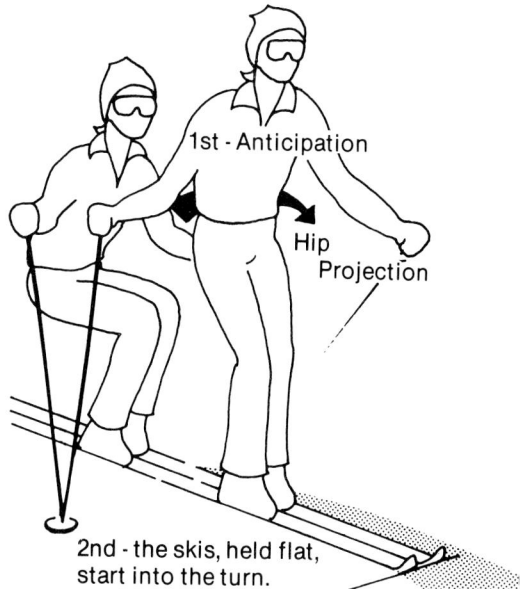

1st - Anticipation

Hip Projection

2nd - the skis, held flat, start into the turn.

"Hydroplane" in genuinely deep snow.

When a layer of powder snow 6, 8 or even 12 inches deep rests on a denser base, you can find a support under the tails of your skis by using a very pronounced back-weighted position. I suggest that we refer to these snows as *"false deep snows"*. You undoubtedly have had the occasion to ski these snows in a very seated position with your chest upright, thighs strained in effort and the tips of your skis rising out of the snow. This technique is effective enough but it is very tiring. I ask that you not consider it as anything more than a stop gap technique because it becomes impossible to use when the layer of powder snow is deeper. You are then obliged to use greater speed to support yourself in the snow by weighting the entire surface of your skis like an airplane weights the entire surface of its wings in the air. We often use the term "hydroplane" but one could just as easily say "planing" because the contact of the skis with light powder snow is certainly closer to gliding in the air than on the water. If you haven't yet discovered hydroplaning, don't miss the next fall of powder snow to initiate yourself and become acquainted with one of the greatest joys that skiing has to offer.

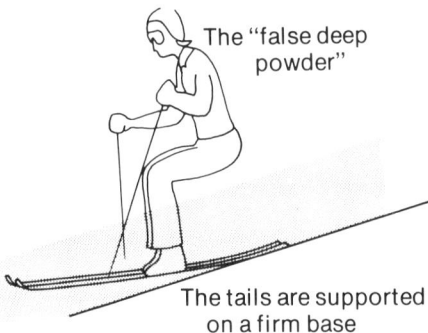

Hydroplaning

The "false deep powder"

The tails are supported on a firm base

How do you discover hydroplaning ?

Choose a slope that is not too steep so that you can ski straight down the fall-line without running the risk of immediately obtaining too much speed. Start straight down the fall line with your feet together in a narrow stance but still free as you weight your heels slightly more than the balls of your feet but avoid pressing against the backs of your boots. You will feel your skis literally "suspended" in a fluid environment. You should also feel that the slightest increase of pressure on your heels immediately tilts the tips of your skis upward and reduces your speed. On the other hand, decreasing the weighting of your heels causes your skis to tip forward and slide faster until ultimately you reach the point where your skis dive into the snow and "submarine". You will understand hydroplaning when you can adjust the weighting of your heels to the minimum necessary to support your skis without slowing down. *Once again, what is most essential is for you to strive for optimal gliding by avoiding all unnecessary braking.*

The distribution of your weight on your skis for hydroplaning demands a constant and very fine adjustment of your balance. Fortunately, this adjustment will become reflexive with practice and no longer require the same strict attention. Ultimately your only intention will be to slide as smoothly as possible to turn and wedel with greater suppleness. Little by little, you will discover the sensation of skiing "on a layer of air..."

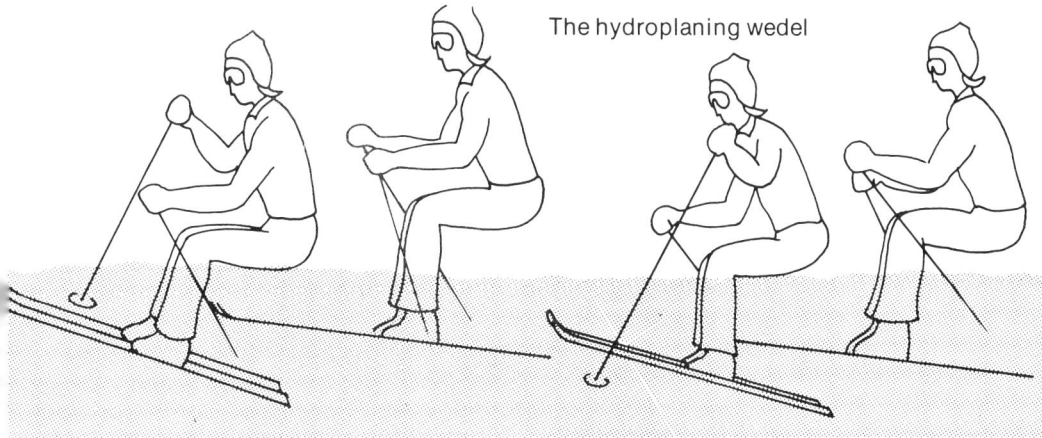

The hydroplaning wedel

How do you turn and wedel while hydroplaning ?

Just like you already know how to turn on packed powder, but balanced more equally on both skis with your feet closer together and more relaxed and especially by prolonging the loading of your skis during your extension and as your skis are weighted again at the beginning of your turns. Also, by keeping your skis flat and pivoting them softly into the turns.

First of all try to make a long wedel down the fall line. By starting with a fast straight run down the fall line, the initiation of the first turn will present no problem. On the contrary, you should focus your attention on what follows this first turn for it will determine the initiation of the following turn. To do this, flex your legs while sitting slightly and distribute your weight equally over both skis which should be held flat in the snow. From this "seated" position you make a very supple kind of rebound which will allow your skis to start into the turn.

Only then should you try to make real turns. Start with long curves and very progressively try to leave the fall line: in this way you will feel the very characteristic thrust that your feet, and more precisely your heels, must assert laterally on your skis so that they slice sideways through the snow. Having experienced this thrust, progressively diminish the radius of your turns until you have mastered them perfectly but don't pay too much attention to how your turns are initiated.

Next, try to make a rounder hydroplaning wedeln down steeper slopes, always aware of the strong lateral thrust exerted by your heels. Then... you can do even better, mimicking the image of today's champions by using modern, dynamic turn initiation techniques perfectly adapted to bottomless deep snows: avalement and the surf technique which I will describe in the following chapter.

Do you know how to "wiggle" with flat skis ?

Can you rapidly pivot your skis, while held flat, to the left and right in either false or genuinely deep snow while your chest continues to move straight down the fall line ? This is an interesting manuever which has a double value. First it allows your feet to isolate the point of the ski which you need to push to most easily pivot your skis (page 78). Secondly, the resistance provided by the deep snow allows you to really feel the so-called "vissage" muscular action which produces the linked pivoting of your feet under your chest.

Without hesitation, you should now alternate long turns, long wedeln and round, flat ski wiggles.

WITH VIGOR AND DECISIVENESS, "CARVE" YOUR TURNS ON HARD SNOW.

You have doubtless become aware of the fact that the least uncertainty, the slightest defensive attitude on icy snow compromises your ability to hold and condemns you to a skidding, imprecise and sometimes dangerous skiing.

If you don't want to submit to the elements, if you want to dominate them, if you want to maintain your line, you must fight a genuine combat against the terrain and against yourself.

The problem posed is as much psychological as technical.

If you dare to ski aggressively by skiing with enough speed and resolutely holding your skis in the line of your turns, or with very little deviation from this line, you can use the directional effect of your skis to make them "hold" on the ice and direct them with precision.

If you are afraid, if you pivot excessively to brake in your turns or while traversing, they will slip away and you are no longer the master of your line.

It is exactly the same with dynamic edge-sets when you want to control your speed or start a turn. If your edge-set is "decisive", sharp, well timed and made with a significantly dominant weighting of the tail of your outside ski, your skis will hold and you will get excellent rebound. But a timid attempt will be totally ineffective and condemn you to a passive sideslipping.

To ski with vigor, you must also have an adaptive technique.

Have you genuinely felt, on steep slopes and icy snow, how your foot blocks your skis onto edge laterally through the three-point pressure of your foot against your boot (ball of the foot - heel - inside ankle bone, *see page 64*)? How by adjusting the position of your outside knee laterally you can adjust the angle of your edge-set? How a firm hip angulation permits you to hold your downhill thigh and knee in proper position? How your upper body is balanced supply over this rigid structure to immediately neutralize any beginning of a fall? If you don't clearly perceive all of these elements, return to the systematic approach that I suggested in the preceeding chapter (page 66).

When the snow is icy, choose easier slopes and during the 3, 4 or 5 seconds during which you control long turns, concentrate on one of the technical elements just mentioned. You will be amazed how quickly you progress and within a few days you can entirely transform your skiing.

THE END
OF THE TURN

Angulation and
inward knee drive

Carving with
tail pressure

First of all, use tail-pressure at the end of your turns to improve "carving".

If you have already acquired good turn control by weighting your edges at the end of turns on normal snow but nevertheless have difficulty on icy snow, try very progressively to use "tail-pressure" on your outside ski. Above all, however, avoid doing this by moving your body backward! Instead, simply push your outside ski 4, 6 or even 8 inches forward under your body. You should immediately feel your edges begin to carve better on the ice. But don't use this tail pressure exclusively when you are having difficulty. Use it at the end of every turn on hard snow. In this way, you will discover a precision in the control of your turns and an acceleration at the end of each turn that will fire your enthusiasm. Soon, this use of tail pressure at the end of your turns by extending your outside foot forward will become a reflex for you as it has become during the last few years for the greatest international slalom specialists.

Then carve the entire turn with tail-pressure. Lateral projection.

Having mastered carving at the end of your turns with tail-pressure, you are now prepared to learn the spectacular technique of the champions that I described 10 years ago and baptised *"lateral projection"*. As you exit a turn with tail-pressure, maintain a carved line by weighting your downhill ski. Rapidly push your uphill ski up the hill and prolong this thrust until you have pushed your body mass up the hill. Then, shift your weight to your uphill ski in preparation to immediately begin a turn down the fall line. This turn is initiated by weighting the inside edge of your uphill ski, applying tail-pressure and carving toward the fall line. Then, try to continue the carving through the turn. It's not easy!

The association of lateral projection and tail-pressure carving at the beginning of the turn is the secret permitting the easy assimilation of these two movements. Make thousands of turns of this type, just as Patrick Russel did on the Sarennes glacier while developing this technique which made him the world's best giant slalom skier when he was already the best slalom specialist. The game is worth it because nothing is more enjoyable than these perfectly carved turns which alone allow the skier to remain glued to the ice on the steepest slopes as surely as flies stick to the ceiling.

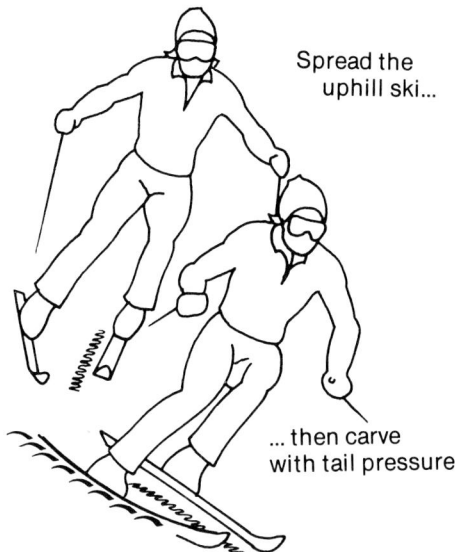

Spread the uphill ski...

... then carve with tail pressure

Also try to wedel by ricocheting on the ice like a flat stone on the water.

Holding a continuous carved turn is one thing. Making precise carved platforms while wedeln is another thing. You can be a virtuoso at one without being that successful with the other.

The lateral holding of the knee, foot and hip is accomplished in the same manner but made easier because the centrifugal force isn't as great. In fact, the vertical pressure exerted on the ski to make it bite the ice is ten times more intense because the period of holding is so brief. It is from the rhythm of the edge-set movement that the rebound is born; it is not a consequence. But beware. One can hop from one thrust on the edges to another thrust on the edges without ever experiencing a genuine rebound rhythm: the platforms are then less elegant and the carving of the skis mediocre.

If you have not yet discovered the right rhythm, keep slaving away ! Strive for intense, precise, almost punctual platforms. In this way, perhaps you will discover the ricochet that the slalom specialists execute on their icy courses.

QUICKNESS AND FACILITY THROUGH LEG ACTION

No matter how good you are at long turns and no matter how much pleasure you get linking them together down the slope, you must not be content with limiting your skiing to one tempo. On snow, just as in music, you must vary the rthythm. The need for this variation becomes even more obvious when, as is frequently the case, a change in terrain lends itself to a change in rhythm. Certainly a series of smoothly linked short turns would be appropriate when a run narrows into a bumpy, tight trail between the trees. A quick series of tight, short turns along the side of the run would make it possible to avoid a short, steep, rocky area. What could be more enjoyable than to finish a succession of short radius turns with a long, diving curve into the fall line in order to start a series of large radius turns ? What would be more natural than changing back to a short turn rhythm in order to avoid a group of skiers stopped in the middle of the slope ?

It is this variety in tempo which will spare you from the feelings of monotony which bother those skiers who repeat the same type of turn regardless of the conditin of the snow or the changes in terrain, their mood or even their desire for a little fun.

Try, then, to vary the rhythm of your skiing. If you haven't yet acquired the technical means to ski in this manner, you will learn them very quickly if you attempt to play with the terrain and alternate between long, controlled arcs and wedeln with independent leg action.

Recognize that there are three types of very different movements described by the expression "independent leg action": the first involves a smooth pivoting of the skis which are held flat in powder snows. The second is used on hard snows and includes bouncing from rapid edge-set to rapid edge-set. Rapid lateral displacements of one ski in wedeln or in the initiation phase of longer turns distinguishes the third type.

Refine the smoothness of your leg action in flat ski pivoting on packed powder snow.

Try to keep your upper body motionless, as if all the movement were taking place not just in your legs but below your knees. Keep your feet relaxed so that your skis are almost free to choose their own path. If you feel your back, shoulders and arms reacting to the movements of your legs, relax, bend forward a bit at the waist, place your hands in your field of vision and watch them. You will quickly learn to keep your upper body stable.

In order to discover the most effective flat ski pivot point, try to gradually accelerate the linked movements. Avoid applying pressure to the fronts or the backs of your boots. Instead, try to keep your weight distributed over the full length of the insoles of your boots. Keep practicing until you have located the central pivot point of your skis (page 135).

If you have the habit of skiing with your ankles flexed quite a bit, push your feet forward a bit, because excessively flexed ankles are always somewhat stiff. This stiffness impedes the discovery and use of the central pivot point.

You will have developed effective leg action once you are able to link 2 pivots together within a few yards between 2 powder snow bumps.

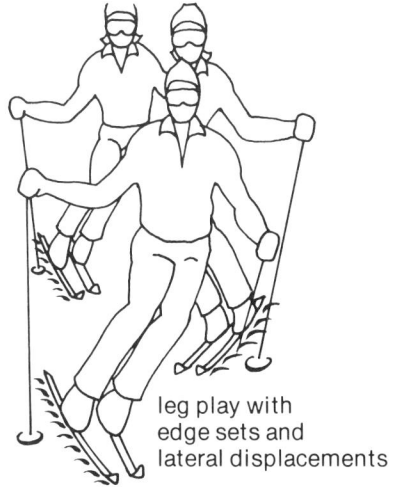

Flat ski
"pivoting"
leg action

Increase the precision and speed of your leg action from edge-set to edge-set on hard snows

I'm always surprised when I see good skiers who know how to use an effective edge-set when conditions require it but who don't know how to use the change in rhythm and bounce which produces a quick edge-set between short turns on hard snow. These skiers are able to wedel only by shooting

leg play with
edge sets and
lateral displacements

their skis laterally from right to left under their bodies. This movement allows only a limited increase in tempo.

I hope this isn't the case for you and I hope that your wedeln technique corresponds with the classic approach in 2 phases which I described on page 84. If you are able to distinguish between the action of your feet and legs in setting the edge and bouncing toward the next turn and the relaxed phase in which your skis describe, almost by themselves, a slight curve, nothing will prevent you from accelerating the rhythm... Edge-set, arc, edge-set, arc. The arc phase can gradually be shortened or even eliminated altogether. This is how good slalom skiers turn through more than two gates in a flush in less than a second. You might not be able to approach that feat, but you can still surprise your friends by knocking out three good short turns for one of theirs. But keep this quickness in reserve. For the most part, retain the arc phase which is the most elegant phase of your wedeln. Consider your edge-sets as only the punctuation which provides adequate rhythm to the movement.

I mentioned the quickness and ease which are provided by independent leg action. Upon further reflection, I've come to the conclusion that this ease or facility exists only among skiers who are agile and quick, and when snow conditions and terrain are favorable.

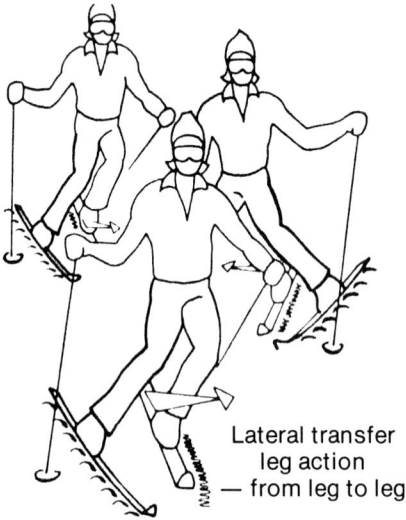

Lateral transfer
leg action
— from leg to leg

Whenever possible, work laterally from leg to leg.

When you are in a bad position to initiate a turn, or if you must react very rapidly to do so, nothing is easier than stepping your uphill ski laterally to start the desired turn. In this manner it takes as little as a quarter of a second. Have you developed this reflex? If not, spend a day or two learning how to use it. Displace the ski uphill and turn. Learn to do it under any circumstance, in any snow condition, and on any run. Step to the side and turn. Learn to enjoy the rhythm. It is very beneficial for you. Were you aware that Perrine Pelen, at the time a young Grenoble University Club skier, didn't know how to make any other kind of turn during a full season? It was at this time that she developed that marvelous independent leg action which is her strength today.

Work on short wedeln turns on steep slopes

Do you enjoy wedeln, in which your skis pivot under your body until they're across the fall line so that you are able to control your speed without broadsliding? Do you have the flexibility in your hips and the muscular relaxation necessary to allow your legs to pivot to the maximum under your pelvis? Have you recognized that the greater the amplitude of the pivot, the easier it is for your legs to pivot back in the other direction?

Be aware that this type of wedeln is reserved for those skiers who have discovered the pivot center of their skis and who know how to take advantage of the natural tendency of the skis to pivot. Contrary to what one might imagine, the mechanism of this kind of wedeln is more passive than active. If you haven't mastered this movement yet, don't try to learn it by concentrating on the movements which must be performed but concentrate rather on this tendency of the skis to pivot almost by themselves under your body. Try to be even smoother with your upper body. Feel your trunk even more motionless than in other types of wedeln. Pay attention to the pivoting of your skis. Even help it to happen, but as soon as the pivoting is initiated, don't make any further efforts. Just let it happen.

This type of wedeln is the miracle remedy for any skier who is accustomed to skiing with his weight distributed over the front of his skis and his shoulders locked perpendicular to his skis.

The use of compact skis facilitates the discovery of this movement but does not allow it to be performed perfectly. These skis pivot more easily at the beginning of the turn but tend to describe the arc of very tight turns less effectively.

Linked
wedeln

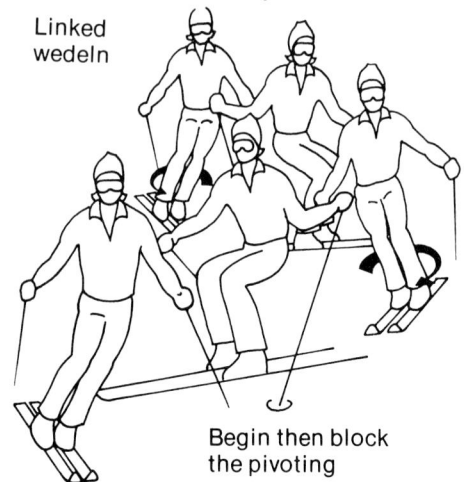

Begin then block
the pivoting

THE SYMPHONY OF THE MOGULS

What do you think when you pass from a wide and smooth run to a field of moguls? Do you feel that it's an unnatural and polluted obstacle that you must contend with against your will? Or do you prepare yourself with pleasure to negotiate as best as possible a different technical problem, more difficult but also more varied, which will tax your muscles, your imagination and your decisiveness?

Admit that it's better to be in the second category. But for this you must acquire an adapted technique; not the devensive tactics that I recommended for beginners (page 46) but a technique of smoothness and ease which I have already described (pages 85 and 88).

There exists a fundamental difference between skiing in moguls and skiing on smooth slopes

Down mogulled slopes you must "absorb" the forces coming at you from the ground, while down smooth slopes you must create these forces.

Down mogulled slopes you must have an extreme sensitivity in your feet to recognize every oncoming compression so that you can immediately relax your legs to flex and absorb the bump. This upward movement of your legs must not be a simple flexion like you might do in a gymnasium to move from a standing to a squatting position because in skiing you are always moving forward. A bump doesn't just stick out of the ground, it comes toward you.

As soon as your feet feel the tips of your skis touch a bump, they immediately begin to climb. If you let your muscles react freely, they will move in two planes: 1. they lift up. 2. they simultaneously move forward. Through this movement they continue to press perpendicularly against the side of the mogul. *You should feel this movement of your feet as being a lifting of your legs not underneath you but in front of you.* You should see your knees lift in front of you with relatively little flexion in the ankles. Over very pronounced bumps, your knees actually come up toward your chest. You also should feel that this lifting of your legs is combined with a forward bending at the waist while your arms are spread wide and pressed forward for better balance. We refer to this flexion as *"passive avalement"*.

This lifting of your legs and bending at the waist reaches a maximum when your feet arrive at the crest of the mogul. You then let your skis dive down the mogul and extend your legs smoothly to maintain contact with the snow. Your legs should stretch out like the feet of a landing bird, feeling softly for the contact. The pressure gradually increases fron 0 to 20 to 50 to 150 pounds and you regain normal sliding until the next bump.

Have you already acquired this modern flexion and extension with the feet in front of your body such as the downhill racers have always known or are you still using the classic flexion, with the feet lifting under the body and often called "balanced" when in reality it isn't? In fact, when the feet lift underneath the body, the ankles flex and the lower legs bump against the fronts of the boots, increasing the pressure on the tips of the skis. Devote a few hours on each day you go skiing to simultaneously adjust your basic stance (page 69) and your technique of flexion. Every time you have the occasion to do so, drop into a schuss; feet forward, upper body and arms relaxed, to run across bumps or a flat or to swallow the "washboard" which often covers a catwalk.

Ski many fast traverses over easy mogul fields

There is no better exercise for you. When traversing across moguls along their steepest sides, you should pay particular attention to the holding of your edges which obliges you to weight your downhill ski almost exclusively by assuming an angulated position. Don't hesitate to lift your uphill ski off the snow on occasion.

Erase the bumps
with flexion-avalement

These fast traverses will make it much easier for you to acquire this special kind of flexion. You will no longer feel your feet lifting and falling in front of you but the foot and knee of your outside leg.

This will make it easier for you to control your trajectory than if you were weighting both feet and allow you to dodge the most difficult moguls. It will also be easier for you to initiate a turn at the end of your traverse using an uphill ski that is ready and available to start turning.

Gradually discover the genuine flexion-avalement to absorb moguls

Once you have understood the lifting of both feet or of your downhill foot by the thrust of the bumps, you will progressively be able to negotiate more pronounced moguls and at higher speeds. Without being consciously aware of it, you will assist the lifting of your legs to diminish the impact of your skis against the bump by physically lifting your feet up in front of you. You should feel a distinct contraction of your stomach muscles before your skis even come into contact with the bump. Your skis,

literally sucked upward, won't regain contact with the snow until you re-extend your legs on the backside of the mogul.

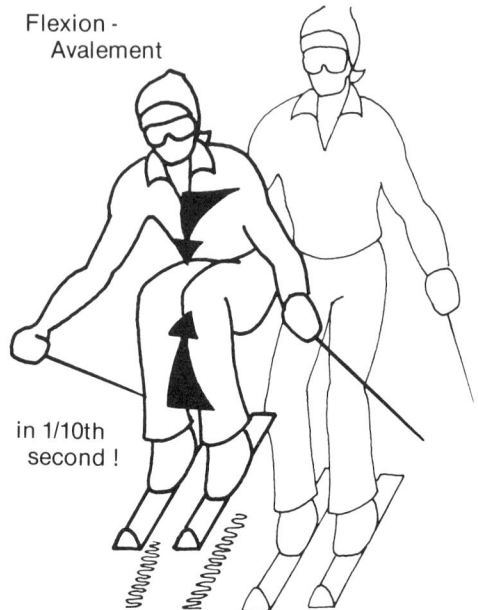

Flexion -
Avalement

in 1/10th
second !

122

Initially you will succeed in using avalement in soft snow. Only later, and provided you have developed the necessary muscle power and can apply a solid pressure to your edges, can you hope to use avalement really effectively to "swallow" hard, icy bumps during traverses or the initiation of a turn.

Alternate long turns and fast traverses down mogulled intermediate slopes.

Begin in a traverse and try to line up as many troughs as possible to give you a smoother path through the moguls. Build up speed and then drift slightly up the hill.

30, 50 or 60 feet later, absorb or swallow a mogul and let your skis dive down the fall line down the backside of the mogul. Smoothly extend, ride a bump or two while dropping straight down the slope and then turn into another long traverse. Frequently you will find smoother terrain on the edges of a mogulled run. This area is usually not so icy and sometimes only half packed. Nothing is more enjoyable than to turn up to the side of the run and then dive into a turn over this easier terrain before dropping once again into the mogul maze.

You can also interspace your traverses with two or three wedels across the fall line or place one or two very supple wedels in the middle of your dive down the fall line. Relax your muscles by allowing yourself to enjoy as many of these fantasies as possible.

Wedel down mogulled intermediate slopes.

Select from among several wedels according to the shape of the moguls, the texture of the snow, your mood and the shape of your muscles.

A flowing wedeln, very close to the fall line using the straightest line possible through the troughs between the bumps gives you such an acceleration in a few turns that you must make a long turn up the slope to control your speed.

Dive down
mogulled terrain

123

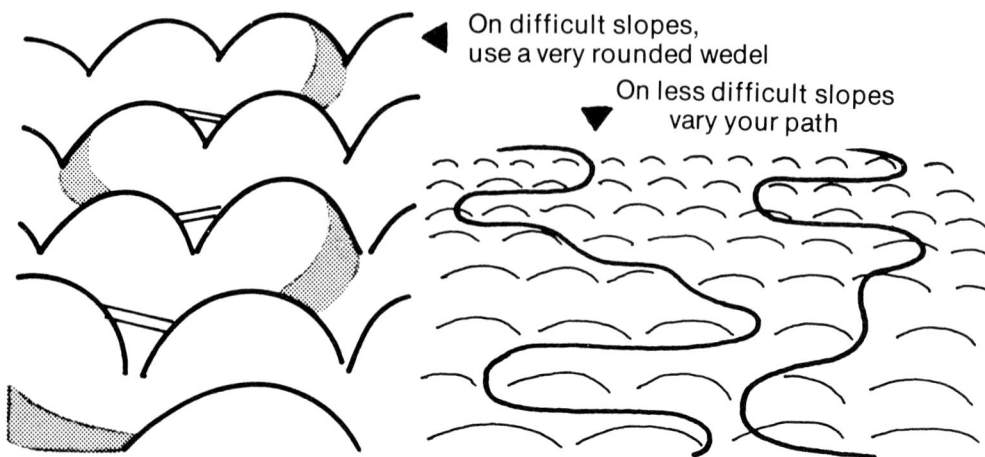

On difficult slopes,
use a very rounded wedel

On less difficult slopes
vary your path

A flowing wedeln can also be very round if it uses the narrow troughs around the big moguls. Let your legs pivot deeply and smoothly under your upper body while your skis make very round turns by sliding flat along the bottoms of the troughs (page 120). This sensation of having the skis led by the ruts, particularly in powder snow, is one of the most enjoyable that you can experience.

Even though you aren't riding over the tops of the moguls, you nevertheless experience an undulating surface. With your legs supple and weighting both skis, your feet and knees lift and fall in front of you while you try to maintain uniform pressure on your skis. It's most likely the combination of these pivoting and flexion-extension movements that gives this wedeln its special beauty and charm.

An "offensive" wedeln directed at the tops of the moguls is also possible. You certainly can't consider this particular wedeln as being charmless if you like dynamic skiing and if you occasionally like to release your fighting instincts.

Dropping straight down the fall line and over the tops of the moguls, overlap the "feet forward" flexion and a solid check with the tails of your skis. Your skis dive down the slope from mogul to mogul while your upper body flexes and extends (page 87). This is beautiful gymnastics !

From time to time, accelerate the rhythm of your wedeln. Turning with ease from bump to bump, you can suddenly find yourself out of step and poorly positioned to absorb the next mogul. Hup, hup ! Squeezing two turns into the space of one, you quickly recover. You also can amuse yourself every now and then by making a series of rapid turns by "wiggling" two or three turns at a rapid rhythm. In this way, you will prepare yourself to overcome all of the traps and obstacles that these mogulled slopes can offer and, in particular, avoid the rocks that are often hiding behind the bumps.

Know how to come to terms with the terrain down steep and very mogulled slopes.

Essentially, your problem is to choose the right route. In this kind of terrain, it isn't unusual to literally find walls of snow in front of your ski tips. The only retreat is downward, thus the need for you to always conserve a certain safety margin to be able to accept without risk, and without fear, a sudden dive down the slope which will accelerate your speed even more.

A sliding and very rounded wedel in the troughs

Have you already discovered the sidehill wedeln, which allows you to escape the fall line and, within one or two turns, provide you with an excellent opportunity to check your speed? Nothing is more useful than this asymmetric, traversing wedeln for dodging those unexpected walls of snow which I mentioned above. This sidehill wedeln is also a good mechanism for diverting your line around obstacles and perhaps to another section of the slope that isn't as steep and therefore not so hostile. It also allows you to reach the sides of the run which usually are less bumpy and have softer snow.

When the moguls are icy the problem of holding with your skis is compounded since the sides of the moguls are twice as steep as the average slope. You are, of course, aware that the quality of your skis, the state of your edges, the lateral support provided by your boots and their design all become im-portant factors. Many mishaps can be attributed to the untimely contact of a wide boot sole and the snow or to a ski brake that protrudes too far from the ski digging into the snow. You are particularly susceptible to these kinds of accidents if you habitually weight both skis and particularly if you ski on your inside ski. By corollary, a distinctly dominant weighting of your outside ski reduces these risks.

In such heavily mogulled terrain, the position of your arms and their balancing pole effect and the quickness and solidity of your pole plants are basic for good balance. In difficult, mogulled terrain 50% of the risk of falling can be nullified by good arm position. After you've been off skis for a few weeks and begin to ski intensely in this kind of terrain again, do you feel a stiffness in your shoulder and pectoral muscles? If this is not the case, you aren't using your arms enough.

125

ATTACK THE MOUNTAIN AS IF YOU'RE IN A RACE

When you play tennis, you don't hesitate to occasionally shift your tempo to a sharper even fiery game during which you attack your adversary placing him on the defensive. This is one of the pleasures of sports, yet why doesn't one see skiers play this game more often on the slopes ? Perhaps you will tell me that competition is this game: the points counted in tennis, the battle against the clock in skiing. This is true, but I always think that competition is more than a game while what I am now suggesting to you is nothing but a game, a game that will perhaps make you smile because of its vanity and childlike character. But aren't the childlike joys the purest of joys ? Give me your confidence and let's take ourselves to the slope.

You're now standing on a slope that is perfectly suited to you. The snow is hard yet it still permits your edges to hold well. You feel in top physical shape and want to give the run everything you have. You're going to attack the mountain as if you're in a race.

"Go!" You throw yourself down the slope with a few flowing, flat ski wedels to pick up speed and gain a rhythm. You then cut across a slope and quickly reach the maximum speed that still allows you to control your downhill ski in a traverse. You carefully control the line of this traverse to hold without slipping or braking and supply absorb the terrain. Holding with your downhill ski, you step off onto your uphill ski and start a long turn down the fall line. You dive smoothly down the slope and then apply pressure to your outside ski to accelerate into a a new traverse. You carry your turn slightly up the slope and then dive again... The slope begins to flatten. You draw out your turns to ski closer to the fall line with flat skis or even slightly tipped onto the tails of your skis which become a rudder. You accelerate even more. Approaching a difficult wall, you make three, progressively rounder turns to reduce your speed. With a last, solid edge-set, you link several turns down the wall into a wedel, much like a difficult slalom. Of course you slow down, but just enough to be able to control your skis between edge-sets and to be able to make as many turns as there are bumps. The end of the wall approaches and you drop straight through the ruts, thereby erasing the last moguls and increasing your speed to make a long, flowing, flat ski wedeln through the flat in front of you. You absorb all compressions and irregularities in the terrain. In a low stance, you make your skis slide like you've seen STENMARK and HEMMI do at the end of giant slalom courses and finally come to a stop...

Your pulse is over 180 beats per minute. You pant for breath. You're happy ! It was a good fight; too bad that there were neither gates, nor stopwatches, nor adversaries. Without doubt you're progressing. You are carving better with your edges and you react faster from one leg to the other. You even succeeded in executing a good lateral projection in the middle of the wall which proves that you still had some reserves. You even surprised yourself by making two turns in a flat ski wedeln between two bumps. And that unplanned flight from one mogul to another at the beginning of a turn that became necessary in the heat of the battle. Bravo ! it was great skiing...

Have I convinced you ?

THE CHALLENGE AVAILABLE FROM FREESTYLE SKIING.

In France, when a skier throws himself straight down a field of moguls, leaping from one to another, wedeling in the air and starting his turns while flying, he is taken for a nut !

In America they laugh and applaud.

I prefer the attidude of the Americans, which shows that they have maintained intact their taste for play, the unexpected and innovation.

I find it admirable that these young people have joined together to practice what they have christened freestyle skiing. Even when codified by rules, even at the highest levels of international competition, this kind of skiing continues to be done in a totally relaxed and jubilant atmosphere. If you have a taste for acrobatics and the necessary physical qualities, I could only encourage you to go and explore this world of acrobatic jumps and freestyle skiing with a few experts.

But even if you don't want to go this far, you should still try to escape the unwritten but, nevertheless, fixed rules of slope skiing.

First of all, take advantage of all of the moguls that are shaped like natural jumps to launch yourself into the air. Before you know it, you will feel so at ease in the air that you will squat with your hands to your ankles and your knees against your chest. Or try a spread eagle with your legs and arms spread wide and your entire body stretched.

These manuevers will give you an explosion of enjoyment. Not just the take-off or the flight itself, but also the landing, where you touch down softly and perfectly balanced over your feet.

You will soon discover that from using moguls as jumps, you will progress to jumping from one mogul to the tcp of another, where you immediately begin a turn down the fall line. Or you can jump off of one mogul, squat as you ride through the air, and then extend your legs to land smoothly on the backside of another mogul to start a turn. These jumps, flights and landings will refine your balance considerably and give your skiing a precision that you could not have acquired in any other way.

You can also learn to use extremely rapid leg movements with a "wiggling" pivoting of your legs on flat skis over a few yards of smooth slope as well as a lateral rebounding from one leg to the other, thrusting against the sides of tightly packed moguls. You can cultivate sudden rhythm changes in your wedeln, shifting suddenly from long turns to an accelerated "wiggling" wedel, from fast traverses to sidehill wedels, from spread eagles to wedels...

Explore these fantasies with a group of friends. Each successful new exploit by a member of the group will lift the entire group. And don't be afraid to ski very close together, even in difficult terrain, because nothing is better for educating your reflexes and emancipating you from the terrain. Carried away by the atmosphere, all members of the group will surpass themselves.

In this way, you can experience the wild skiing of all mountain children who discovered long before you that skiing is a game to be played in a group.

TWO CHAMPIONS PRACTICE CARVED PLATFORMS.

Don't be distracted by the bizarre instruments that **PERRINE PELEN** and **PATRICE CIPRELLI**, two champions from the Grenoble University Club, are wearing around their waist. These are small "hangers" which allow them to use the club's lift at 10,170 feet above Alpe-d'Huez. Patrice and Perrine are still practicing their scales, but this time on very steep and very hard snow where they are making wedeln with carved platforms to minimize skidding between turns because in racing every skid is a braking — a few hundredths of a second lost.

This "carving" is made by quickly thrusting their feet forward relative to the mass of their upper body at the instant of the edge-set. They then enter the next turn in a "feet forward" attitude.

USE "FEET FORWARD EXTENSION" TO ENTER A TURN MORE SMOOTHLY

This is one of the latest technical evolutions of giant slalom racing as demonstrated perfectly here by **INGEMAR STENMARK**. Ingemar moves his feet forward, relative to his upper body, at the peak of his extension, allowing him to return to the snow with very progressive tail pressure. The turn can then be initiated with flat skis and a slight pivoting effort of the feet or, as Stenmark demonstrates in the photos, by returning to the snow on the inside edge of the outside ski in order to smoothly carve the trajectory from the beginning of the turn. In both cases, the return to the snow is made in a slightly angulated position and with knee angulation on hard snow. The skier then has a great deal of flexibility available to control the turn and smoothly absorb the compression that will occur after crossing the fall line.

TURNS WITH AVALEMENT

Avalement is the opposite of extension. It consists of a rapid flexion and a pivoting and forward pushing of the feet. It permits **INGEMAR STENMARK** (top photomontage) to shorten his turn as much as possible and and **PIERO GROS** (upper photomontage) to absorb a bump at the beginning of his turn. Don't confuse the folding that follows this flexion with the extension at the beginning of the turn.

PERRINE PELEN is shown at age 14 in a junior race in the sequence below execuling an excellent avalement with a change of support foot. Many at first judged her movements to be extreme. Time has proven Perrine to be correct...

THE ART OF "MODERN" SKIING

THE LATEST TECHNICAL INNOVATIONS

Avalement has been the most important technical innovation of the last 20 years. It has profoundly influenced all of today's national teaching methods and, of course, all of the technical elements that will be discussed in the following pages.

But avalement is an entire technical complex that can be acquired globally without having mastered each of the constituent elements and can be arrived at from any of several different approaches.

This is why I base this chapter on:

• the forward thrust of the feet, a decisive new technical element that will improve your effectiveness now and prepare you for avalement,

• the surf technique, the latest refinement of "leg action", equally as effective for handling difficult snow or sliding smoothly down the moguls or picking up fractions of a second in a race course.

• a refinement of vertical action — flexion and extension — which can be overlapped with the techniques of avalement and controlled carving.

Ever since 1957, I have suggested to my readers that they ski "modern".

Today, as much as ever, my insistence in suggesting new technical elements born from the inventive genius of a few champions has been proven to be right !

In 1956, at least in France, I had to reject the official commandments of the era: "don't plant the ski pole, don't extend, don't angulate, ski with forward weighting..." and suggest a flexion-extension, balanced platforms, leg action with vissage, the "egg" position...

In 1963, I began to demolish the myth of skiing with the feet together, circular projection, and create — or rather rehabilitate — foot steering and the easy leg action which it permits.

In 1966 I suggested a lower position and avalement for racers.

By 1970, avalement had already overflown the realm of top international competition with the first 'S' turns, the sliding jet turn and the "jet" wedeln.

Today on the slopes, as in this book, the position and the gestures which are inspired by certain elements of avalement have become commonplace for skiers of all levels, even beginners.

Should one slam on the brakes and try to retreat, like the French Ski School, or should one force on ahead toward the spectacular, if not realistic, innovations to try to become the "locomotive", like the Austrian Ski School?

I will leave these problems to those ski technicians who are responsible for these heavy machines that the national ski schools have become...

For me the answer is simple.

You are a good skier and you want to be current? You are not used to seeing young people in outrageous costumes ski with ease where you are having problems? While racing, are you passed by racers who you don't believe are as good as you but who have discovered new "tricks" to ski faster? And you don't know what you can do to ski like them? Then you are thinking like my students at the University of Grenoble. Since your desires are the same as theirs, I have many years of experimentation to bring to your assistance.

FORWARD THRUST OF THE FEET

In order to ski more smoothly, push your feet forward through the turn.

If you have learned to ski, or if you have improved your skiing, with the use of this book, you have already developed two valuable automatic reflexes: an uphill climb before starting a turn and the use of heel pressure during counter-turns in preparation for upcoming turns.

If you haven't already developed these skills, go back to Chapter II pages 70 and 72-76 and learn to apply them on the hill. Then try this new turn which includes a counter-turn and which I have christened the 'S' turn.

Make 'S' turns on a smooth slope

The 'S' turn is the logical next step in the modern technique of turning from a platform or, as it is often called, a counter-turn.

It involves an uphill pivoting of the skis, a feeling on the part of the skier of being compressed onto his skis as a result of his forward displacement, a platform phase with a pole plant and a rapid change of direction of the skis into the up-coming turn.

In order to learn the 'S' turn, simply modify your traditional counter-turn by thrusting your feet forward in the line of

travel of your skis through the platform phase of the turn. After a few unfruitful attempts, you will begin to feel:

1. Your skis holding better because they carve uphill. Your edges penetrate the snow more effectively.

2. Your skis accelerate forward, especially your outside ski which has more pressure on it.

3. Your skis become light or unweighted at the same time that they begin to move forward and pivot unaided into the up-coming downhill turn.

4. Your weight distributed over the tails of your skis after the unweighting phase as they start into the next turn. (In particular you will feel pressure exerted on the tail of your outside ski).

If you have been able to do as I describe in the preceeding paragraphs, you have felt how important the use of a "modern" position is to smooth and balanced skiing, to the smooth absorption of bumps with your legs which bend up in front of your torso, to a carved edge-set on the tail of your ski in icy conditions, as well as to the rapid repeated edge-sets also on the tail of your ski in quick

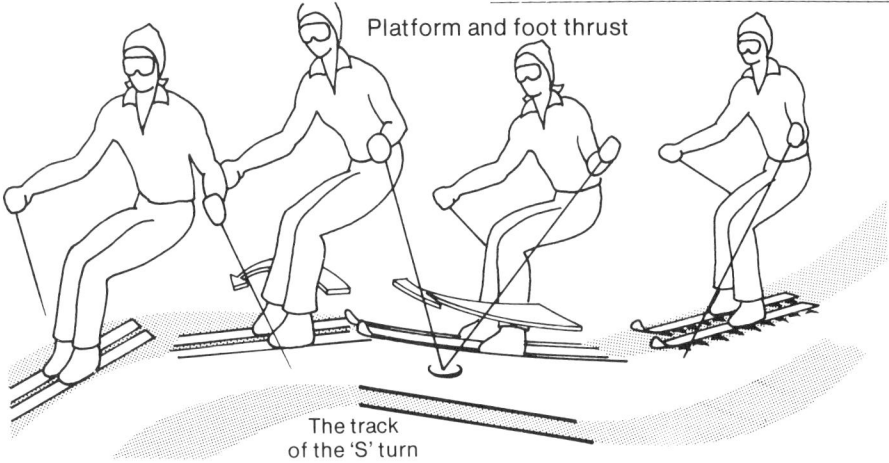

Platform and foot thrust

The track
of the 'S' turn

rhythm short turns. From this position, you have moved into passive avalement at the beginning of your turns in moguls. If you are naturally aggressive, you have even been able to use actual avalement in bumpy terrain and in deep snow through a jack-knife type motion and a projection of your skis into the up-coming turn in the manner of Gustavo THOENI. However, this last step is not necessary to the systematic use of the technical element which we call forward foot thrust, nor to the development of what is certainly for you a new element, "surf technique".

The 'S' turn corresponds to a new type of leg action which I have termed the "gliding double pivot" (up the hill then downhill). This movement is comparable to two pivoting actions which occur in the linking of a counter-turn with the downhill turn. However, it is distinguished by pivoting movements which are linked together so smoothly that they form a single whole. This is the origin of the name 'S' turn.

Practice this turn hundreds of times. In each traverse, make sure to pivot your skis uphill a good deal before they start into the downhill turn.

Don't forget to plant your pole during the platform phase. The pole plant will help you to regain your balance if your forward foot thrust is excessive and your skis squirt out in front of you.

Your pole plant is also a bit more prolonged than normal. As a result, it helps to place your upper body in a more an-ticipated position during the uphill pivoting of your skis. You should feel the result of this anticipation as your skis pivot into the turn without any particular effort on your part.

It is through a careful adjustment of the forward thrust of your feet and the pivoting of your skis that, little by little, you will acquire better balance through the begin-ning of your downhill turn.

Get used to exerting pressure on the tail of your outside ski at the beginning of the downhill turn. As you improve, you will notice that the initiation of an 'S' turn will result in the pressure on your outside ski being distributed slightly toward the tail of the ski at the beginning of the turn without your actively trying to place the pressure there. This tail-pressure is a valuable result of the 'S' turn technique and if you have modern skis you will soon discover how easy it is to control the arc of the turn perfectly in this position.

Note: It is possible that in your first at-tempts at 'S' turns you will lose your balan-ce backwards. This isn't a grave error. You will soon learn to use the elastic reaction resulting from this by quickly pressing against the backs of your boots.

The double pivoting of the 'S' and the forward thrust of the feet up the hill in the direction of travel of the skis forms a single whole movement, the 'S' initiation.

131

Check

Foot thrust
and platform
against a bump

Climb the backside of the bumps with the 'S' turn

If you're having trouble with 'S' turns on smooth slopes, don't be too concerned. Moguls will help you to learn this manuever.

Select a very moderate slope, well within your ability, and with large and well-spaced bumps as well as snow conditions which permit your edges to hold easily.

In a narrow stance, you are going to try to make your skis climb sharply up the hill for a yard or two as you reach the backside of a mogul. You will then turn downhill on the crest of the bump after planting your pole. You should feel your body compressed by the bump at the very instant that you thrust your skis forward and up the hill along their line of travel. In the following instant, you should feel your skis practically take off by themselves as they reach the crest of the bump and pivot down the hill. You then smoothly extend your body in order to regain the pressure on your skis and control the rest of the arc of your turn with slightly more pressure on the tail of your ski. Once again in the traverse, you aim at a new bump, you pivot your skis up the hill and push them forward again up the side of the mogul.

You will quickly discover a rocking movement which I sometimes describe as being similar to that of a rocking chair and which will help you to make 'S' turns. Be careful, however, not to over exaggerate this rocking motion as it will lead to an excessive use of your upper body whereas the 'S' turn depends simply on an action of the legs under the trunk which leans slightly forward in a completely relaxed position. The arms are spread wide apart in front and act as does the balancing pole of a tight-rope walker.

Be very careful !

Once you have passed over the crest of the mogul, reapply pressure sharply, particularly to the outside ski of the turn. It is the outside ski, in fact, on which the pivoting of the 'S' turn is most effective (533-h). If you place too much weight on your inside ski during your edge-set *your skis will skid out from under you, your inward lean will become excessive and you will fall.*

Don't forget to plant your pole each time your skis pivot down the hill and don't hesitate to prolong this pressure on your pole. A strong push on the planted pole can save you from a fall as your skis dive behind the bump. Don't let this concern you. You are passing through a normal stage in the learning of the 'S' turn.

Bumps facilitate 'S' turns by accentuating the two pivoting actions and the forward thrust of the feet.

132

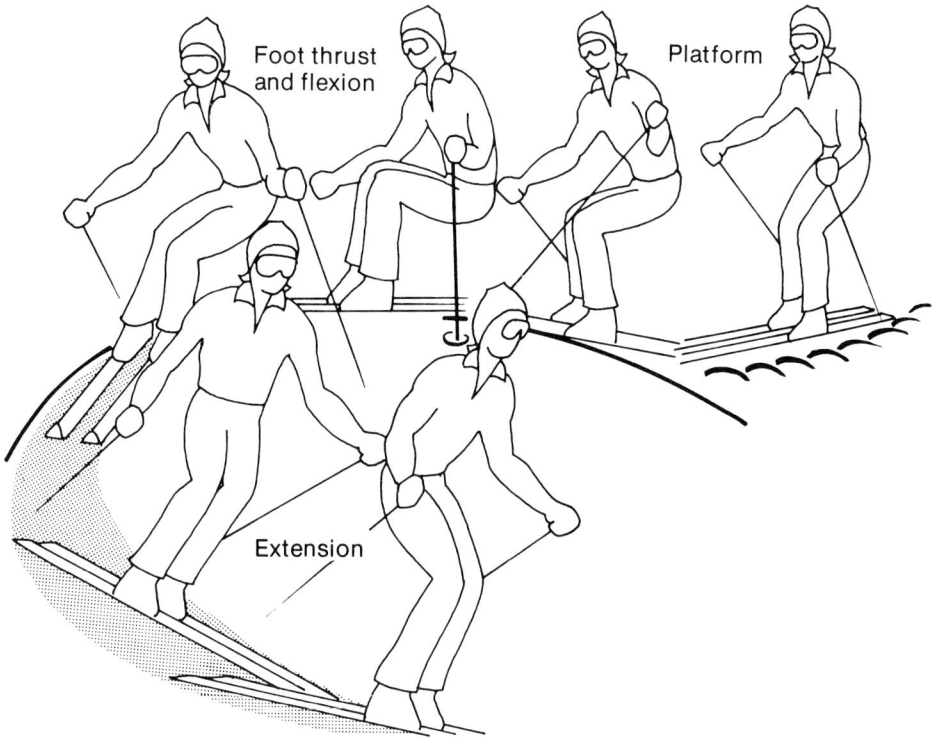

Foot thrust and flexion

Platform

Extension

Practice the extension which follows the double pivoting action and the forward thrust of the feet.

While making a series of linked 'S' turns, try to resist the thrust of the bump under your feet a little bit less and allow your legs to bend up in front of you a little bit more. You will thus reach the crest of the bump in a slightly lower position and the ensuing extension of your body will be greater as your skis dive into the turn. This extension will help you to regain your balance over your skis. From bump to bump, you will thus be able to develop an even smoother leg action. The action of your skis over the bumps will also become smoother because you will almost completely eliminate the compression exerted by the bump under your feet.

In summary, you will be able to use moguls in order to develop two fairly different types of 'S' turns:

• *The dynamic 'S' turn* which I described first includes a true platform phase against the backside of the bump, a flexion while the unweighted skis climb to the crest of the bump and an extension behind it.

This type of turn relates to the carved rebound described on page 135 and to the giant slalom turn with extension and a forward position of the feet described on page 139.

• *In avalement type 'S' turns*, the compression is absorbed partially or completely and is linked with a very full extension after passage of the crest of the mogul.

This type of turn is very similar to some slalom turns performed in soft snow and ruts as well as to short turns with avalement performed in very deep snows and which I have labelled "porpoising" (page151).

Do not confuse the extension in 'S' turns with the up-motion which preceeds certain other types of turns.

133

Thread your way through the bumps with your feet in a forward position

You have skied bumps frequently enough to have tried, perhaps successfully, to thread your way through the narrow channels which wind between the moguls. These intertwining channels form true labyrinths. It is possible to thread one's way almost straight down the fall line or, on the contrary, to follow an extremely sinuous path in very short, tight turns.

I am going to suggest a "secret weapon" for approaching this second type of line. This movement is very similar to the preceding 'S' turn. It also employs a double pivoting action and a forward thrust of the feet.

In order to be most effective, you must be in a flexed body position, feet pushed sharply forward, and trunk bent fairly well forward from the waist. Your arms should be wide-spread in front. You should be ready to control the direction of your skis with your feet. Begin by skiing in a field of moguls in your accustomed manner. Make your turns as short and tight as possible. Then, little by

little, try to remain in the channels between the bumps. Keep your feet in front and use them to control the path of your skis. You should discover very quickly that each time you turn your skis out of the fall line along the path of a lateral channel while thrusting your feet forward in their direction of travel and up the hill, that you are performing an extraordinarily tight turn. You should also recognize that to each upward climb of your skis is linked automatically a downhill dive during which your body remains in a well-balanced position. During these turns, you plant your pole as usual and keep your trunk relaxed and facing down the fall line.

Once you have understood this movement, you will feel that it is performed more easily in a narrow stance. You will feel a new kind of leg action in which your feet pivot and move forward with your skis almost flat on the snow while your knees ride and fall in front of you.

After a few thousand turns of this type, you will approach the surf technique (page 141).

Nothing will improve the double pivoting action better than practicing tight complete turns through the channels between moguls.

Use forward foot thrust to develop your ability to carve

I have already indicated several times that modern skis will hold better when the skier exerts slightly more pressure on the heel of his foot. I mentioned a dynamic pressuring of the heel during quick, repeated edge-sets and a sustained heel pressure on the outside ski at the end of a turn in order to avoid excessive sideslipping. I also mentioned a type of heel pressure which can be exerted at the very beginning of a carved turn on hard

snows after a lateral projection, for example (127).

You should now discover that more important than being in a position which exerts pressure on the heel of your foot, it is the forward thrust of your foot or feet which results in this heel pressure. The forward thrust of the feet initiates the carving action of the skis and once the carving action is begun it is easily sustained.

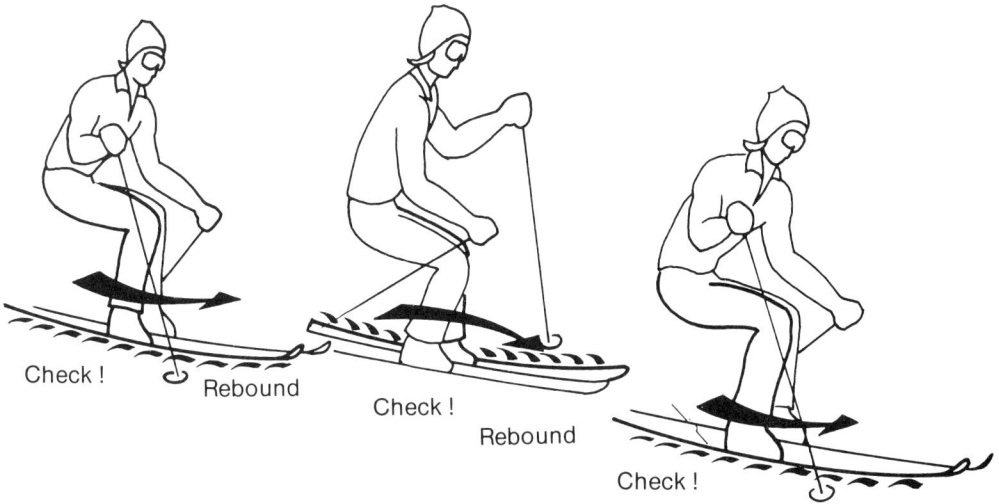

Check ! Rebound

Check !

Rebound

Check !

Discover carved wedeln with rebound

During the past few years, carving with continuous steady pressure on the edge has become so popular that most advanced skiers don't use any other manner of free skiing on hard and icy snows. They seem to prefer long radius turns to wedeln turns. It is sometimes useful and even occasionally indispensable to react very quickly from one ski to the other or to displace both skis laterally from edge-set to edge-set as is done currently by slalom racers. In the past, this type of movement resulted in edge-sets which chattered laterally. This is why slalom racers have tried to avoid the movement and advanced skiers have imitated them.

However there is a means of bouncing from edge-set to edge-set in wedeln or short turns without slowing down or chattering by using a quick forward and slightly pivoted thrust somewhat like that used at the initiation of 'S' turns. I think that the skier who used this element most effectively was the international ski racer from France, Jean-

Noel AUGERT. His forward and pivoted thrust was so quick that very few coaches recognized it. At present, a whole new wave of very aggressive slalom racers led by Piero GROS of Italy employ with equal skill the sustained carve as well as the quick carved edge-sets.

How are these rapidly carved edge-sets performed ?

First you must master the 'S' turn. Then try to make 'S' turns on very hard snow. Gradually try to shorten the period in which you thrust your feet forward and pivot them until the displacement of the skis up the hill in their direction of travel takes no longer than a traditional edge-set. You will automatically begin to rebound from the edge-set and your skis will pivot downhill during the rebound. Having experienced this incisive initiation in longer turns, you are now ready to apply it to wedeln. Take off straight down hill and set your edge with this thrusting motion in order to start a slow

---

Carving rebound and avalement are two extremes of the same technique: modern technique.

rhythm wedel. Rebound laterally from one side of the fall line to the other. Set your edge with another thrust and rebound again. Link these movements together. Your skis begin to pivot each time while they are suspended above the snow and once pressure is exerted on them again they carve while continuing this pivoting action. Then rebound again into the air and begin to pivot in the opposite direction.

In my chapter on "Classical Skiing" (page 119), I suggested a "ricochet" type wedeln for hard snows. In that case, the impact of the edges on the snow resulted in sharp, lateral shocks with each edge-set, while in the case of the forward thrust of the feet, the shocks are transformed into a series of inimitably smooth, carved edge-sets

Avoid excessive sideslipping at the finish of your turns by pushing your feet forward

As I have mentioned several times before, it is at the finish of your turns where it is most difficult to make your skis hold. This is especially true if the radius of the turn is short, the hill is steep and the snow is hard. In this case, you feel yourself literally crushed onto your skis and pulled down the hill.

These extreme conditions are encountered in slalom, but also on hard snow, steep slopes or very bumpy terrain.

Under these conditions, skiers are easily divided into two groups: those who "hold" and those who can't make their skis hold.

The secret of "holding" at the finish of the turn.

If you want to be among the group of skiers who hold, you must develop the automatic reaction of pushing your feet forward as soon as your skis have passed the fall line and you feel yourself compressed onto your skis.

You will then feel the edge of your skis begin to carve, and you will be able to sustain this carving action through the finish of the turn. You can also perform this push and carving action with your outside ski exclusively. Nine times out of ten, this is the best way to obtain an effective carving action.

Even though this movement occurs at the end of the turn, it shares certain characteristics of the 'S' turn initiated on hard snows in bumpy terrain (page 132). If you have become accustomed to analyzing your movements, the displacement of your skis, the compression and unweighting which you experience, you have certainly felt that at the finish of your turns you are com-

The maintenance of
tail pressure by
a forward thrust of
the feet allows the skis
to carve.

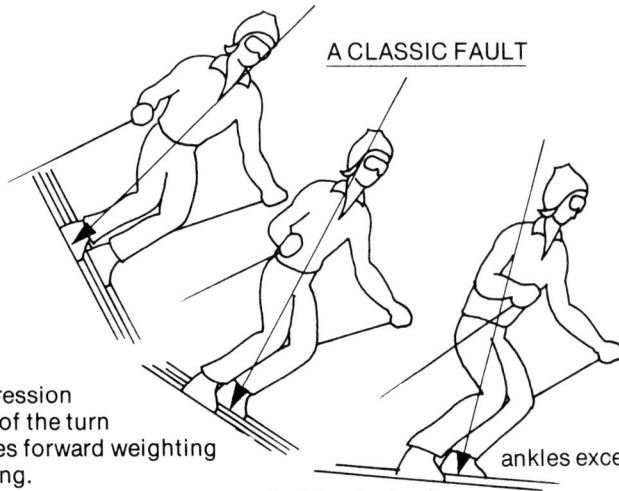

A CLASSIC FAULT

The compression
at the end of the turn
accentuates forward weighting
and skidding.

ankles excessively flexed

feet too far back

pressed onto your skis just as you are by the climb of your skis up the backside of a bump. If this is not the case, practice your skiing until you become aware of it, because in your short turns this feeling of being compressed should become the signal to push your feet forward through the turn.

You will then recognize that each time that your skis sideslip at the finish of your turn, you have allowed yourself to be compressed into a position of gradually increasing for-ward lean accompanied by excessive ankle bend in your outside leg which trails too far behind your inside leg (218). Unfortunately, we become accustomed to such feelings and are no longer aware of them until we acquire new feelings to replace them. The finish of any turn tends to compress the skier into an excessive forward lean. By pushing your outside foot forward through the turn, apply this pressure to the tail of your outside ski.

The finish of any turn tends to compress the skier into an excessive forward lean. By pushing your outside foot forward through the turn, apply this compression to the tail of your outside ski.

1st - spread

2nd - the uphill foot is
pressed forward and pivoted
to initiate a carved turn.

Forward push of the outside ski at the beginning of a carved turn

Whether performing a powerful lateral projection with either a maximum or a minimum extension or simply stepping uphill 8 inches to a foot in order to smoothly initiate a turn on icy snow, you are faced with the same problem. You must initiate the carving action of the ski on edge in order to avoid excessive sideslipping. Once again, the answer is the same: *you must push your foot forward and pivot it slightly in order to make the edge bite.* In this type of turn, you can really feel your leg and foot work with your ski as if it were a tool. If the ski begins to carve immediately on the hard snow, it will continue to do so. If, on the other hand, it begins to sideslip at this point, it will continue to sideslip.

This action of the outside ski at the beginning of the turn is possible only from a wide stance, or after a lateral projection, because it almost always involves an inward displacement of the outside knee. If your knees are in contact with one another in a narrow stance, this movement is impossible. If the start of the turn is accompanied by a full extension, the inward movement of the knee is often replaced by a movement into hip angulation.

In order to discover this movement, practice on a moderate but icy slope and, in a slightly flexed position, step your ski uphill about a foot to 18 inches in order to start a moderately large radius turn. Try to make the inside edge of the displaced ski bite immediately so that it starts into the turn without sideslipping excessively. After a little trial and error, you will discover that a slight forward push and pivoting of this outside ski will start it carving into the turn. Once you have felt it, you will be able to perfect the movement in higher speed turns as well as turns initiated more aggressively.

This method of starting a turn is also possible on soft snows. You will become aware of this fact once you have mastered the movement on hard snows. Then, on soft snows, you can step up to your uphill ski, placing it flat on the snow, and then gradually push it forward and pivot it slightly as you gradually apply a light pressure on the inside edge of the back half of the ski. You will then experience a directional effect which is half carved, half slipped as the ski starts smoothly into the turn. We will encounter this movement again in our discussion of the surf technique (page 154).

The forward push and pivoting of the outside ski at the beginning of a turn permits a very effective carved turn initiation.

foot-forward
extension

edge-change

ample extension

progressive re-weighting

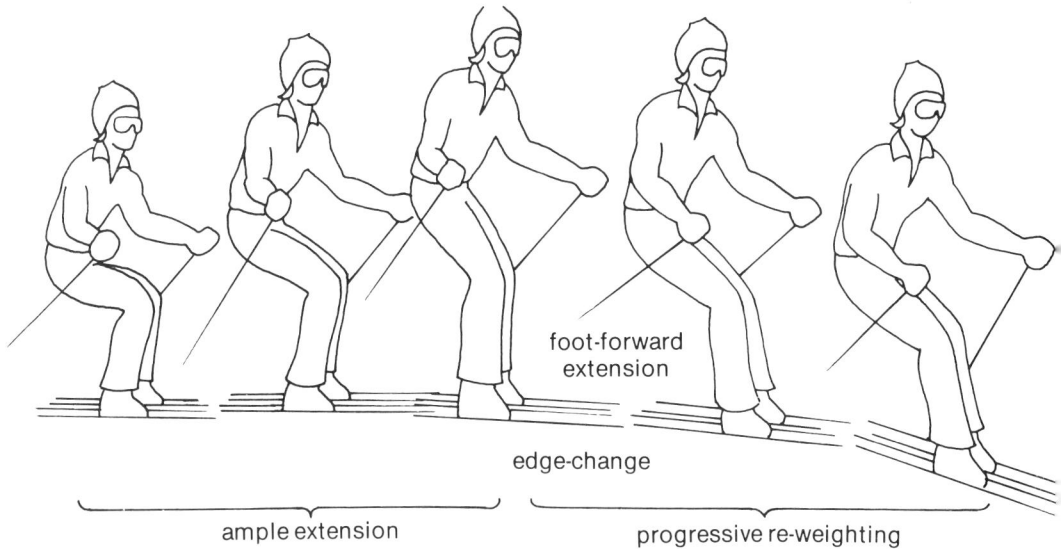

This movement is distinctive in two ways:

Turn with up-motion and a forward thrust of the feet.

This type of turn was in fashion in 1976 and 1977 in international competition. Misunderstood, it reaked havoc among the members of certain national teams then filtered through the regional racers, always in search of the latest moves, and ended up among the best advanced free skiers. Correctly applied, however, it allowed great giant slalom skiers like the Swiss Heini HEMMI to dominate their competition.

The movement is simple. It begins like a normal turn with an extension but the stance is generally wide. During the traverse, the skier unfolds vertically with a thrust of his legs. His upper body remains relaxed and his arms spread wide in front. At the end of this upward thrust, the skier pushes his feet slightly forward and pivots them into the turn as the pressure develops along the tails. The skier then controls the arc of his turn and is able to flex through a large range of motion in order to absorb the compression force which is exerted on him as a result of centrifugal force and his turn out of the fall line.

• Pressure builds gradually and smoothly under the heel of the ski following the extension. On hard snow, and particularly in competition, the tail-pressure can be exerted on a well edged ski, whereas it is also applicable to a reduced edge angle on soft snows. The skier angulates slightly as the pressure builds.

• Because of the higher position of the skier's center of mass, produced by the extension, the sensation of being pulled into the fall line at the beginning of the turn is heightened.

In order to feel this movement, begin again some moderately large turns with an ample extension followed by an increase in pressure over the tail of the ski and light angulation. Work almost in slow motion, then begin to change your rhythm. Tighten your turn and complete it by carving with the tail of your ski by a sharp forward thrust and pivoting action of your feet accompanied by a full flexion while maintaining the pressure on the tails of your skis. In other words, begin a fairly long radius turn with an extension into a relaxed, high body position. Then complete the arc and finish your turn in a flexed and angulated position, compressed over your skis with your feet forward and with most of your weight on your outside ski.

This movement can lead in many directions

Once you have gotten the feel of the two phases of this turn, you will have acquired the key to a series of slightly different turns.

• *Longer radius turns:* The extension is the same. The pressure builds even more gradually and not quite as far back on the tail. The skis are pivoted less and the edge angle is more reduced and increased gradually. Because the compression force is reduced, the flexion takes place more slowly and the arc of the turn is controlled more like that of a normal turn. An attempt is made to maximize the acceleration at the finish of the turn.

• *Turns started with an extension and projection from one ski to the other.* This turn is the most frequently used today. It does resemble lateral projection even though vertical movement is emphasized more than lateral movement. The upward thrust results largely from the action of the downhill leg. At the end of the unweighting phase, when the feet are pushed forward, the uphill ski, which was displaced slightly uphill, comes smoothly back into contact with the snow before the other ski. It is by a slight pivoting action and push of the uphill foot that the turn is initiated, either with a reduced edge

angle on soft snow or with carving action on the tail of the ski on hard snow.

This movement is fairly closely related to the extension and change of support foot that is instinctively discovered by many intermediate skiers (page 75).

The most frequent errors associated with the performance of these turns are of three types:

1. An incorrect extension; principally by extending only at the waist and often accompanied by an unnecessary upward or even backward movement of the arms.

2. An extension accompanied by a projection of the upper body in the direction of the upcoming turn. In this case, the skier regains contact with the snow in the middle of the turn with his skis pivoted excessively and his body facing his skis. He is therefore unable to make his skis carve. This error is particularly common among those skiers who insist on using an extension under all circumstances, even when there isn't enough time such as in a mogul field or even moreso in a tight slalom.

Women seem to have greater difficulty performing this manuever than men. They tend to flex too quickly and energetically after the extension and lock their shoulders into a position perpendicular to their skis.

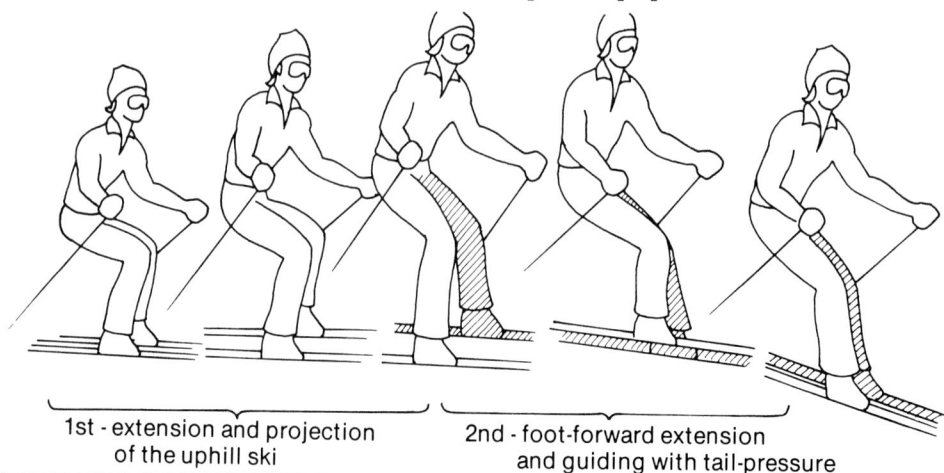

1st - extension and projection of the uphill ski

2nd - foot-forward extension and guiding with tail-pressure

The combination of extension and a forward push of the feet permits a more gradual reapplication of pressure to the ski and occasionally a more effective carving action, but it requires that the skier have several yards before he must initiate the turn.

THE SURF TECHNIQUE, A NEW KIND OF LEG ACTION

The search for optimal gliding with flat skis has led the "all terrain, all snows" specialists and the virtuoso gliders of the race courses to a particular kind of leg action which I have baptised the "surf technique". This leg action has the unique characteristic of dissociating the lateral displacements of the knees from the pivoting movements of the feet. Its acquisition, even if just partial, can improve the finesse of your leg action considerably, not only for flat ski contact with the snow, but also for carving on the edges.

The surf technique, just as rotation, flexion-extension, vissage, avalement and the forward thrust of the feet, is not the invention of a technician !

Even a long time ago, virtuosos and other inspired skiers began to use the surf technique in certain specific situations without actually understanding what they were doing. There are even photographs that were taken of these skiers during the fraction of a second that they assumed a position very different from the other skiers and magazine editors and advertisers used these photographs, exploiting this new image. I can think in particular of a photograph of Stein ERIKSSEN clearly using the surf technique over 20 years ago.

My attention was drawn to the characteristic position of the surf technique very early, but I never fully recognized the implications of it until I had my first opportunity to see the latest of the ski virtuosos, the Swede Ingemar STENMARK. This slalom and giant slalom specialist doesn't use the surf technique exclusively, but in very quick turns on hard snow this technique has assured him a superiority over all of his competition for several years. This technique is also one of the potent weapons of the young star of the 1977 season, Perrine PELEN.

The surf technique is derived from the technique of avalement which was executed perfectly during the years 1968 and 1969 by Gustavo THOENI and Patrick RUSSEL. But the surf technique adds an extreme rapidity of movement and a possibility of riding a flat ski that has been heretofore unobtainable. Since 1973, specialists of

avalement and of gliding, such as Gustavo THOENI, tried to increase the tempo of their turns by using dynamic platform movements against the ground. Another Italian, Piero GROS, turned this into his specialty.

The young Swede Stenmark, howevever, began his technical progress beginning with the foundation which the classical avalement represented for him. His leg action in a very low position and his ability to glide, on flat skis as well as on his edges, struck me as early as 1974. Today his technique is even more varied and is less differentiated from the techniques of other racers. I recognized very early the connection between his leg action and the leg action of some of the powder snow virtuosos and ultimately of the mogul skiing specialists of the freestyle skiers.

I then analyzed this gesture at my leisure and attempted to explain it to and instill it in good skiers. I met with failures, semi-failures and then semi-successes. I believe that I have mastered this technique and its instruction sufficiently today to be able to attempt to pass it on to you in the following pages.

It was during discussions with students that we adopted the name "surf technique", as much for the similarity of some of the positions to positions of surfboard and skateboard riders as for a certain similarity in the sensations perceived during these types of activity.

Caution ! Do not consider the surf technique as an exclusive technique !

Certainly the surf technique can be adapted to skiing in deep snow, in bumps, on icy slopes and to wedels and long turns, but it should be only a supplementary element of your total technique. It is not a question of your depriving yourself of extension,

avalement, extension during turns, carved platforms, rebounds, etc...

In this circumstance, the surf technique will impoverish you instead of enrich you.

Discover the surf technique in difficult snow.

The surf technique is a leg action which involves essentially the feet and the knees. Therefore, it is a quiet leg action that is related to the action of your skis and to discover it you must sense what is happening under your skis. It is an exceptionally effective technique in difficult snow and this is why I insist that you make your first attempts at the surf technique in difficult, poorly packed or deep snows in which you have great difficulty making your skis pivot and sideslip.

If you are already accustomed to using this book, you will follow me easily. If you are reading me for the first time, you will accuse me of being obscure. I am sorry, but I am trying to explain as simply as possible to you a gesture that unquestionably is very complex. If you have a methodical, scientific mind, perhaps you will be helped by the more precise analyses which I have made at the end of the book (534,535). In any case, before tackling the surf technique, review the 'S' turn (pages 130 and 132) which constitutes a very good approach for learning the "surf".

Discover the "surf" leg placement by making a quick 'S' down the fall line.

First, assume a seated position with your feet very far forward and flexed strongly in the knees, moderately at the waist and slightly in the ankles. Use a narrow stance and spread your arms wide for better stability. You should have the impression that your feet are distinctly forward relative

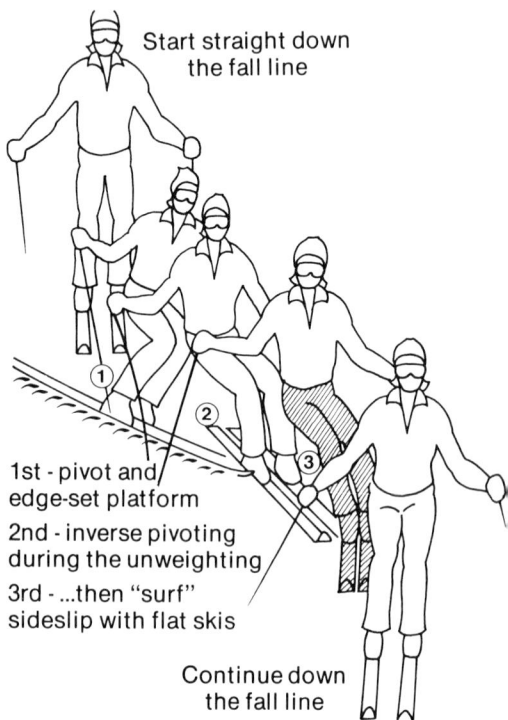

Start straight down the fall line

1st - pivot and edge-set platform
2nd - inverse pivoting during the unweighting
3rd - ...then "surf" sideslip with flat skis

Continue down the fall line

to your body. Weight your heels but without pressing against the backs of your boots. You should feel your ankles completely free and your feet relaxed and mobile.

On poorly packed snow, make 'S' turns with platforms down the fall line.

Drop straight down the fall line in the stance described above. After 10, 15 or 20

You will discover the surf technique through a search for greater effectiveness in difficult snow.

142

yards, pivot your legs and thrust your feet forward to leave the fall line and make an 'S' which then returns your skis to the fall line again. This turn should consist of an 'S' with a platform and unweighting. Slide straight down the slope for another 5 or 10 yards and make another 'S' in the opposite direction. Link these movements together. Of course, you should plant your ski pole at the instant that you make the platform between the turns as for all 'S' turns.

You will notice immediately that you can easily make this turn in snows that you wouldn't dare to approach with a wedeln or more classic turn.

I now ask you to make this 'S' turn more dynamically in order to feel the pressure and unweighting at the middle of the 'S' and especially to feel your skis sideslip laterally and perfectly flat on the snow as they dive back down the fall line. Emphasize your leg flexion to soften the re-weighting of your skis and thereby facilitate their sliding. Repeat this manuever 100 times.

If you execute this exercise properly, the track you leave in the snow should look like a square wedeln. The 'S' turns that seperate the straight runs down the fall line are a bit brutal, but they will lead you to discover the secret of the surf technique.

The secret of the surf technique is the special position of your knees during the second pivoting action of the 'S'. In the first pivoting, your knees and feet have pivoted together up the hill, but during the second pivoting only the feet pivot down the fall line, placing you in a position typical of the surf technique. It is this special position that allows you to regain your balance more easily with your skis flat on the snow following the 'S'.

Evolve your surf 'S' into a surf wedeln with a platform.

Now discover a genuine surf wedeln in difficult snows which hinder the pivoting and

lateral displacement of your skis.

1st step

Slide straight down the fall line and make an 'S' as described above. Slide another one or two yards down the fall line and make another 'S' in the opposite direction. Slide another one or two meters and repeat the 'S'... Now you should feel the position of your knees carried slightly to the outside of the turn at the end of each 'S'. It is this position which permits your skis to ride flat on the snow and to sideslip slightly after

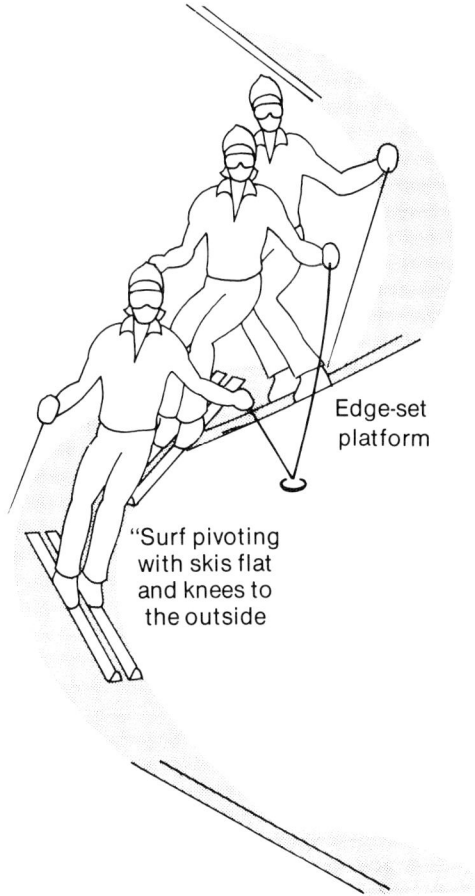

Edge-set
platform

"Surf pivoting
with skis flat
and knees to
the outside

The unique feature of the surf technique is the independent utilization of the pivoting of the feet and the lateral displacement of the knees.

each unweighting.

You should also feel your knees return to a normal position after each sideslipping until the beginning of the next 'S'.

2nd step

You will now make the same 'S' turns but as soon as your skis arrive at the fall line, accentuate their pivoting with your feet but keep your knees positioned as before. You leave the fall line with your skis flat and sideslipping and can then begin a new 'S' in the opposite direction with your knees.

Little by little, you will be able to diminish the dynamism of these 'S' turns by emphasizing less and less the platforms and the unweighting of the skis. You will then be able to evolve toward a surf wedeln without platforms.

What should this first surf wedeln with platforms feel like?

• Above all else a flat ski action with relaxed and mobile feet.
• Additionally, a desynchronization of the pivoting movements of the feet and the lateral displacements of the knees. At each turn you should feel: 1. a pivoting of your knees and feet up the hill and a slight platform; 2. your feet pivot down the fall line and your skis dive down the slope; 3. you absorb the landing while your feet continue to pivot; 4. both your feet and knees pivot uphill again as you set another platform, etc...

Discover a more flowing surf wedeln with flat skis in easy powder snow.

You have learned to surf wedel while searching for greater effectiveness in difficult snow. Now that you have "felt" the movements and mastered the characteristic leg action of the surf wedeln, you should try to adapt it to less demanding conditions while preserving the flat ski action: light powder snows or light layers of powder snow over a hard base down relatively flat or intermediate slopes. These snows offer a slight resistance to the pivoting of your skis which will allow you to better feel your muscular pivoting efforts. Proceed methodically in the following three steps.

First step: surf wedel by a simple pivoting of the feet.

Try to wedel with flat skis by making linked, very short turns in a rapid rhythm using a stance that is even narrower than you used for the preceeding 'S' turn and with your knees practically glued together and in the very low position as described earlier.

First, try to use your knees as little as possible. This will force you to use only your feet to achieve a pivoting of your skis. It's

GLIDING SURF WEDEL

1st step

Torso and thighs immobile

only the feet pivot under the knees

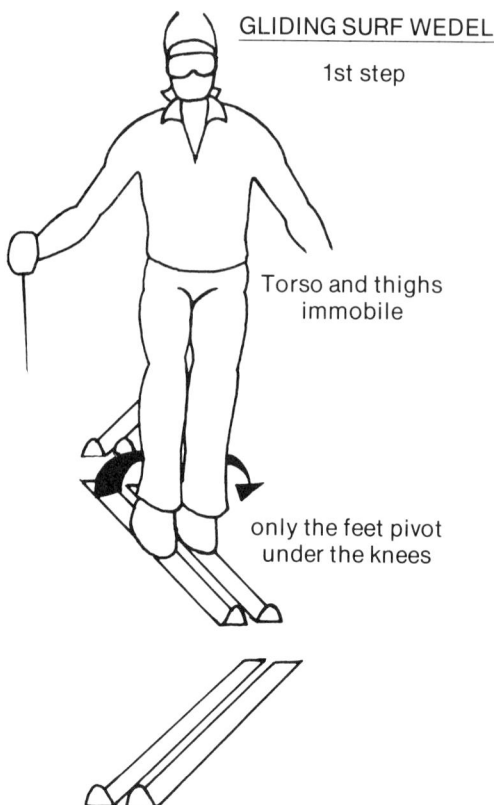

144

possible to practically avoid using your knees at all to make short "serpent" type turns while your body moves straight down the fall line. Your lower legs and feet do all of the work underneath your knees.

You can then try to accelerate the rhythm of these turns to make them as fast as you can. You can achieve an amazing tempo and, using a mogul for a jump, you can even make two or three of these quick pivoting turns in the air before landing, just as the freestyle skiers do as they jump from one bump to another.

This exercise is particularly useful for helping you to feel the movements in your joints which most skiers don't know how to use. Even at the top levels of international racing, some racers who are successful on hard snow are poor gliders because they aren't aware of the range of movement in their joints.

Second step: a round surf wedeln by a pivoting of the feet then a lateral displacement of the knees.

Having succeeded with the previous wedeln, you are now going to try to progressively pivot your skis more to make your turns rounder.

If you have genuinely felt the pivoting of your feet, this will be easy. Pivot your feet to the left and your skis will begin to turn to the left; then displace your knees laterally to the left. Next, pivot your feet to the right... then displace your knees laterally to the right. Your movements will likely be too quick for you to count: "1. the feet, 2. the knees". Nevertheless, you should be able to clearly feel the "feet first — then knees..." desynchronization.

While the surf wedeln with a platform is executed in a three step rhythm, this wedeln has a two-step rhythm.

Do you feel the difference between this surf wedeln and a wedeln with classic leg action ?

In the classic wedeln you globally pivot your lower limbs underneath your pelvis: you pivot your thighs, calves and feet simultaneously which causes the skis to pivot and bank onto edge. This movement is easier in a relatively upright position.

In the surf wedeln, made from a very low position, the pivoting of the feet under the knees is the dominant movement. The lateral displacement of the knees follows this pivoting of the feet and serves to keep the skis flat. In fact, the thighs no longer even pivot under the hips (534).

It's difficult for the skier to feel just what kind of a pivoting he is using during a wedeln. On the other hand, it's relatively easy for him to feel if the pivoting starts to bank the skis onto edge. Once again, I ask you to really try to feel what is happening between your skis and the snow.

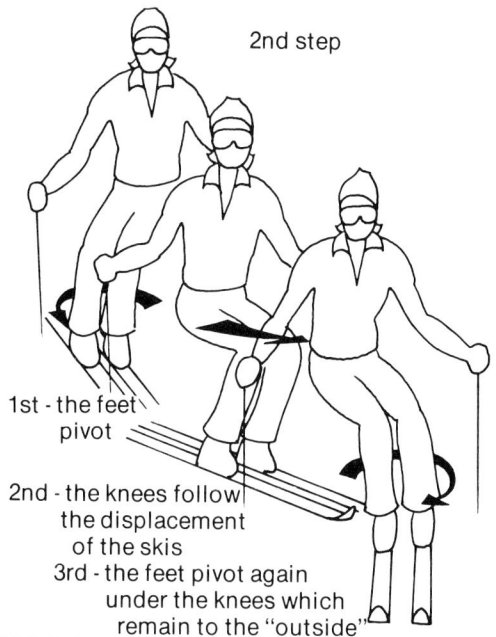

2nd step

1st - the feet pivot

2nd - the knees follow the displacement of the skis

3rd - the feet pivot again under the knees which remain to the "outside"

In the surf technique, the feet turn and slide the skis — the placement of the knees assures their remaining flat.

**Third step: surf wedeln at higher speeds
with a forward thrust of the feet.**

As soon as your speed increases, you will
feel a moment between your turns where
your balance is very delicate as your skis are
pivoted down the fall line and bump against
the unpacked snow. The resistance that must
be overcome at this moment tends to make
you stiffen your legs and feet.

If you have mastered the forward foot
thrust technique that I described at the
beginning of this chapter you should have
no problem in overcoming this situation. As
soon as you begin to pivot your feet, thrust
them forward by extending your calves under your knees. You will then be able to absorb the compression totally relaxed and
then return your feet to a normal position.

From the side, the surfing skier gives the
appearance of shifting from a position with
his ankles directly underneath him to a
position with his ankles stretched out in
front in each turn. When the braking of the
snow increases, the lower legs actually
"whip" forward under the knees and when
the snow causes an unweighting, the forward
thrust of the feet coincides with the platform.

Note: When your speed increases you rein-
stitute the forward thrust of the feet that you
used in the 'S' turns to introduce yourself to
your first surf turns (page 142). But the forward foot thrust that you use here isn't accompanied by a banking of the skis onto
edge and can be made without the use of a
platform.

*During these surf wedels, you should feel the
lateral movement of your knees and a sliding
straight down the fall line.*

As you master this flat ski wedeln you will
accept the speed and discover the importance of the lateral displacement of your knees.
It is this lateral displacement of your knees,
in fact, that permits you to place your skis
alongside your body and thereby balance
the centrifugal force generated by the turn. I
will speak of this "placement of the skis to
the outside" later when describing the

initiation of long surf turns.

*Make hundreds of these wedeln turns in
good snow.*

Start by making wedeln surf turns in a low
position with your upper body relaxed and
your arms spread wide and without using a
pole plant. The pole plant, in fact, has a tendency to put too much rhythm into this
wedeln and introduce unnecessary platforms. Don't add a pole plant until you have
completely mastered the leg action and
reduced all movements of the upper body to
a minimum. Your pole plants will then serve
only to improve your balance. Have you
noticed, for example, that the slalom
specialists who are good gliders are planting
their poles less and less in the sections of
courses that are flowing and can be skied
with flat skis?

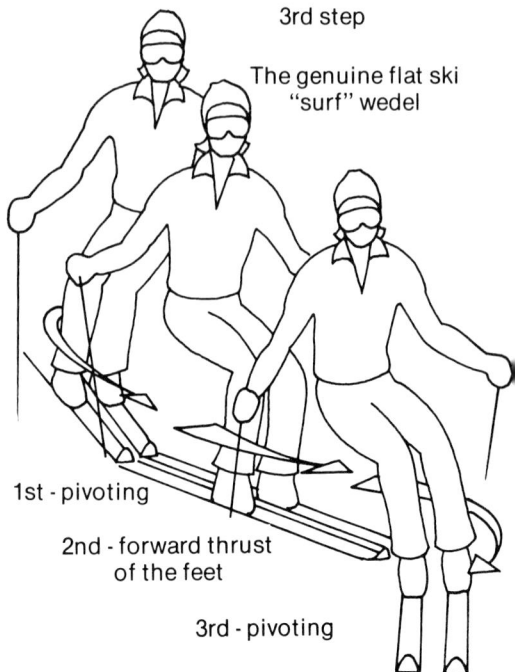

3rd step

The genuine flat ski
"surf" wedel

1st - pivoting

2nd - forward thrust
of the feet

3rd - pivoting

Make beautiful, gliding turns with the surf technique

Having mastered the surf wedeln, both with and without platforms, you will undoubtedly derive new pleasure in skiing difficult snows which paralyze many good skiers. You can profit in particular from the semi-packed areas outside of the bumps on the edges of runs to smoothly make a few surf wedels before joining the traffic again.

You will also find pleasure in using these flat ski wedels to change the rhythm of your skiing. For example between long turns when you encounter a bumpy, poorly packed section or between two turns of an elongated wedeln or even between two successive moguls to better position yourself for the terrain that follows.

You can also discover other very interesting movements with the surf technique: wedeln down mogully terrain or in very deep snow or even carved platforms spaced between flat ski turns.

Surf wedeln in the troughs

The surf wedeln is so well adapted to flowing through the ruts of an extremely bumpy slope that one can consider it to be another way of learning the technique. I have seen very good skiers discover the surf wedeln in this kind of terrain when I told them no more than to ski "in a low position with your feet very far in front of your body and try to make a very round wedeln in the troughs with flat skis". The shortcoming of this approach as a teaching method is that the skier sometimes doesn't succeed in transferring the technique to other terrain and snow situations.

Flexion-avalement
and flat ski surf pivoting
in the bumps

What, in particular, should you try to do down the troughs ?

1. Add a vertical movement to very large surf pivots. Sliding straight down the fall line between two moguls you can thrust your skis into a turn and arrive on a flat which will compress you onto your skis. You should feel your knees climb together in front of you and to the side to absorb this compression until they follow your feet down the hill into the next turn. At the instant that the upward movement of your knees is at a maximum and your feet begin to pivot, you are in the characteristic surf position. As your knees climb upward, you plant your pole and twist your upper body down the slope in anticipation. The climbing of your knees and pole plant allow you to ski from one turn to the next while absorbing the compression mentioned above and the flat ski sideslipping doesn't hinder your surf technique. This surf wedeln in the troughs is distinguished from the wedeln with forward foot thrust described on page 134 by the constant holding of the skis flat on the snow. This results from a different knee position and allows for better sliding and the possibility of making even rounder turns, but the wedeln with forward foot thrust remains a good means of preparing for the surf wedeln.

2. Control your speed exclusively by rounding out your turns. Never scrape away at the sides of the bumps with your edges during the turn. If you must, you can let your skis sideslip a little bit in the flats between turns as you absorb the compression which we just mentioned. This slight sideslip with flat skis should not disturb your surf behavior. This surf wedeln down the troughs is differentiated from the wedeln with forward foot thrust described on page 134 primarily by a striving to keep the skis flat on the snow. It is the result of a different positioning of the knees, better gliding and the possibility of making your turns rounder, but the wedeln with forward thrust of

the feet is a good preparation for the surf wedeln.

Surf to turn smoothly over moguls covered with fresh snow.

It is easy to make normal length or even longer than normal length turns down a field of moguls that is covered with a layer of fresh snow and which slows the forward sliding of the skis. On the other hand, a problem arises as soon as the snow no longer slows you sufficiently and you are obliged to check your speed by sideslipping in your turns. Sideslipping becomes difficult in such snow conditions, therefore I advise you to turn on the tops of the bumps, letting your skis climb as far as possible in front of you and then sideslip in a "surf" position down the back side of the mogul. Here again, the outside positioning of your knees allows you to place your skis flat and minimize the resistance to pivoting and sideslipping. This is impossible using any other technique.

Moguls and Fresh Snow

With skis flat, the snow is pushed out to the side

By trying to wedel through the troughs with flat skis, you can discover the surf wedeln and improve your gliding ability.

This surf sideslipping with the feet forward and the knees to the outside can be cultivated during long traverses through the repetition of surf garlands; a short, slightly pivoted sideslipping.

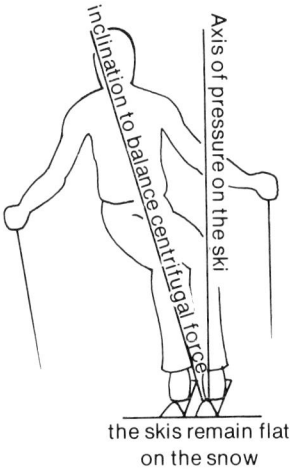

Axis of pressure on the ski

inclination to balance centrifugal force

the skis remain flat on the snow

Make an elongated hodroplaning surf wedeln.

I have spoken a great deal of balance while hydroplaning and prolonging the vertical movements to permit a flowing wedeln and finally long gliding turns (page 114). I have emphasized that the difficulty inherent in this wedeln and these kinds of turns is in overcoming the resistance of the snow when displacing the skis laterally. This difficulty arises from the fact that because of your speed you must incline your body to the inside of the turn to balance the centrifugal force and this inclination places your skis on edge when you really need to keep them flat on the snow. You can throw your hip to the outside of the turn to flatten your skis or you can use the surf technique.

Try a hydroplaning wedeln by using a slight platform that is prolonged through the turn to give you just enough unweighting to simultaneously pivot your skis and position your knees to the outside of the turn. Then absorb the compression on your skis and make another prolonged platform, unweight and pivot your skis and position your knees to the outside of the turn... I'm sure that many of my readers, who are avid deep powder specialists, will discover while reading these lines that they have already surfed...

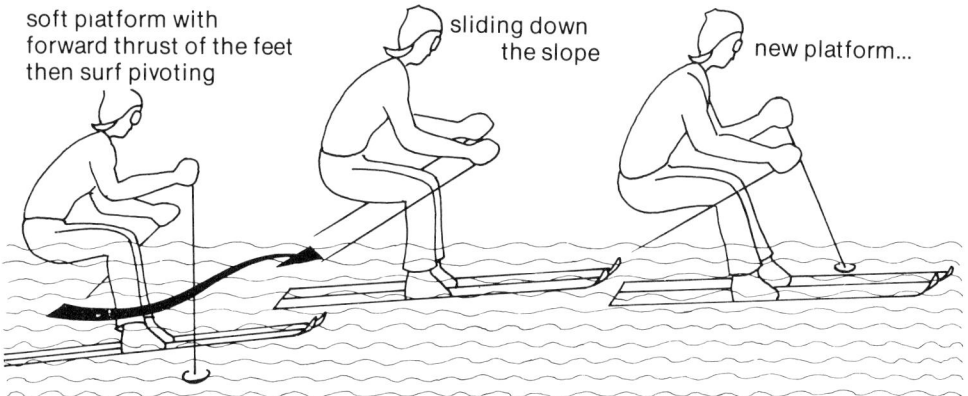

soft platform with forward thrust of the feet then surf pivoting

sliding down the slope

new platform...

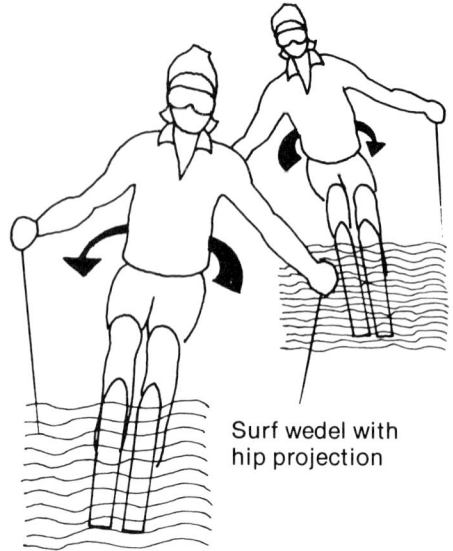

Surf wedel with
hip projection

The porpoise wedeln down steep slopes in bottomless snow

Have you ever seen those amazing Japanese and American ski films where they show skiers dancing an astounding ballet in snow so deep that they sink in to their ears ? Since these skiers are filmed with backlighting we can only distinguish their silhouettes in the cloud of powder snow that surrounds them. What is so fascinating about these films is the overlapped rising and sinking movements of the skis and the alternating pivoting of the skis from side to side and the stretching and folding of the body. Perhaps the most striking feature is the upward and forward thrust of the feet and skis and then the release when the skis dive turning down the slope again. The similarity between this kind of skiing and a porpoise jumping and twisting out of the water comes to mind...

You will rarely find these bottomless snows in France but it can happen, particularly if you leave the packed trails where you can find snow over four feet deep in

Surf wedeln in deep snow can be linked to hip projection

The combination of these two movements can help the skier accustomed to skiing deep powder with hip projection to discover the surf technique. Of course it's necessary to make a slight platform and then simultaneously thrust both the hip and knees to the outside of the turn from this platform. The hip projection can then be gradually reduced.

As could be foreseen, the surf technique is particularly well suited to hydroplaning.

The skis are thrust up and forward...
..then "surf" pivoted into the turn

snow packed
by the skis

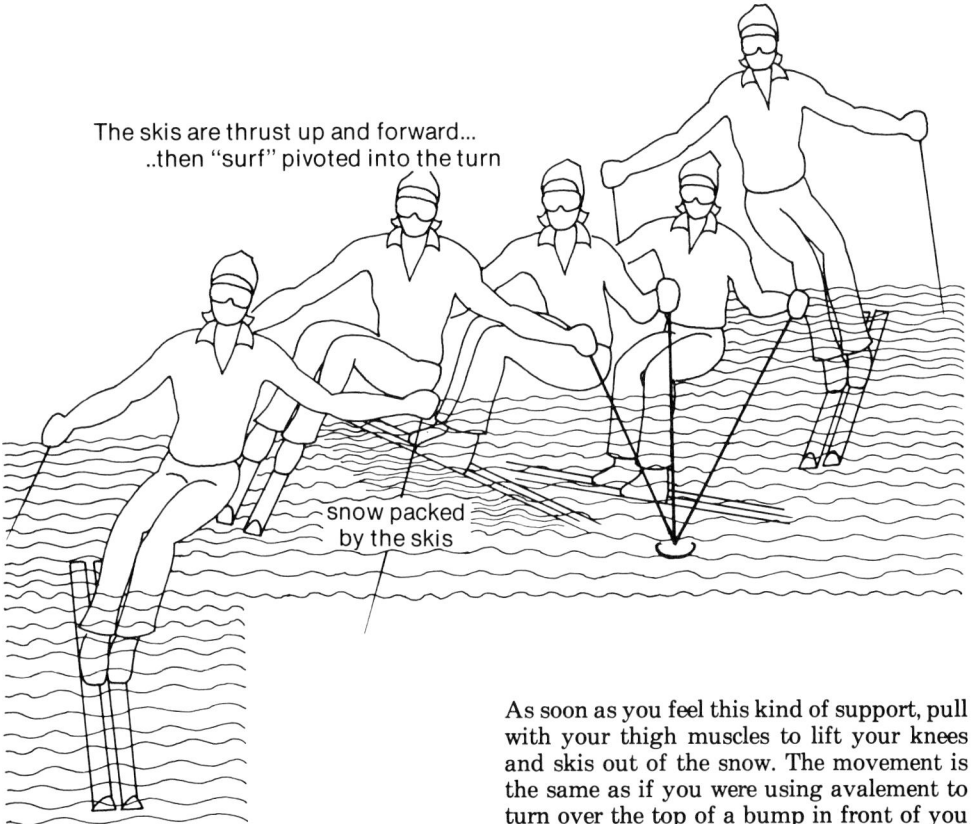

which you will not be able to find a support from the firmer base underneath. If the slope is too steep, you won't even be able to hydroplane. It is in just such a condition that you must use a surf technique which uses a lot of avalement.

The principle is simple.

From a traverse, begin a smooth flexion while exerting a downward thrust on the tails of your skis. Your tails will sink in and your ski tips will pack snow in front of them.

As soon as you feel this kind of support, pull with your thigh muscles to lift your knees and skis out of the snow. The movement is the same as if you were using avalement to turn over the top of a bump in front of you that is as high as the surface of the snow (page 88). Your skis will pivot by themselves down the fall line although, of course, you use a surf pivoting so that the skis can still move laterally and flat into the turn if they have not been lifted entirely out of the snow. As your skis pivot toward the fall line, you stand up relaxed and pivot them on through the turn. You then flex smoothly and thrust on the tails of your skis to finish the turn. As the snow packs in front of you again, use avalement to begin another turn...

Of course you use your ski pole for support, although in very deep snow it hardly ever gives you very solid support, and twist your upper body down the slope in anticipation.

The porpoise is the perfect association of avalement, the forward thrust of the feet and the surf technique; but you have to be in good physical condition to execute it properly.

You will be more successful with the porpoise wedeln if you have already been able to link a pivoting of the skis, a flexion-extension of the body and a lateral thrust of the skis in a surf position in moguls.

By the same token, it is indispensable that you have already mastered active avalement (pages 88 and 164) with a dynamic action of the stomach muscles.

Start long surf turns with flat skis

If you are not an accomplished wedeler but more of an "all snow, all terrain" skier, you can still succeed in using a surf initiation in long turns before knowing how to surf wedel.

Nevertheless, it's still necessary that you first understand the surf initiation by making an 'S' starting from a straight run down the fall line (page 130). This exercise will help you to feel the key to this turn initiation, the surf position with feet pivoted toward the fall line and the knees to the outside of the turn, a low, almost seated position with the upper body relaxed and the arms spread wide for balance.

You will have to overcome two problems: how to initiate the turn and find the surf position just described and how to control the turn using this position.

How to initiate a long surf turn

You can choose from among several solutions:

• An 'S' similar to that already described but more extended and started from a traverse. The double pivoting of your skis is prolonged and the platform from the flexion-extension more pronounced because of your higher speed.

• A forward thrust of the feet (page 139) which produces an unweighting of the skis followed by a landing with tail pressure and pivoting. In this case, the pivoting is produced by the feet and the flexion at the landing is made without pivoting the thighs into the turn (that is without displacing the knees to the inside). This again will result in the surf position and this particular approach is well adapted to difficult, poorly packed and heavy, deep snows.

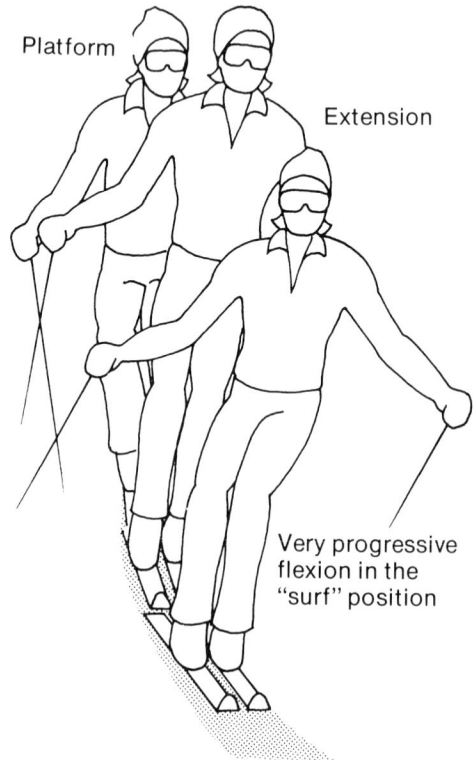

Platform

Extension

Very progressive flexion in the "surf" position

• The two movements above can be linked. The skier makes a forward thrust of the feet during the platform obtained in the 'S'. In this case there often is a simultaneous outward projection of the hips and the knees.

• A turn can be started simply by a flexion and forward thrust of the feet and pivoting of the feet — but without pivoting the knees — in certain situations: packed powder snows or light, deep powder; straight turns and turns made over large moguls.

Knees in =
greater edge-set angle

Knees outside =
flat skis

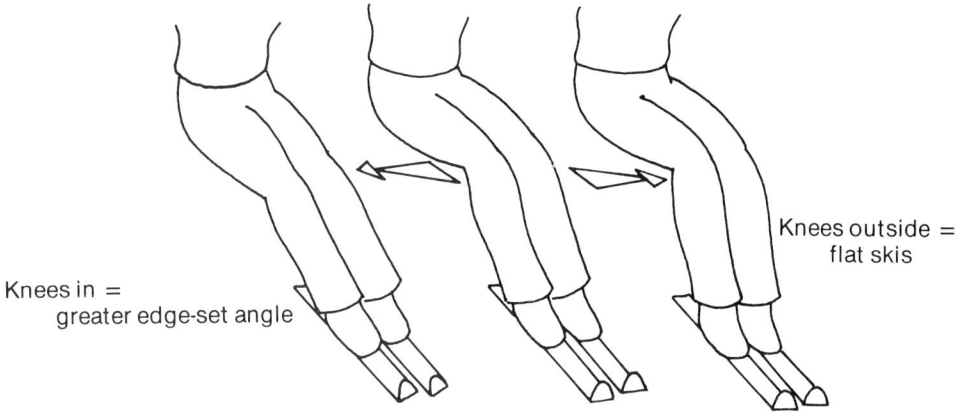

How do you control long surf turns?

By piloting your skis while precisely adjusting your surf position.
• Adjust the pivoting of your skis with your feet.
• Adjust the angle of the skis on the snow by adjusting the position of the knees laterally. This is similar to the adjustments of angulation for balance.

A perfect knee position is unobtainable. The position of the knees must, in fact, compensate for the inclination of the body toward the inside of the turn; an inclination that is a function of speed and the radius of the turn. The knee position must also be adjusted to account for undulations in the terrain in order to keep the skis flat. Ultimately, it shouldn't vary as you flex to absorb the compression at the beginning of a turn or as you cross a change in terrain.

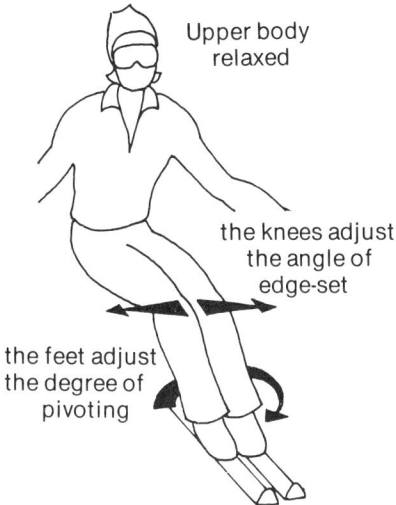

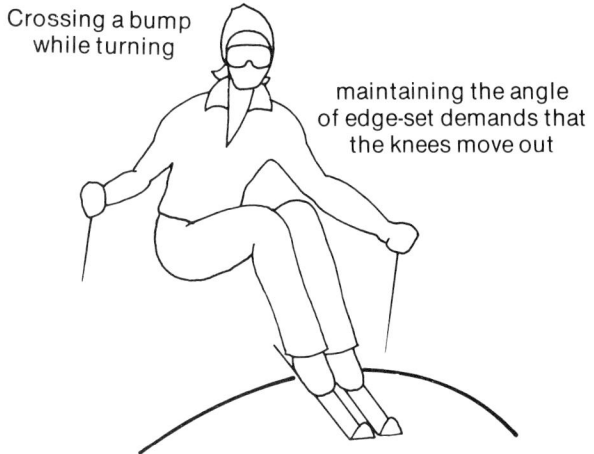

Upper body relaxed

the knees adjust the angle of edge-set

the feet adjust the degree of pivoting

Crossing a bump while turning

maintaining the angle of edge-set demands that the knees move out

The control of surf turns demands a greater sensitivity to the lateral position of your knees.

153

Use the surf technique to improve your carving effectiveness

Discover the relationship between "flat skis" and "carving with tail-pressure" in the surf technique

Start straight down an intermediate or even flat slope and make long turns (of 15, 20 or even 30 yard radius) in a low surf position. Start your turns by spreading one ski. Each time you spread a ski you will find yourself weighting it with your knee positioned similar to the surf position. You should feel how this flat ski slides and how both skis slide flat once you have brought them together.

After having started the turn with flat skis and in a semi-wide stance, press the knee of your outside leg in and push your outside foot forward to apply tail-pressure. You will note that the outside ski, by banking only a few degrees onto edge, begins to carve the turn while sliding distinctly better. You will feel a genuine acceleration. Continue.

You will gradually feel that you have developed a new weapon to slide better through long turns. You are, in fact, not making a new movement but discovering a fine tuning of the angle of edge-set and tail-pressure which permits you to fully exploit the attributes designed into modern quality skis. The tails of modern skis are designed to produce an astounding directional and carving effect.

At the international level, this gesture often coincides at the beginning of the turn with a forward thrust of the feet and lateral projection. It has become one of the most ef-

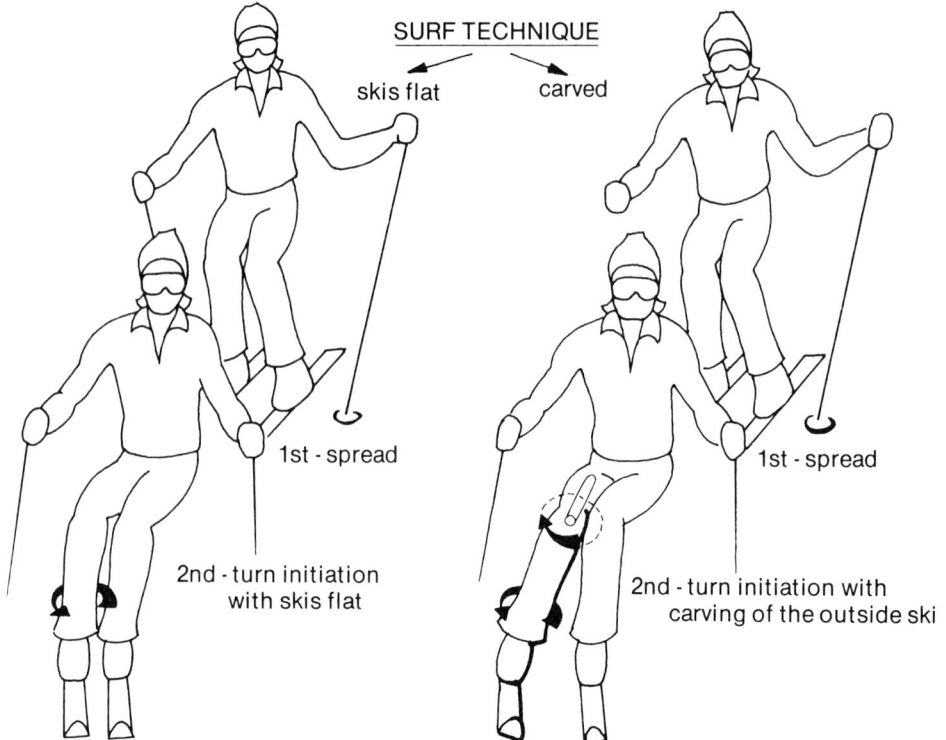

SURF TECHNIQUE

skis flat   carved

1st - spread

2nd - turn initiation
with skis flat

1st - spread

2nd - turn initiation with
carving of the outside ski

fective weapons of giant slalom specialists in easy gates on flat slopes and is used with great success by Ingemar STENMARK and the skiers of the "new Swiss school" and its leader Heini HEMMI.

In a wide stance, discover the instantaneous carved edge-set on one ski through the surf technique.

Undoubtedly you have already learned how to carve edge-sets which permit you to rebound on even the hardest snows (page 135). But these rebounds require large vertical movements and, therefore, a relatively long period of time. The time required for the downward acceleration of the body mass to produce the compression and then the rebound prevents the rapid linking of these movements.

You can make quicker rebounds by using the surf technique. Slide straight down an intermediate slope with very hard snow in a low surf position but in a wide stance. You are going to try to make a quick platform on only your outside ski.

With a very quick movement of your outside leg simultaneously:
• Move your outside foot forward and pivot it to place the ski in a narrow stem,
• and make the ski tip onto edge by pressing your knee inward.

In a very low and flexed position, a pivoting of the femur pushes the foot laterally and places the ski on edge.

Because of your forward speed, you will be instantaneously compressed onto the tail of your outside ski which then makes an extremely brief carved edge-set and begins into a slight turn.

After several yards, you can make a carved edge-set with your other ski and then link these movements together to make a new kind of elongated wedeln down the fall line.

This platform is instantaneous, very brief and very precise. On the other hand, it doesn't permit a large, prolonged movement.

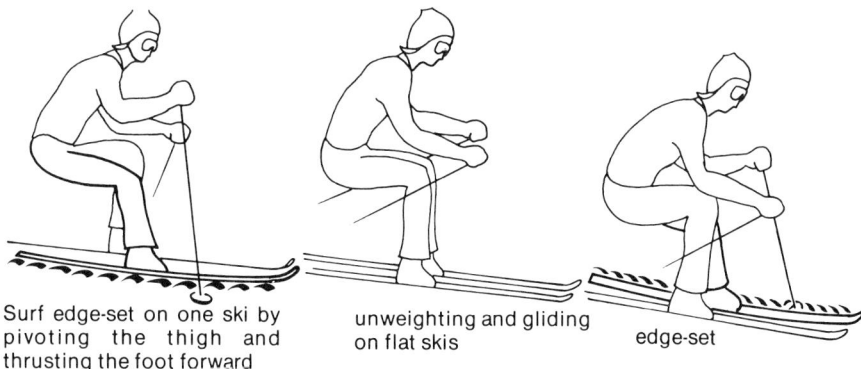

Surf edge-set on one ski by pivoting the thigh and thrusting the foot forward

unweighting and gliding on flat skis

edge-set

The surf position and surf platforms permit faster and more precise carving than any other technique.

Carved platforms
with tail-pressure
and rebound from
one ski to the other

Carve wedeln at an ultra-fast tempo with the surf technique

Having mastered the quick, carved edge-set in a wide or semi-wide stance on one ski as I have just described, it should be easy for you to now link edge-sets of the right foot with the left foot, with the right foot... Since these platforms are practically instantaneous, they can be linked at a tempo that can not be attained in any other way.

The mass of your body moves in an almost straight line down the slope and you ricochet from carved thrust to carved thrust moving only your feet and lower legs.

You can also "surf" carve wedel with both skis and with your feet together. This is the same movement as described before except that the legs are held together and the feet move in unison. This movement perhaps isn't as fast, due to the greater inertia, but it sometimes permits better sliding. It is more of a slalom racing technique whereas the movement described above is more for freestyle skiers.

You will recall that I have already pointed out the use of flat ski surf wedeln at an extremely rapid tempo by freestylers.

Combine carved and flat ski sliding with the surf technique

For ski competition, this is the ultimate outcome of the surf technique, particularly for skiing easy slalom and giant slalom gates.

In some situations, the ideal is to make a sharp, carved platform of minimum duration and then be able to follow this with a feet relaxed, skis perfectly flat sliding. This is the secret to the superiority of some slalom skiers who ski through very tight gates in a low position.

When discussing the forward thrust of the feet, I insisted on the extension and flexion action of the modern giant slalom skier. Here I insist on the "surf" technique in a low position. These are the two extremes of the technique of the best slalom specialists today.

II EFFECTIVENESS OFF THE TRAIL AND IN COMPETITION

GET A TASTE OF EXTREME SKIING

If you are a mountain climber and already a good skier...
If you like to meet challenges...
If you are obsessed with efficiency...
Then as soon as possible confront snow conditions and terrain which are at the limit of your capabilities. But to do this, you must forge some specific technical weapons.

What do I mean by extreme skiing?

The "skiing of the impossible" as brought to the attention of the public with great fanfare by the media and the large equipment manufacturers? Certainly not. This kind of a challenge on the highest and most terrifyingly difficult terrain has pushed back the limits of human possibilities but this kind of activity is strictly for a few of the most exceptionally gifted skiers who are also exceptionally competent mountain climbers.

Do I mean skiing off the marked runs? Yes, in certain cases but not in others. A beautiful deep powder or slightly surface softened corn snow that permits each skier to leave tracks outside the marked runs consists more of beautiful skiing than extreme skiing.

For us, we will define extreme skiing as being skiing on terrain and in snow conditions that are at the extreme limits of our individual capabilities. In competitive skiing, man confronts the stopwatch. In extreme skiing, he confronts the entire scale of objective problems posed by nature.

This kind of skiing is beyond the "learning" skier, that is to say the skier who is still searching for his skiing balance. For him it would even be harmful. But the intermediate skier can — and frequently does

— make it an objective. Again and again I listen to the new Grenoble citizen who has just taken up skiing and dreams of what is for him the ultimate skiing achievement: skiing the "tunnel" run of upper Alpe d'Huez or the famous "couloirs of Saulire" in Courcheval or even the couloir of the Grand Diable in Les Deux Alpes.

The opportunities for extreme skiing frequently confront you. If you are naturally athletic, you have occasionally been tempted to make an excursion down that horribly steep slope which drops straight down under the cable car, or which hangs over the "L" in Val d'Isere. Or simply to go and "prod the monstor" ten yards outside the marked run on a day when the very idea would seem crazy to the "prudent" skiers sideslipping over the packed snow. Don't resist the temptation. Leave the run and fight against all the difficulties. After a few unsuccessful attempts you will have a breakthrough, and experience a new source of joy.

In the preceeding chapters, I have already given you weapons proven effective for surviving every kind of terrain. First of all, I will help you to sharpen these weapons and then suggest movements which are situated at the extreme limits of human possibilities... at least for now.

Your number 1 weapon: the check wedeln on very steep slopes.

The virtuosos of extreme skiing can ski slopes as steep as 55°, that is to say all slopes and chutes in the Alps capable of holding snow. With the appropriate technique, even an intermediate skier can succeed in wedeling on slopes of 35° to 40° which is the steepest that can be found within the boundaries of the ski resorts.

I have already described (page 83) how intermediate skiers can adapt a standard wedeln with platforms to steep slopes to improve their security. I suggested to them, in fact, a check wedeln which I will now describe in greater detail.

Down very steep slopes and icy chutes: 1st objective — slow down; 2nd objective — make the edges bite.

At the extreme limit, a check wedeln becomes a series of lateral sideslips seperated by platforms which stop the sideslipping and permit a pivoting rebound to start a sideslip in the opposite direction.

1. How do you slow down?

By sideslipping with your skis placed precisely across the fall line in a very wide

158

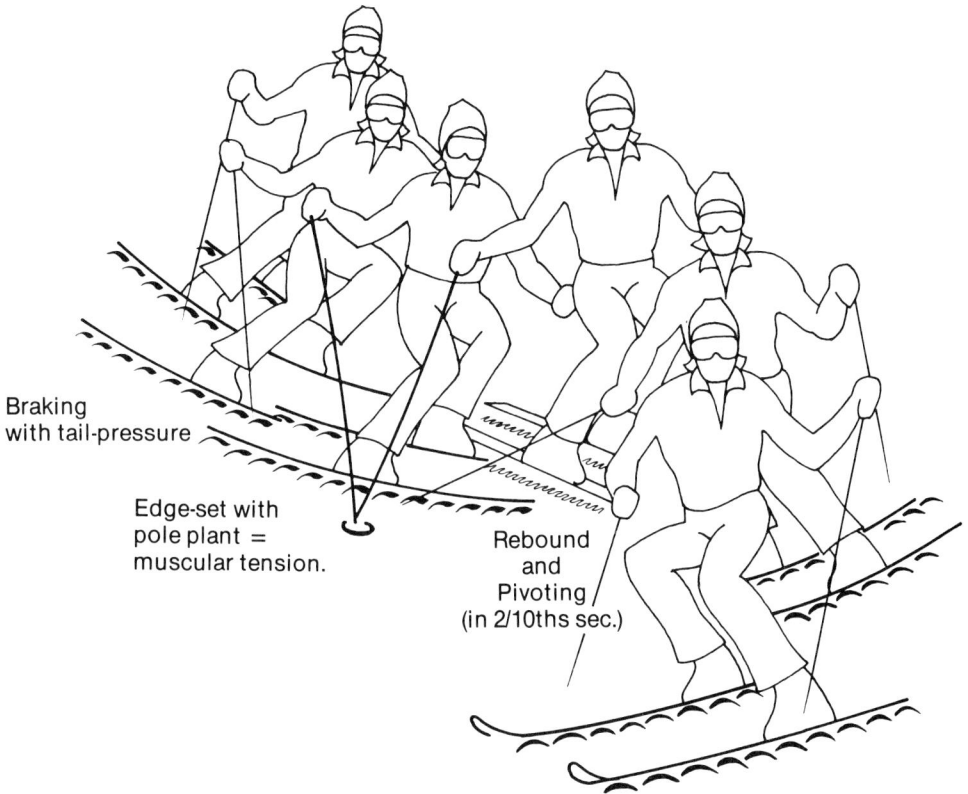

Braking
with tail-pressure

Edge-set with
pole plant =
muscular tension.

Rebound
and
Pivoting
(in 2/10ths sec.)

stance and with your legs flexed and with pronounced knee and hip angulation and your upper body twisted to face down the fall line. It is essential that your weight be placed on the heel of your downhill foot so that the ski sideslips in a balanced manner and doesn't tend to pivot (157-182).

Begin by assuming this stance in a standing position and then start a lateral sideslip and begin to wedel.

2. How to make the edges bite ?

If you are in the position described above, you can stop your sideslip by simply flexing deeper and pressing your outside knee in. The compression that helps the edge of the ski to bite into the hard surface of the snow should come more from your stopping the sideslip than by a vertical movement of the

legs. The briefer this check, the more the edges will bite into the snow. This is why an excessively deep flexion isn't recommended.

Planting your downhill pole is obligatory at the instant that the edges bite. This permits you to stabilize the upper body and absorb the downward momentum of your body mass.

Some good advice: To prepare yourself for the check wedeln, first of all practice on very steep slopes and on very hard snow. Start with a proper stance and make precise, lateral sideslips seperated by very sharp edge-sets with a pole plant to check your sideslips. This will enable you to succeed in making pivoting rebounds with greater ease.

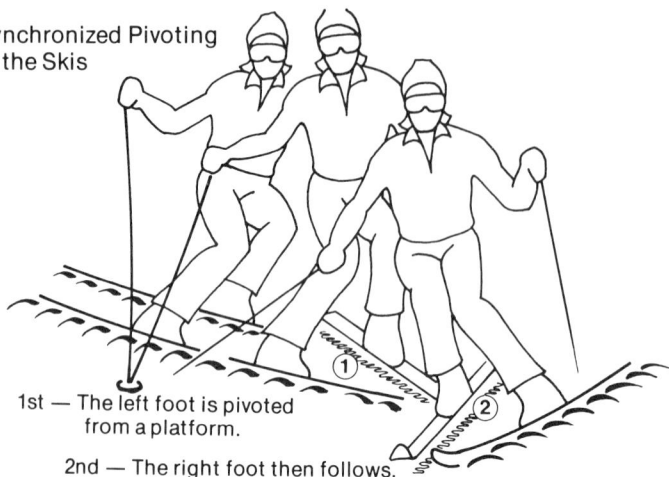

Desynchronized Pivoting of the Skis

1st — The left foot is pivoted from a platform.

2nd — The right foot then follows.

3rd objective: pivot your skis very quickly.

Specialists of the check wedeln develop a pivoting of their skis that is at maximum speed at the beginning of the turn and then progressively slows to zero at the instant of the platform. They also have reduced their vertical movement — extension then flexion — to a minimum. These two elements together contribute to facilitate the biting of the skis during the following edge-set.

On the contrary, many skiers who extend excessively at the beginning of the turn have a pivoting action that starts too slow and then accelerates toward the end of the turn. They then have a great deal of difficulty in making their skis hold.

How can you make your skis pivot rapidly ?

By sideslipping in a proper position and knowing how to make your edges bite precisely, you should automatically discover the wind-up movement that is the key to the check wedeln. This "wind-up" is the compression that you must resist with your entire body and with your torso twisted to face down the fall line. The "recoil" is the rebound of your skis which leave the snow and move up the hill and also their pivoting down the fall line as they are unweighted.

Caution ! The pivoting "recoil" occurs withing 2/10ths of a second after the plat-

form is set. Your skis must be pivoted in the air, otherwise you must extend your legs to pivot your skis with leg thrust and steering and *"projection circulaire"*. It's this delayed and slow pivoting of the body followed by the skis that obliges many skiers to accelerate the pivoting of their skis at the end of the turn.

Immediately following your edge-set platform, you should feel your skis begin to pivot rapidly under your body as if they were propelled by an unwinding spring. Ski hundreds and thousands of these wedels bringing your skis across the fall line each time to refine the rhythm of the rebound. This manuever is simultaneously one of the fundamental elements of the technique of extreme skiing and of slalom racing.

The desynchronized pivoting of the skis.

If you ski in a wide stance as I have asked you to do, you should have felt that your uphill ski starts to pivot before your downhill ski following your edge-set. This is very beneficial because it allows you to start your skis pivoting even quicker. If you have not felt this desynchronization, I can assure you that your stance is not wide enough. It is also possible that, among other problems, the inward push of your knee at the instant of the platform is not pronounced enough.

160

PRACTICING AVALEMENT IN RUTTED SLALOMS

It is by training in rutted slalom courses on the glaciers that Grenoble University Club racers, following the example of their colleague **Patrick RUSSEL**, have become specialists in avalement.
Avalement is executed with the weight distributed evenly over both skis when the snow is soft and would risk giving away under the pressure of one ski as demonstrated perfectly in the photomontage above by **Patrice CIPRELLI**, second ranked giant slalom racer in France according to the 1977 world classification.
The skier must use avalement with projection from one ski to the other at the instant that he is catapulted from one rut to the next in order to absorb the bump between the ruts as demonstrated excellently in the photomontage below of **Yves HOTTEGINDRE**, French University Champion.

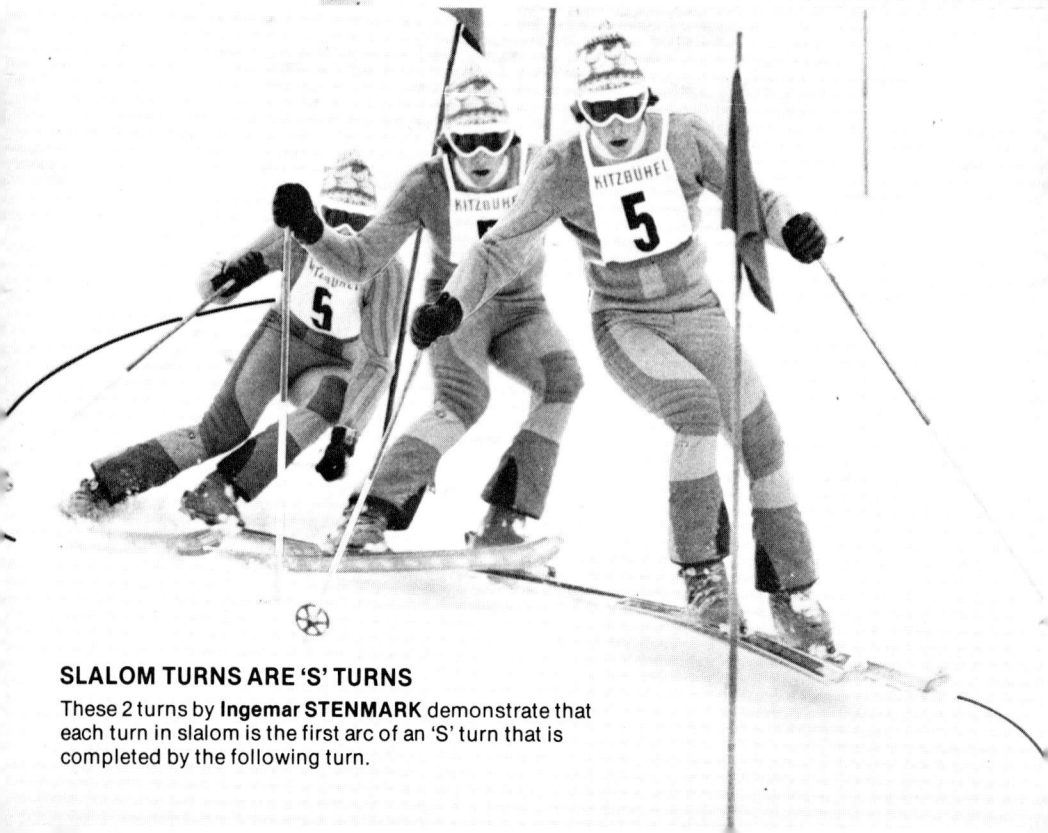

SLALOM TURNS ARE 'S' TURNS

These 2 turns by **Ingemar STENMARK** demonstrate that
each turn in slalom is the first arc of an 'S' turn that is
completed by the following turn.

PRACTICE THE 'S' TURN WITH A FORWARD THRUST OF THE FEET.

Bernard REPELLIN, regional ski coach from Grenoble, executes a typical 'S' turn exercise in the photo-sequence above. One can see that he literally climbs up the slope as he sets a platform and thrusts his feet forward. Once released, his skis pivot into the turn by themselves. The two linked arcs constitute an 'S' turn.

THE SURF STANCE — THE SURF EDGE-SET

A well flexed position allows for the independent mobility of the feet under the knees and the thighs under the pelvis which characterizes the technique of **Ingemar STENMARK**, the premier slalom racer and principle technical innovator of the past 7 years.

I have called this leg action the "surf technique" because of its characteristic use in deep snow where it allows the skier to keep his skis flat by rolling his knees to the outside of the turn. It also permits an exceptional rapidity in pressing on the edge of the outside ski with the "feet thrust forward" in relation to the mass of the body. The Scandinavian's technique is already becoming universal among the international slalom specialists. Note the striking similarity of the movements of one of his more dangerous rivals, the American **Phil MAHRE**.

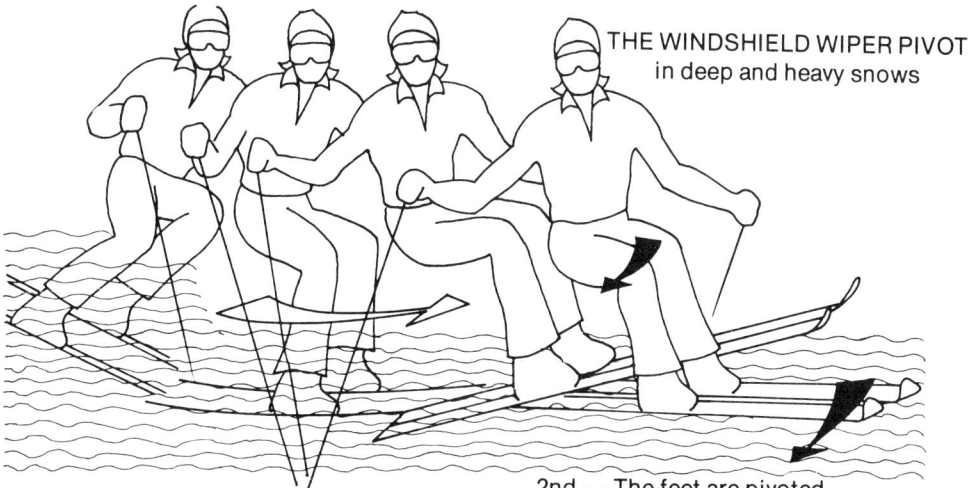

THE WINDSHIELD WIPER PIVOT
in deep and heavy snows

1st — A platform with a forward thrust
of the feet.
The tips rise.

2nd — The feet are pivoted
and the knees are banked
down the fall-line
around the tails of the skis.

How can you control the pivoting of the skis which follows ?

Your pivoting rebound should bring your skis into the fall line or even slightly beyond the fall line. Your skis will then continue to pivot in a braking sideslip by themselves. By assuming the proper stance as described above, it is relatively easy for you to control this braking sideslip and pivoting either to continue your sideslip — with your skis across the fall line — or to facilitate the next edge-set and rebound.

In difficult snow conditions, use a check wedeln with forward thrust of the feet and a "windshield wiper" pivoting.

How do you wedel on a very steep slope covered with unstable or even avalanche prone snow ?

By adapting your check wedeln to the conditions. The first problem regards your platform. If you thrust vertically on your skis as you do on hard snow, they will sink in and there will be no recoil. The solution is to make a vertical thrust that is not so sharp and combine it with a forward thrust of the feet. You will notice that your skis make a little bit of a platform during this thrust

from which they can then begin to pivot. This forward thrust of the feet resembles the forward thrust we described on page 130 for the 'S' counter-turn but here there is little or no counter-turn. The forward thrust of the feet is also similar to that used in the porpoise wedeln (page 151) but is slower and the legs are pushed further forward. It produces a genuine backward leaning of the body.

The pivoting of your skis that occurs after the forward thrust of the feet is essentially the same as the pivoting produced after the 'S' counter-turn. It, likewise, is an automatic response but is more deliberate, as if in slow motion, and by itself will not give a sufficient pivoting of the skis.

You are about to discover what Sylvain SAUDAN, the great skier of the "impossible" has called the *"windshield wiper"* *movement of the skis.* But be careful. Even though this movement consists exclusively of a leg action, it is impossible if you have not planted your ski pole during the platform and if you don't maintain pressure on your pole throughout the pivoting of the skis.

How is the windshield wiper pivoting made ?

It is at the end of a forward thrust of your

161

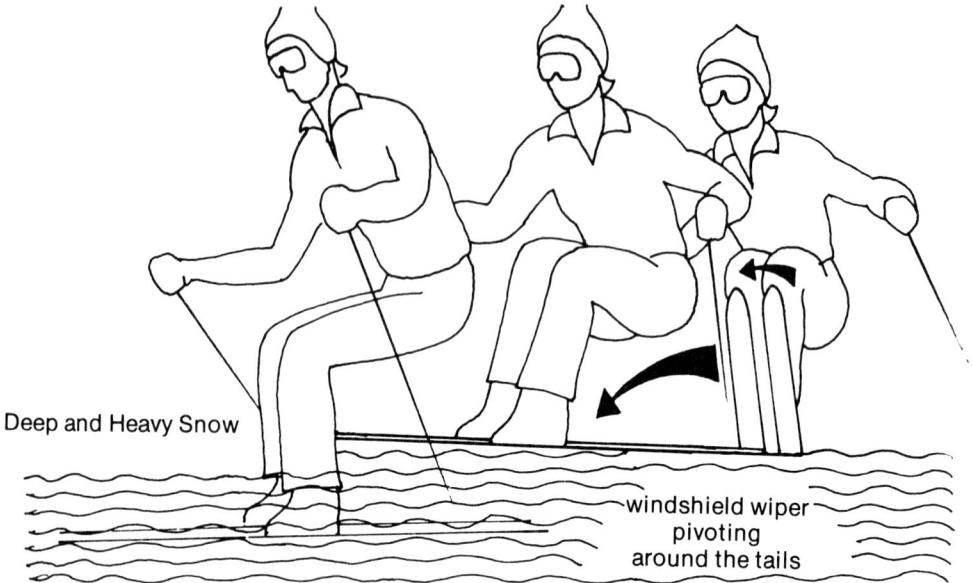

Deep and Heavy Snow

windshield wiper
pivoting
around the tails

feet when only the tails of your skis are pressing against the snow that you use the "windshield wiper". Use the support that the tails of your skis give you to bank your legs and your skis, pivoting them into the turn. This pivoting movement should be very rapid.

When you try this manuever do you feel as if you are sitting back and even nearly fall over backward despite pushing vigorously against your planted ski pole? You will notice that as your skis pivot rapidly through the turn the forward movement of your body brings you back over your skis

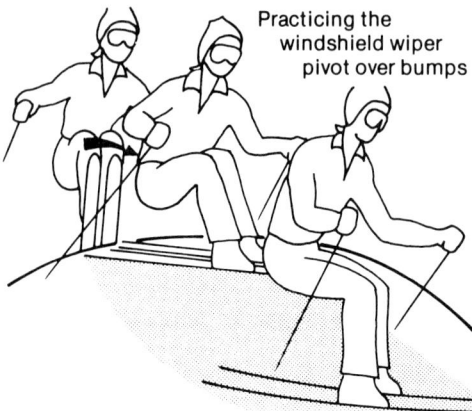

Practicing the
windshield wiper
pivot over bumps

and assures your balance.

The windshield wiper pivoting technique demands good muscular power, decisiveness and an ability to use the forward foot thrust. It is easier to learn in slightly bumpy terrain with difficult snow conditions. The end of the forward thrust of the feet should coincide with the moment when only the tails of the skis are in contact with the crest of the bump. The windshield wiper pivoting is then much easier to make.

Many good skiers discover the windshield wiper pivoting while making 'S' turns over bumps (page 130) in an excessively back-weighted position. They should then apply this technique to heavy, deep or even avalanching snows where it it a particularly effective weapon.

Hopped wedeln with "feeling" of the snow on landing.

This is a wedeln that is particularly well suited to irregular or even crusted snow in which you never really know how well your skis are going to be able to sideslip and pivot into the next turn.

HOPPED PIVOT AND "FEELING WITH THE TAILS".

1st — hop

platform

2nd — touch down
with the tails
then control the pivoting
around the tails of the skis

skis are lifted more than the tails and in this way the tails will touch down first on landing. Gradually you will learn to sense during the fraction of a second that the tails of your skis first make contact with the snow whether or not you can still "windshield wiper" pivot your skis and how far. You will also learn to land smoothly by flexing your legs to absorb the landing and eventually learn to finish your turn with a sideslip.

On very difficult snow, use a hopped wedeln and test the snow with the tails of the skis.

Some virtuoso skiers have discovered that by using a check wedeln with a strong platform, they are able to pivot their skis above the snow until their skis are pointed straight down the fall line and then, by landing on the tails of their skis, can sense the condition of the snow before deciding whether it is prudent to attempt to keep pivoting the skis. I have called this *"feeling with the tails"*.

Depending on the condition of the snow, the skier decides whether to try to pivot the skis a lot, a little or not at all. This pivoting is made somewhat like the windshield wiper pivoting but is distinguished by the very deep flexion of the legs used to absorb the landing.

To discover this gesture, first of all practice making hopped check wedeln with a large extension of the body and a slight rotation into the turn. Then try to make a slight forward thrust of your feet at the end of your extension so that the tips of your

Your number 2 weapon: an extension with tail contact for intermediate radius turns.

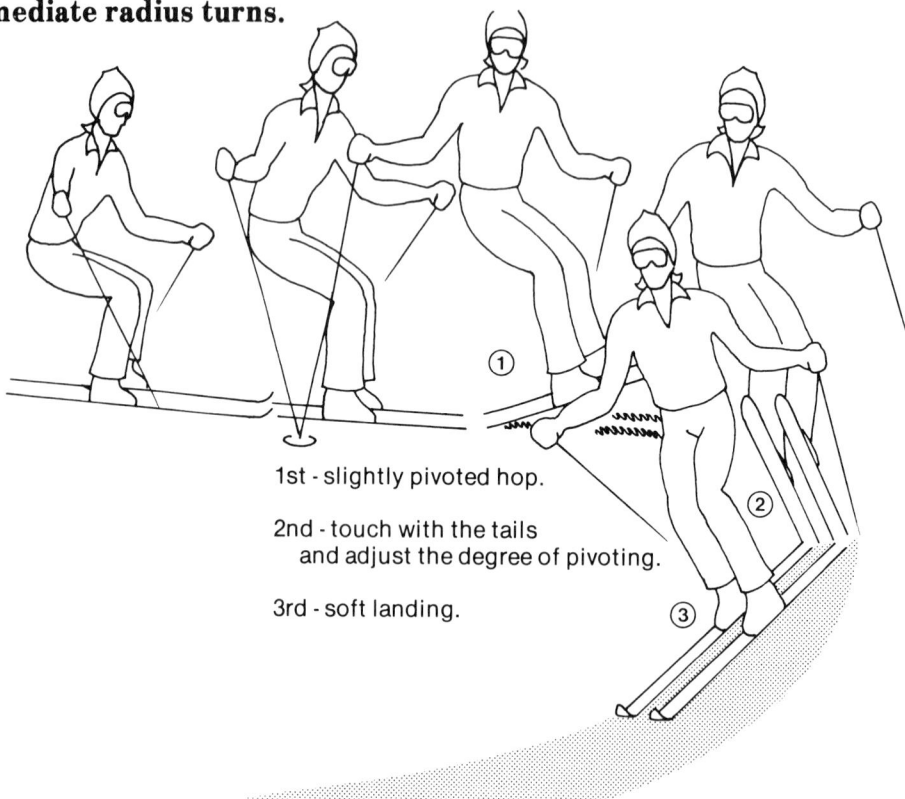

1st - slightly pivoted hop.

2nd - touch with the tails
    and adjust the degree of pivoting.

3rd - soft landing.

I already described this "secret weapon" for handling extremely difficult snow conditions, like breakable crust, on the preceeding page because it is just as effective in the linked turns of a wedeln as in intermediate radius turns. Many skiers, in fact, learn it more easily with a wedeln because of the repetition of the same movement which allows it to be more progressively developed and practiced.

In intermediate radius turns in the same kinds of snow conditions, use an energetic flexion-extension with a pole plant to feel your body thrown upward and into a slight pivoting movement into the turn. A little bit of a forward thrust of your feet at the end of the extension allows your skis to take off above the snow with your tips higher than the tails.

Try to feel relaxed in the air and concentrate on your feet. As you feel your tails regain contact with the snow, judge its consistency in a fraction of a second as you flex to absorb the landing and pivot your skis 5°, 10°, or 20° as seems indicated. You will then finish the turn in a sideslip.

How do you pivot your skis after the tails make contact?

In shorter turns and in very heavy and dangerous snows, use the windshield wiper pivoting (page 161).

In longer turns in snow that is not so difficult and through which you can push your skis when held flat or nearly flat, you can use a surf pivoting (page 142). Your feet will then pivot more than your knees with your knees remaining "outside" your skis to allow you to hold your skis flatter.

164

The ultimate weapon for extreme skiing: avalement.

When I first analyzed the avalement movement and recommended it to racers in my book *HOW TO SKI THE NEW FRENCH WAY* (1967), I didn't realize that the global movement that I baptised with this name contained so many distinctive technical elements and that each one of these elements could fundamentally influence teaching and training methods.

As a matter of fact, everything that I mentioned regarding the forward thrust of the feet, the flexion with upward movement of the legs in front of the body, the pivoting of the legs — or only the feet — in front of the body, and even the landing with tail pressure followed by windshield wiper pivoting *are all included in the global gesture of avalement*. But a genuine avalement demands a dynamism, a decisiveness and athletic capabilities which not all skiers possess. But each of the elements which constitute avalement and which we have mentioned can be used with much greater ease and nearly as much effectiveness in less extreme situations.

What are the essential characteristics of avalement ?

Avalement is a turn initiation technique that is instantaneous and therefore requires no time.

• It requires no platform and therefore insures better gliding.

• It incorporates an unweighting, a change of edges and a pivoting of the skis which are the three essential elements of the initiation of every turn down the fall line.

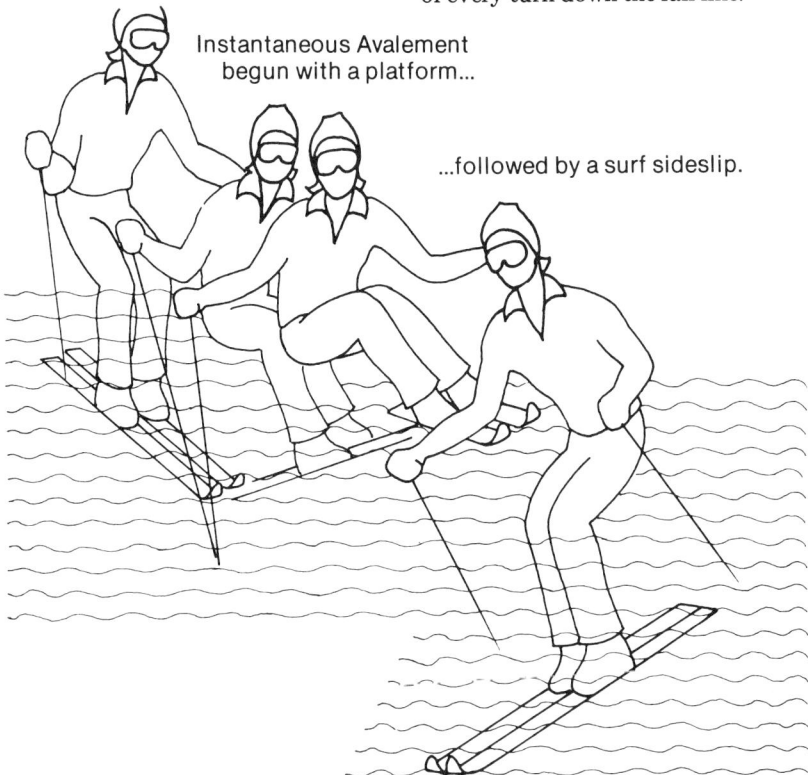

Instantaneous Avalement begun with a platform...

...followed by a surf sideslip.

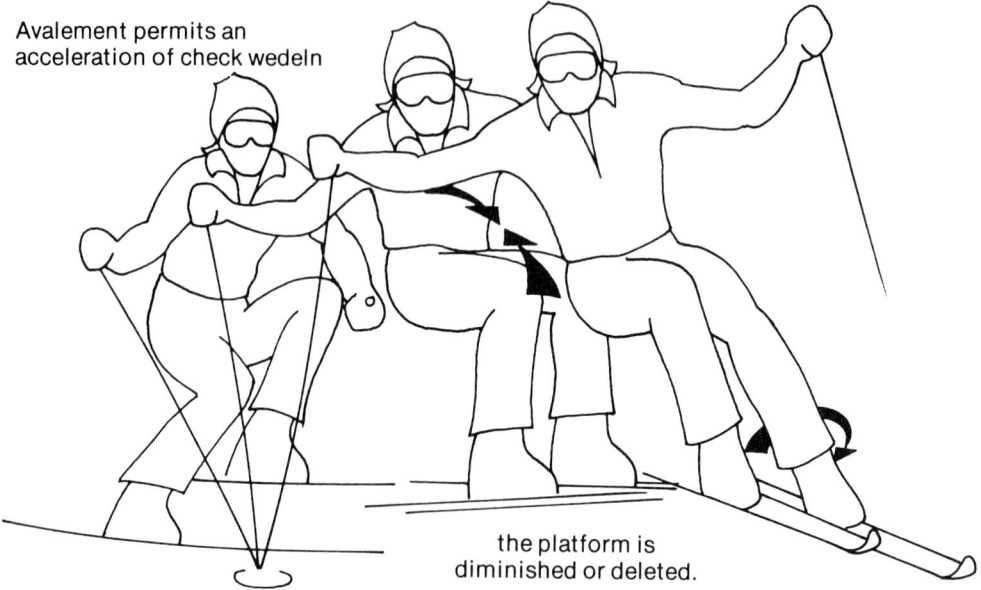

Avalement permits an acceleration of check wedeln

the platform is diminished or deleted.

• Avalement produces tail-pressure at the beginning of the turn which facilitates the control of the turn and permits better gliding at the beginning.

If you have already more or less mastered the essential elements of avalement but not the integrated movement as I suggested at the "intermediate" level, then try to discover the movement globally in specific yet not extreme situations.

• Fast skiing over very bumpy terrain. First make a platform in the trough followed by avalement; then only avalement (page 88).

• Simple but very rutted slalom courses: try to weight only one foot — the outside foot of course — in each rut, and between these supports absorb by pushing first one and then both feet forward. This results in a kind of a lateral projection from one foot to the other with avalement between the platforms. Also try it with a simultaneous action of both legs in a semi-wide and semi-narrow stance.

• Wedeln in easy but deep snow down a steep or very steep slope with little or no platform.

How do you improve your avalement ?

By systematically trying to use it to make rounder turns at higher speeds down terrain containing large bumps. Also in either light or heavy deep snows making long or short radius turns while avoiding any overloading of your skis. Since avalement is not a technique that allows you to conserve energy, don't attempt to link hundreds of turns. Unless you are a racer and are trying to prepare yourself athletically, you need to limit avalement to a few dozen turns at a time.

Skiing very fast with the avalement technique is a very intensive training for building muscle power and speed in the muscle groups which are used most in competitive skiing. As a training method, it has the added benefit of simultaneously cultivating your sense of gliding. Could you imagine anything more useful ?

What does the surf technique, introduced in the "Technical Innovations" chapter, add to avalement ?

• Better gliding at the beginning of the turn over soft or deep snow by refining the placement of the skis flat following the avalement.

• An indisputable advantage for piloting the skis and gliding during the phase of the turn which follows.

• It also has appeared to me that the passive surf wedeln through the bumps can permit dynamic skiers to instinctively learn avalement as their speed increases. Perhaps experience will show that this is the easiest way to learn avalement.

• Some skiers also learn avalement more easily starting from 'S' turns, others by trying to make a porpoise wedeln (page 151).

Edging with the inside ski: sometimes effective, always dangerous.

Some virtuosos of extreme skiing and of competitive skiing recommend this technique for improving the holding of the skis on very steep slopes and very hard snows. Some modern ski technicians consider edging with the inside ski, particularly at the end of the turn, to be a panacea. I do not share their opinion.

I admit that this use of the inside ski can be effective for certain skiers who are morphologically well suited for it, particularly those with bowed legs who are accustomed to weighting the outside edges of their feet. I also admit that it can be useful for all skiers in certain very extreme situations which, fortunately, occur only rarely: the sudden beginning of a skid, the necessity to tighten the radius of a turn at the very last moment or catching a fall to the inside which began at the beginning of the turn (banking).

But I have noticed that the systematic use of the uphill or inside ski at the end of the turn, even by skiers with bowed legs, often presents more disadvantages than advantages.

The disadvantages of holding with the inside ski.

• Poorer gliding resulting from a lack of finesse in piloting the turn. The foot seems to have less sensitivity when the outside edge is weighted.

•Losses of balance to the inside are more frequent. If the support ski suddenly slips more than anticipated there is little or no opportunity for the skier to catch his balan-

ce.

• There is a tendency for the skier to bank excessively to the inside at the beginning of the turn when he tends to weight his inside ski. If this banking becomes *too* pronounced, it leads to a loss of balance to the inside of the turn.

• A tendency toward a loss of balance to the rear at the end of the turn when the skier would like to weight his inside ski. Often the skier can not bring his body sufficiently far forward and up the hill and the inside ski then escapes in front of the skier.

• Contact of the outside of the boot sole — which extends out over the ski — against the slope. This then results in a brutal loss of edging and a fall.

167

• Pedagogically, this edging with the inside or uphill ski can not be recommended to skiers other than those at the very end of the teaching progression since the basic principle of skiing balance is weighting the outside ski of a turn and the downhill ski of a traverse. I have even observed, in fact, that when introduced at the end of the teaching progression, the weighting of the inside ski can very quickly become habitual for some racers and their softness and effectiveness decrease; first on soft snow and in round turns and ultimately on ice.

What should you conclude ?

Well aware of the dangers of this technique, it is up to you to determine what advantages it may hold for you. It is indisputable that the bony "architecture" of the foot makes it possible for you to hold with your uphill ski at the very extreme limit when you can no longer hold with your downhill ski. You should be able to use this technique, but use it only deliberately.

Extreme skiing with compact or intermediate skis.

Both good skiers with solid athletic qualities and intermediate skiers have become interested in using the so-called compact skis, which are more manueverable, to confront terrain and snow conditions which are at the very limits of their capabilities. They have been particularly interested in using the "all terrain" compact skis.

To the contrary, the experience of the "skiers of the impossible" proves that very good skiers should use either normal length skis or the intermediate length skis which are situated between the normal and compact lengths and have flexible tips and tails. Granted, these skis aren't as manueverable as the compacts, but they give the skier greater stability.

But you should be careful. Excessive flexibility will compromise the skis stability. The central zone of the ski should have sufficient stiffness to diminish the effects of slight errors in forward and backward weighting, but the ends of the skis should be flexible.

Extreme skiing outside the marked runs demands the competence of a mountain climber and extreme prudence.

Even if this book is only involved with motor behavior — or psycho-motor behavior to use the more fashionable expression — I can not end this brief chapter without drawing your attention to the safety problems posed by extreme skiing off of the marked runs; security for yourself, perhaps also for your friends who have confidence in you, for other skiers who might be endangered by an avalanche that you could start, and ultimately for the rescuers who will surely come to your aid if needed.

If you do not have extensive experience skiing off the packed run, a great knowledge of the terrain over which you are going to ski and a good understanding of snow conditions, meteorology and the multiple dangers of avalanche and the behavior necessary to avoid these dangers, don't ski outside the resort boundaries unless you are accompanied by a professional guide or an experienced amateur. You should also be aware that even in the best of circumstances such an adventure is not without risk. Some avalanches remain perfectly unforeseeable.

Even if you only go looking for your extreme skiing within the boundaries of the resorts, be prudent and respect the "run closed" signs. These runs can be closed because they aren't packed — or because of extreme avalanche danger. In any case, such runs aren't patrolled at the end of the day and any accident might be "overlooked"...

GET A TASTE OF RACING

To discover a new pleasure, to accelerate your progress, to "measure" your efficiency, get a taste of racing.

Perhaps, like many other skiers, you consider competitive skiing to be something entirely special, reserved for skiers born with skis on their feet.

Even though you participate in Nastar races on occasion you may not consider these to be genuine competitions where the racer should be totally involved, giving battle. Perhaps you only enter these races to "measure" yourself, just as you might measure your height or weight. You are then interested, but certainly not obsessed.

I would like to convince you to view competitive skiing in the same way that you look at a tennis match against a friend of yours whom you have vowed to some day beat. In other words, take ski racing seriously and view it as something which takes minute preparation and demands a total involvement followed by serious reflection in order to draw a useful lesson for the following competition.

In this way you will be able to cultivate a love for competition, regardless whether it consists of a Nastar race, a Citizen race, or a United States Ski Association race from a club event to a major national competition. You will become a member of the big family of competitive skiers. Perhaps you will one day even enter that elite group of racers who are "classified" by the International Ski Federation!

BEGIN WITH GIANT SLALOM

If you have never entered a ski competition, begin with a giant slalom. You should prefer giant slalom to slalom because it more closely resembles the linked turns that you make when free skiing.

Most of the ski areas in the United States regularly run Nastar races and many of the local sports clubs run Citizen races. These races are usually run on well controlled giant slalom courses and licensed racers are prohibited from entering.

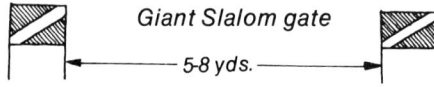

Giant Slalom gate

5-8 yds.

Horizontal gate

2 round turns

Vertical Gate
(skied over)

Oblique Gate
(skied underneath)

minimum distance
10 yards

Giant slalom courses.

Two rectangles of cloth of the same color and each supported by two poles make a gate. The course consists of alternating blue and red gates and the racers must pass through all of the gates. The minimum distance between the closest poles of two successive gates is 10 yards.

A new rule specifies that the number of gates must be equal to 15% of the vertical drop of the course in meters plus or minus 5 gates. The race is run in two successive runs on different courses and the results are then determined by combining the times for both runs.

A starting gate, opened by the skiers legs, triggers a timer situated at the bottom of the course. A light beam placed along the finish line electronically stops the clock as soon as the skier breaks the beam.

Point calculation.

In each race sanctioned by the United States Ski Association (USSA) or the International Ski Federation (F.I.S.) a skier can earn two kinds of points: race points that are calculated according to a formula that takes into account the length of the race and the difference in time seperating the skier from the winner; and points by which a skier can be "classified" by the USSA which are an average of each skier's 2 best performances over a season in each of the alpine disciplines. The points used to compute a racer's classification points are equal to the race points plus a handicap for that race. This handicap is calculated by a formula that compares the previously acquired classification points of the 5 top classified racers who finished among the first 10 finishers of each race and the race points which they earned in that race.

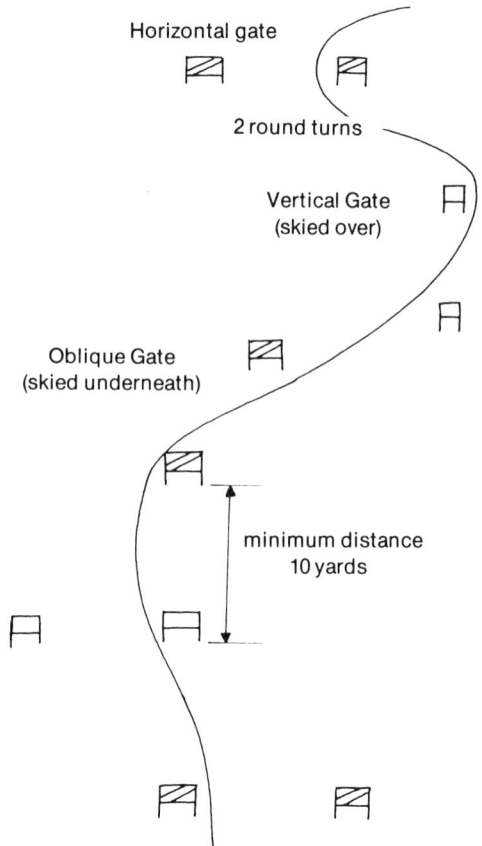

Unlike free skiing, however, the line of the turns in a race course is very strictly determined by the position of the gates but you will have little difficulty adapting your skiing to the race course if you have learned to control the arc of your turns, to start your turns with precision and if you have learned to smoothly link your turns together as we have advised you throughout this book.

Of course you won't have to think about all of this while racing. The technical fundamentals that you have mastered, along with your muscles and body, constitute your weapons; the engine that you are going to pilot through the course. Your task will be to drive this engine well, drawing out all that you can, and in doing so you will gain something that you can't achieve in normal slope skiing. Something just as exhilarating as an automobile race... with fewer risks and less expense !

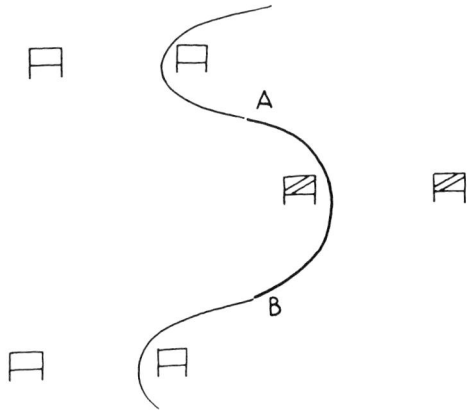

The shape of the turn from point A to point B is determined by the positions of both the preceeding and following gates. This is true for all slalom and giant slalom turns.

Five preliminary suggestions.

1. Before the race, inspect the course paying particular attention to the terrain, snow and speed. Prepare yourself psychologically.

An essential part of the competition takes place before the race itself. It consists of the inspection of the course which should always be set a few hours before the first start.

Caution ! Contrary to a widely held opinion, you should *not* try to learn the entire sequence of gates by heart; nor the peculiarities of each of the 8th, 13th, 27th, and 31st... I have often remarked that 99% of the time the beginning racer has forgotten all of this by the time he starts. For you, inspecting a giant slalom should consist of an awareness of the speed, the eventual problems created by this speed for holding with the edges or with flat skis or the linking of turns that are close together.

Only in very certain situations, and for only one or two sections of any course, should you decide beforehand on a particular behavior (ie. slow down, check, turn very high or take a gate backwards...). In

these situations, find a couple of reference points in the course to identify these sections, for example — three gates after the beginning of the steep section, or two gates after the beginning of the flat... But don't select reference points alongside the course because you won't see them while racing when your attention is focused on the gates ahead.

Beware also of the advice of friends, and even of coaches and instructors who don't know you well. This advice will only be useful if you can integrate it perfectly into the plan of action that you are formulating for yourself. Don't let yourself be distracted by the advice of others which won't even help to calm your anxiety. You will be alone while racing; therefore be alone as you prepare for the race.

2. Liberate yourself during the race, but never let yourself be overcome by the events.

The race shouldn't be a tornado that carries you from gate to gate and leaves you on the other side of the finish line stunned and remembering nothing.

Neither should it be a pleasurable promenade through the gates...

You should go as fast as possible and brake as little as possible. Judge the difficulties, see the "openings" and sometimes even anticipate them. To be successful you must "liberate" your muscles and reflexes. You should feel yourself totally involved in what is happening but still remain aware, in control of yourself and events. Each failure should become an instruction. Don't look for excuses but instead look for the error you made — either a technical error or a behavior error — and why you made this error and draw appropriate conclusions for your next races.

3. First tactical suggestion: Turn far above the gates.

If you turn too late at each gate, you will soon be overwhelmed. As a general rule, try to turn high in each gate so that most of your turn is completed by the time you pass the gate.

4. Second tactical advice: If you have to check, check before the turn and not during the turn.

I have mentioned this repeatedly throughout this book, but it is even more important while racing even though it is rarely applied ! The snow surface at the end of the turn is rutted and chatter marked by the earlier racers who have tried vainly to brake. If you try to check your speed in the same place, you multiply your risk of falling. Instead, control your speed before the turn so that you can cross this difficult section with ease.

5. The only technical advice applicable to all circumstances: ski with your weight balanced over your outside ski.

You will be better able to hold your line and will run less risk of losing your balance. You will be better prepared to react to any situation.

This advice is even more important for racing than for free skiing because the site of the inside pole of the gates will provoke an almost irresistable tendency in you to lean to the inside of the turn and perhaps to weight the tips of your skis excessively. Anticipate this error by skiing with all of your weight balanced over your outside ski. Don't hesitate to lift your inside ski, not only at the beginning of the turn but throughout the turn and, in particular, at the end of the turn as you enter a traverse. You should feel that your weight is distributed equally over the front and back of your outside foot (rule of 2 support points). Only in this way can you succeed in piloting your turns (page 108).

I won't give you any further technical advice because until you have accumulated sufficient experience in racing you won't be able to concentrate your attention on technical details other than to correct gross errors. If you try to do so, it will be to the detriment of your performance, and competition is, above all, ... performance.

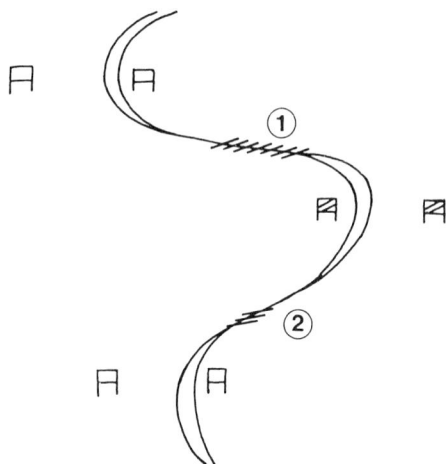

To slow down. One can not slow down without risk except in the traverses which seperate the turns. With a downhill stem or braking sideslip for a prolonged braking (1). With a parallel skis or downhill stem edge-set for a brief braking (2). In both cases, the reduction of speed should assist the initiation of the next turn.

To slow down without braking: round out the turns

What difficulties are you having ?

Do you skid away in the turns ?

Do you have difficulties holding your line in the course as soon as your speed increases ? This is a common sensation among racers who are accustomed to letting their skis determine the radius of their turns while free skiing. To compensate, these skiers accentuate the pivoting of their skis, bank even further to the inside of the turn... and skid even more. To keep from falling into this trap, find out why you don't hold and correct your faults.

• If your speed is generally higher when you enter than when you exit a turn, you should use a slight check — eventually in the form of a couter-turn — before starting down the fall line (see page 46 for the "brake then turn" reflex). No longer skidding away in the turns, you will be able to carry more speed out of each gate and this can translate to gaining several tenths of a second per gate. Gradually you will learn to diminish the check.

• You don't try, even subconsciously, to control your speed during the turn by pivoting your skis excessively do you ? This is the worst time possible to control your speed. Slow down during the traverse, or by making a counter-turn, but try to slide cleanly through the turn by holding your skis as much in the line of the turn as possible.

• Do you aim at the gate and then turn afterwards ? If so, your turn is made below those of the other racers and you cross their tracks bumping against the ruts that they make. It's only logical that you then skid away. Aim 4 or 5 yards higher than the gate and complete ⅔ of your turn before passing the gate.

• Do you find that you can hold the first half of the turn but unavoidably skid away at the end of the turn ? Do you have good skis ? Have you sharpened the edges (at least once

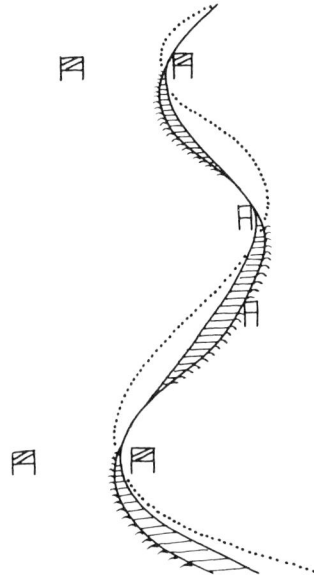

The skier who runs straight at the gates and then turns (solid line) skids away. He brakes and runs the risk of falling. The skier who completes ⅔ of his turn above the gate (dashed line) avoids these difficulties.

every 8 days of skiing) ? Do you have good boots ? Are they properly canted for you ? Are you weighting your outside ski sufficiently ? Have you felt the effort required by your outside foot to hold the ski on edge (ie. the rule of 3 support points, page 66) ? Are you properly angulated (page 67) ?

If you are committing a technical error, you should be aware of it and try to correct it. But at the same time, when you are training in gates you should try as hard as you can to hold on with your edges so that you can accelerate through the end of your turn and dive into the traverse that follows. You will find that only a sufficient level of involvement in what you are doing will help you to overcome some technical problems. This is one of the greatest advantages of competition.

• Do you feel that you hold poorly from the very beginning of your turns ? This is due to a serious technical error. An excessive extension creates an unweighting that is too prolonged and often results in a skidding of the skis upon landing. Rotating into the turn creates a pivoting inertia which hinders the holding of your skis. Starting your turn with forward weighting or a combination of forward weighting and extension or rotation results in the skis tending to pivot around their tips. An excessive banking to the inside at the beginning of the turn, whether conscious or not, always disturbs the holding of the skis.

To correct all of these technical errors, I suggest that you make several hundred turns initiated by spreading your uphill ski and control your turn exclusively with pressure on your outside ski. Your inside ski should be lifted off the snow. You can even run your giant slalom like this until your mistakes are corrected.

Are you so intimidated by the speed that you always ski out of the course ?

Identify your situation:

• Are you perfectly relaxed, almost euphoric, brushing by the gates up until the moment that you are catapulted out of the course ? Your sin is an excess of optimism ! You can not claim that you are at ease in the course until you can run it without problem. For the time being, make your turns a little rounder and even slow down if you must to force yourself to finish.

• Would you like to slow down but find that you can't because the course is too rough or the smoother sections too short to give you time to check your speed ? I suspect that you are trying to use a stance that is too narrow and high, using a technique that is, perhaps, elegant but inefficient. Return to a more utilitarian approach: a lower position, wider stance and more dynamic movements. Rediscover the rudimentary checks by leg action and stem platforms (downhill stem and foot steering sideslipping, page 46) and

use these techniques to initiate turns with a change of support foot and foot steering. Then, and only then, can you enhance these gestures with the ornaments of a more elegant technique.

• Are you momentarily indecisive at the start of your turns ? The remedy is simple. Cultivate the "brake then turn" reflex (page 46) and then discover a turn initiation with a platform; first with a downhill stem and ultimately in a wide stance. Don't hesitate to begin your turns with a check.

• When the gates are set down the fall line do you become incapable of controlling your speed and become afraid ? Get more experience schussing. If you are used to top speeds of 30, 40 or 50 miles per hour, you won't be afraid of 15, 20 or 30 miles per hour in a giant slalom. If the course isn't too rutted, you can also reduce your speed by making your turns rounder. You can't slow down by sideslipping, but don't be afraid to open your skis into a stem and even use a wedge braking. Even very accomplished racers use this technique in certain circumstances.

Are you unable to "liberate" yourself and glide ? Are you too slow ?

• Perhaps your basic technique is a braking technique, even when you are skiing outside of the gates. If this is your case, you should methodically reacquire the essentials of a gliding technique: a soft control of the skis in a schuss and in serpent movements (page 78), a smooth dive into turns down the fall line, a sliding phase in the middle of every turn down the fall line and a piloting of your skis either held flat or on edge (page 64). Beginning with these fundamentals, ski miles and miles of long turns and flowing wedeln down easy slopes while cultivating good gliding. Only then should you return to competition.

• Perhaps just the fact that you're in a race course makes you contract and brake against your will. This is a psychological problem that can only be resolved by seeing yourself clearly. Are you afraid ? Afraid of what ? If

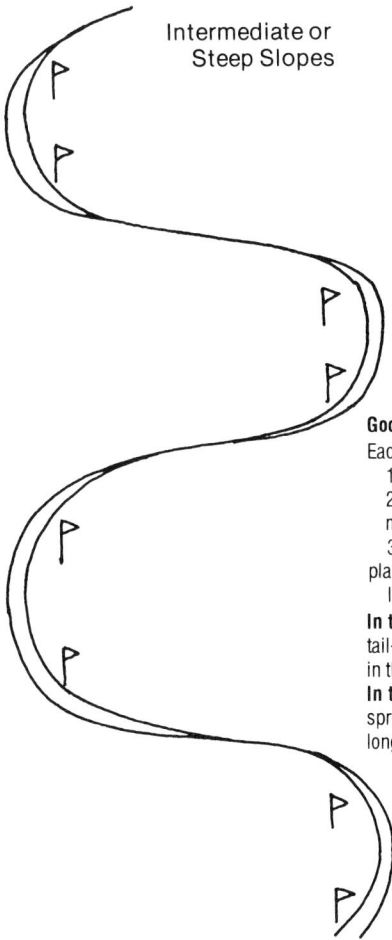

Intermediate or
Steep Slopes

Flat
Slopes

Good giant slalom training
Each turn is made by two poles. Advantages:
1. You are obliged to make round turns.
2. You are obliged to accept a dive down the slope in the middle of the turn.
3. You must be balanced in both the fore-aft and lateral planes. Banking becomes impossible.
It is easier to carve the end of the turn.
In the left course, the long traverses oblige the skier to use tail-pressure to carve the line and not lose too much height in the gate.
In the right course, the skier is encouraged to use a lateral spreading or even a lateral projection which will allow longer, straighter turns.

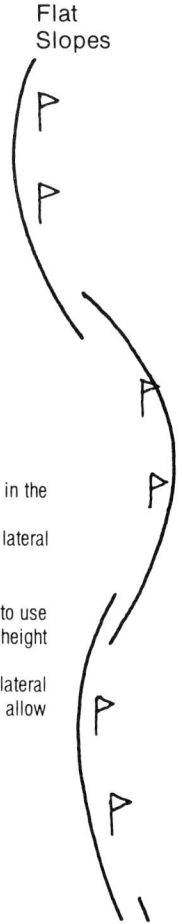

you're afraid of speed, try to free ski faster. If you're afraid of the gates, find some way of getting some training; first in very easy courses which will give you confidence and then progressively train in more difficult courses. If you're afraid of an accident, have your bindings checked over by a competent ski technician.

In any case, try to create a relaxed environment. Even if it disturbs your concentration a little before the race, such an atmosphere will have a positive influence on your performance.

Also try to make 2 or 3 fast runs just before the race. Try to remain mentally at the rhythm of the turns you made during these runs up until the moment you start the race. This will free you to do better.

I am going to give you one last piece of advice which will seem very simple but isn't: while racing, use the traverses when the course is smooth and straight forward to check out your progress. You may be surprised to notice that you are slowing down without being aware of it. Perhaps because you're already thinking about the upcoming turn. Instead, concentrate on your gliding in the traverse. You will be impressed by the time you can pick up in this way.

Are you unable to ski in ruts ?

When the competitors who have preceeded you dig a deep trench down which you must ski, you will confront increased difficulties. These kinds of toboggan runs increase your speed, present new balance problems and make it difficult to check your speed. I can only give you a few general suggestions.

• First of all, be aware of the fact that the only place where you can slow down is between the turns where there usually is no rut.

• Flex down low in the ruts and adopt a semi-wide stance with your arms spread wide and let yourself go. Don't try to slow down. It will be your doom.

• Enter the rut at the very beginning of the turn. Eventually you will use a lateral step to do this. If you enter the rut later, you will "bump" against the wall and this can be very unbalancing.

• If your speed seems to be too fast, turn along the outside of the rut every now and

In rutted courses. Aim for the beginning of the rut and press against it as quickly as possible (solid line). If you go "straighter" (dashed line) you will hit the rut sideways and risk losing your balance.

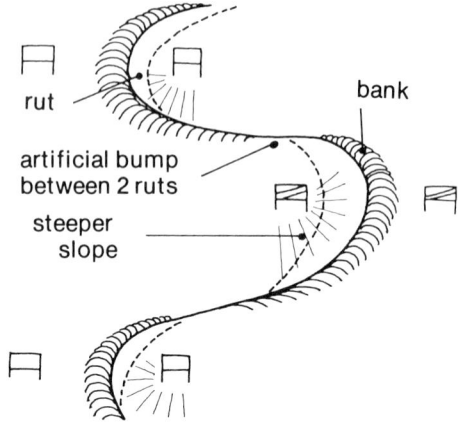

then in an easy gate to slow down.

• By skiing down intermediate, mogulled slopes, you can make long turns in the troughs and become accustomed to skiing in ruts.

GET A TASTE OF SLALOM

After having raced a few giant slaloms, you can now attempt a slalom. The easiest for you will be to enter various kinds of Citizen slaloms. Choose a time when the slalom hill is not too icy and when there aren't too many competitors. This will give you a better chance of finding a course suitable for your first attempts. I strongly recommend that you get in a few hours of training before your first race.

Even though you are very competent at the wedeln, the simple fact of having to turn in gates poses new problems for you. Not

only will you have to learn to control the trajectory of your skis more precisely but you will have to learn to judge the gate, the terrain, the shape of the turn to be made and the turn that follows from just a glance. In short, you will have to hone your reactions to a very new environment. A certain familiarization is necessary for this.

Once you have run several Citizen races, and have experienced some success, I would advise you to enter the United States Ski Association races and gradually work your way up the ladder of licensed racers.

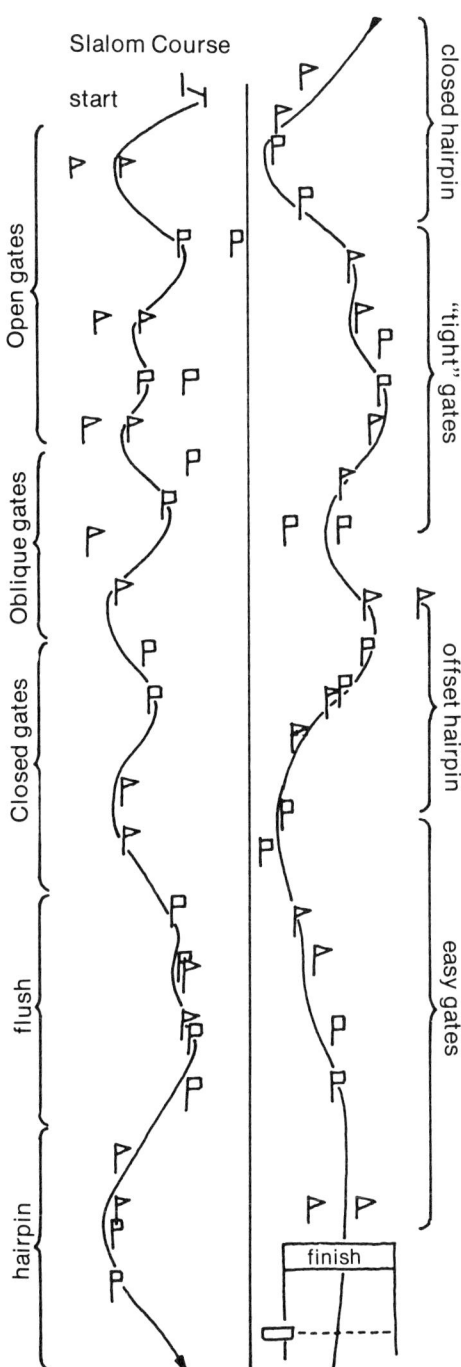

Slalom Course

start

Open gates

Oblique gates

Closed gates

flush

hairpin

closed hairpin

"tight" gates

offset hairpin

easy gates

finish

Slalom courses.

The gates consist of 2 poles with small flags. These poles are spaced 4 to 5 yards apart. The gates are alternately red and blue. The closest poles of two successive gates must be at least 2½ feet apart and at most 15 yards. The minimum vertical drop of a slalom is 395 feet. The maximum vertical drop of international slaloms is 720 feet.

The race is always run in two runs. The results are determined by combining the times of the two runs. U.S. rules demand that the winning racer's time be over 30 seconds per run. International slalom races, which generally contain nearly 60 gates, are run in approximately 50 seconds.

Six preliminary suggestions.

1. Before the race, inspect the course and pay particular attention to the terrain, snow and how fast the course is. Prepare yourself psychologically.

I can offer you basically the same advice that I did for the giant slalom. Make several runs 10 or 20 yards to the side of the course in a wedeln rhythm that approximates the rhythm of the turns in the course. Look for snow that has essentially the same consistency of the snow in the course, even if this means making your warm-up runs 100 or 200 yards away on one of the tourist runs. It is impossible for you to evaluate the difficulty of the gates if you can't feel what is happening under your skis at approximately the same speed that you will experience in the gates. As you examination the course, note no more than 2 or 3 particular difficulties and find reference points that will allow you to easily locate these sections while racing. Don't get carried away. Avoid pessimistic observations which will only increase your anxiety. Be positive and concentrate on only a few important features.

2. During the race, don't let yourself be overcome by the events.

My advice here is the same as I gave you regarding giant slalom. But be careful ! The gates come at you much faster in slalom and therefore increase your risks.

177

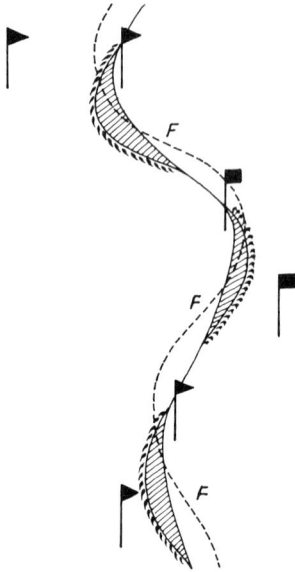

Good (dashed) **and bad lines.**
See the caption to a similar drawing regarding giant slalom turns on page 173. A checking of the speed can be made at point **f** but must be brief and accompanied by a pole plant. It should assist the beginning of the following turn.

3. Turn above the gates. Learn a proper racing "line".

You need to turn high just as you did for giant slalom so that you have sufficient time to complete your turn before the gate and thereby avoid having to turn in the area just behind the gate where the snow is the most deteriorated. Then too, if you are a little late in one gate you will have a better chance of recovering and not skiing out of the course. You can then try to aim above the next gate to regain your line. Always look far ahead because the line of each turn is determined by the position of the gate to follow. A failure to ski the best "line" often results in technical faults which can only be corrected by correcting your line.

4. Ski with constant weighting of your outside ski.

I mentioned this with regard to giant slalom but it is even more important in slalom because the tendency to lean in against the gate is greater in slalom. If you are balanced over your outside ski, it will be easier for you to move from one leg to the other and to move faster from one turn to the next.

5. On hard snow on intermediate or steep slopes, use a platform and a precise pole plant between each turn.

This platform, which I discussed with regard to wedeln and short turns (pages 70 and 81), allows you to control your speed at the conclusion of one turn and to position your skis and body for the start of the next turn. In the heat of the competition you won't be able to pay attention to your body position at this critical moment but by systematically using platforms you will increase your security.

6. Don't hesitate to use a slight stem on soft snow and flat or intermediate slopes.

This isn't only the surest method for threading through the gates but the one that will give you the best gliding. It's curious that despite the fact that children will readily use a slight stem, most adults are loathe or incapable of using one.

What difficulties are you having ?

Are you overwhelmed by the rhythm of the turns and unable to keep up ?

• When free skiing do you have a leg action that is rapid enough for the kind of snow you will encounter in racing ? If this isn't the case, practice wedeln with flat-skis pivoting in powder snow (page 78) and with platforms on hard snow (page 81). If you don't succeed, you are committing a serious technical error. Refer to pages 99 and 100.

• If, on the contrary, you have already developed a sufficiently rapid leg action on every kind of snow while free skiing, it remains for you to learn how to direct your skis with greater precision. In a free skiing wedeln, for example, one pays little attention to the positioning of the skis and, in fact, tends to swing the skis the same distance away from the fall line with each turn and to ski with the same rhythm all the time whereas a slalom course is constantly varying. A good skier also finds it easier to make a free skiing wedeln in a narrow stance but this is no longer true in slalom racing. All slalom skiers use a semi-wide stance and move frequently from one ski to the other, something that is rarely done in a free skiing wedeln.

• To acquire the behavior of a slalom racer you can either train a lot in gates or, having understood the 4 gestures of slalom skiing, refine them on bumpy slopes, steep and icy runs, over flats... Make series of 20 to 40 linked turns with total concentration and going all out. You can get as much out of this type of training as training in gates.

• Do you find that you must make a movement with your arms before your legs will function? This is a common problem and the reasons for it can be many and diverse. Perhaps your arms are poorly placed. If you have to perform an arm movement of a given amplitude to plant your pole, you will turn later and later with each gate. Try to correct your arm position while free skiing and feel that your hands are always alert, ready to plant the pole. If your pole plant is not brief and precise, then it is no longer useful as soon as the turns accelerate. Practice a wedeln at a very rapid rhythm while free skiing and accelerate the wedeln by first accelerating your arm movements.

• I won't dwell on all of the gross faults of beginning slalom skiers: jumping from one gate to the next with both feet, standing to erect and skiing with the legs held together. Before trying to ski slalom, you must first acquire a fairly solid and complete technique. One of the virtues of slalom is

that it constantly reminds this truth to those who might forget it.

THE FOUR TYPES OF WEDELN WHICH PREPARE YOU FOR SLALOM.
On flat slopes — sliding wedeln
  1. By opening a sliding stem at the beginning of the turn;
  2. By spreading the uphill ski and change of support foot.
On intermediate slopes — wedeln with platforms.
  3. By downhill stem platform and pole plant;
  4. By edge-set in a semi-wide or wide stance with dominant pressure on the outside ski and pole plant.
On steep slopes: check wedeln.

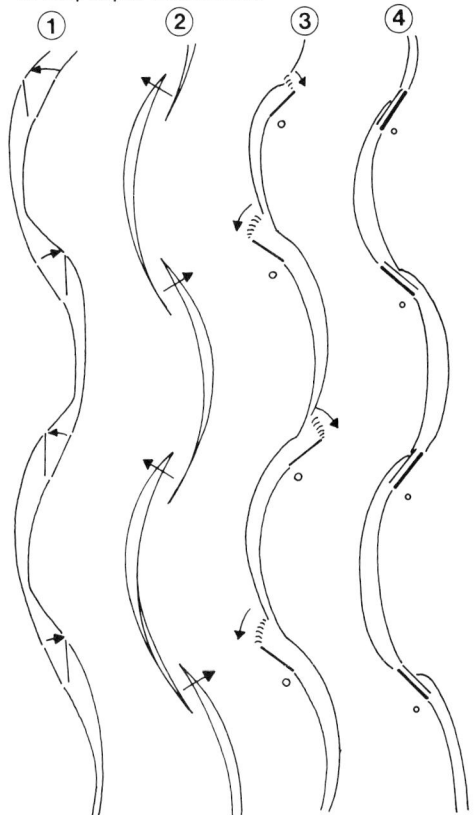

Are you unable to complete the course ?

• It is possible that you are trying to carry too much speed. This frequently happens to gifted skiers who are used to fast, sharp free skiing. I propose two remedies: 1. Round out your turns every time you can by skiing 1, 1½, or even 2 yards from the inside pole of the gate, even outside the tracks of the other competitors if necessary. You may still be able to post a better time than them if you are a good glider. In any event, never try to touch or brush the poles. 2. Do you know how to make a brief check ? You must know how to reduce your speed by 10 miles per hour within 2/10ths of a second using a precise edge-set (pages 70 and 72). Or, even better, use a downhill stem edge-set starting from a wide stance. 9 times out of 10, the skiers who don't know how to quickly slow down are those who ski in a narrow stance, in a position that is too upright and don't know how to move from one ski to the other.

• It's also possible that you are committing a fault that 30% of all adult skiers make compared to only 10% of the children: "banking".

This is an excessive, subconscious leaning to the inside from the beginning of the turn; either a leaning of the entire body or a collapsing of the hip against the gate. This mistake was studied on page 100. If you are guilty of committing it, correct yourself. I can offer only one suggestion which happens to be applicable while free skiing as well as in a slalom course — in each turn and throughout all of your turns, feel that you are perfectly balanced with *all* of your weight riding on your outside ski.

Are you too slow ?

This isn't as serious a problem in slalom as it is in giant slalom. With a little training you will improve because, even if the problem is psychological, it can be resolved to a great degree through technical solutions. First of all try to reduce the duration of your braking between the gates be evolving these checks, which tend to stif-

fen you, into platforms which will give you just as much security but leave you more relaxed and supple (page 70). Then try to let your skis slide better between these platforms. You will dare to do this as soon as you have confidence in your platforms. It then only remains for you to decrease the braking produced by your platforms and ultimately to make your turns shallower by passing closer and closer to the poles. In skiing, as well as in tennis, eagerness and total involvement only play a decisive role when you start from a very high technical level.

Are you unable to hold on ice ?

Do you have the same difficulty when free skiing on ice ?. If yes, refer to page 101. If, on the other hand, you only have problems holding in courses, you are inevitably banking to the inside of your turns, a mistake already analyzed above. It's also possible that your failure to hold on ice is due to a bad line. If you go straight at the pole and then try to turn you end up pivoting your skis on the part of the course that has been chattermarked by the earlier runners and you won't be able to hold on. But if you complete most of your turn before passing the gate your skis will carve through the rough section.

Are you unable to ski in ruts ?

The problems posed by skiing in ruts are basically the same as in giant slalom but are magnified and more difficult to solve.

One good solution is to become accustomed to skiing in ruts by skiing a lot of rutted giant slalom courses. In fact, since you must develop new balance mechanisms, you will find it easier to accomplish this in giant slalom where the ruts are longer and spaced further apart (refer to the giant slalom chapter, page 175).

There still remains a problem peculiar to slalom: the ruts tend to make you start your turns late. The solution almost always consists of working laterally from leg to leg. Do you have this kind of good lateral independent leg action ? (page 120)

GO ALL OUT WITH RACING

In the chapter GET A TASTE OF RACING I addressed myself to the masses of intermediate and good skiers who today constitute the majority of all skiers.

Here I address myself to very good skiers who have already skied hundreds of slalom and giant slalom courses. These skiers can be city-dwellers who have worked very diligently on their skiing. They can also be mountain dwellers who were born with "skis on their feet" and instinctively discovered skiing in the most varied terrain and snow conditions or in the race courses which they were introduced to at a very young age.

Conscientious city-dwelling skiers, either young or not so young, don't have to feel inferior to the mountain-dwellers. Through a more rational and more systematic training program, you can achieve or even surpass the level of the mountain-dwelling skiers, particularly if they don't likewise impose such a training regimen on themselves. And by keeping abreast of the latest technical evolutions, you can even hope to surpass the mountain-dwelling skiers in a few years.

Even if you aren't this ambitious, I warmly invite you to play the racing game for a few years. Racing can heighten or renew your interest in skiing. I know one athletic individual who began skiing at 40 years of age and has made a respectable career as a regional racer. You can, of course, set your goal at accumulating a collection of Nastar gold and silver medals, but I would encourage you to become involved in the races of the United States Ski Association. Each race is handicapped according to the levels of ability of the top ten finishers. You will receive race points depending on the amount of time you finish behind the winner. Your points, when added to the handicap, will fairly precisely define your level of performance. Your two best results in each of the three disciplines — slalom, giant slalom and downhill — will allow you to be classified in the national or regional point lists of the United States Ski Association.

With 100, 200 or 300 points you can compare yourself to Ingemar STENMARK or Perrine PELEN who have 0 points.

Nevertheless, I don't recommend that you become fanatical about skiing in gates. I know many racers, both city and mountain dwellers, who no longer appreciate skiing outside of the gates. This is unfortunate for them and besides it's absurd because most experts today admit that free skiing is an important part of training for racing. Very fast free skiing, while letting the skis "run", skiing all kinds of terrain and snow conditions including ice or very bumpy terrain can give free rein to a racer's sense of improvisation and athletic qualities. And free skiing in beautiful powder snow can preserve a racer's joy in skiing without which it is difficult to remain a competitive skier.

In other words, make racing increase the fulfillment that you get from skiing. This will be easy if you don't place excessive emphasis on the gates and if you set as your only goal to improve yourself. In this way you can progress until 50, 60, perhaps even 65 years of age with your technique making up for the unavoidable loss of athletic qualities.

One large French ski area has created competition training weeks for skiers of all ages. This initiative should spread. And why not training weeks by point level ? Or camps for the young, the not so young and the "veteran" skiers.

In any event, it's in a club atmosphere where you can best taste the joys of ski competition. Oftentimes access to the clubs in the resort areas is difficult but there exist clubs in most of the cities. Learn about them through the United States Ski Association but take the precaution of writing these clubs to learn of their activity program before becoming a member. Another option will be the formation of clubs in the resort areas expressly for tourist skiers who want an athletic experience. Some experiments are underway; they should be successful.

But returning to the principle objective of this book: you have discovered competition and you want to improve. I won't have to propose new techniques for you in slalom and giant slalom but simply help you to transfer the behavior that you have developed in free skiing to the race course. The sum accumulation of your experience on the slopes will help you to progress more than anything that I could say.

I am assuming, of course, that you have already acquired a solid technical foundation and understanding from this book.

The reader who begins with this chapter will not understand what I am talking about. I'm sorry, but I can only invite him to return to the preceeding pages. If the reader is already a good skier, and if he is willing to study this text very diligently, I am confident that he will pick up some useful information.

With regard to downhill, I will offer some advice for beginning and improving in this event and an analysis of what the champions are doing, but I have often remarked that progress in this event can often be meteoric. Furthermore, training in downhill will improve your slalom and giant slalom. This is why I strongly urge you to become interested in all three of the alpine disciplines.

IMPROVE YOUR GIANT SLALOM

You have already made the first steps and are now looking for ways to improve your effectiveness. You can do this by better understanding giant slalom, your technique, your race tactics and strategy but also your concentration during the race and your physical preparation. It requires an entire program. Perhaps one day I will develop it in a book devoted exclusively to competition. Here I can only brush the surface of these subjects.

Before approaching the technical problems posed by giant slalom, I would first like to point out that all of the technical elements which I recommended to you in the preceeding chapters are directly applicable to competition.

Through your exposure to ski racing you may very well develop a fuller and deeper appreciation for some of the techniques discussed earlier which you may have considered to be of marginal importance.

The first problem that confronts the good skier who begins to compete in genuine giant slaloms is the speed. Not only the speed imposed by the course, but also the speed to be accepted and even to be sought in order to be successful.

The search for speed.

Giant slalom racing doesn't mean making turns at a given speed but to ski at maximum speed in spite of the turns. I'm not toying with words. These represent two types of behavior that are distinctly different psychologically and, to a degree, opposites.

The former essentially represents the use or putting into use of previously acquired turning techniques. The latter, above all, is a combat from start to finish in which the racer draws upon his will, courage, athletic qualities and his entire repertoire of technique. The essential difference is the state of mind of the racer. If you have learned to ski or refined your technique through the use of this book, it should now be easy

for you to focus your attention on speed, and put all of your technical attainments to the goal of skiing faster. I have, in fact, insisted throughout on gliding, the dive down the fall line, the acceleration out of the turn and the precise use of pressure and carving, all elements which belong more to a search for speed than to an elegance of the gestures.

Nevertheless, without a sufficient and solid technical foundation, will, courage and concentration will be of little use and sometimes can even disturb the racer's behavior. This can be the result of a technique that is not adaptable to the combat conditions of racing as are most of the ski school techniques which have been essentially formulated for the needs of tourists. Or it can just be the matter of a technique that, in the heat of battle, is not appropriately adapted. A ski racer can be fiercely aggressive, but he must nevertheless maintain a light foot, a soft edge and velvet smooth contact with the snow. *Softness in violence* in short is the desirable attribute of the effective competition skier.

Again, I emphasize that this shortcut encompasses an entire program of technical, physical and psychological preparation which I can not develop adequately in this book.

Adapt to the terrain.

Beautiful, flowing giant slalom courses are set over varied terrain with drop-offs, compressions, banked turns in hollows or fall-away turns... Your major concern is the same as the downhill specialist's: to distribute the overloading and unweighting of your skis as much as possible by extending as soon as you experience an unweighting and flexing as soon as pressure begins to build on your skis. Over rolling terrain, the amplitude of your vertical movements will depend simultaneously on the terrain and the turns. For example, a turn on the crest of a bump will be made with a flexion at the beginning of the turn followed by an extension. A turn in a hollow, on the other hand, will be made with an extension followed by a flexion. If you have adhered to the principles recommended in this book, and if your sensations of the ski snow contact, as perceived by your feet, play an important role in your behavior, you will have little difficulty in instinctively adapting your movements to the terrain. You won't fall prey to the fault committed by "constructed" skiers who think in terms of stance and gestures instead of adaptation to the snow, the terrain and the speed.

At the same time you make instinctive and subtle adjustments to the position of your hips and knees (see the surf technique, page 141) to keep your skis as flat as possible and yet maintain enough angulation so that your edges hold precisely as much as they need to. If these reflexes begin from below, then you have little chance of committing the grossest errors. But at higher speeds you must always anticipate the need for movements, for example by flexing before actually feeling a bump or even standing up to allow a greater flexion.

This play with varied terrain can be fascinating and brings the joys of downhill racing to the intricate turns of slalom.

The "standard" shape of giant slalom turns.

The higher speeds that you will encounter in serious giant slalom racing can pose new problems on the initiation, control and completion of your turns. The elite racers counter this problem by skiing tens of thousands of gates under the most varied of conditions. They then acquire "situation" conditioned reflexes that allow them to cope with all possibilities. The amateur racers who don't have these opportunities, however, must use a very fast and varied free skiing to familiarize themselves with the speed. Unfortunately our young French racers from the cities don't recognize this.

3 objectives determine the shape of your turns.

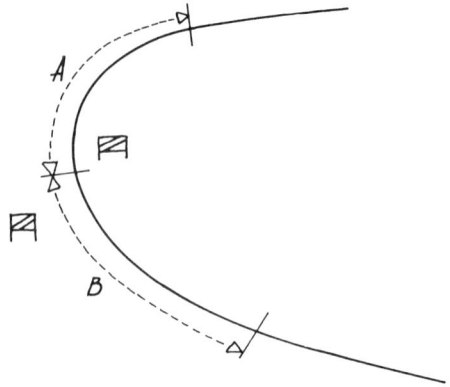

The shape of a typical turn.
The shape of the first part of the turn (A) and, therefore, the precise point where the turn must be started are essentially determined by the need to carry as much speed as possible out of the second part of the turn (B). The advice to turn very high above the gates is, therefore, not always valid for good skiers.

What I mentioned in an earlier chapter (page 170) is no longer valid for good racers. In fact, good racers give themselves 3 objectives: 1. To hold the turn by sideslipping and braking as little as possible. 2. To shorten the turns as much as possible by diminishing their radii while continuing to respect the first objective. 3. To complete as much of the turn as possible in the first half of the turn to then be able to make an accelerating dive into the following traverse. This concept of trying to accelerate out of the end of a turn is an extension of the notion of accelerating down the fall line in the middle of the turn which I have always tried to instill in beginning and intermediate skiers (page 63). Don't hesitate to backtrack if you have problems in achieving this objective.

Adapt to the snow conditions.

The same course will be skied entirely different depending on whether the snow is soft or hard. If the snow is soft, the skier must keep his skis as flat as possible (pages 65, 107, 110), avoid the use of harsh platforms and counter-turns, edge-sets and occasionally even lateral projections. On hard

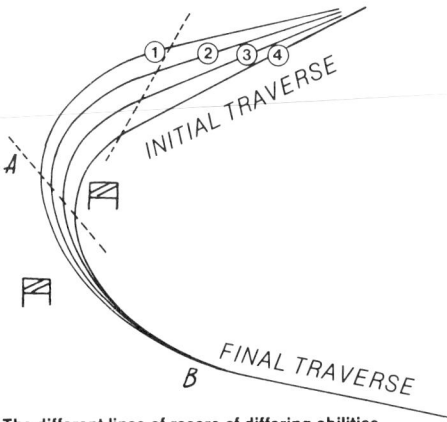

The different lines of racers of differing abilities.

The problem that each racer must resolve is to "hold" in part **B** of the turn without sliding away. The best racer will enter the turn along line 4. His initial traverse will be steeper and will represent the most direct and shortest approach and therefore will cause him to enter the turn with greater speed thereby compounding the diffiulties of holding in phase **B**. The less skilled racers will be compelled to take a higher and less direct line (as indicated by lines 1, 2 and 3) in order to negotiate the turn as well as possible.

snow, the skier must carve the line of the turns (pages 66, 116) and find solid supports that will permit him to accelerate by stepping from one leg to the other (page 120). It's rare that a racer doesn't prefer one type of snow over the other. This preference can originate from his technical baggage, his neuro-motor capabilities and even his racing "personality", but all of these elements can be "trained" and I have often observed that by improving your ability to handle snow conditions where you are weak, you can still obtain even better results on the kind of snow you prefer.

The traverses between the turns.

The tracks that a racer leaves in a traverse are a better indication of how successful he will be than his behavior while turning. I became aware of this while working with international calibre racers and having them make large, carved turns down very steep and icy slopes. The racer who is more successful in making a smooth traverse without sideslipping at the end of the turn will have

better results because he reduces the obligatory braking which occurs in every turn and lengthens the traverses where he can gain more speed. In order to resume a traverse as soon as possible at the end of a turn requires the skier to "set up" his turns so that he can carve through the end of his turn, making it a genuine acceleration ramp to allow him to carry more speed out of the turn.

An ability of the edges to hold in the traverses and in turns on steep slopes and on hard snow is also a key factor for success in giant slalom racing. I have repeatedly insisted on the skier being aware of the rule of three support points (page 66), hip angulation (page 67), tail-pressure (page 117), and the quality and the maintenance of the skis, their edges, and the boots. All of these elements play a major role in holding in the traverses and turns.

I have already remarked that a great many racers, who don't appreciate the importance of the traverses, lose precious seconds where it should be easiest for them to gain.

Elongated turns.

Elongated turns can allow you to gain time far easier than round turns, provided you have already developed the technical repertoire described in the pages of this book. From the very beginning chapter, I have underscored the importance of elongated turns — eg. the "long serpents" — for cultivating gliding in turns.

On soft snow I have recommended the use of the sliding directional effect with flat skis (page 64), then a sliding that is only slightly carved with tail-pressure (page 66) and then a gentle movement from one ski to the other with a smooth extension and progressive weighting (turn with lateral projection and turns with a forward thrust of the feet, page 139). Ultimately, I recommended the latest development in the realm of flat ski or slightly carved sliding: *the surf technique* (page 141).

For these kinds of snows, I have mentioned a balanced distribution of pressure

**A classic fault:
banking the turns**
either by allowing
yourself to lean
laterally against
the gate...

or by letting
your hip collapse →
against the pole.

One can hit the gates,
but only when in a
balanced position.

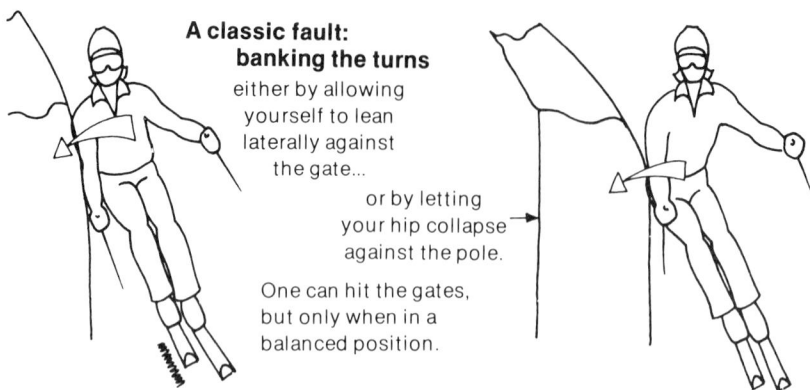

over both skis or with slightly dominant weighting of one ski, a uniform pressure on the skis by flexion-extension movements and a balanced or slightly back-weighted pressure. It is up to you to sense with your feet which solutions offer optimal sliding....

On hard snows I have first of all recommended carving with the edges while weighting the center of the skis and then improve upon this carving by increasing the pressure on the heel of the foot at the end of the turn (page 66). Then, by weighting the heels of the feet following a lateral projection at the beginning of the turn and, finally, I have insisted on a forward thrust of the outside foot to begin carving with tail-pressure (page 136). I have underscored the use of an extension while moving laterally from one ski to the other preceeding the turn to permit, with a forward thrust of the feet, a better carving. This is the type of turn that has proven to be the most effective through a series of round turns in giant slalom on hard snow in international competition (page 140).

Should one hit the gates ?

Yes, if you brush them while trying to make your feet pass as close as possible to the pole and while maintaining a perfectly balanced position. No, if you try to hit the pole with your hip and without regard to where your feet are passing because this leads to an inward fall which must be prevented in each gate by braking with your skis. If you can clearly dominate the course,

and if you have equipped yourself with suitably padded racing pants and sweater to protect yourself from the impacts, then don't hesitate to go for the poles.

The classic giant slalom turns.

These turns are generally set on the steepest sections of the course and constitute the essential technical difficulties of giant slalom racing. They require that the skier resist a considerable centrifugal force — particularly at the end of the turn where centrifugal force and gravity both pull in the same direction and increase the possibility of a skid. The two objectives of the skier in these kinds of turns are: 1) complete as much of the direction change as possible during the first half of the turn. 2) Maintain a solid holding of the skis on the snow during the second half of the turn.

Four techniques are currently used with success by the most brilliant international class racers:

• Turns begun with lateral projection.

This necessitates a good purchase on the snow of the outside ski, good carving and a powerful thrust with the downhill leg.

Lateral projection should be a thrust off of the downhill leg to move the uphill ski laterally and smoothly across the snow, not a lateral and vertical hop as is often seen. The uphill ski should then be placed flat on the snow if the snow is soft or on the inside edge if the snow is hard, but never on the

A few types of giant slalom turns...

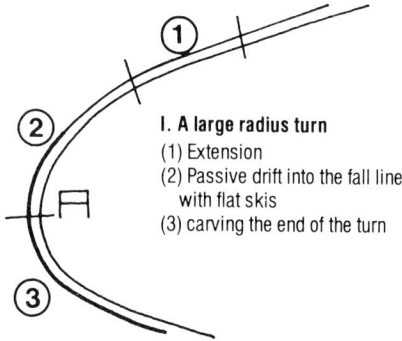

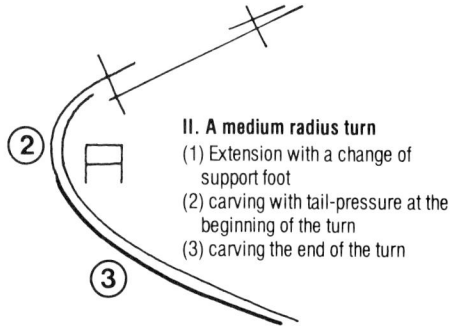

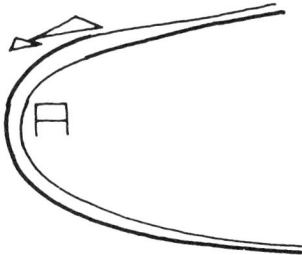

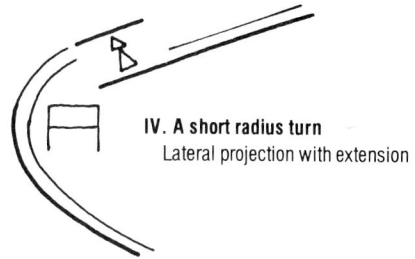

I. A large radius turn
(1) Extension
(2) Passive drift into the fall line with flat skis
(3) carving the end of the turn

II. A medium radius turn
(1) Extension with a change of support foot
(2) carving with tail-pressure at the beginning of the turn
(3) carving the end of the turn

IV. A short radius turn
Lateral projection with extension

III. A medium radius turn on hard snow
A change of support foot and pivoting of the outside ski with a forward thrust to make the tail of the ski carve.

V. A short radius turn at high speed
Avalement with a change of support foot

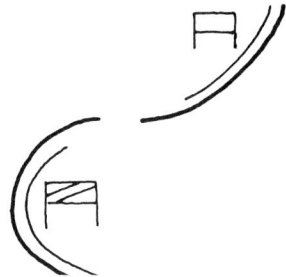

outside edge.

I have already analyzed lateral projection because, in addition to its usefulness in racing, it has enormous educational value for recreational skiers (page 140).

The particular advantages of lateral projection on hard snow are:
1) It allows the skier to gain height in the turn to thereby increase the turn radius.
2) By placing the outside ski onto its inside edge, the edge change is made at the same time as the lateral displacement.

3) Provided the lateral projection is sufficiently dynamic to allow an immediate weighting of the outside ski, carving can be started very early in the turn.
4) By allowing the carving of the turn to be started earlier, there is a greater possibility of preventing a skid on very hard ice where every compression can cause the skis to slide away.

On soft snow, lateral projection allows the uphill ski to be placed flat on the snow which in turn facilitates a smoother and softer entry into the turn.

Don't confuse lateral projection and finishing the turn on the inside ski with cramponnage.

These two movements are more often confused in slalom than in giant slalom. Some specialists have made cramponnage their preferred way of turning. I think this is a mistake for several reasons. For turns that are close together, lateral projection, which is briefer, simultaneously allows the next turn to be initiated whereas cramponnage on the inside ski must preceed an extension then a change of edges before the turn can be started. For turns further apart, is lateral projection slower than cramponnage ? No. Moreover, both gliding and security are almost always better when skiing on the outside ski.

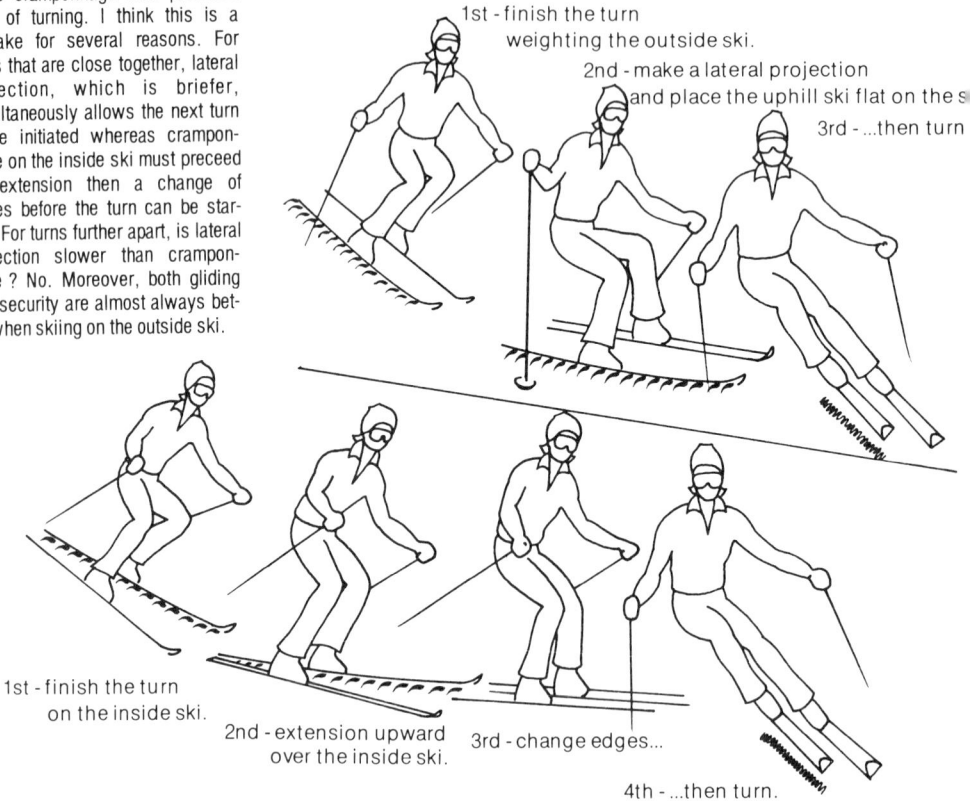

1st - finish the turn weighting the outside ski.
2nd - make a lateral projection and place the uphill ski flat on the s
3rd - ...then turn

1st - finish the turn on the inside ski.
2nd - extension upward over the inside ski.
3rd - change edges...
4th - ...then turn.

The most commonly committed errors are:
1) A failure of the downhill ski to hold as the skier projects off of it.
2) Excessive inward lean at the end of the preceeding turn which prevents the skier from thrusting vigorously with his outside leg and leads to *a simple transfer of the mass of the body to the uphill ski.* (See turns with cramponnage). This gesture is often confused with lateral projection and 9 times out of 10 gives the skier no advantage.
3) Trying to accelerate by projecting forward. This is only possible very early at the end of a turn where it is possible to project in a perpendicular direction off of the support ski and into the direction of the next turn. The thrust can only be made in a direction per-

pendicular to the support ski — otherwise the support ski is merely pushed backward. This therefore implies that a lateral projection at the very end of a turn or in a traverse must be made in a truly lateral direction and not forward. Many very good racers and experienced coaches have failed to understand this mechanism and speak very vaguely about "accelerating out of the turn" which can include just about everything.
4) Transfering to the outside edge of the uphill ski. This is often the result of a short lateral movement that doesn't last as long as the extension. This seldom gives the skier any real advantage and is far less effective than a genuine lateral projection.

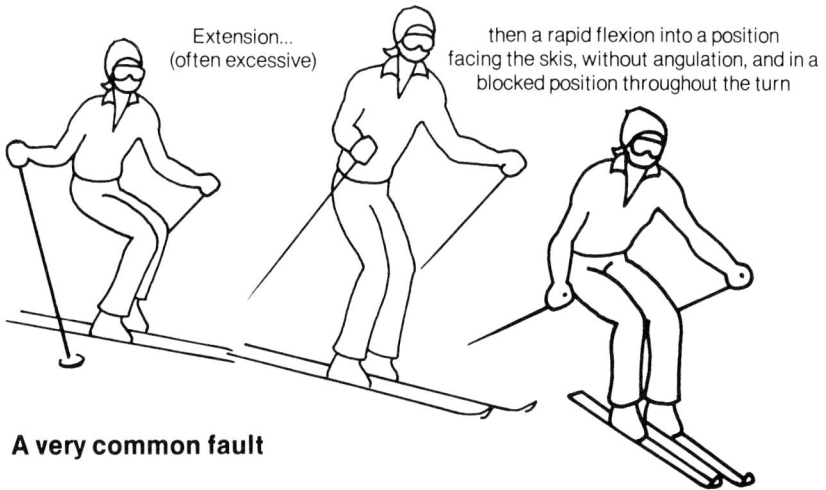

Extension...
(often excessive)

then a rapid flexion into a position
facing the skis, without angulation, and in a
blocked position throughout the turn

A very common fault

• **Turns with a forward thrust of the feet.**(page 139)

This particular turn, which is usually associated with a slight lateral projection, allows the highly skilled skier to re-weight his skis more progressively at the beginning of the turn and thereby insure better sliding. By first gaining contact with the snow with the body extended and then flexing and angulating, they are able to use the vertical fall of their body mass to place even greater pressure on their skis to carve dynamically at the end of the turn. The primary difficulty is making the skis hold on the snow and therefore it is imperative that the skier assume an angulated position early in the turn to place the skis on edge.

• **Carving with the inside ski — cramponnage.**

Two methods of cramponnage — carving with the inside ski — at the end of the turn must be distinguished: 1) on hard ice it is sometimes impossible to "hold" without edging both skis. Some skiers are able to get a more secure hold with their inside ski by weighting this ski without totally unweighting their outside ski and letting it shoot out down the hill. At the end of the

turn, these skiers can still thrust off of their downhill ski and produce an unweighting of both skis or even a lateral projection. 2) On the other hand, carving with the inside ski can correspond to a progressive transfer of the mass of the body to the inside of the turn with the skier completely balanced over his inside ski. This is done in a flexed, very low position with the outside ski turning less than the inside ski. The outside ski is then lifted and brought parallel to the inside ski. From his low position, the skier can use an extension to prepare for the following turn, provided he has enough room. On the other hand, it is impossible for him to use a lateral projection. I have already reviewed the numerous advantages and disadvantages of this type of turn on page 167.

I have noticed that many coaches don't distinguish between the two types of carving with the inside ski just described. This is unfortunate because I believe that the virtuoso giant slalom racers today are using the first type more than the second. It is difficult to estimate the magnitude of the centrifugal force by studying isolated photographs and one often concludes that a skier is weighting his inside ski when, in reality, nearly all of his weight is on his outside ski. One is usually able to avoid this error by studying photosequences instead.

• Turns with avalement.

Avalement remains the most effective technique when several very round turns must be quickly linked. It permits the skier to avoid the overloading and braking which every platform between two turns produces. Furthermore, when a turn is made over a bump or within a few yards after a terrain transition, avalement allows the skier to maintain contact with the snow and better pilot the turn. Avalement is very frequently associated with a lateral projection or a simple lateral step.

To master round turns perfectly, and hopefully to achieve excellent results, you must also know all of these movements, understand their advantages and their risks, their adaptation to all the different kinds of snow, terrain and turn shapes. Then, in a reflexive manner, you will select the most perfectly adapted movement for each and every circumstance.

But you must also be aware that in order to make the proper selection reflexively requires that you accumulate a lot of experience. Furthermore, every new movement that you learn will tend to dominate your technique and you will tend to use it all the time until it becomes perfectly assimilated in your technical repertoire and assumes its place and only its place. Because of this, some great champions have experienced entire months and even years of failure...

Rutted turns.

I have already discussed this problem on page 175. But while ruts are the obsession of beginning racers, they can be an exquisite delight for very good racers. The skis can, in fact, be held flat against the bank of the rut through the entire turn and thereby attain optimal sliding. A lateral projection and extension, with the feet forward, allows a very early positioning for the rut. The greater flexion that is available allows the skier to better absorb the contact and then accelerate even more in his dive down the fall line and from the middle of the turn the rut forms a natural ramp for sliding with skis flat and feet forward into the next traverse.

The mistake that must be avoided is systematically trying to ski along the inside of the rutted turns and refusing the support of the bank. Almost invariably any gains that could be made by skiing this straighter line are lost by the braking produced by trying to make the edges bite on the side of the steep wall at the foot of the pole. After a race, throw yourself down the course "with reckless abandon" after the last racer has run. No other experience can be as enriching and prepare you as well for the modern techniques of avalement and forward foot thrust.

The linking of giant slalom turns.

It is very esthetic and sometimes very efficient to link giant slalom turns by going immediately from one to the next with the end of each turn constituting a counter turn for the following turn. But as soon as the turns are further apart the skiers who try to maintain this kind of rhythmic swinging start to initiate their turns too early and then sideslip at the end of their turns. They don't profit from the tail-pressure carving at the end of a turn which can accelerate them into the traverse.

This is the same for racers who systematically project into a new turn from the end of each turn. If these racers are incapable of delaying their projection and profiting as much as possible from the acceleration into the traverse, they exit each turn slower than they might and risk starting their next turn too early. Certainly by emphasizing or prolonging the extension it is possible to increase the distance between their platform and the initiation of their next turn but often this distance is too great.

This is a classic error which forces the skier to move from one foot to the other at the end of the turn and often will result in a loss of balance to the inside at the beginning of the turn or very early in the turn.

On the contrary, the skier who is perfectly balanced over his outside ski and concentrates his attention on sliding smoothly at the end of the turn can easily select the most appropriate time to start his next turn. If the

1st-jump and lean forward

dive forward by pushing on the poles then swing the feet forward.

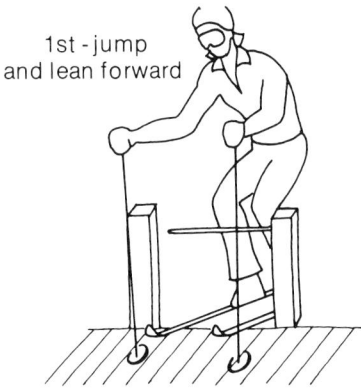

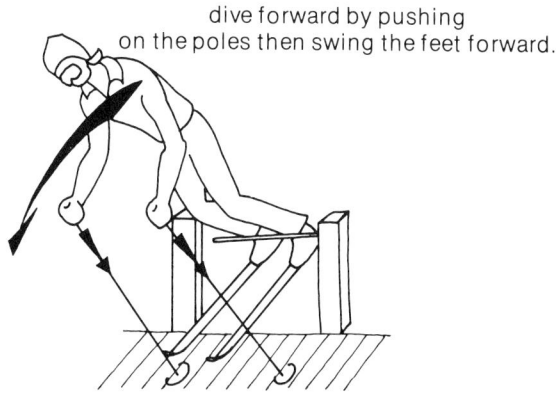

flexion at the end of the turn is sufficiently prolonged, it can be smoothly linked with the projection. I have noted that the correction of this error requires that the racer get out of the habit of using an even rhythm in all of his turns. This is what poses the greatest problem for very good racers.

The starting gate.

You should practice starting from a starting gate. This is more of a gymnastic manuever, similar to an exercise on the parallel bars, than a skiing type manuever. Unless you have exceptional abilities, don't count on your start to gain 5 or even 10 hundredths of a second over your competitors. On the other hand, you should recognize that a poor start can cost you 10, 20 and occasionally even 30 hundredths of a second.

With your legs flexed and your poles planted in a solid support in front of the starting gate, wait for the starter's signal. Go ! React in two steps. 1. Thrust with your legs to lift your skis off the snow. 2. Dive forward with your chest and push firmly on your poles so that your feet trip the starting wand at the last possible instant. This kind of a start will allow your feet to swing forward underneath your body within the next few yards.

Crossing the finish line.

A few yards before crossing the finish line, thrust your feet forward by flexing your knees and dropping your hips and torso backward. This will allow your lower legs to break the beam of the timing light while your body mass is still a foot or a foot and a half behind the finish line, thereby allowing you to pick up a few hundredths of a second.

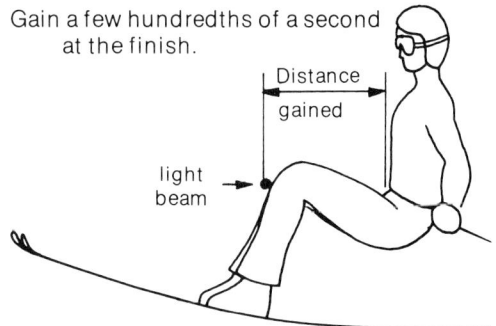

Gain a few hundredths of a second at the finish.

Distance gained

light beam

Giant slalom tactics.

Course inspection.

Course inspection should be approached seriously. You shouldn't attempt to memorize a map of the terrain but rather try to inscribe in your memory a film of the run you are about to make in this course. This film should star the gates, the terrain, the variations in snow and also the acceleration that will bring you with your skis flat into one series of gates, the gates you will hit and the gates you will turn widely around. Likewise, the speed checks that you must make before certain combinations of gates... You can even devise two versions of your race film; one that you will use if all goes well and the other a spare solution. With your program now well adjusted and verified by a few warm-up turns or wedeln near the course, you should be able to relax more confidently.

Warming up before the start.

An adequate warm-up is indispensable both for physiological reasons (greater muscular efficiency) and psychological reasons (preparation for action).

Concentration before the start.

The intense and solitary concentration which most great champions impose upon themselves before races and in particular during the few minutes preceeding the start has often been poorly interpreted. The supporters of relaxation techniques see this as some kind of meditation. This may be true for a few hyper-nervous individuals who need to find a few calm moments before the race. Nevertheless, most often the champions will use this period of concentration for intensification; to sharpen their senses and their will to win, a concentration of all of their physical, nervous and psychic powers toward the same goal.

If you very objectively recognize that it is unrealistic for you to race to win, you shouldn't consider your situation as being any different than the racer who races to win. If you want to progress, to achieve a performance that is good for you, you too must learn to concentrate yourself, to eliminate all negative thoughts — the difficulties of the slope, the risk of falling — and focus all of your powers on the test that is coming. This is part of competition.

Tactics are essential.

I have already mentioned (page 171) that you can become too caught up in the race. It is essential that you be alert and able to think clearly during the race. After a fall, for example, the good skier should be able to tell his coach precisely what happened. The coach must correct this analysis if it is mistaken. Far too often, young skiers are encouraged to believe that they will one day become champions by trying the impossible. They should be asked to only brush the impossible without going so far that they see failure more than once in every three or four competitions. I believe that they can be educated more effectively in this manner.

In the paragraphs above I already mentioned the imaginary movie of the race which the racer should create before his start. This movie should be adaptable. By observing the previous racers and listening to the comments of racers who have already run and/or coaches standing alongside the course, you can pick up valuable information with which to adjust your program, but do so only in moderation and with absolute certainty. Many racers have lost races because they changed their tactics at the last moment. Many others have lost because they were unwilling or unable to modify a tactic during the race and in the heat of the battle when it proved to be inappropriate.

Giant slalom training.

I don't address myself in these paragraphs to racers who are members of a team and already are involved in a rational training program.

THE LIMITS OF POSSIBILITY IN SLALOM.

Only a few years ago, a racer finding herself in the position **Perrine PELEN** is in in the fifth frame of the photomontage above, filmed during a slalom on a very steep slope, would inevitably have slipped away and lose all chance of victory. Today, the technique and physical power of the racers and the quality of their skis have pushed back the limits of possibility.

Perrine catches herself without skidding by applying all of her weight to her outside ski, allowing her to then step up to her uphill ski and achieve a better line for diving into the following turn.

A PLATFORM ON THE TAIL OF THE OUTSIDE SKI WITH A FORWARD THRUST OF THE FEET INTO THE TURN.

Klaus HEIDEGGER of Austria, one of the top-ranked giant slalom racers in the world in 1978, executes a platform at the end of a carved giant slalom turn to launch him into the next turn. Heidegger's ability to hold his line at the end of the turn is his greatest strength.

GIANT SLALOM TURNS REQUIRE BOTH TECHNIQUE AND POWER.

Klaus HEIDEGGER executes a giant slalom turn on irregular and difficult terrain. Did you know that the racer's legs have to withstand compressions that can exceed 450 pounds during the intermittent ricochets that constitute giant slalom turns ? Without exceptional strength, the racer isn't able to resist the pressure on his outside ski, an indispensable condition for precise control of his turns. Yet despite Heidegger's fierce determination as seen in his facial expression, his stance and movements are relaxed, permitting him to cultivate optimal gliding.

USING KNEE ANGULATION TO HOLD WITH THE OUTSIDE SKI.

In the 4 individual photos, one can see **Ingemar STENMARK** complete a turn on solid ice during the giant slalom of the last World Championships by using a progressive knee angulation to maintain the carving of his outside ski. In the photo-montage below, Stenmark's very brief knee angulation produces a rapid edge-set. Applied with tail-pressure, his knee angulation allows for maximum holding.

Giant slalom training should consist of both technical and athletic training.

The technical training should be made both in courses and during "technical" free skiing, that is during very fast free skiing with precise control of the trajectory and sliding of the skis. The proportion should vary from half free skiing and half gate training to ⅓ of one and ⅔ of the other depending on the circumstances. Your free ski training, just as your training in gates, should be made in all varieties of snow and terrain conditions possible. The search for technical improvement, particularly in the gates, should be made at speeds as close to maximum as possible (eg. short courses run in 31 or 32 seconds instead of the 30 second maximum speed). From time to time the maximum speed should be attempted or even surpassed — which will result in the skier not completing the course — in order to become familiar with the limit.

The athletic training can be made on the track, in the gymnasium or by very intense skiing in the gates or while free skiing. It's impossible to "go all out" while skiing as you can do by running 4 series of 400 yards around a track, but it is possible to completely fatigue the quadriceps and buttock muscles with a minute or a minute and a half of very intense skiing down a mogul field or in a course. For the weekend racer it is even more important to acquire good specific muscular conditioning than a general cardiac and circulatory system conditioning. It remains no less a truth that an ability to involve all of one's energy in one minute of intense effort is more effectively developed on a track than on a ski slope. Too many international racers and coaches seem to have forgotten this principle of training today...

Even if you are not a "professional" skier but can ski as much as you like, you can assure yourself of athletic training by skiing. You can alternate a series of 3, 4 or 5 intense runs of 30 seconds to 1 minute duration with isolated longer runs of 2 or 3 minutes. Before and after these intense 2 or 3 minute runs allow yourself to rest with 5, 10 or even 15 minutes of very relaxed skiing. Profit from the runs you make when fatigued to control any irregularity in your technique. In this way you can determine if various technical elements have become perfectly assimilated.

I will treat the subject of physical training a little later for those skiers who are even more involved in competition.

The role of the coach on race day.

A coach can play a fundamental, useful, useless or even harmful role depending on his level of competence.

Competition is first and foremost an activity of the individual skier. If the coach has prepared the athlete properly, the athlete should be able to assume all of his responsibilities on race day from the course inspection on.

Of course it's perfectly alright for the coach to bring particular details to the attention of the racer that have been overlooked, but it's only a hindrance if he spews out banalities and disturbs the racer's concentration. Yet the nervous racer usually loves that reassuring but useless rhetoric, that friendly presence.

During the minutes preceeding the start, the good coach speaks only when he has something important to say and when he is sure he is right. He might say, for example, "you can attack all out" or "take it easy in the second flush" or even "race to win". But this silence shouldn't stop the coach from offering as much material help as possible; particularly in preparing the equipment.

After the race, and while the racer is still feeling the effects of the competition, the coach can summarize the lessons to be drawn from the success or failure in just a few well-chosen words. This evaluation can result in a sharp reaction from the racer but usually will have a profound effect on him. It is better to extract a living, enriching lesson from a failure than to find the many different excuses which every racer is capable of inventing for himself — and run the risk of committing the same error in the next race...

IMPROVE IN SLALOM

Almost all the information which I have given you for giant slalom is valid for slalom.

I have emphasized giant slalom up to this point because the fact that competition is a veritable battle becomes more obvious through giant slalom than it does in slalom. Slalom can appear to be a simple exercise in virtuosity. However, if one approaches it from this point of view, nothing is accomplished. The idea that competition is a battle does not mean that the skier should attack the poles ! Not all combat is a fight to the death. A game of chess can also be a battle. It is the top international slalom racer's ability to combine audacity with caution, tactical sense, aggressiveness and touch that excites the experienced spectator.

How can the international racer be imitated ?

Slalom is not a mad dash to the finish line.

In spite of the fact that the International Ski Federation has increased the distance between poles in a slalom gate, and in spite of slalom course setters setting smoother, more open courses, it is still not possible for the racer to attack continuously at top speed. Excessive speed, which threatens to throw him out of certain portions of the course, remains the greatest problem facing the slalom racer today.

The most important characteristic of the slalom racer today is, therefore, the precision with which he is able to judge the maximum speed possible and with which he is able to remain in control. This precision requires a complete mastery of technique. Equally important are the sureness of his balance on the edge, the carved quality of his turns, the projection from one ski to the other, and sometimes the quick checks in speed which then allow him to "let his skis run".

Centrifugal force and lateral supports.

When one watches a top slalom racer from

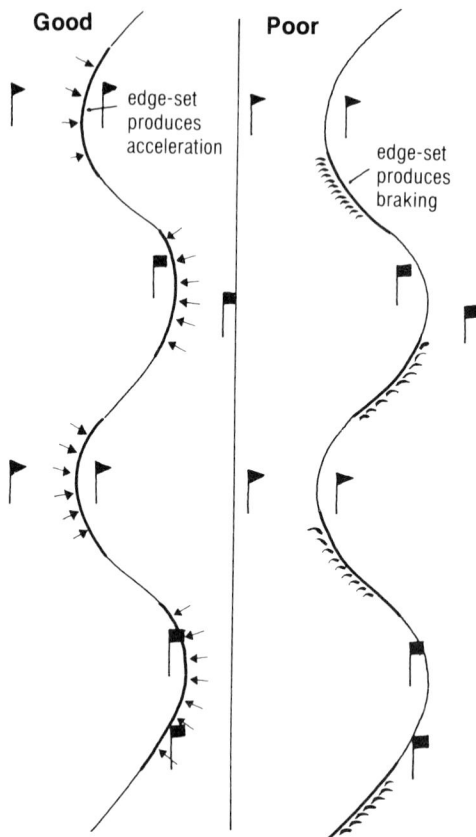

Good — edge-set produces acceleration

Poor — edge-set produces braking

Resisting centrifugal force.

The beginning slalom skier has a tendency to set his edges between the turns and to throw himself into the next turn, thereby compounding the lateral thrust of centrifugal force. He risks being thrown out of the course (left track).

On the other hand, the good slalom skier tries to hold onto the snow when he is in the fall line or even before and has consequently reduced his edge-set.

The excellent slalom skier is even able to retract his legs in the traverse, in effect using avalement at this precise moment. He is also able to accentuate his holding with a very dynamic edge-set when he is in the fall line or just as he leaves the fall line.

behind, it becomes obvious that he is essentially resisting centrifugal force, which tends to throw him laterally out of the course. He exerts the greatest pressure on his edges during the carved phase of the turn which occurs when his skis are farthest to the outside of the turn. In the extreme, it is possible to imagine the slalom racer projecting from "lateral support" to the opposite "lateral support", and eliminating all of the elements which normally occur between these phases of greatest pressure on the skis.

A mediocre slalom racer, on the other hand, sets his edges between turns, that is when his skis are closest to a horizontal traverse or when they are across his general direction of travel.

Certainly it would be difficult for you to progress directly from the former to the latter! However, you can begin to move in this direction by taking care to: 1) carve your turns as early as possible after their initiation; 2) exert greatest pressure on your skis earlier in the turn, before they are across your general direction of travel; 3) little by little, decrease these "lateral supports" each time you feel comfortable in a course and replace them with a lateral projection from one ski to the other.

An effective learning aid would consist of visualizing yourself projecting laterally from one ski to the other while continuing to face in the general direction of the line of the course. However, in competition this goal will be out of reach for you until you are skillful enough to control your speed precisely by delaying the lateral support by a few tenths of a second in order to accomodate the difficulties of the course and the terrain on which it is set.

The "best line".

There is no such thing as a single ideal line for any given slalom course. Depending on his physical ability, his technique and his temperament, each slalom racer has his own ideal line. On the other hand, there are lines through a course which could be called incorrect, or at least ineffective. It is not a question of a value judgement, but rather of an objective determination.

The best line through a slalom course for any given skier is the line which permits him a minimum loss of speed. Whereas one tends to believe that it is the shortest or most direct line.

The No. 1 error: aiming at the slalom poles.

The most common error in slalom is aiming at the slalom pole. The racer attempts to cut as closely as possible, even hitting it, and then to rapidly pivot his skis in order to dive into the upcoming pole.

First of all, this rapid pivoting of the skis slows them abruptly, unbeknownst to either the skier or the observer.

However, this slowing effect is very real.

In preparation for this slowing effect, the racer had to begin an inward lean so extreme as to unbalance him. As a result, regaining his balance during the edge-set becomes a risky chore and often results in an additional slowing effect as his skis chatter through the turn.

Do not confuse aiming at the slalom pole with the dive to the fall line.

In the discussion on turning techniques, I strongly emphasized the dive into the fall line which allows the skis to start into the turn without slowing down and which diminishes the need to resist centrifugal force. One simply takes advantage of the resultant of gravity which acts in the direction of the fall line. This passive plunge into the fall line should be used each time the radius of the turn is rather long, and when the difficulty of making the skis hold in the second part of the turn is reduced. However, take note. This dive results in a downhill arc. The skis are unweighted and you are in perfect balance. Conspicuously absent is the excessive inward lean which characterizes the previously described turn.

Economy of motion and balance.

These 2 traits are characteristic of the technique of the best slalom skiers in the world today. This observation has guided my technical analyses toward the study of balancing mechanisms. These mechanisms are so complex that I have lost any hope of working effectively at this level. However, I have come to the conclusion that certain technical voids are effectively filled thanks to my observations. Through an indirect approach, it is also possible to apply them practically. Thus, I have carefully avoided suggesting certain movements to my readers or have recommended that they be approached cautiously.

As a first example, let's return to our discussion of aiming at the slalom pole in slalom or giant slalom. Nine times out of ten this preparatory inward lean corresponds to the mechanism which I have termed the change of support foot (page 80). In suggesting this movement to my readers I described its disadvantages and how to avoid them, either by pivoting the outside ski and balancing on it or by spreading one's ski to the side and pivoting it. In the same manner, a slalom racer can not correct this error without bringing new and different balancing reflexes into play. Even a minimum lateral projection at the initiation of the turn will neutralize this excessive inward lean. Of course, this must involve a true lateral thrust and not simply a lifting of the inside ski, a peddling motion, which corresponds to an inward lean and change of support foot.

A second example is the use of forward lean and sideslipping in order to slow down. The skier loses his balance in such a forward lean position if the slowing effect of his skis is increased abruptly. If the pressure increases enough, the skier might even be thrown forward and into an uncontrollable mad dash through the slalom poles. Human balancing reflexes, as well as current ski design, result in a tendency toward incessant movement between the balance point and positions in which more or less pressure is exerted over the tails of the skis (117, 127, 135). This differs from the forward balancing position advocated in the past in many teaching methods.

In our third example, we will consider the need to exert pressure on the tails of the skis in order to make them hold at the end of the turn (pages 67, 138). In this manuever, the

knees and ankles are heavily flexed so that the position has sometimes been interpreted as one of forward lean ! This misinterpretation has occured to such an extent that I had to label what is in fact a balanced position, a position with "heel-pressure". At that time everyone was accustomed to seeing a foward lean position as a balanced position !

It has occured to you, perhaps, that I have been ignoring the concept of economy of motion. This is not at all the case. Economy of motion is the result of perfect balance. It is a goal and not a means. In order to attain it, one must construct a technique from the feet up. All the movements must be conditioned to create those mysterious forces which occur between the base of the ski and the snow and create turns. In this technique, more or less natural balancing reflexes result from the unstable human structure as it rides on sliding supports. If these conditions are met the skier can simultaneously attain economy of motion and effectiveness in slalom. This is true because slalom is an exercise in which the skier is exposed to a maximum number of outside constraints. His actions are responses to problems posed from the outside. There is no room for artificial movements which do not resolve the problems of maintaining balance.

This is why skiers who have learned to ski by themselves are often better prepared than those skiers whose techniques have been "constructed" by teaching methods which are not oriented toward competition.

Glissement

Glissement is, above all, an intention, a state of mind or a desire. "To want to ride a fast ski" is very different from the idea of "wanting to go fast" and even more different from the idea of "going all out". These last two forms of behavior imply the idea of doing something. The first, on the other hand, is more appropriately expressed in negative terms: to avoid slowing down. Contrary to what one might imagine, it requires just as much and perhaps even more aggressiveness on the part of the racer, but it is a contained aggressiveness that is perhaps even more ferocious than that displayed in an open brawl with the slalom poles.

Ingemar STENMARK demonstrates this kind of tranquil aggressiveness which seems to relate naturally to the relaxed muscular power of the shotputters of track and field.

Next to the psychological aspect of riding a fast ski is the technical. Glissement, flat ski leg action, riding a flat ski, carving through edge-sets and rebounds, avalement or absorption of abrupt increases in pressure and adaptation to constant changes in the relief of the terrain constitute the essence of the teaching methods presented in this book.

A few specific movements.

In slalom, one encounters the same types of movements as those in giant slalom, especially in the wider, looser turns, but the tempo is quicker and the rhythm more precise.

It would seem to be an inability to adapt to two different kinds of rhythm which prevents specialists of one of the two disciplines from performing successfully in the other. A lack of quickness can constrain the giant slalom specialist in slalom just as the tendency to react too quickly can impede slalom specialists in giant slalom.

• *Standard turns adapted to the snow conditions, traverses, carved turns with lateral projection, turns with forward thrust of the feet, turns with cramponnage with the inside ski: see the chapter on giant slalom.*

• *Flushes: surf technique, flat ski and carved.*

Currently the best technique in these gate combinations is the surf technique. The skis are used with a reduced edge angle or carved with a greater edge angle with movement from one ski to the other or carved on both skis or with rebound from one carved edge-set to another. These movements are described at length on pages 142 through 156 and (534) to (537).

I would like to make a clarification at this point regarding flat ski surf technique. In competition, taking into account the in-

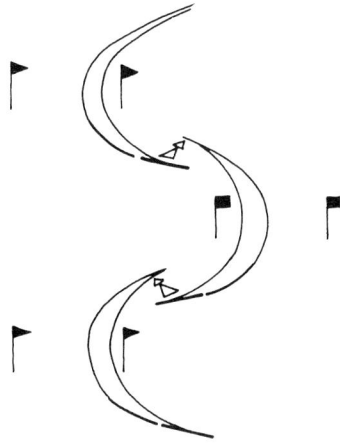

Steep slopes
Round turns

A pole plant and lateral projection make it possible to execute the turns by placing the skis in the turn. The skis, therefore, follow a rounder path than the trajectory of the center of mass.

Fall line turns
Flat slopes

By projecting laterally from one ski to the other, you can modify the arc of your turns until your skis are effectively sliding straight down the axis of the course. This is not possible when carving on the tails of the skis at the moment of the projection or while steering long turns.

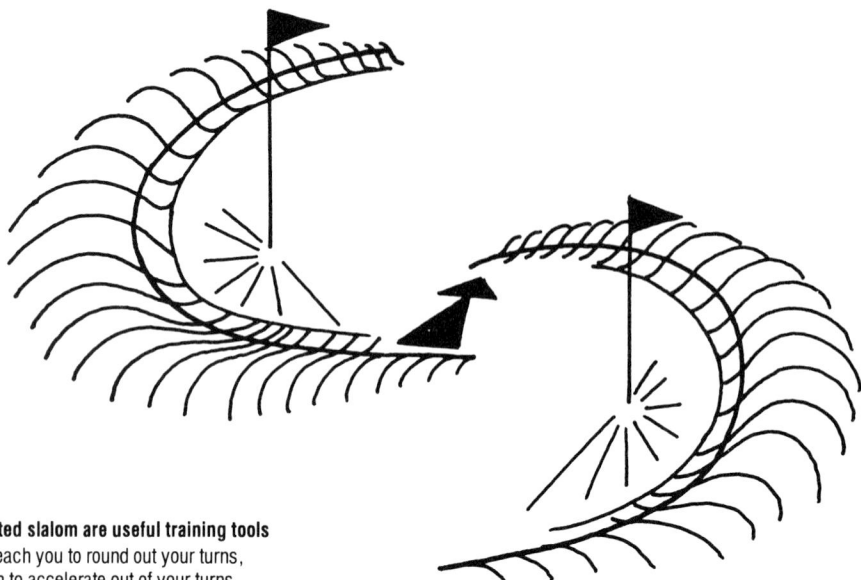

Very rutted slalom are useful training tools
• They teach you to round out your turns,
• to learn to accelerate out of your turns,
• to use avalement between the turns in order to absorb the bump which always seperates 2 ruts,
• to combine lateral projection and avalement to gain a few hundredths of a second.

creased effect of centrifugal force and the quality of the snow which is always packed hard even when it is powder snow, there can be no question that the "outward displacement" of the knees is simply a diminished inward pushing of the knees resulting from independent action by the feet, knees and hips.

Furthermore, surf technique in slalom, even on soft snows, is never performed with the skis perfectly "flat". The skis are relatively flat at the beginning of the turn which is then finished with a slight carving on the back half of an edged outside ski (page 156).

It seems that some talented young international ski racers have begun to use the surf technique in a slightly higher stance (537 d).

• *Quick, complete turns with avalement-deploiement.*

If one considers the slalom skier as being alternately displaced from one side of the axis of the slalom to the other while con-

tinually facing down the axis of the slalom, it's possible to develop a special understanding of the instant when the racer passes from one side to the other.

In this phase, the skis are slowed because they are placed somewhat across the fall line and the skier is compressed and unbalanced in a manner similar to that which occurs when skiing over a bump.

The solution would then be to avoid this phase of the traverse. In fact, this is what slalom racers do, at least partially, thanks to avalement. However, even the best slalom racers can not do so 100%. They are not exerting maximum pressure on their skis when the skis are headed straight down the fall line in the middle of the turn, but at the earliest possible moment during the finish of the turn. From this base of support they "retract" their legs while maintaining their balance on their ski pole which is planted downhill and thus avoid the phase between the two turns in which the skis are slowed. They absorb, so to speak, the "bump" which exists between the two turns and which I have already described. Carried on by their speed and acted upon by gravity, they plunge into the following turn and must un- fold their bodies, extending their feet down- ward in order to renew contact with the snow which falls away under their feet (again just as if they had crossed over a bump). This renewal of contact with the snow in an ex- tended body position slightly angulated with the outside leg pivoted in order to carve early in the turn relates to the movement described in turns with a forward thrust of the feet.

Gliding wedeln without platforms

(1) A medium or tight gliding wedeln with flat skis, both skis weighted and without perceptible pivoting of the skis. Preferably a surf wedeln.

(2) the same in a longer wedeln with a very light edging of the back half of the outside ski at the end of the turn.

(3) With tail carving and exclusive weighting of the out- side ski. Eventually surf carving.

Slalom training

Because slalom seems to be a rather acrobatic discipline, one might conclude that the young slalom racer, like the gymnast, should practice as much as possible, or in other words should run as many gates as possible.

A great deal of slalom training can be done outside the gates. However, this kind of

Use wedeln to prepare for slalom

Wedeln with platforms

(4) Rebounds from carved platforms on the outside ski with tail-pressure. Ultimately surf platforms.

(5) Check wedelns with carved platforms on steep slopes.

(6) The same with a transfer from one ski to the other.

Note: All of these wedelns can be used in rutted slaloms.

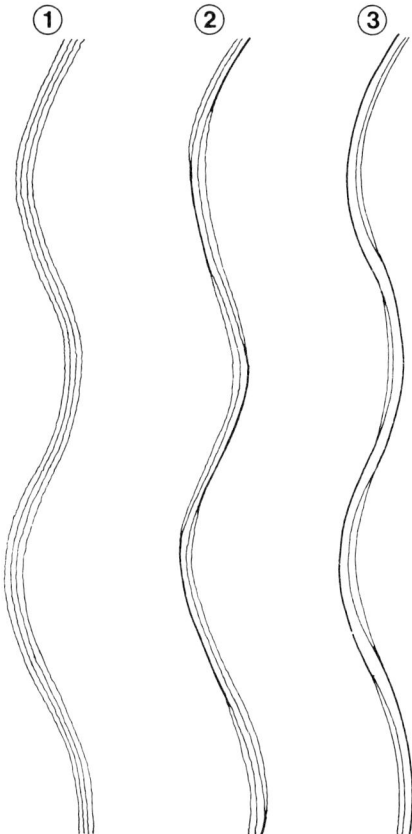

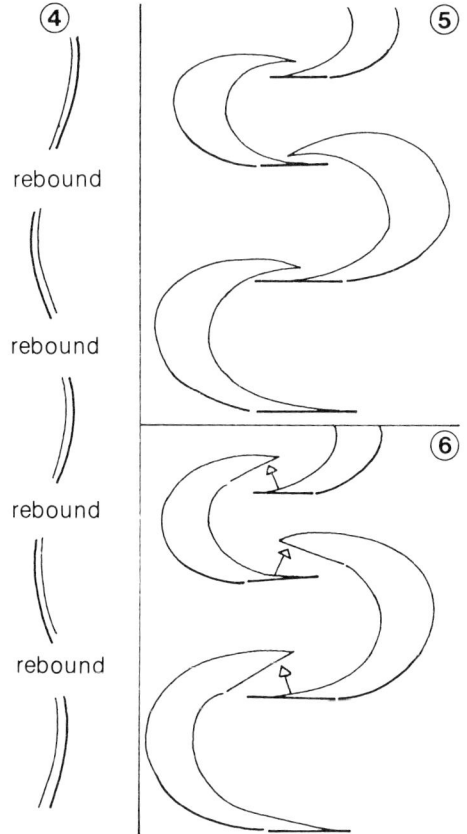

training can often be of little value.

The essential quality of the training session is the spirit in which it is approached. However it is not simply the quality of aggressiveness which is important, as many coaches seem to think. Equally important is the systematic approach to the development of observation, deduction, movements and behavior during your successes as well as your failures.

Among slalom racers who dominated the international circuit in past years, there were two groups — the super talented and the super workers. Today the super talented are no longer able to dominate unless they are capable of a systematic and intelligent as well as hard-working approach to training.

As a result, the task of the coach has become very much more difficult! Oh the happy days when it was enough to ski 5,000 more slalom gates than the others in order to be better than them. In order to be successful today one must not only work but work more intelligently than the opposition!

Your problem certainly doesn't correspond to that of the top international racers but be aware that it is very similar. The aspect of quality in your training is just as important as the aspect of quantity. Also be aware that the only way to withstand large doses of gate training is to become interested in technique. Many young international ski racers today have acquired an attitude common to professional athletes. They complain of being "stale" whereas their real problem is one of disinterest. Future slalom racers will train more and better than those of today. This fact is obvious to those who are familiar with the intensity of training common among other and older technical sports, sports which have developed to a higher level of sophistication than ski racing.

• *All of my comments concerning giant slalom training remain valid for slalom training.*

I will only add a few thoughts concerning the quickness and tempo of the turns.

• *Quickness is an essential characteristic of the slalom racer.*

Quickness includes reaction time, which is hereditarily determined and subject to little if any improvement, but also other characteristics which can be improved:

1). The first is the ability to understand the nature of the obstacle to be overcome and to determine the best solution to the problem. Training improves this ability but only if the racer concentrates and makes the effort to learn from his successes and failures. The racer must be faced with as many varied situations as possible. He must be called upon to improvise, that is to react spontaneously (courses should be changed frequently and set in such a manner as to provide unusual problems).

2). Quickness also includes the ability to react rapidly and effectively with a large number and variety of motor skills. Without a rich technical development the skier relies on mechanisms which are less appropriate to given situations and therefore slower. One means of creating this richness other than the systematic study of the many types of movements such as those presented in this book results from systematically varying the training courses as much as possible. I would also like to emphasize the fact that it is necessary to then practice repeatedly the same types of situations so that it is no longer necessary to improvise 100% each time. I know that some technical experts won't agree with my opinion but it is my practical on-slope experience as a coach which has led me to this conclusion. I have also found agreement with this opinion among fencing coaches, and fencing is a technical sport which has evolved over several centuries.

3). Coordination, which is the ability to link movements together smoothly, is considered by many to be a characteristic that is improved by participating in a large variety of activities and sports whereas others believe that it can only be improved in a specific sport. There undoubtedly is some truth in both of these opinions, but I believe that the frequency of balancing reflexes occuring simultaneously with other motor skills requires that coordination in skiing be developed by practicing the greatest possible variety of snow conditions, terrain and courses. Good coordination results in a relaxation of the inactive muscles and this relaxation is a key factor in quickness.

4). Finally, quickness requires a state of mind that results from concentration but also intuition and a taste for risk taking.

• *When should you try to be quick ?*

You should always be working to develop quickness. In free skiing, for example, make 2 or 3 ultra-quick turns when the terrain allows you to do so. You can do the same thing in a slalom course, for example when an easy flush allows you to link a few quick turns together even though you may have to check your speed immediately afterwards.

But be careful ! Don't confuse the concept of quickness with aggressiveness. A desire to attack the course often results in the racer being too "harsh". Quickness, on the other hand, is more closely related to riding a flat ski. You can more easily succeed in being quick in three or four sections of a course if you take them at a slightly slower speed rather than at your very limit.

You will improve your speed as you improve your technique, that is the linking together of your movements or, more briefly, your coordination. It is the improvement of coordination which is the greatest benefit of this type of practice.

The varying tempos of running gates.

You must not systematically try to link your turns together at the highest possible tempo when you're practicing slalom.

First of all, the attempt to increase acceleration of the tempo does not always result in a gain in time. I have proven this fact a thousand times to racers during training.

In attempting to ski in a very quick rhythm you make small technical errors which slow your skis. Even if you have gained one second, the slowing effects can represent a loss of as much as two seconds.

In addition, you have not been able to concentrate on correcting your bad habits.

On the other hand, if you devote a portion of the year, for example the summer, or a few runs at the beginning of a session of training to eliminating bad habits and developing an ability to ride a fast ski, you can then benefit from an attempt to develop a maximal tempo.

You should even push to the very limit of your quickness in order to become very familiar with your limits.

Tactics in slalom

Recall the points I made concerning giant slalom.

When racing slalom, it is perhaps even more important to avoid taking risks than it is when racing giant slalom. However, this requires a precise knowledge of your limits and a long and difficult development of the ability to judge your performance to within a second of your maximum. One second is only 0.8 to 1% of the total time spent in a slalom course, but it is a margin easily judged by an intelligent slalom racer who is trained with this goal in mind. It is just the correct amount of margin to permit him to eliminate the risks of the more dangerous or difficult sections of the course. In fact, the regular winners in top international slalom competition are those who race at a pace just under their maximum. To be convinced of this fact it is enough to watch them in the second run of a slalom in which they are behind by a greater margin than they like. The fact that slalom and giant slalom races are held in two runs presents a difficult tactical problem. Except for the top champions, whom I mentioned above, each run should be treated in the same manner. If you are very slow in a first run, you can try to ski at the limit of your ability in the second. However, if you are only able to finish one out of 4 or 5 runs you are trying to go to fast. You are overestimating your abilities and it is more likely that you will become discouraged than you will succeed in the brilliant fashion to which you aspire.

Many young racers have destroyed their careers in precisely this way.

DOWNHILL

Even though it remains the king of ski competition, downhill is becoming less and less a pastime of the average skier. It even seems as if downhill is gradually becoming a "sports spectacle" which prohibits rather than encourages participation. I deplore this because downhill represents speed, sliding in the purest state and in a way the very essence of true skiing whereas the linking of braked turns is only a charicature of skiing.

It is unfortunately true that the good amateur skier who would like to get a taste of speed must contend today with crowded slopes, moguls that tend to appear within hours and slope etiquette — the amateur who skis at 30 miles per hour is considered a dangerous nut — and occasionally even the skis themselves since it is much more difficult to schuss at higher speeds on compact or intermediate skis or excessively soft skis.

It seems paradoxical that good skiers tend to frequent the steeper slopes and more difficult terrain over which it is impossible to experiment with speed. It has become almost childish to ski on the wide flat or intermediate slopes where speeds of 60 miles per hour can be handled without danger, even by intermediate skiers.

A few racing oriented ski areas have attempted without success to close off downhill stadiums for tourists. But in order to be taken seriously, these stadiums are often too steep. For such slopes to be safe, the trails must be perfectly maintained and groomed resulting in prohibitively high cost. Likewise, the steady increase in the number of skiers and the resultant overcrowding of the slopes prohibits a slope being reserved exclusively for downhill unless enough skiers would appear to take advantage of it. For the moment at least, this is extremely improbable.

Then must the notion of proposing downhill for the tourist skier be abandoned ? No, absolutely not ! Because before experiencing true downhill, one must first experience speed, schusses, long slopes skied non-stop from top to bottom at high speed, for example during the morning or evening when the crowds have diminished. The joy that can be obtained merits the few sacrifices that have to be made to acquire the minimum indispensable technical baggage.

This technical baggage is very similar to that of the World Cup downhill stars who you see on television.

BEGIN DOWNHILL

How do you learn to accept speed ?

99 times out of 100, it is the subconscious refusal to accept speed that results in a fall.

Every skier has his own individual speed threshold which, when passed, will create anxiety. This is more than a simple fear in that it leads to a contraction or blocking of the muscles, to a numbness in the legs, a loss of balance, and an abandonment of the fight...

This reaction is natural. At high speed, without the protection of the frame of an automobile, a crash can be dangerous. But you must be willing to accept the challenge to be convinced !

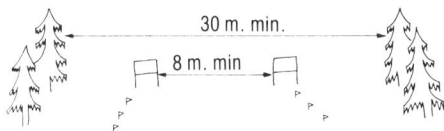

30 m. min.

8 m. min

The Downhill Course

Downhill gates have red panels on mens' courses and alternating red and blue panels on womens' courses. Their purpose is to orient the skier's trajectory and occasionally to oblige him to check his speed to insure his safety. The character of the downhill is determined, therefore, more by the features of the terrain than by the placement of the gates. For safety considerations, downhill trails must be approved before competitions can be organized on them by meeting a number of criteria relating to, among other things, the width of the trail, the vertical drop and length, terrain features and the proximity of obstacles or other dangers.

Downhill competitions sanctioned by the United States Ski Association must have vertical drops of at least 400 meters for both men and women with a maximum vertical drop of 1,000 meters for men and 700 meters for women. International downhill races must have minimum vertical drops of 500 meters and major international competitions for men (eg. World Cup, FIS Championships, Olympic Games) must have minimum vertical drops of 800 meters. These races are generally run in times of from 1 minute 45 seconds to 2 minutes 30 seconds.

Become familiar with the "terminal velocity".

Are you aware that you will not continue to accelerate indefinitely on a slope with a constant pitch ? You will quickly attain a certain speed and then plateau. Pulled down the slope by gravity but slowed to an equal extent by the resistance of the air, you will move at a constant speed. This speed will diminish or increase if the slope flattens or becomes steeper, but you will then attain a new terminal velocity. As you stand more erect, this terminal velocity will decrease but the more you crouch down the more it will increase (see page 93).

This constant terminal velocity is a sensation which you should fully explore: it will give you greater confidence. Of course you should first experience it on flat then intermediate slopes but soon become aware that it will not increase proportionally with the steepness of the slope (the air resistance increases as the square of the speed).

You should also discover that, contrary to a widely held opinion, one must not lean forward to resist the thrust of the air as the speed increases (211). Perhaps this idea evolved to encourage the kind of relaxation in the chest and the arms which one must have to slice through the air like the wings of an airplane ?

Learn to adjust your state of mind.

If your technique allows you to maintain your balance at 60 or 75 miles per hour, your brain must not disturb the functioning of your body and your movements. As you accumulate mileage, you will be able to eliminate these negative reactions but you can do better.

The desire to go faster will help you to become accustomed to the speed. For example, on a speed trial track, where there are several start points and over which your speed is clocked for 100 or 150 meters, you have attained a speed of 60 or 75 miles per hour. Rather than starting right away from a higher take-off point, make numerous runs from the same start point, always trying to go faster. *Just by wanting to go faster, you will gain 5, 10 or even 15 miles per hour.* Finding a more positive attitude is a far surer way of avoiding negative reactions.

The support of a group will help you to accept speed.

You will be able to surpass your limits by skiing behind a friend, provided that he doesn't blind you with the snow flying off of his edges. But you should then ski in front of him to discover a new kind of stimulation. Then you should attack alone...

A rivalry among the members of a group to go faster and faster can play a positive role within certain limitations. Afterward, there will be an introversion, a refusal. Therefore, you should know how to select your group.

Take advantage of the days or hours when you are optimistic and sure of yourself. Top speeds are often achieved in the runs immediately after a good meal in one of the restaurants at the top of the slopes where one is bathed in sun, pure air and sometimes a well chilled wine...

203

DOWNHILL POSITIONS:

UPRIGHT

SEATED CROUCH

LOW SEATED
OR "ROUND" POSITION

Have a solid technique which can be adapted to high speed.

The specific advice that I can give you regarding downhill will not necessarily permit you to modify your technique for high speed skiing. On the contrary, a good deal of the information that I discussed for good or intermediate skiers will permit you to acquire the basic elements indispensable to balance at high speed. Here, I believe we find some of the most interesting aspects of the evolution of ski technique with regard to sliding.

The essential technical elements seem to be:

The gentle control of flat skis.

This implies, of course: a wide or semi-wide stance, relaxed feet, a clear distribution of pressure on the ball and heel of the foot, and lateral mobility of the knee.

The "modern" position.

A stance with the ankles straight and the chest tilted slightly forward should help you to relax your feet. This stance also prepares you for the flexion-avalement and a supple movement of your feet forward and backward under your body.

Your arms should be spread wide in front of your for better balance and you should

lean slightly into the wind with your chest and arms to balance the pressure of the air.

Modern flexion and the flexion-avalement.

All of the compressions and shocks on your skis as they slide across the snow should be absorbed: your skis should be able to freely deflect upward in front of your body with your knees climbing up toward your torso and your chest and arms moving forward to retain your balance.

The forward-backward mobility of your feet under your body.

This kind of leg action is developed from your first balance reflexes and your most elementary leg action. In prior times, turns involved gross forward or backward movements of the upper body mass which were too slow and imprecise and which seriously compromised good balance. If you have followed our advice, your balancing mechanisms are constructed beginning from your feet and their movements relative to the mass of your body. You are, therefore, capable of instantaneously neutralizing any situation which throws you out of balance.

The dive down the slope and the directional effect of the skis.

THE AERODYNAMIC POSITION: THE "EGG"

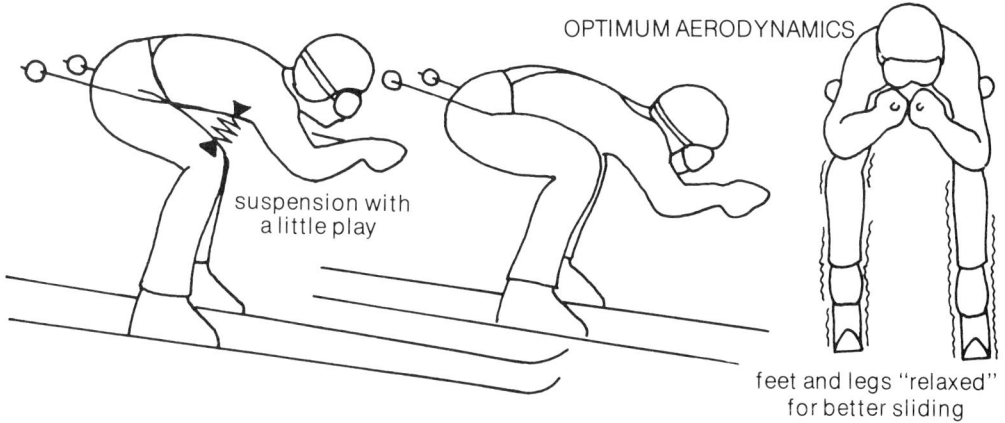

OPTIMUM AERODYNAMICS

suspension with
a little play

feet and legs "relaxed"
for better sliding

I'm not refering to what we spoke of before as "piloting" your turns because at high speeds you should use your skis to "negotiate" the arc of your turns rather than try to impose it. This is a very fundamental nuance of behavior of high speed skiing and explains why some giant slalom experts are only mediocre in downhill or vice versa.

The habit of always diving down the fall line will permit you to prolong your turns as you need whereas many apprentice downhillers always turn too short. You should eventually get into the habit of drawing out the ends of your turns without trying to hold excessively with your edges which would cause you to slow down. This constitutes an essential difference in the techniques of downhillers and of giant slalom skiers.

The "egg" position.

The egg position is an aerodynamic position. It gives the skier the best opportunity to penetrate the air. It diminishes the vertical mobility of the legs but still allows for smooth flexion and extension movements and a forward and backward displacement of the feet.

It is in this position where many skiers learn to maintain their balance over terrain variations or during sudden decelerations by adjusting the position of their feet under their body.

The only inconvenience — and occasional danger — of this position is that it limits the amount of flexion that is possible to adjust for bumps or other obstacles in the terrain. It is often impossible for a skier in an egg position to absorb some bumps without transmitting excessive pressure to the tips of his skis which, therefore, results in poor sliding. This fault becomes more serious when the skier has stiff boots.

The skier must learn to stretch out while approaching a bump so that he may immediately flex by dropping his hips into what I have called the "round" position.

The "seated-flexion" and the "round" position.

The "round" position is a position that is assumed momentarily to absorb terrain features. You have already experienced this position if you have followed our advice for skiing in bumps. It is derived directly from what we have called the passive flexion-avalement and active flexion-avalement used to absorb bumps in a schuss or during long turns (page 93). Nevertheless, the technique is somewhat different at higher speeds due to the distinctly different balance problems.

— First of all, you must learn to let your knees climb up in front of your body by simultaneously flexing your hips and lower back in such a way that your back, your buttocks and hamstrings form a perfectly rounded silhouette. This is to prevent you from leaning back excessively.

— When passing over a bump or the edge of a drop-off at high speed, there must be a very sharp change in the rhythm of the flexion-extension. The flexion should be quick and dynamic and the flight and extension for the landing should be slow. You all have seen the long flights of the downhill champion Bernard RUSSI in a perfect "round" position with his knees glued to his chest and his skis always held parallel to the profile of the slope.

What are the advantages of the round position ?

The round position doesn't give better aerodynamics. It is merely the outcome of a forward thrust of the feet which is somewhat different and which I have called "seated-flexion". The objective is to avoid an excessive weighting of the skis and particularly the shovel of the skis while crossing over a bump.

Then why is this position used over drop-offs which are not preceeded by a bump ? Simply because the accomplished skier, upon approaching the transition to a drop-off, stands slightly then flexes so that his center of mass follows a more even and rounder trajectory than that of the ground. Relative to the trajectory of the skier's center of mass, the drop-off represents a genuine bump. The skier absorbs it by allowing his skis to climb up in front of his body or by retracting his legs quickly, a gesture that is related to what used to be called a "pre-jump" but is less brutal because one no longer finds such pronounced terrain features on downhill courses today as before. The skier flies through the air in a round position and continues the forward banking of his chest begun during the take-off to maintain himself in a position which will permit a perfectly balanced landing. This landing is made by stretching the legs forward and down in order to absorb the

SEATED FLEXION FOR ABSORBING A BUMP

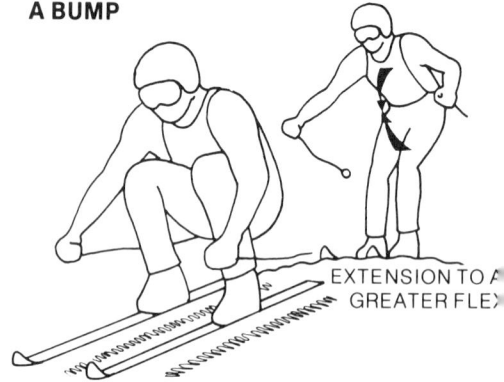

EXTENSION TO A GREATER FLEX

compression of the landing and maintain the skier's balance.

Avoid two common mistakes.

Don't automatically assume the egg position.

As soon as many skiers start to slide in a schuss, they automatically assume an egg position with their hands in front of their nose. They believe they use the egg position to go faster, but in reality the wider stance, limited ankle flexion and forward-backward mobility of the feet make them feel more stable. What is absurd, however, is that they don't feel at ease in any position between their basic stance and the egg. Consequently, they are unable to use the wind check: the best technique for slowing down. This is why one often sees inexperienced skiers use the egg... and the snowplow. You should feel perfectly at ease in all of the positions intermediate between the modern high position and the egg. This will allow you to adapt your stance to brake with the air as much as you need to as well as to the size of the bumps to be absorbed.

You should also be aware that your stance in a high position should only be semi-wide. As you assume a lower position, your stance should become progressively wider.

Avoid blocking movement in your joints.

A stocky, short skier who is accustomed to skiing in a low position can hold a schuss by more or less blocking the degree of articulation in his joints. But he soon reaches his limits, and his subsequent fall will be hard.

This skier, moreso than others, must learn to ski in a higher, more relaxed position so that he can supply absorb the terrain and prevent himself from blocking his body which is a solution only in very extreme cases.

Refine 4 defensive weapons.

You won't dare to go fast until you have learned to master speed.

• I have already mentioned that learning to ski at high speed in an upright position is indispensable. This allows for an *aerodynamic braking* which is very effective because it lowers the terminal velocity by as much as 10 to 25 miles per hour. This braking technique isn't as easy as you might expect. You must get used to it.

• *In downhill, as in all other circumstances, a check made before a turn is usually preferable to a check made during a turn.*
Nevertheless this isn't always true. The ability to slow down during a turn is indispensable in downhill.

• *Learn how to use tail-pressure to slow down during a turn.*
This is only possible if you don't "bank" your turns. I remind you that banking is an excessive inward lean during the turn. Only when you feel perfectly balanced throughout your turns can you slow down by pivoting your skis a little bit more and placing more weight on the tails of your skis which will increase the compression that results from your speed and the centrifugal force generated by your turns.
If you master this braking technique, you will only be able to use it at the beginning of the turn in order to then slide better if the turn leads onto a long flat.

• *Learn how to make a hockey stop by quickly steering your skis across a narrow course.*
Learn the hockey stop by starting from a schuss on a smooth slope. Pivot your skis rapidly across the slope and edge them in a very wide stance to stop as quickly as possible along the axis of the slope. This is the most effective way to stop quickly on a narrow slope. Repeat this manuever hundreds of times because it gives you a considerable guarantee of safety. Unfortunately, however, it is ineffective on bumpy terrain. I don't recommend the braking snow plow to all of my readers because in the last few years I have noticed that only a few very skilled skiers are able to use it successfully to slow down, whereas the majority can quickly learn the hockey stop.

Where and when should you start downhill ?

There are 3 different kinds of training.

Schuss as often as you can.
This is easy to do because the steep walls are usually followed by flats. The flats allow you to carry the speed generated by your schuss and cultivate gliding.

When the steep slopes are mogulled, use the edges of the run which are generally smoother and have softer snow, or start straight down the bumps in a very upright position, swallowing them as long as you can, and ultimately ricochet off the tops of the bumps. Little by little you will extend your possibilities.

Make one or two long turns down a wall and end in a schuss.
Start by gradually arcing a schuss that you have already made several times into one long curve. Then, starting from a traverse, pick up speed and let gravity pull you down the slope to finish in a schuss as above. Next, make a big 'S' which ends in a schuss. The fact that you can always recover by diving straight down the slope will give you confidence.

Occasionally, when the slopes are un-crowded, run the entire length of an easy slope.

You have already skied down the most direct line of this trail section by section. You know it well. You know exactly where to ski, taking into account the snow, the terrain and the places where other skiers usually stop. Nevertheless, you must be alert, because arriving at places where you usually stopped, you will very likely see mild bumps or drop-offs suddenly become nasty. This is unimportant because it is evident that you are about to experience a new adventure. You will run a few risks but you will be repaid over a hundred times by the few minutes of intense skiing which you are going to experience !

If you have followed the advice that I have given throughout this book; if you have learned to feel and react with your feet and legs, if your technique respects the fundamental principles of balance, you will rapidly become an accomplished downhiller and you will gain confidence for every circumstance you encounter.

IMPROVE YOUR DOWNHILL

I can't pretend to cover here, in a few pages, the problems posed by elite downhill competition regarding courses, racing psychology, technique, equipment, training and/or the influence of the enrionment. I regret this because the subject is fascinating. I therefore will only skim over a few of these problems.

Accumulate hundreds of miles of training.

• As I discuss in the last part of this book, the balancing mechanisms of skiing and the transmission of the thrusts from the ski-snow contact constitute the essence of the technique of a skier. The regulation of these balancing mechanisms imply constant micro-adjustments; particularly at 50, 60 or 80 miles per hour. Finesse in these balancing adjustments is only attained through thousands or millions of repetitions under the most varied conditions.

• I will recall the use of weights to train the downhiller, but it must be remembered that through 20 to 30 miles of downhill training each day, the racer is training himself for the specific effort which the low downhill position requires.

• The profound adaptation of human behavior to the world of high speed skiing, with its phases of weightlessness and then extreme compression, with its slow motion and then rapid rhythm, requires living as much as possible in this new environment.

• All of this represents less a matter of gestural technique than of responses adapted to the demands of the slope. To the contrary, it is evident today that the basic position of the downhiller, the position from which the responses appear, plays a fundamental role. This is a position which we called the "modern" position when we proposed it to beginning skiers. Nevertheless, it isn't surprising that the same problems confront these two extreme categories of skiers because the essential problems for both are balance and the quality of gliding.

Eliminate all unnecessary braking

I have insisted throughout this book on the elimination of braking. I will emphasize it even more here.

In a schuss: 1) by standing over the point of the ski which allows the best compromise between sliding and directional stability, a point that is slightly behind the normal

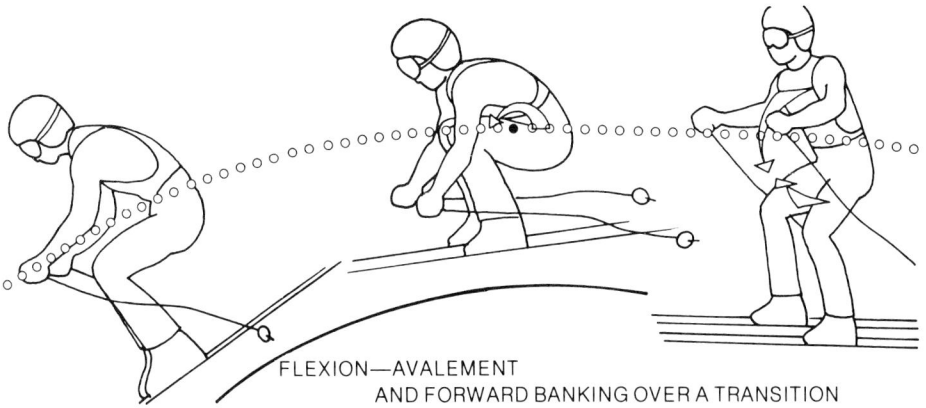

FLEXION—AVALEMENT
AND FORWARD BANKING OVER A TRANSITION

pressure point; 2) by relaxing as much as possible the muscles of the ankle and feet so that the ski is free to move in every plane; 3) by keeping the lower legs as supple and independent as possible so that the smallest ripple in the terrain can move one or both skis with minimum resistance; 4) by moving the feet forward or backward as required to maintain balance without producing even the slightest amount of pressure against the tongue or back of the boot and therefore on the tip or tail of the ski; 5) by flexing and extending vertically as much as possible to ab-

sorb the compressions produced by the terrain.

Turn with flat skis or with carving. I have already mentioned the desired progressiveness of the initiation of the turn, of the smooth dive down the fall line, of holding the skis in the line of the turn, of prolonging the compression and the carving at the end of the turn, and of the accelerating dive into the following traverse. I attach importance, however, to only one peculiarity of the downhill turn.

Carving turns with "ricochets" at high speeds.

The term "carving" is less appropriate when applied to downhill turns where the skier, constantly striving for optimum sliding, tries to give as much liberty to his skis as possible. Nevertheless, in shorter turns on hard snow, there is carving.

Unless the slope is exceptionally smooth, this carving is never as regular as that made in giant slalom. This is for 2 reasons which have an accumulative effect:

— During the control of a carved turn, the overloading created by centrifugal force is absorbed entirely by the muscles instead of being dissipated by the skis scraping away against the snow. The skier absorbs this extraordinary compression with the muscles of the thigh, the buttocks and the lower back when carving at speeds of 50, 60 or even 80 miles per hour. Compressions as great as 550 pounds have been measured. These muscular contractions can only be maintained for several seconds and only with great difficulty.

— At very high speeds, and because of the overloading mentioned, the slightest ripple on the ground produces a spring board effect and the racer ricochets over the snow instead of carving continuously. These carving ricochets undoubtedly account for the extreme compressions which have been measured.

Carved ricochets require of the skier:

1) A perfect forward-backward balance to prevent any banking movement as the skis leave the ground. Some giant slalom specialists, who are accustomed to carving with a slight tail-pressure, have difficulty remaining in balance in downhill.

2) A perfect lateral balance with almost exclusive weighting of the downhill ski and with supple angulation in order to position the weighted ski precisely where it must be to begin carving again after each ricochet.

3) Considerable power and flexibility. At the rate of several such ricochets per second, the skier must absorb an impressive compression during each one through a flexion

turning with carved "ricochets"

movement and then extend supply to regain contact and then resist again. A lack of sufficient power will result in the skier blocking his joints instead of flexing to absorb them and result in harsh braking and poorer sliding.

A major mistake committed by many coaches is to avoid training in the kinds of terrain which will prepare the skier for this kind of carving: slightly bumpy courses or

Supple extension at the beginning of a turn

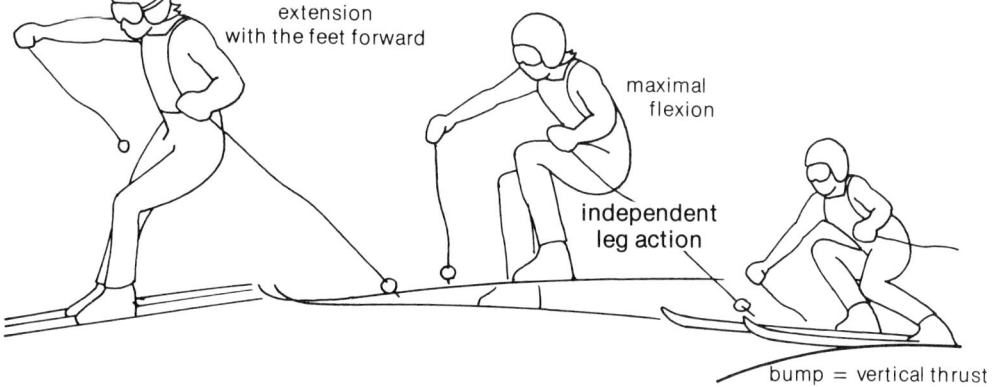

extension
with the feet forward

maximal
flexion

independent
leg action

bump = vertical thrust

large turns which are already rutted. It is often better to ski at 50 miles per hour over such terrain than at 60 or 75 miles per hour over a course that is too smooth.

The essential element of downhill turns: weighting the outside ski.

Nothing in theory is simpler than weighting the outside ski. In reality, nothing is more difficult. The speed and the chattering of the skis tend to cause the skier to bank to the inside of the turn; or at least to weight both skis. It is only through constant effort that you will succeed in the supple angulation and relaxed arms which will allow you to remain balanced over your out-

side ski in an upright as well as in a low position.

Turning in an egg position.

By simply tilting the outside ski onto edge in a wide stance, it is possible to turn on very smooth slopes in the egg position. A higher position is recommended as soon as the terrain has slight undulations or ripples.

Take advantage of every acceleration.

Avoiding every unnecessary braking is all very fine but is, today, insufficient for downhill racing at the international level.

To be among the best, one must want to go faster, want to slide better.

Controlling the turn
with tail-pressure and flat skis

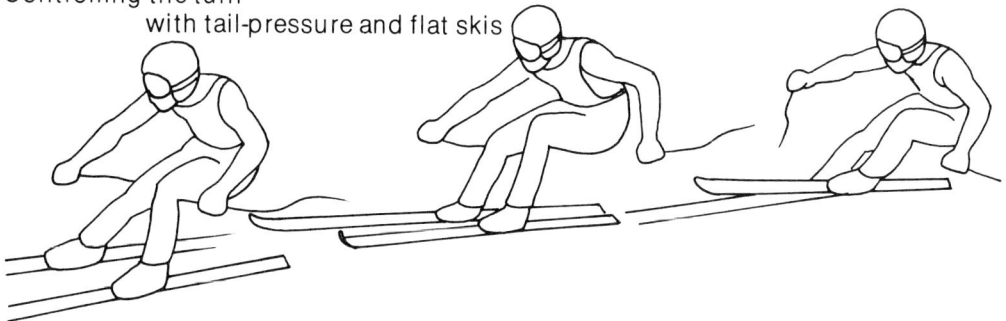

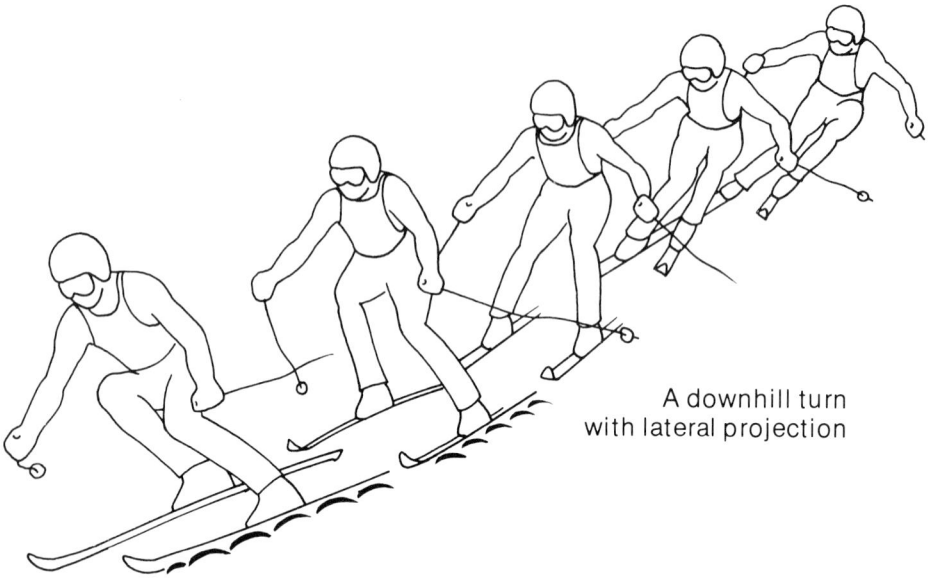

A downhill turn
with lateral projection

How can one best use gravity, the only motor force of the downhiller ? How can one improve his performance by using the best line, by eliminating all checks ? I don't think that the answer can be given by mechanics. Then by a highly skilled downhiller ? Unfortunately no, because no more than the creative artist can the champion clearly analyze what he does.

I am going to present you with a theory born from observations of the greatest champions, and with conversations with some of them or with their trainers.

— First of all, it is more or less evident today that the braking produced by a sudden but slightly brutal overloading is greater than the braking produced by the increased air friction that results from skiing in a slightly higher position but which allows for a more progressive loading of the skis.

— The downhill racer perceives the systematic and subconscious extension to prepare for a prolonged and voluntary flexion as an accelerating dive down the fall line.

— This dive is experienced at every drop-off and at the beginning of every turn down the fall line. It also allows the skier to absorb

certain bumps and to displace certain pressure zones...

— It allows the downhiller to redefine the profile of the slope, to a certain extent, which his center of mass follows, to a profile which is more in harmony with the trajectory of his skis and allows for greater speed.

Of course this "flexion-dive down the fall line" is not a cure-all which precludes all of the technical elements mentioned before. It is more of an embellishment.

The skis slide over the slope with a minimum of overloading, held either perfectly flat or on edge. In the air, the skier's body mass follows the most direct and fastest trajectory. Between these two extremes, the skier's legs act as extraordinary shock absorbers. This is the image presented today by the greatest downhillers.

The desire to go faster is always a psychological attitude. It isn't just the will to win or the will to fight or even the desire to glide which I contrasted to the former two when speaking of giant slalom. It is the sharpening of all of the skills in training as in racing, to determine at every moment what must be done to gain a hundredth or even a thousandth of a second; and it means

212

stretching out
to absorb
the landing

doing this all of the time. This incredible tenacity of the champion who is making a great performance, provided it doesn't effect his suppleness and the fluidity of his movements, is evident even to the spectators and arouses their enthusiasm.

But I must repeat one more time that desire can do nothing if the mechanics don't allow it, and the mechanics are simultaneously the athletic characteristics of the skier, his technical baggage, his aptitude for adjusting his movements to the snow conditions, the terrain, his speed...

Friction through the air and over the snow — the skier's morphology.

Is aerodynamics of less importance now than it was during the era when, with my friend Jean VUARNET, we first described the egg position? No. We confirmed 20 years ago that gliding should be developed both through the air and over the snow. It is only because coaches have somewhat neglected the latter to the benefit of the former that they have had to take a step backwards. In reality, it's difficult to estimate the relative contributions of air friction and ski-snow friction. Nevertheless, it's possible today to see the problem a little more clearly because of the use of radar guns to instantaneously measure speed. This has allowed coaches to better localize and estimate braking. Because of the performances of the great champions like Franz KLAMMER, it has

been proven hundreds of times that it is far more important to absorb even the slightest overloading of the skis on the snow during a take-off or landing than to maintain a perfect aerodynamic position in the air.

But one day there will be a skier who will leave his skis just as free, to slide just as well, while remaining in a more aerodynamic position... This skier will unavoidably go faster... at least until he again neglects the gliding of his skis on the snow.

Two decisive elements: weight and power.

Downhill racing fans are amazed by what appears to be a continuing increase in the physical size of downhillers. Today they are heavy athletes. Will they eventually be built like football players? Is it known that today's football players are among the fastest sprinters over 40 yards? Is it known that the modern techniques of weight training develop speed as well as power?

Over the last few decades, the small or intermediate size athletes seem to have been favored in skiing, a fact which perhaps has banished numerous potential champions from downhill racing. The following considerations perhaps will restore confidence to racers who have been eliminated from elite competition at a young age when their size still constituted a handicap.

I have already discussed the "terminal velocity" or speed plateau for a given slope which every skier hits somewhere between 30

213

and 70% of the distance down the slope. A skier's weight, which is his driving force, increases as the 3rd power of his linear dimensions; or the square of his surface area. It is evident that the force relationships will favor the larger skier. The terminal velocities of two skiers with the same body morphology, and assuming the same position, will vary in proportion to their size. For example, a skier 5'7" and weighing 130 pounds will have a terminal velocity that is 10% slower than a skier 6'3" and weighing 194 pounds and on any slope.

Yet it is well established that the heavier an individual is, the more difficult it is to maintain the power to weight ratio. The compressions sustained by the skier against the terrain or during the turns is a direct function of his body weight. Therefore, the heavy downhiller must develop more power and a better technique than the intermediate size downhiller. First of all, because the slightest errors will have greater consequences but also because he will tend to arrive at the difficult sections at higher speeds and must, therefore, overcome greater problems.

Furthermore, he must work on cultivating quickness of movement because it is more difficult to move long body segments to absorb a succession of rapid bumps than to mobilize shorter segments.

Nevertheless, the evolution of downhill courses to courses with less pronounced terrain, longer turns and higher speeds on flatter slopes favors the heavyweights.

PHYSICAL TRAINING FOR COMPETITIVE SKIING
THE YEARLY PROGRAM — THE COACH

If you are an "amateur" racer

There are "amateur" ski racers, even at a mediocre level, who are far more serious about their physical training than the professionals. I don't address myself to them. Instead, I am going to preach to the others. First of all, in favor of what I believe to be an absolute minimum...

The indispensable minimum: be in good physical shape.

A certain minimum level of physical conditioning is absolutely necessary. A lack of this is totally incompatible with competition. It creates inhibitions and poor reactions and can be the cause of serious accidents.

Before even considering racing you should at least regain a minimum level of physical conditioning. In a few weeks of physical activity practiced two times per week — hiking, jogging, bicycling, tennis, calisthenics — you will develop a minimum level of over-all physical conditioning and muscle tone.

Your skiing efficiency will be distinctly better if you develop two qualities.

1. Aerobic and anaerobic conditioning.

A ski race lasts 1 or 2 minutes. Untrained, you arrive at the bottom of the course out of breath with a high heart rate and with your leg and hip muscles fatigued. Every intense effort involving your legs for a duration of 1 or 2 minutes will prepare you to support this effort. It is preferable to train at a lower work load for a longer period of time than to use an effort that is more intense but too short in duration. Jog, bicycle or even play tennis where you go all out for 1 or 2 minutes.

214

Eventually, repeat this performance 3 or 4 times spaced with intermediate rests of a few minutes. Of course, you should select efforts which involve particularly the muscles of the thighs, the buttocks and the lower back because at the same time that you develop your heart, lungs and circulatory functions your muscles will improve in tone and they will develop better circulation for eliminating the toxins which create fatigue.

In essence, you are helping your body to turn better and at a higher RPM, but it still remains for you to develop maximum "torque"...

2. Muscle power.

Whether you are aware of it or not, your power limits your technique. Many movements made by the champions are impossible for you because you don't have sufficient power in your feet, thighs, buttocks and lower back. This is particularly true among women.

What does this power consist of?

In mechanics, power is the work that can be done during a unit of time; the work being produced by the force of a movement. The notion of muscle power is somewhat similar. It isn't the same as pure force, which can be the capacity to staticly resist another force; for example blocking a flexion to resist a compression. Muscle power, however, is a dynamic quality: it is a force creating a movement. Power is necessary to start a lateral projection, especially at the moment when the skier is in compression.

But the power of a skier has the particular characteristic of being a "decelerating" power. The skier must decelerate compressions ten times as often as he projects with his legs. The muscular characteristics of these two movements are very different (411-412). For example, the skier must develop his maximum power in a low position whereas this is usually developed in an upright position.

How to develop power?

First of all, you should recognize that this is the physical quality which can be improved in the most spectacular manner.

But it is improved only if it is taxed very close to its maximum level. This is the major discovery of modern sport and that which makes weight training one of the fundamental elements of the training of all athletes.

How do you tax your muscles to 80 or 90% of their maximum without recourse to bar bells, weight machines and other gymnastic equipment? Very simply by pushing your exercises to the maximum: jumping as high as possible from a crouch, landing from these jumps with the briefest possible flexing, deep flexions on two or even one leg while carrying a friend piggy-back. While skiing over mogulled terrain, and with good snow, make wedeln turns with checks and maximum compressions in the ruts between the moguls, especially when you are tired. The principle is simple: try to attain the limit of what is possible and see if you can go further... This, in general, is the system utilized today to develop all physical qualities. The principle is simple but its practice is difficult because it demands a maximum and constant involvement.

Be determined, because you shouldn't forget that power is just another aspect of that essential quality of a competitive skier, *flexibility.*

The training of the champion.

Physical training.

It is no longer sufficient to "get into shape" as it was 20 years ago, nor is the "physical preparation for skiing" of 10 years ago still valid. Physical training today is a constant and continuous development of the physical qualities which are involved in skiing. Each year the potential champion must develop better conditioning, more power and greater speed. The improvements gained each year must be added to those of the previous years, just like the technical developments and psychological mastery and experience.

In this domain, skiing must borrow considerably from the evolved sports, in particular from track and field and especially from the throwers, the strong men of the stadium.

On the cardio-vascular level, ski competitions don't seem to stress the organism to the degree that foot races of an equal duration do. In spite of this, the training methods used in track are very valuable for a skier. The ability to go all out over four repetitions of 440 yards to the point of nausea represents an intensity that is difficult to attain in skiing, especially in training. It is, therefore, good, while developing the conditioning of ski racers to have them discover the limits of total involvement in a time duration that corresponds to that of ski competitions.

Endurance, another essential quality of athletes is equally useful for ski racers. It will allow them to endure the fatigue of repeated training sessions and racing, long trips and the occasional periods of low health. Endurance for a ski racer should assume a somewhat specialized form. It should be accompanied by what I call hardiness; the tolerance of cold, wind, stormy weather, fog, of changes in altitude, of changes in food and of irregular physical training. With regard to the development of *speed,* a distinction must be made between the speed of a sprinter and that of a skier. The sprinter creates his speed whereas the skier must cope with the speed created by gravity. I have discussed at length the quickness of the slalom skier. Nevertheless, the downhiller must absorb compressions on the order of 400 to 500 pounds several times per second and the slalom skier must ricochet from one leg to the other in a low position, creating pressure of the same magnitude as that absorbed by the downhiller to make his skis bite on the ice. We find here an action similar to that of the sprinter which demands power to the highest degree.

Power is unquestionably the most characteristic attribute of the skier — and of the female skier — of today. I have already discussed this at length while addressing myself to the needs of the amateur racer. It is inconceivable to me that some coaches, particularly in France, can still doubt this. This quality doesn't seem to be sufficiently developed merely by skiing, even in the most difficult of conditions. Thus the necessity of a systematic weight training program, either in a well-equipped gymnasium or through the selection of suitably adapted exercises. This training, to be both efficient and safe, must be lead by a specialist in physical training.

It is important that the physical training specialist have a good knowledge of skiing. For several reasons:

— First of all to design a training program which utilizes positions similar to those encountered in skiing. Flexed, low positions with the feet and legs moving in parallel forward-backward planes when both feet are weighted and an emphasis on balanced, angulated positions with the weight concentrated on one foot.

— Also, to insist on eccentric work which is generally seldom used in weight training programs. For example, while carrying a

216

friend piggy-back, flex rapidly in the legs, abruptly stop this downward flexion and then slowly stand up.

— To emphasize the training of muscle groups which play a critical role (rotators of the feet under the calves, the calves under the thighs, the thighs under the hips, lateral fixators of the feet and hip, adductors and abductors of the hips) in addition to the muscle groups which are more generally thought of to be associated with skiing (extensor muscles of the lower back, buttocks, thighs, calves, abdominals).

The annual program of the champion.

It is absolutely unrealistic today for a skier to aspire to reach the national or even moreso the international level of competition if he doesn't impose upon himself a year-round training program and even a multi-year program with distinct objectives to be obtained over the short, intermediate and long term. These objectives can even be quantitated, at least the objectives relating to purely physical performances.

The different phases of an annual training program can be:

• *Spring:* The spring period includes several weeks of active rest with general physical training and perhaps a compensation of the insufficiencies sometimes created by skiing. Eventually, this period should include free skiing, concentrating on corrections of technical faults to allow a more productive training during the summer months.

• *Summer:* The physical training levels are accentuated to lead to peak athletic performances at the end of September.

The summer period should also include intensive technical training on snow using both free skiing and gate skiing, but at a conservative tempo (approximately 3% of the highest possible speed). Technical refinement should be directed along precise training objectives with the results in each one constantly evaluated.

This training period should include several weeks of semi-rest during August to break up the summer. The physical training is alternated with glacier skiing: 5 days of one, 5 days of the other. This seems to represent an optimal quantity of each activity when the trips are not too long.

• *Fall:* The fall period consists of progressively more intensive skiing. The physical training is directed toward the development of maximum resistance and power. The ski training is done in gates at racing tempo and in conditions duplicating competition.

• *Winter:* During the winter months it's necessary that the skier maintain, through his skiing and physical training, a level of physical capacity (specifically endurance, resistance and power) in spite of the competitions, the inevitable travel fatigue and the irregularity of the daily routine. Even with a great deal of intense skiing, two sessions per week of physical training seem to be necessary: one directed at maintaining aerobic and anaerobic conditioning, the other directed at maintaining power.

The efficiency of such a training program isn't manifested only in the physical and technical characteristics.

The motivation of the athlete, far from weakening due to what some mistakenly refer to as "burning out", is enhanced by the setting of a series of specific goals. Burning out, nine times out of ten, is only a loss of interest.

With regard to psychological preparation, confidence in a training program, accomplishing intermediate objectives and eventually doing more and better than the competition will only add to the confidence generally produced in an athlete who improves his physical potential. Certainly this approach is more productive than all of the purported 'psychological' training techniques that are being proposed today. Of course those rare cases of real psychological imbalance will require professional assistance.

What makes a champion ?

As a coach with years of practical experience, moreso than as a technician, I will not tell you "it is technique which makes a champion" any more than I will tell you "it is the psychological profile or preparation or psychological 'set' the day of the competition" or "physical qualities" or "the environment"... All of these factors intervene. It isn't a matter of attributing a percentage to each factor any more than to pretend that the champions of today have exploited certain factors to the ultimate degree and that only by cultivating some factors more than others can they do better, even though this may be confirmed by specialists trying to advance their own specialties...

The ski champion indisputably has innate physical and character qualities. He or she has generally benefited first from the family and then from the immediate surroundings; from an atmosphere supportive of sport and competition. He has trained a great deal and has benefited from favorable material conditions. 9 times out of 10, he has had to impose extreme efforts and sacrifices upon himself. He is highly motivated and generally unsatisfied with results obtained previously.

He is not a superman, merely an individual who is slightly more gifted than those who preceeded him in a particular endeavor.

The myth of the born champion, who automatically became a champion, is absurd and discourages many athletes who could become champions if only they believed less in fate and more in the efficiency and effectiveness of an intense and rational training program.

The coach.

For you, the racer, he should be:
• the man on the hill who always knows how and where to find the best possible training conditions in every circumstance,

• the technician who knows how to ransack your technique, find solutions, see in others what makes them win and make use of it for you,

• the organizer who knows how to plan your season in your own best interest,

• the indefatigable disciplinarian,

• an intelligent, forthright and sensitive individual who can understand and admit everything but who can't be fooled,

• the ultimate authority when things go wrong and when your confidence is shattered.

The objective of the coach must not be to become indispensable to the racer. To the contrary, it should be to create an athlete who is sure of himself, confident and willing to assume responsibility for himself. In this way, the coach can hope to help his pupil, not only in his racing career but also in his life as an adult.

This is very different indeed from the long-suffering, coaxing, subservient coach or the self grandizing coach who abounds in international skiing and is attracted more to the perfume of glory which reigns in these high places than by the genuine duties and responsibilities of a coach.

Where can you find such a coach ?

They exist, but they are rare !

If you fail to find this miraculous individual who possesses all of the qualities described above, try to find one who responds best to your needs; and having chosen, give him your confidence.

Only by doing so will you be able to reap the maximum benefit of his help.

III DO YOU WANT TO TEACH ?

In sports large numbers of amateurs help their friends to discover love for their sport and improve their technique.

The experience is a rich one on the human as well as on the technical level.

It can provide you with deep satisfaction if you like to help others.

It will also help you to improve your technique, to refine your movements and to clarify your ideas.

You might even become caught up in the experience !

And why not ?

YOU CAN WORK AT EITHER OF TWO LEVELS

The problems differ depending on whether you are working with beginning and intermediate skiers or with advanced skiers. We will approach the problem, therefore, in two parts.

Beginning and intermediate skiers.

If you enjoy being helpful, and if you have developed a fairly good understanding and feeling of what you are doing yourself on skis, perhaps in part through reading the chapters of this book which apply to you, I wouldn't hesitate in answering yes !

I might even be able to eliminate the condition of having attained a certain competence in technical theory or first-hand experience. If you do nothing more than inspire confidence you will accelerate the rate of improvement of those you teach.

First of all because the true secret of all good teachers in skiing, just as in other activities, results from the quality of the relationships which they are able to develop instinctively with their pupils. Their technical competence, as well as their knowledge of the basic sciences, for example the psychology of learning, neurophysiology, sociology and even psychoanalytic concepts, are of only secondary importance.

This is also true because skiing is learned essentially through skiing. No matter what you say to your pupil, if you have him ski more on slopes and snow conditions appropriate to his level, sometimes challenging him with a line corresponding to the limit of his abilities as you lead him down the mountain, you will speed up his improvement. You will not have taught him a specific movement or movements, but you will have helped him to acquire and then refine the balancing reflexes which are relatively unnatural for man. As these reflexes are infinitely more complex than the motor skills involved in slowing, turning and linking turns together, your pupil will be able to learn these movements without being aware

of them.

Gradually gaining experience, reinforcing his "muscular awareness", he will eventually acquire what we term today "motor behavior" which is adapted to varying conditions, varying terrain and a variety of movements. All of that, perhaps, without any conscious awareness of the movements he performs.

Of course your pupil could develop certain bad habits which could slow his improvement. He could also develop in a manner which would not permit him to become an excellent skier very easily. However, you can be sure that instructors working within strict, standardized teaching methods risk developing far greater problems.

Common sense is the single most important characteristic of the amateur instructor at this level.

Common sense is needed in the choice of runs, the choice of speed and possibly in the selection of the path skied by the pupil a few yards behind the tails of your skis. Common sense is required in determining the manner of stimulation or cautioning or in more general but appropriate directives like, "try to be more gentle", "let your skis go", "make your edge bite"... !

Finally, common sense must be applied to the technical suggestions which must correspond to the level of knowledge of the instructor as well as within the limits of comprehension of the pupil.

I will return to this delicate subject again.

Advanced skiers

Even if you are an excellent skier, working with your friends at this level becomes more difficult.

Certainly you can give them confidence, take them to slopes and types of snows which they would not dare to approach by themselves or give them tips, make them ski faster or teach them to choose a better line through skiing a few yards ahead of them.

If your general stance on skis is superior to theirs, it is possible that through conscious or subconscious imitation that theirs will improve. Also, if you use certain motor skills which they do not yet possess, you can help them to discover the movements by skiing in front of them and emphasizing the movements.

Here again, it's a question of common sense.

And in most cases, common sense should dictate that you avoid long, involved technical explanations which would certainly contribute more to a great admiration for your "science" rather than to a clear understanding of what you're trying to explain. There is a very great difference between the development of your understanding through explanations, lectures and numerous experiences and the understanding which you can develop in your pupils through explanation. I will return to this subject in the chapter on teaching in the discussion of the process of learning and the act of teaching. There is one undeniable fact: the introduction of a technical element at an inappropriate time or the simple conscious or subconscious imitation of a technical error could compromise the development of proper technique forever.

You must use caution and mature reflection when you give technical aid to your friends.

Your technical competence can develop in stages.

I am not referring to the pseudo stages which correspond to the successive layers of exercises at each "level" in ski schools. Rather, I am concerned with the level of your comprehension of ski technique.

1. With a satisfactory ability to demonstrate the movements to be taught and corrected and ten sentences corresponding to general suggestions and uttered at the correct moment, it is possible to help a majority of skiers to improve without risk of teaching them something incorrect. The rest require a more sophisticated teaching approach.

2. Action on this second level involves a deeper understanding of the movements targeted and of the imperfect movements performed by the learner. It requires a certain level of knowledge of ski technique, a certain feeling for observation as well as a systematic approach to observing. It also involves a certain competence in teaching: knowledge of effective and appropriate suggestions, the ability to formulate suggestions clearly for the learner as well as the ability to demonstrate essential details in a target movement. It includes the types of help given by instructors and professional coaches if they do not allow themselves to be limited by the catch phrases of the standard teaching method or of the informed amateur interested in problems in technique and possessing a solid common sense.

3. The third level corresponds to a true mastery of ski technique and teaching methodology.

This technical mastery makes it possible to instantly analyze all of the components of the behavior of the skier. It also makes it possible to judge the relative importance of each of these components within the individual skier, taking into account his physical ability and morphological characteristics. Technical mastery and long practical experience are involved in the ability to imagine what type of movements a given skier should adopt in order to become most effective or, if he so desires, to become more elegant.

Mastery of teaching methodology allows the selection of the most appropriate approach for a given skier, what suggestions, what type of terrain, the most effective approach for accelerated improvement. This type of mastery depends largely on practical experience, systematic research on snow as well as exchange of information between instructors or coaches so that they may profit from each others experience. Unfortunately, it must be recognized that this type of exchange is still rare in this field.

In the rest of this chapter, I will concentrate on the first two levels.

In the last part of this book, I will provide a certain number of documents which will not interest my normal reader.

First, I will include a few documents concerned exclusively with teaching methodology and indispensable to the qualified instructor or coach who desires to understand the why and how of the suggestions which I made to my readers in the first part of this book.

I will end with a series of technical documents organized into what I hope is as rational an approach as possible to that extraordinary field — ski technique.

There is no better approach to mastering the nuances of ski technique than teaching skiing yourself.

If you are interested in ski technique, and if you enjoy helping your friends, if you have a taste for teaching, don't hesitate — go ahead and teach. You will definitely benefit from the experience.

But beware that once you decide to help a skier to improve or to modify certain details in his techique which prevent him from improving that you are taking off into a veritable adventure or, more exactly, into a "search" which will undoubtedly be rewarded with half successes and half failures but which, in any case, should prove fascinating for you.

You can be sure that there is no such thing as standard exercises or progressions of exercises which, when suggested to the learner, will solve all his problems. You can even help the learner to improve without a single specific exercise simply by providing him with the opportunity to discover technical nuances through your advice and your judicious selection of terrain. In this manner, you will gradually modify his behavior on the snow. In fact, these "nuances" in technique are what teaching methods attempt to provide through exercises. Instructors who use these exercises are often only aware of their exterior form and teach without any understanding of their real impact on the behavior of the learner.

Teaching, then, is an attempt to understand more clearly the behavior of the learner and to invent appropriate ways to fill in the voids and help him to improve. How could it be possible for a teacher to avoid analyzing himself and consider himself his most important source of practical experience?

In other words, teach intelligently and you will improve your own skiing!

If you are reading these lines, and if you are still in the process of learning to ski, take note. Avoid instructors who do not themselves improve. Unfortunately, some are attracted to teaching not in a spirit of investigation but rather through a taste for playing an interesting role...

DON'T CONFUSE THE OFFICIAL TEACHING SYSTEMS WITH THE WAY PEOPLE REALLY LEARN TO SKI.

In nearly all countries, the official teaching system of the national ski school has defined that the best way to ski is not the way of the current champions but a technique that has been artificially constructed and is demonstrated by its certified ski instructors and that the only legitimate way to learn how to ski is through the sequence of exercises of the national ski school's teaching method.

The ski instructors become the priests of this curious religion and so it was in 1956 when Emile ALLAIS commented during a meeting of the directors of the French Ski School that he was shocked to see that instructors in France were still teaching the official French technique which was developed in 1937. One of the directors replied, "even

222

Emile betrays us... "

It's incredulous that this approach is still used by a good number of instructors even as they seriously study the skiing of the champions and even of the young racers in the clubs in their resorts and then pass these observations on to their students.

How do you really learn to ski ?

I emphasize the word *really* because many skiers assume that they turn because they perform certain manuevers — for example by planting a pole and extension — whereas in reality they turn by subconsciously using an entirely different mechanism — a change of support foot, for example. Evidence of this can be seen in any resort: a ski instructor descends a slope in front of a class of intermediate students making perfect turns with his skis close together while his students follow in his tracks with their skis apart and using an array of elementary mechanisms to keep up...

It's interesting to observe the international ramifications of ski school techniques. In Austria, Italy, Germany and Switzerland, for example, where the instructors teach their own national ski school technique, the majority of mediocre and intermediate skiers use virtually the same mechanisms. Only the movements of the arms or differences in posture, which have no effect on the turning mechanisms, allow them to retain their national character. This becomes even more evident among the more proficient skiers of these national ski schools who, little by little, become more distinguishable to the point that the silhouettes of the better skiers from these different countries are far less uniform than the silhouettes of the current great international racers from all countries.

Outside of the influence of the ski schools, can it be said that all skiers evolve toward the most efficient technique? No, because every individual, whether he recognizes it or not, is profoundly influenced by the technique he sees in his immediate surroundings; the techniques used by his friends in the resort he frequents in the country where

he skis. All individuals, subconsciously or otherwise, select a model for themselves and try to imitate it.

All of these external influences effect the skier superficially but could eventually block or, on the contrary, accelerate his technical evolution.

There exist, furthermore, a number of overall technical schemes along which all skiers are trained. For example, the official French technique of 1937-57 had skiers make turns with forward weighting and rotation and without a platform or pole plant. From 1957 to 1969, the official technique called for a turn made with a pole plant, extension and *projection circulaire* followed by a slight forward weighting (christiania leger). From 1969 to the present, a turn made with a platform, pole plant, extension, then a slight pivoting of the feet and steered braking with forward weighting. The experience in recent years has definitely shown that because of the monolithic character of the French Ski School it has been unable or unwilling, with few exceptions, to adapt to the technique of the times to make its students progress. Naturally, it's the second, determinedly more modern technique, which has been sacrificed !

Can one avoid this trap of all teaching methods ?

Yes, I think so. First of all, by constantly striving to adapt your teaching method to incorporate the real reasons why the greatest number of skiers are presently progressing. Further, by using the currently best racers and the skiers who are most effective in all terrain as a final model. These skiers have presented remarkable similarities throughout time and are also the most elegant skiers to watch. Between these two extremes, it's important to avoid any motor behavior in your students that could risk an impasse or a direction in technical evolution that is not compatible with the best technique of the time.

After numerous observations and experiences, we have tried to define with precision a certain number of technical features which will permit the construction of a coherent technique by fragments. We refer to these fragments as technical elements.

We have researched as scientific an approach as possible. With collaborators and students — graduate students in physical education and sports and students in the ski diploma program of the College of Science and Medicine of the University of Grenoble — we have launched programs of systematic observation with statistical analysis of the bahavior of skiers of different levels on different kinds of slopes. For 6 years we have been able to study the mechanisms most habitually used by these skiers and to observe the changes in the faults most commonly committed by skiers as the slopes themselves have changed over the years in France.

What has been the result of this work? What is the conscious or subconscious benefit of this pedagogical analysis to the student? From our investigations we have arrived at the essence of what constitutes this book and, in particular, the pages that follow.

BASIC SUGGESTIONS FOR TEACHING

In which major directions should you help your pupils to progress ?

Whether you are working with mediocre skiers, intermediate skiers, the advanced or the very advanced, it is possible to identify four major directions for establishing precise objectives:

1. Riding a fast ski, or a flat ski, in complete, long, controlled turns.

2. Quick, flat ski leg action.

3. Leg action with edge-sets in order to slow the skis or develop platforms permitting a dynamic reaction of the skis on the snow.

4. Carving on the edges in longer turns and wedeln.

5. Precise control through the arcs of the turns using the skis as precision instruments.

I would have preferred suggesting as a first general direction the development of the skill of schussing which, when properly applied, is the best preparation for riding a fast ski. However, I know that schussing slopes as they exist today is difficult and out of fashion. I would not risk making a selection to all of my readers which only a few would be tempted to accept.

I didn't mention the use of sideslipping which generally forms the basis of intermediate skiers. Your problem will be that of helping them discover an entirely different form of skiing.

In each of these 5 major directions, you must observe the development of your pupil, or pupils, and carefully regulate the manner in which your goals are met. You can suggest the approaches which I have presented to my readers throughout this book or you can take the initiative to develop some of your own, but be careful...

WHERE IS SLALOM GOING ?
ANDREAS WENZEL: SURF TECHNIQUE IN A HIGH POSITION.

This young champion, from the exceptional training ground that is the tiny country of Liechtenstein, is notable for his relaxation and his drive. He is a specialist of surf leg action in a position that is higher than that used by **STENMARK** and the other great slalom specialists of the world. He sometimes is able to extract even greater finesse and softness at the beginning of his turns. Does this open the way to a new technique ?

INGEMAR STENMARK: TAIL PRESSURE AND FORWARD THRUST OF THE FEET.

These photographs, taken during the final of the World Series at Montgenevre, France, illustrate how dynamism and power can be used in modern technique.

One can, in fact, see in this series of photos: the surf position, an initiation of the turn by carving of the outside ski with knee angulation, angulation and tail-pressure on the outside ski at the end of the turn, and lateral pressure control with the feet in a forward position to direct pressure to the tails of the skis. This is a perfect illustration of what many coaches call "tail-carving" but without fully understanding the mechanics involved.

BERNARD RUSSI: A "CLASSIC" DOWNHILLER.

Olympic Champion **Bernard RUSSI** is shown as he absorbs perfectly the most difficult bump in the men's downhill course of the 1976 Olympic Games. In the second photo, the Swiss champion is in a positin which I believe to be ideal for absorbing a bump because it permits a maximum retraction of his legs in front of his chest - and not under his body. Perfectly balanced in the air, he extends his feet as he regains contact with the snow.

FRANZ KLAMMER: AN "INSPIRED" DOWNHILLER.

On the same bump, **Franz KLAMMER**, who hasn't sought the easiest line but perhaps the fastest line, is launched into the air out of balance. But of greater importance, he reestablishes his balance while suspended, like a cat thrown into the air, and hurtles on down the slope to victory.

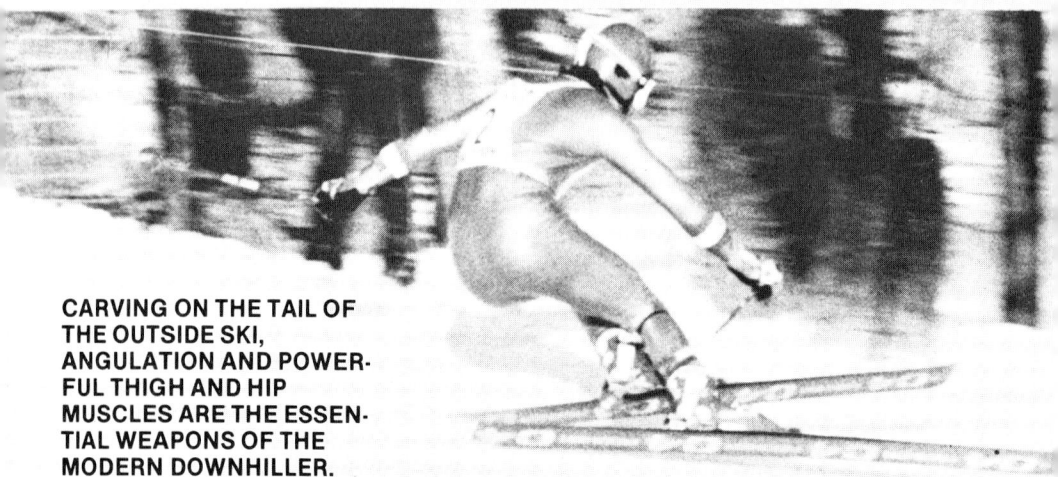

CARVING ON THE TAIL OF
THE OUTSIDE SKI,
ANGULATION AND POWER-
FUL THIGH AND HIP
MUSCLES ARE THE ESSEN-
TIAL WEAPONS OF THE
MODERN DOWNHILLER.

How to improve the ability to ride a fast, flat ski ?

This "flat" ski is that of children which seems never to bite into the snow. It is that of talented young girls who turn and wedel while giving the impression of doing absolutely nothing, that of those virtuosos whom you admire so much when they seem to caress the snow as well as that of the deep snow specialist whose skis move in the snow with the ease of fish in water.

It requires a certain "relaxation", a gentle but attentive manner, muscular suppleness, the absence of any stiffness, and the smooth continuity in the linking together of all movements.

This is as true for the beginner, even the athletic beginner who wants to make phenomenal progress, as it is for the advanced skier who has become accustomed to skiing defensively on difficult runs.

To help your students to understand this state of relaxation is as important as suggesting an appropriate approach on properly selected terrain and with appropriate types of snow conditions.

Approaches suggested in this book:
Concerning turns: pages 22-27, 34-37, 60-65, 105-115, 152-153 and 164.
Riding a flat ski close to the fall line: pages 30-32 then flat ski leg action.

For a more sophisticated analysis:
Refer to technical analysis chapter: 14-39, 111-119, 131-142, 420 to 437 and 439.

How to improve flat ski leg action.

This leg action is the type used by children. Have you never been impressed by the mobility of their legs as they move down the hill in a group, ceaselessly crossing back and forth across each other's path without ever hooking skis ? This type of leg action is also used by slalom skiers on soft snow. It is taken to its extreme limit by freestylers when they thread their way through enormous bumps and when they link 2 or 3 ultra-quick wedeln turns together at the top of a giant bump.

Flat ski leg action provides the variety and rhythm changes necessary to bring joy to any skier who links long radius turns through beautiful powder snow on variable terrain.

This type of skiing involves the same relaxed state of mind as that of long, flat ski turns but also requires a sharper state of arousal, muscles ready to react, a sharpened awareness of a well-balanced position over the pivoting center of the skis, feet completely relaxed because flat ski leg action begins with the feet.

This technique requires appropriately flexible ski boots and perfectly flat ski bases.

A wide stance and low body position as well as a stable trunk and arms facilitates the acquisition of this technical element.

In order to teach independent leg action, you must spur the learner on. Don't hesitate to count out the rhythm. Ski right at the heels of the pupil and don't hesitate to exhort him to be more dynamic and more decisive. Don't worry; he will be grateful to you later !

The greatest obstacle to this type of leg action is forward lean. Its greatest advantage is the discovery of balanced support from the ski which provides the basis for all further improvement.

Approaches suggested in this book:
Riding a flat ski down the fall line: wedeln pages 33, 78-90, 118-119, 122-124, 134, 142-151.
At the beginning of the turn: pages 86-88, 132-133, and 152.

For a more sophisticated analysis:
Refer to the technical analysis chapter: 40-47, 93-94, 534-535, 541-543.

How to improve leg action in carved, short turns.

This type of leg action corresponds to the idea of quick tempo. It is characterized by a fairly brief noise produced by the skis preceeding a single turn or produced in each turn of a series of wedeln turns. The noise is produced by the edges of the skis which bite into the snow. It is a bit longer when the skier wishes to slow his speed and extremely brief when he wishes to shoot himself into the upcoming turn with more precision.

This type of leg action is perfectly compatible with the concept of riding a fast ski which we just discussed in a previous section. On the contrary, it makes the concept even more obvious. Once a learner starts to ski steeper slopes, harder snows and more difficult bumps, he must first learn to defend himself and later to dominate the terrain. He must not simply resign himself to surviving it as do some 80% of most skiers who adopt a very defensive checking technique which quickly becomes a very static approach lacking in both elegance and real effectiveness.

This type of skiing requires a certain psychological tension, even a certain aggressiveness — a sharpened state of muscular arousal which transforms the muscles into powerful, elastic bands without effecting, however, their ability to relax completely instantaneously. Even more than flat ski leg action, this type of leg action involves the ability to react rapidly without abruptness just the same because the movements of the advanced skier must never become disconnected.

Leg action involving carved edge-sets should be discovered first at the beginning of turns and it is possible to try to develop it in wedeln only once the rhythm has been well assimilated. In fact, 50% of most skiers confuse this rhythm with the tempo of wedeln, whereas the rhythm refers to the brief movement which starts each turn of those linked together in the wedeln. Wedeln may be performed slowly in rhythm or rapidly with no rhythm.

Approaches suggested in this book:
At the beginning of turns: pages 40-41, 46-47, 69-76, 130-133 and 143.
In wedeln: pages 81-84, 120, 155-156, 158-161, 531 and 533.

For a more sophisticated analysis:
Refer to the technical analysis chapter: 60-89, 151-185, 438, 534, 551-556.

How to improve the carved phase of your turns.

There is a fundamental difference between the wide, carved arcs performed on hard snows by racers and advanced skiers and those performed by intermediate skiers. The former describe the turns without sideslipping. The skis slide "in their direction of travel". The tips seem to be pulled into the arc of the turn whereas intermediate skiers seem to scrape sideways across hard snow. They lack precision and security as the terrain throws them about.

Carving, just like leg action involving carved edge-sets, requires a certain psychological attention, almost an aggressiveness, as well as a high state of arousal, an intense concentration on the feelings transmitted from the inside edge of the outside ski.

Don't try to work on carving with your pupils very early, particularly if they seem talented in this direction. An ability to ride a fast ski must be mastered first and the concept of gliding must continue to be developed as you improve carving. This is easy: on soft snows and in deep snow develop the use of a flat ski and flat ski leg action as well, whereas on hard snow and ice you should develop carving and carved edge-sets. On the bumpy terrain which has invaded our ski areas you should make a conscious decision to either work with a flat ski in the channels seperating the bumps or with a more edged ski in checked wedeln, slowing the skis with each edge-set, or in long turns carved over several bumps.

Approaches suggested in this book:
For turns: pages 66-68, 116-117, 136-138, 154, 167.
In long radius carved wedeln: pages 135, 155-156, 536-537.

For a more sophisticated analysis:
Refer to the technical analysis chapter: 48-59, 121-127.

How to develop the ability to control the arcs of turns.

The most beautiful examples of controlling the arcs of turns are given by certain great champions — I think especially by

Ingemar STENMARK. This happens particularly when they are running a slalom or giant slalom course to their liking and putting in the best performance of the day without the slightest outward indication of any aggressiveness, seemingly without attacking at all. More and more frequently, we see the great international champions at intermediate speed carving arcs as perfect as those left by figure skaters during compulsory figures.

On soft snows, riding a "flat" ski as well as on hard snows with a greater edge angle, these skiers constantly regulate the placement and movement of their skis so that they describe an arc which seems as if it's programmed. I am using computer terminology on purpose because the skier who controls the arc of his turn leaves nothing to chance: he creates and controls the pressure on his skis to the tenth of a second and the thousands of actions indispensable not only to the control of the arc of the turn but also to maintaining a balance that is just as delicate as that of the high wire artist — the tight-rope walker.

Once the learner is ready to approach the skill of controlling the arcs of his turns, he must develop a state of mind which is above all a state of extreme concentration from a psychological point of view and one of maximum mobility from the physical point of view. Even during the control of the arc of a carved turn, which involves a high degree of rigidity in the foot, leg and hip in the lateral plane, the muscles of the trunk must remain completely free to balance the mass of the upper body to the very millimeter over the hip and to allow the leg to absorb the changes in terrain smoothly in the sagittal plane so that a perfectly continuous pressure is maintained on the surface of the snow.

For a more sophisticated analysis:
Refer to the technical analysis chapter: 17, 23, 25, 16, 53-58, 561-565.

How to approach teaching.

The approach that you will use will depend on your personality, on the nature of your relationship with your students, on their personalities, on your understanding of human relations, on the circumstances... Nevertheless, I think it will be useful to give you a few specific suggestions.

From the very beginning be simple and clear in your thoughts as well as your words.

Thus what you propose will appear to be easy and your students will have the best opportunity to discover globally what you want them to do.

A complex movement analyzed and explained in detail has an infinitely less chance of being fully understood than a movement that is demonstrated in a simple manner.

Don't try to give your students more than one new thing at a time.

This is what I have attempted to do throughout this book. In order for your students to develop properly, they must focus their concentration on only one new manuever at a time. Insist that they add only one new concept or movement, and not two. Correct them on this new movement and concentrate on it until finally, once they have discovered it, it can be totally assimilated without risk of loss.

Never demand that your students attempt a new movement in terrain or snow conditions or at a speed where it will not be used.

The effectiveness of what you present to your student is the most important factor for its acquisition and, equally, for its complete and total acquisition. Your student, therefore, learns at the same time both the gesture and the terrain and snow conditions under which it is used.

The snow and terrain that you have available to you place strict conditions on what you are able to teach.

You are, therefore, never able to strictly program your teaching plans in advance. You must retain a certain flexibility in your planning. By trying to develop your students along the 5 general principles presented on page 224, you will be able to teach one or another principle under these varying conditions. In working on each of these principles, you must have a precise objective.

In any event, you have the option of selecting the appropriate slopes to use and even selecting the terrain features on each slope which are most suitable for practicing the various technical elements you want your students to concentrate on.

Once again, I would like to emphasize the merits of practicing on flat slopes where it is possible to cultivate gliding. Unfortunately, this is too often ignored by skiers whose goal is always to confront steeper and more difficult slopes.

Teaching very young children.

Up until the age of 9 or 10, skiing should represent nothing more than play.

The ideal situation is to have a specially constructed "terrain garden" for children which, in spite of its Disneyland appearance, is an extremely sophisticated teaching instrument. I'm not referring here to the corners of the teaching slopes of many ski schools where children are "parked" by their parents out of harm's way to perform precise exercises in long caterpillar-like lines under the supervision of an instructor. Instead, I'm speaking about large, well planned areas designed exclusively for teaching children to ski and including numerous features built into the terrain to provide the youngsters with a multitude of technical problems, the solutions of which will make them complete skiers. The role of the instructors becomes one of orchestrating the activities of the children with actual technical instruction reduced to a minimum.

Lacking such a genuine "kindergarten", is it still possible to teach young children successfully ? By all means yes ! First of all, select skis that are well suited to the child; not little skates but short skis that are very soft yet well designed. A special base or mechanism to prevent the skis from sliding backward seems to accelerate the child's progress considerably and avoids many of the failures encountered with timid children.

Secondly, insist that the child ski on slopes that are flat enough that he will never lose control of his speed. Use slopes with a 3% to 5% gradient before the child knows how to turn and then stick to slopes of 5% to 10% for a full week before progressing to the 10% to 20% slopes which the child should remain on for several years. The criteria for progress should be the development of speed and sliding in the child's skiing, not the steepness of the slopes skied or the capacity to brake. This is one reason, for example, why I find the first, second and third star tests of the French Ski School to be so absurd.

How do you introduce turns and serpents to very young children ?

In particular by not trying to teach them. Simply slide down a relatively flat slope with packed powder in front of the child and draw out a very long arc but without making any noticeable movements. The child will follow you. As you slide straight down the slope with the child directly behind you, gradually deflect your trajectory to the right, then to the left. The child will do the same. Do this exercise with your skis parallel if the slope is very flat and with your skis in a gliding wedge if it is steeper.

Fortunately, the wedge that young children make, even on slopes that are a little too steep, seldom evolves toward a braking snowplow with the thighs and hips blocked which paralyzes so many beginning adult skiers.

Is the hyper-backweighted position, with the child leaning against the backs of the boots, a serious problem ?

According to Professor KHOLER, who has directed a marvelously constructed kindergarten in Kitzbuhel, Austria for more than ten years and which has provided him with an exceptional vantage point from which to address this problem, this position should not be systematically corrected. He notes that as soon as the youngster succeeds in accelerating his leg actions and incurs balancing difficulties which must be quickly resolved, for example in bumpy terrain, he will immediately adopt a more prudent stance. Some youngsters who habitually skied with extreme backweighting have gone on to become excellent racers and develop a technique that is at the peak of refinement.

Furthermore, it's not difficult to imagine that skiing with pressure against the backs of the boots in a wedge allows many of these youngsters to complete their turns with tail carving and, hence, better sliding. But when the end of the turn is made in a wedge with the ankles flexed, as used to be common among children, the result will unavoidably be excessive pressure on the tips of the skis and braking in what amounts to a very inefficient stance.

Teaching children.

From the age of 10 or 11, children can profit fully from the same advice that I have directed to adults throughout this book. Up until the age of 13 or 14, or perhaps a little later for unathletic children, the technical elements of gliding and flat ski leg action should be emphasized. As muscle power is developed it becomes progressively more possible to orient the training to emphasize leg action with edge-sets and carving control.

It's primarily within the realm of teaching methodology where your approach should be adapted to the specific needs of teaching children. Using competition as an objective, even if limited only to Nastar or Family Challenge races, can be very productive. You will soon discover that children and even adolescents seem to have a sense for efficiency that is far more pronounced than in adults and as a result they tend to evolve easily toward technically correct movements. Perhaps this is because they are generally less concerned about the form and elegance of their movements.

The many different kinds of adults.

I'm referring here less to the variety of morphological types or differences in physical aptitudes than I am to the diversity of motivations which prompt the adult skier to seek the aid of an instructor or the advice of a qualified friend.

This diversity tends to be the greatest in the group lessons at ski resorts where the beautiful women who have come to the resort for a tan rub elbows with the timid skiers who don't dare to ski alone, the chronic technical "retards" and, finally, those who genuinely want to progress and among these the gifted and the not so gifted...

You claim that this is the insoluble problem of every class lesson ?

No, not when a resort has 2 or even 4 or 5 classes of the same level running concurrently. I would propose 4 kinds of lessons within each level and with these four lessons falling into 2 main categories; one category a "technical training lesson" and the other category called a "normal lesson" to avoid offending anyone. There would be two technical training lessons with one reserved for the young and the other for the "still young". A third kind of lesson, in the "normal lesson" category, would consist of intensive recreational skiing, discovering and challenging all of the slopes of the resort and guaranteeing physical effort. The fourth type of lesson, also in the "normal lesson" category, would consist of skiing at a more reserved pace without fatigue and with an instructor who has been selected for his good humor, charm and rapport with his students.

Even in a private lesson, you should take inventory of the genuine motivation of your student!

Nothing is sorrier than to see a talented instructor give of himself freely and untiringly for a student who has no desire to progress. I'm not speaking, of course, of those charming couples where "he" progresses rapidly with little assistance but "she" skis tranquilly as always and flattered to receive so much attention...

The first step to helping a friend — or, a much tougher problem, your spouse — to progress is to make them interested in what lies before them. This can simply be a desire to be "more elegant" or "not so ridiculous" or "more effective" or to be better than a friend, or to be able to tackle a slope they've always wanted to ski, or to "not risk breaking a leg", or to "have less difficulty down the slopes" or to learn to look more modern... I believe that the best argument is to make them understand that the skier, like the musician, draws more and more pleasure from his art the better he becomes. Even though most people rarely love "technique for the sake of technique", they readily accept an effort that will better allow them to taste the pleasures of life.

With regard to adapting your instruction to the capabilities of your students, if you fully understand the 5 teaching principles that I have already described and if you fix only limited and accessible objectives, you will deceive neither your students nor yourself.

Teaching groups of students is more difficult.

How does one teach a group of students without falling into the trap of communally learning a series of standard exercises which are only to a limited extent adapted to each of the students; without holding back the progress of the most proficient students while at the same time pushing the less capable too fast; without the seemingly inevitable inefficient use of time which reduces the effective skiing time of each student in a 2 hour group lesson to no more than a few minutes ?

20 years ago, I was responsible for training the club instructors of the French Ski Federation and as I gave them my last few words of advice I suggested, "Above all else, see to it that your students progress faster than those skiers who are not taking lessons. For this to happen, insist that your students ski a lot during your lessons. Don't forget that we learn to ski by skiing."

The same advice could be addressed to all instructors, even the fully certified ski instructors and the ski professors in physical education.

Ski instruction has a genuine technology all of its own. A knowledge of technique and the movement patterns of skiing is only a part of this technology. Unfortunately, I have only been able to scrape the surface of this subject in the pedagogical documents presented in the remainder of this book. If you genuinely want to experience teaching groups of students, I recommend that you familiarize yourself with the instruction plan which I outline in these pedagogical documents.

IV TECHNICAL DOCUMENTS FOR SPECIALISTS

The last section of this book is addressed to specialists: instructors, coaches, technicians of the ski equipment industry... and to the passionate lovers of the technique of skiing.

I don't have sufficient space here to even superficially cover all of the problems posed by skiing. Consequently, I have had to make choices and this book, therefore, contains omissions. For this I beg your pardon.

PEDAGOGICAL INFORMATION

Even if pedagogy is not a science, it has a certain number of fundamentals which can direct the instructor in his work. More specifically in the domain of sports, the instructor can have the attitude of a specialist of the so-called experimental sciences where hypotheses are verified through repeated experiments.

I believe, therefore, that I have gathered here a few concepts which will permit the reader to better understand the profound nature of athletic skills and specifically the movements of skiing. Likewise, these concepts will allow the reader to better understand the process of learning and the role which an instructor can play in this process.

I will also present a somewhat new theory which makes a more or less complete picture of the global technique of skiing and a more or less coherent unit of elements, completely individualized, which we have baptized units of acquisition or "technical elements".

This pedagogical information could suffice for a good number of instructors for whom pedagogy is more of an art than a science. This is why I have placed in a chapter "Inventory of Technical Elements" a number of discussions which could have found their place in the following chapter, "Technical Documents".

THE PROCESS OF LEARNING TO SKI

1. What is a movement (or more precisely a "motor performance") ?

Every movement of the body uses muscles to displace body segments. The muscles do not contract unless they are elicited to do so by a "nerve impulse". The distribution of the nerves to the different muscles implies the existence of a "center of distribution". As everyone knows, this center of distribution is involved in the so-called reflex movements or, alternatively, specific movements solicited by the will of the subject or "voluntary" movements. The repetition of voluntary movements can ultimately lead to their being made without conscious control or direction at which time they become habits or "automatisms".

It's evident that if we want to intervene directly on our own movements, or on those of a subject we wish to teach, it is indispensable that we develop a better understanding of

what a movement is, not only from its exterior aspect but in its totality.

Psychologists, psychophysiologists and neurophysiologists study this problem but, at the present time, can only present theories. The research and data in cybernetics seems to provide some information. I will present in a very simplified form what one can suppose a motor performance to be.

The global concept of a "motor performance".
The "stimulation-reaction" or "information-action" circuit.

The genuine nature of a motor performance seems to reside, for all living organisms, in the relationship between the environment and the subject.

This was first described as a

"stimulation-reaction" relationship. An action from the environment is made on the subject which then reacts. A unicellular organism, stimulated by a bacteria, absorbs it. A blow to the patellar tendon of the knee will make the quadriceps contract and the knee extend.

In man, this type of elementary reaction plays an important role in the adjustment of muscular contractions, but the majority of movements imply a stimulation and a reaction that is more complex. For example, when a skier crosses a bump at low speed, he perceives sensations under his feet and in his legs and in a reflexive manner flexes his legs while at the same time maintaining his balance. This implies a multitude of muscular interventions.

At higher speeds, the skier must anticipate his reaction when seeing the bump, that is before touching it. In slalom, he reacts upon seeing the slalom pole. In these cases, the stimulation is visual but in both kinds of situations the skier can react voluntarily or subconsciously without the profound nature of the motor performance differing.

This, what we have called a performance, is in reality usually a series of successive motor actions. A turn on skis is, simply; an initiation then, as a function of the snow, a carving of the skis, an adjustment of the angle of edge-set and an inward lean which balances the braking and centrifugal force. Skiing is, therefore, a long chain of "action-reactions".

One can readily see that the term "stimulation-reaction" is not perfectly suited. The relationship is better described as an "information-action", a more commonly used term today.

2. A schematic representation of body movement.

Refer .to the diagram on the following page. Each one of the following paragraphs is related to one of the numbered elements in the diagram.

I. Object of the movement: to ski.

This can mean maintaining balance while sliding over easy terrain.

It can also mean executing a certain turn as decided by the skier. Beginning with the initial decision, the action consists of constantly adapting the movements to the conditions imposed by the terrain.

II. The sensory receptors.

These are the sensitive nerve endings under the feet and on the surface of the feet, ankles and legs where they contact the ski boots; sensitive terminals located in the muscles and tendons (in particular the extensor muscles of the limbs of the lower body but also in the upper body). The muscles of the neck, for example, appear to play an essential role.

The inner ear (in addition to other structures the *utricle* which perceives sensations of acceleration and the semi-circular canals which perceive movements of rotation in every plane...).

The eyes (the retina alone has 140 million nerve cells).

— These receptors communicate information regarding the pressure exerted on the feet, the position and movements of the body segments relative to each other, the speed of sliding or braking of each of the two skis, the degree of edging on the snow of different parts of the skis.

— At each instant, the sum of all of this information being transmitted is changing. *A multitude of messages are transmitted every instant.*

IIIa - IIIb. Organization and comparison of sensory information.

a) Organization.

The multitude of messages must be organized, perhaps in reference to schemes already placed in the memory (there is an increasing tendency to speak of "programs" in analogy to the programs of computers).

b) Comparison.

The organization of sensory messages must be made relative to sensory messages already assembled.

For example, a subject seated in a standing train sees another train leave. He may then have the impression that it is his train which is moving. As a result, he then perceives all of the sensations which he would perceive in an advancing train. This is the same phenomenon that occurs when we are stopped in powder snow in the fog while in reality we are still sliding. Stopping provokes a fall.

IV. Interpretation of sensory messages.

This generally occurs subconsciously.

It nearly always involves a selection of information, a selection partially made at level III.

It appears that the ability to interpret these messages must call on programs already interpreted and placed in the memory. A rich sensory experience seems to increase this capacity of interpretation considerably. This capacity is nonexistent in the beginner who perceives such messages for the first time. An interpretation is necessary in order to make a decision to act and the resultant movement will be inappropriate if the information received is erroneous. For example, a turn is executed which is inappropriate for the snow conditions which, in turn, have been poorly judged by the subject.

V. The intervention of cognitive and intellectual processes.

In skiing, we are principally concerned with the following factors:

— Attention: can save the skier from being "unsaddled" by a bump by improving the information and accelerating the action.

— Deduction: will allow the braking resulting from passing from a packed to an unpacked surface to be predicted.

— Imagination: allows a patch of ice or a rock hidden behind a bump to be anticipated.

— Global technical intention: will allow the skier to avoid sudden skidding on patches of ice by concentrating on holding his skis on their edges.

— Fear: of the slope, speed, ice, unpacked snow, or other skiers to the rear...

— Excess of confidence.

— Motivation: acts on previously mentioned factors, such as attention, but also seems to modify numerous other factors, even psychological.

SCHEMATIC REPRESENTATION OF THE MOTOR ACT

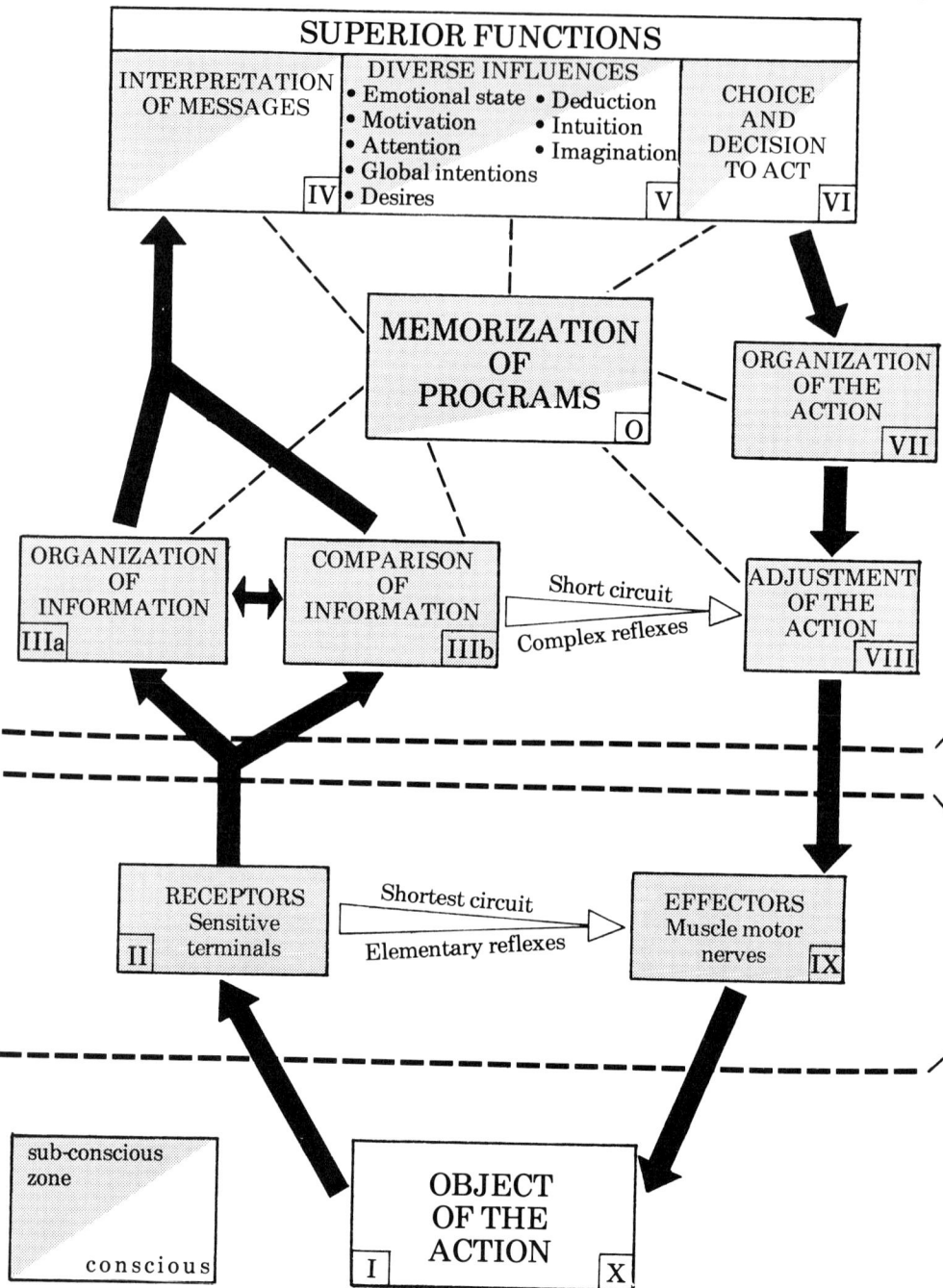

SUPERIOR FUNCTIONS

INTERPRETATION OF MESSAGES	DIVERSE INFLUENCES	CHOICE AND DECISION TO ACT
IV	• Emotional state • Deduction • Motivation • Intuition • Attention • Imagination • Global intentions • Desires V	VI

MEMORIZATION OF PROGRAMS O

ORGANIZATION OF THE ACTION VII

| ORGANIZATION OF INFORMATION IIIa | COMPARISON OF INFORMATION IIIb | Short circuit Complex reflexes | ADJUSTMENT OF THE ACTION VIII |

| RECEPTORS Sensitive terminals II | Shortest circuit Elementary reflexes | EFFECTORS Muscle motor nerves IX |

sub-conscious zone

conscious

OBJECT OF THE ACTION I X

234

These factors intervene at the level of the interpretation of sensory messages (IV) and of decision making (VI). Their involvement is generally subconscious.

VI. The motor decision.

The motor decision can be either conscious or subconscious.

We often assume that it is made consciously when, in reality, the conscious motor command plays only an infinitesimally small role in the global motor impulse which creates the movement. For example: in order to turn the skis in a certain way, the skier consciously decides to make a platform, an extension and a pole plant. In reality, the global program of the movement also includes pivoting of the legs and torso, a lateral thrust, a setting and releasing of the edges, etc... In other words, there is an intervention of the balancing mechanisms during the numerous forward-backward and lateral bankings which accompany the initiation of the turn. These complex interrelationships are modified during each and every fraction of a second.

It is difficult to seperate what we have called the superior functions from the levels VII and VIII already mentioned in the decision to act.

One can, nevertheless, surmise that:

• The choice between different possible motor decisions seems to be made at the superior level.

• For already well established movement patterns, only the "decision to act" seems to be taken at the superior level.

• The important features of certain actions which we will classify as "constructed" seem to be defined at the superior level.

• For new movement patterns, the intervention must be greater and, consequently, the movement is generally less coordinated. For example: a student wishes to turn by making: 1) flexion, 2) extension, 3) pivoting of the legs; he starts... and falls. But gradually, the programs which have interfered with the balancing mechanisms become established and the intervention at the superior level is diminished.

VII. The organization of the movement or codification of motor impulses.

The decision to act, supported by the use of memorized programs, is coded and transformed into coherent motor impulses (the juxtaposition and succession of impulses which begin the hundreds of muscular contractions necessary for the execution of the movement).

These motor impulses are modified each fraction of a second in relation to the sensory messages received during the movement.

This continuous modification of the motor messages can be linked to the unfolding of the different steps of the motor performance of which the skier is conscious. For example: the linking of short turns in a wedeln. Or, on the contrary, a simple adjustment during a continuous motor performance to exterior conditions which are varying. For example: changing the angle of edge-set during a carved turn. In the second case, one preferentially speaks of an "adjustment" of the movement.

VIII. Regulation of the movement.

Certain regions of the brain (the *cerebellum*, among others) play the role of movement regulators. At the level of the cerebellum, there is constant comparison of the motor messages transmitted and sensory information of these movements received from sensory terminals. Automatic readjustments will be made at this level.

Note: One cannot conceive of adjustments during the course of certain very rapid movement (for example: three turns of a flush). The subject can perceive that the movements are being poorly executed as they occur, but he can do nothing to modify them. In such a circumstance, he must simply put a program into play which unfolds without any possibility of adjustment.

IX. The motor elements.

These are the muscles or, more precisely, the "motor units" which they consist of. Each of these units includes a nerve fiber and a bundle of muscle fibers which are actuated simultaneously. Each muscle fiber bundle contains numerous motor units which can be fired simultaneously or

sequentially. Some muscles consist of many such fiber bundles oriented with different directions of pull on the tendons. Every movement, even apparently simple movements, puts into action many muscles. Now we can begin to appreciate the complexity of motor behaviors.

The nerve fiber transmits a precise motor message to the muscle fibers which then contract. The exact nature of the transmission of this impulse from the nerve to the muscle is still unknown, but the electrical nerve impulse serves to detonate the oxidative chemical reactions which are responsible for the resulting muscular contraction (or, more precisely, the shortening of the part of the muscle that consists of contractable material).

Placed parallel to the fibers in the muscle bundles are a special type of fiber known as *intrafusal* fibers which contain many types of sensitive terminals. These sensory terminals transmit impulses giving information regarding the lengthening of neighboring muscle fibers or the force of the traction and permit the adjustment of the contraction. In skiing, for example, a contraction of muscles created by fear impedes fine balance adjustments.

X. The memorization of programs.

This is a simple theory which has the advantage of greatly facilitating the understanding of the mechanisms of a motor act. It seems, anyway, that these memorized programs should probably consist of movement fragments instead of complete movements, in this way permitting thousands of combinations.

This memorization must play a major role in what some psychologists and educators call the "experience" of the student. In this "experience" can enter, among other things, a certain number of operations which we have designated as levels IIIa, IIIb, IV, V and VI.

Direct circuit III-VIII.

The performance of certain movements, in particular those strictly conditioned by the intervention of exterior elements (eg. balancing mechanisms in skiing), do not seem to imply the complete circuit. The sensory messages assure an adjustment by the intervention of structures placed at the deeper levels of the brain.

Direct circuit II-IX.

This circuit emanates from the stretching reflexes of the muscle (the sensation of stretching conditions the contraction). It involves simple reflexes which can only activate the nerve cells of the spinal cord. These reflexes are extremely rapid (a few hundredths of a second). This rapidity seems to allow their intervention during even extremely quick movements which one could not consider as being "adjustable" during their execution. This circuit is exemplified in skiing by the control of the angle of edge-set or the degree of pivoting of the skis during turns or sideslips.

Conscious and subconscious motor acts.

There was a tendency earlier to clearly differentiate the two. Subconscious motor acts were often considered to be at the level of "automatisms" which led to the belief that subconscious motor responses could only be responses programmed in advance. In fact, there also exist subconscious behaviors such as driving a car or skiing while the mind is preoccupied with something else which implies the interpretation of sensory messages, deduction, and making of complex decisions. One must admit that even in a subconscious act the level of attention or inattention is a factor. The consciousness of the operations performed by the superior nerve centers in a motor act seems to establish itself at different levels between clear consciousness and total subconsciousness.

During the conscious motor act, the subject could create a certain image of the motor act which he will perform or which he wants to perform. One then speaks of a "motor image". The subject declares that he can actually "feel" the movement which he will make. More than "seeing an image of the movement", he "feels it in his muscles". This does not imply, however, that he will execute it correctly. This "constructed" motor image can be inaccurate or faulty.

Reflexes and automatisms.

In contrast to reflexes, which are only slightly organized, simple motor responses, automatisms are complex responses often resulting from a learning process which can be situated in the domain of consciousness and which in some cases are substituted by motor responses of will. In fact, the simple reflex in which a stimulus directly provokes a muscular response is very rare. Other than the sudden stretching of a muscle which provokes its contraction in response, it is difficult to find reflexes which are not a part of a coordinated action of many muscles (each one containing numerous motor units contracting with complete independence of each other). Even in reflexes considered simple, such as a skier relaxing one leg to absorb the push exerted by a small bump under his foot, the organization of information and the organization of the motor responses don't permit a clear differentiation of "reflexes" and "automatisms".

Regarding well organized, acquired automatisms, which can be substituted by a voluntary act of the subject, it seems that the hypothesis of a memorization of programs of action can bring an instant solution to the problem as well as satisfy the intellect: the automatic response preceeds the voluntary response and, in this way, substitutes itself for it.

3. Remarks concerning motor performance in skiing and learning skiing.

1. Every movement made by a skier is directed toward two goals;
• One conscious or subconscious consists of the realization of a precise objective: brake, turn, jump, try to slide better...
• The other, always subconscious: to remain balanced over the skis (ie. to prevent a fall).
In other words, a global movement executed by the skier has both mechanisms directed toward a particular objective and mechanisms directed toward maintaining balance.
It seems that during every ski manuever the balancing mechanisms are infinitely more complex than those mechanisms put into action to produce the movement. It also seems desirable that these two categories of mechanisms are interwoven as much as possible, that some of them are superimposed yet never oppose each other.

2. The sensations perceived in the foot and ankle and the reactions of adaptation at this level are very different in skiing than normal activity (the non-flexing of the foot, the relative immobilization of the ankle, the contact with the walls of the boot).

Good skiers are extraordinarily sensitive to such feelings which permit them to adapt to braking, to changes in the terrain, and to different snow conditions.

For the beginner, therefore, this implies a genuine reeducation at the level of the feet that must be made.

3. A slightly flexed stance results in constant muscular tension which is abnormal and which requires very precise muscular control to maintain balance. This muscular control places additional muscles under tension.

4. The sensation of sliding, which reduces the range of fore-aft support, is anxiety producing and can inhibit some muscular activity.

5. Since a skier's movements are, to a great extent, always composed of subconscious balancing mechanisms, it is very difficult for the skier to feel his movements and have a correct motor image.

The skier can even have an image which doesn't correspond at all to the movements which he, in reality, makes. This image can, for example, greatly resemble the silhouette of the ski instructor... consequently the deception of many skiers when they see themselves on video or film for the first time.

6. The analysis, deduction and contemplated action of a skier often have very little effect on the quality of the execution of a gesture which the skier

will perform.

The superior functions often have a more negative than positive effect. The adjustment mechanisms are often inhibited as soon as the skier plans to control his actions voluntarily. This remark is as valid for the intermediate skier as it is for the international racer.

The ability to correct movements or to acquire new ones is disproportionately distributed among individuals. This aptitude seems to be educable with best results obtained when the education is undertaken during childhood (10-14 years).

7. Emotional factors have a very important influence on the quality of the gestures performed (301-320).

8. If there is, in fact, a memorization of programs at the level of sensory messages as well as motor, these programs are most certainly very varied to account for the vast variety of snow conditions, slopes, terrain, speed and turning radius.

Except for very mediocre skiers, it's possible to conceive of skiers adopting "stereotypes", that is movements defined to the finest detail and exactly reproducible. It seems as if the uniformity of movements one sees used by mediocre skiers consists of the systematic utilization of a few elementary motor mechanisms used independently or in combination according to the problems posed by the terrain.

9. The individual rhythm of a movement is an integral part of the motor image (or motor program) which the skier must have. It can even constitute one of the essential features of this image.

OUR THEORY OF TECHNICAL ELEMENTS

1. What does technique consist of ?

— The technique of a skier, or more precisely the sum of behaviors which the skier displays on snow under the most varied or circumstances, can be considered to be the overlapping of a sum of indivisible acquired elements which we call "technical elements".
— These elements fit together like the pieces of a puzzle.
— These technical elements are the same for all individuals.
— They can be acquired in different sequences.
— The personality of the skier is expressed by the preferential utilization of certain technical elements or of certain combinations of elements. This, in fact, can even allow one to determine different characteristic types of individual behavior.
— Not all technical elements are compatible. For example: the automatic turn initiation reflex with side-slipping in a slightly forward position is incompatible with the automatic turn initiation reflex sideslipping in a back-weighted position.
— Some technical elements have an affinity for others. The obligatory choice to be made between two technical elements which are incompatible can condition the possibility of the later acquisition of certain other

elements.

For example: the reflex of sideslipping in a forward position is easily associated with circular projection, banking to the inside of the turn and the carving of a turn but precludes other elements which generally accompany a slightly back-weighted sideslipping: pivoting of the feet under the legs and the legs under the thighs, pushing the feet forward, or carving the turn with tail-pressure.
—Some individual techniques, even when incomplete, are perfectly coherent. It is difficult to enrich them. They do not seem to contain any "holes".
— It is impossible to instill certain technical elements in subjects having a coherent technique by using technical elements incompatible with those which one wants to introduce. One must then succeed in substituting a unity of technical elements for another unity of technical elements. Returning to the same example, one must substitute "slight back-weighting plus a pivoting of the feet" for the unity "forward weighting plus circular projection".
— Some of these elements are generally found associated and can often be considered to constitute a compound technical element. For

example: an excellent platform made at the beginning of a turn can be considered to be composed of the following individual elements; 1). movement of the feet under the body, 2) lateral blocking of the ankles, 3) setting a platform and simultaneously recoiling vertically and laterally, 4) pivoting wind-up movement, and 5) maintaining a specific rhythm. A platform can consist without all five of these elements. Nevertheless, it remains a recognizable unity.
— A succinct technique can be developed by the side-by-side placement of several compound technical elements. The technical "puzzle" constructed in this way contains empty spaces between the compound elements, spaces which can be bridged by other compound elements. There also will exist empty spaces at the interior of each one which can be bridged by individual technical elements which remain to be assimilated.
— A technical element taught by using two or three movements will usually tend to be transferred to a great number of other movements. This theory of technical development brings a certain clarity to the problem of "transfer" in physical and athletic education.

2. How did we arrive at this theory ?

— At every stage in their progression, skiers display certain precise technical deficiencies and these deficiencies can stay with them throughout their development. An excellent skier, or a highly skilled racer, having such a deficiency in his technique will display it throughout his repertoire. There is a "gap" in his technical baggage. For example: one will find the same rhythm of a dynamic platform with recoil in both turns with downhill stem platforms and in check wedeln.

If one corrects this deficiency at one level, it will be rapidly corrected everywhere.

— The learning process in all skiers appears to take place in steps. First, there is the sudden discovery of a new element followed by a phase of assimilation and then of maturation which undoubtedly corresponds to the restructuring of balancing mechanisms. The acquisition of a new technical element, or of several new technical elements in the form of a "compound" element, is a step in the technical progression which occurs in all skiers.

— Not all skiers cross these steps in the same order, an observation which precludes the concept of a "ladder" of elements of increasing difficulty.

— There also exist certain global behaviors which are very similar for groups of subjects during a given era. For example: a poor understanding of avalement has resulted in skiers all over the world using an extreme back-weighted position. The use of this position has led these skiers to discover a new way to pivot their skis, aided by planting the ski pole to the side and toward the tails of the skis. In attempting to correct these skiers, if has been effective to preserve certain useful elements of their movements, such as the forward thrust of the feet. Their initial movement, therefore, was fragmentable, consisting of a compound element or coherent grouping of compound elements.

— Highly structured techniques (ie. national instruction techniques) trap the students in a set of movements which are too rigid and exclude the acquisition of other gestures. We have attempted to identify the compatabilities and incompatibilities of such techniques and in the process evolved toward the concept of what we have referred to as "technical elements".

— During our investigations, we at one point identified a set of "fundamental elements", the acquisition of which would have a decisive effect in facilitating the acquisition of other elements. It has become apparent to us, however, that elements that are of greatest importance to some individuals are of only secondary importance to others as a function ot the personal benefit which each individual derived from its acquisition. A missing element, which otherwise would make a technique complete, is critical, but an element added to an already coherent whole will be perceived as having a lesser importance.

3. The theories used in teaching.

— To analyze a skier's technique is to make an inventory of the technical elements which he possesses and those which he lacks. This inventory can be general and restrict itself only to those groups of elements which I have labelled "compound elements".

This inventory can be even more general by limiting its scope to a global compilation of the skier's capabilities by assessing his aptitude in the following 6 areas: 1) the flat sliding of the skis in turns; 2) flat ski leg action; 3) side-slipped and braked turns; 4) platforms and the corresponding leg action; 5) carving; and 6) precision in turning and wedeln.

For a student to progress in a methodical manner amounts to adding the most easily acquirable technical element, taking into account those which he already possesses. The ideal is to propose no more than one element at a time to the student.

— A "compound" element can be assimilated globally but is often learned in an incomplete form with one of the elements missing (This element is often one which has already been omitted during the acquisition of other compound elements). Consequently the necessity for fully understanding all of the technical elements if one should attempt to develop an excellent skier.

— The level of understanding of the affinities and incompatabilities of the technical elements will define to a great extent the methods to be used by the instructor.

—Teaching experience (and sometimes theoretical knowledge) permits the instructor to anticipate toward which type of "unity of elements" the student will most readily evolve as a function of his personality and the elements which he already possesses. It then only remains to determine the order in which these elements can be most favorably acquired.

— A clear understanding of technical elements (both simple and compound) allows the instructor to act in a more precise manner to facilitate their acquisition: for example, by selecting the appropriate snow conditions, terrain features, speed, etc...

In conclusion

This theory is nothing more than a simple construction of thought. Nevertheless, I have been able to observe that it is enriching for the instructors I have trained. First of all, it has the advantage of directing their attention away from the exterior form of movements so that they can concentrate on the genuine technical development of their students. It leads them to analyze their students at depth and to discover remedies other than mere critiques of form which usually have no real effect.

The notion of technical elements which can be added in increments greatly facilitates the learning of the self taught skier.

And, finally, I have been able to ascertain that a clear understanding of the nature of the technical element which they are missing and which they can differentiate from other technical elements which they use can help excellent skiers and even international class racers to correct a deficiency which they could not overcome in any other way. An awareness of this "missing element" can effect the behavior of the skier in a latent and permanent manner when a correction of the form of a movement requires a distinct effort with each execution of the manuever.

For example: a skier who wants to integrate the "forward thrust of the feet" technical element during counterturns into his technical repertoire assumes an adequate position (with his ankles only slightly flexed), accentuates his counterturns and feels the platform under the tails of his skis which accompanies a well-balanced counterturn. He can then gradually progress to a forward thrust of the feet whereas if this new movement had been attempted alone, he likely would have risked falling into an exaggerated imitation of this movement as is seen so often on the slopes.

An inventory of technical elements is presented at the end of this chapter.

III. THE STUDENT - TEACHER RELATIONSHIP IN SKIING.

1. A schematic representation of this relationship.

Refer to pages 240-241.

2. Concerning the intervention of the instructor.

• The instructor must try to develop the student's skiing balance. This can only be done indirectly:
— by having the student ski a great deal in varied snow and terrain conditions,
— by having the student adopt a favorable basic position: wide stance, legs flexed, arms spread and feet and ankle muscles relaxed.
— by trying to eliminate all inhibitions.
— by giving preference to the use of mechanisms which disturb balance very little; for example by keeping the upper body quiet.
— by avoiding movements which pose particular balance problems which the skier has not yet resolved.
• The strict adaptation of the movements to be performed to the nature of the snow and terrain implies the use of what is known as "situation instruction". Rather than learn specific gestures, the student learns to find solutions to specific problems.
• An analysis of the behavior of the

student and the approach to be undertaken in order to make the best progress were examined in the preceeding paragraph "Theory of Technical Elements".
• When an instructor wishes to introduce a movement using a new technical element, he must:
— be assured that the student can make a similar but somewhat more elementary movement. Eventually, the student is made to perform this movement several times.
— propose in a clear manner and in few words a gesture which does not contain more than one new element.
— demonstrate the movement in a way that the student can actually perform it himself and which illustrates the new technical element.
— be certain that the student has a clear understanding of what he is going to attempt to do.
— use verbal signals during the student's attempt to define the proper timing or rhythm of the movement.
— critique the student's execution by concentrating on the technical point

under study.
• The new technical concept (or technical element) should be practiced in different situations or through the execution of many repetitions. If not, the technical element may become identified with a specific gesture and no longer be transferable to other movements or situations.
• The instructor should be ready to admit failure in a learning attempt. Don't insist in vain. Instead, consider other technical elements which perhaps could be learned more readily and then facilitate the learning of the first element.
• A few manuevers on skis allow a good instructor to help his students discover a great number of technical concepts. Long, carved turns and check wedeln on steep slopes can suffice to round out the techniques of intermediate and even good skiers. We have experienced this in a systematic manner during training on glaciers.

A SCHEMATIC REPRESENTATION OF THE STUDENT-INSTRUCTOR RELATIONSHIP IN A SKI LESSON OF THE PAST

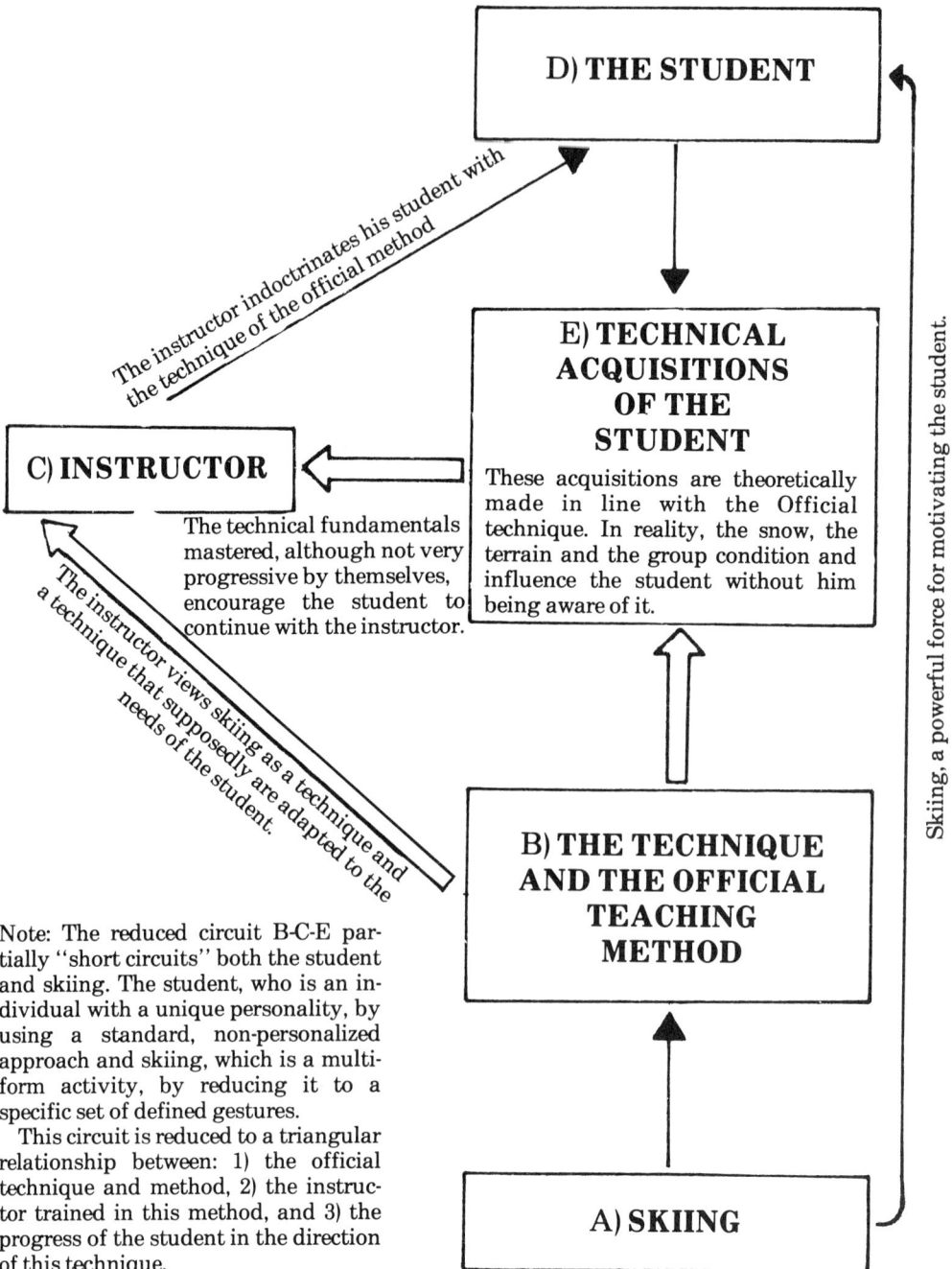

D) THE STUDENT

The instructor indoctrinates his student with the technique of the official method

E) TECHNICAL ACQUISITIONS OF THE STUDENT

These acquisitions are theoretically made in line with the Official technique. In reality, the snow, the terrain and the group condition and influence the student without him being aware of it.

C) INSTRUCTOR

The technical fundamentals mastered, although not very progressive by themselves, encourage the student to continue with the instructor.

The instructor views skiing as a technique that supposedly are adapted to the needs of the student.

Skiing, a powerful force for motivating the student.

B) THE TECHNIQUE AND THE OFFICIAL TEACHING METHOD

A) SKIING

Note: The reduced circuit B-C-E partially "short circuits" both the student and skiing. The student, who is an individual with a unique personality, by using a standard, non-personalized approach and skiing, which is a multiform activity, by reducing it to a specific set of defined gestures.

This circuit is reduced to a triangular relationship between: 1) the official technique and method, 2) the instructor trained in this method, and 3) the progress of the student in the direction of this technique.

A SCHEMATIC REPRESENTATION OF THE STUDENT-INSTRUCTOR RELATIONSHIP IN A MODERN CONCEPT OF LEARNING TO SKI

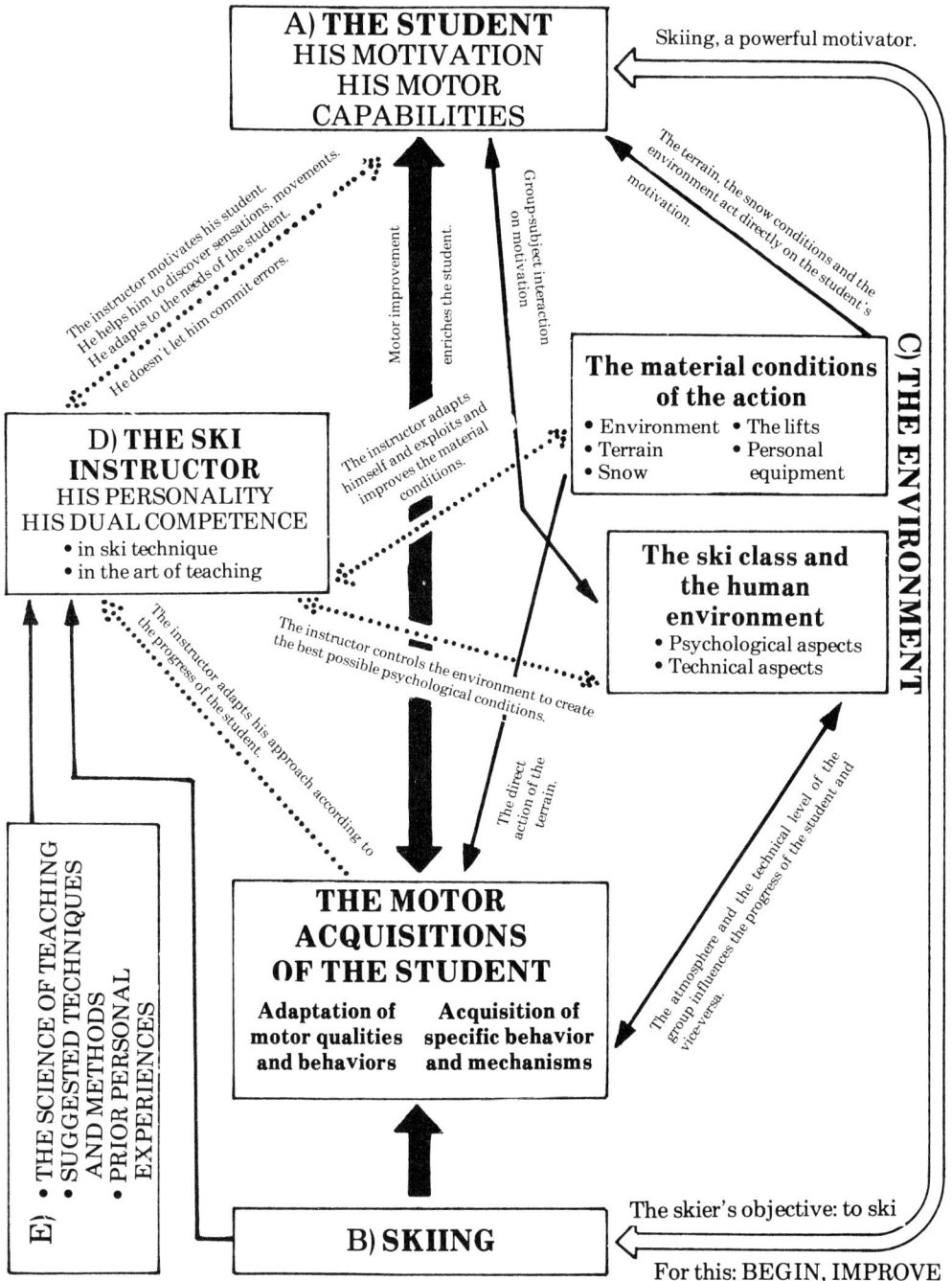

A) THE STUDENT
HIS MOTIVATION
HIS MOTOR
CAPABILITIES

Skiing, a powerful motivator.

The terrain, the snow conditions and the environment act directly on the student's motivation.

The instructor motivates his student.
He helps him to discover sensations, movements.
He adapts to the needs of the student.
He doesn't let him commit errors.

Motor improvement

enriches the student.

Group-subject interaction on motivation

The material conditions of the action
- Environment
- Terrain
- Snow
- The lifts
- Personal equipment

C) THE ENVIRONMENT

D) THE SKI INSTRUCTOR
HIS PERSONALITY
HIS DUAL COMPETENCE
- in ski technique
- in the art of teaching

The instructor adapts himself and exploits and improves the material conditions.

The ski class and the human environment
- Psychological aspects
- Technical aspects

The instructor adapts his approach according to the progress of the student.

The instructor controls the environment to create the best possible psychological conditions.

The direct action of the terrain.

The atmosphere and the technical level of the group influences the progress of the student and vice-versa.

E)
- THE SCIENCE OF TEACHING
- SUGGESTED TECHNIQUES AND METHODS
- PRIOR PERSONAL EXPERIENCES

THE MOTOR ACQUISITIONS OF THE STUDENT

Adaptation of motor qualities and behaviors

Acquisition of specific behavior and mechanisms

The skier's objective: to ski

B) SKIING

For this: BEGIN, IMPROVE

3. Remarks regarding the instructor's behavior

1. The "constructed" skier, the "reflexive" skier, and the "instinctive" skier.

When there is learning by the systematic application of an instruction method, the mental processes and even the mechanical linking of movements can be very different from what they would be during a learning born from a simple confrontation with varied situations. One often describes the result of the first case as a "constructed" skier and the result of the second case as a "reflexive" skier.

— *A "constructed" skier is judged by the quality of his "construction"*, that is to say:
• by the correctness of his body positions and acquired mechanisms,
• by the quality of their combinations,
• by the possibility of their adaptation to exterior elements.

Few skiers can generally be considered to be "constructed" because, during the course of their training, a great part of their learning was necessarily "reflexive". I believe that the ideal for a constructed skier is to have a technique very similar to that of the reflexive skier but free of every technical fault and already prepared for an evolution toward the ultimate techniques of the era with, among other things, the assimilation of new movements.

Note: Too often it is forgotten that the "constructed" skier likely has the handicap of having started the sport late in life.

— *The "instinctive" skier* is the term most often applied to the skier who has educated his reflexes and constructed his automatisms from a young age when the nervous system has a greater capacity for adaptation. This capacity is at a maximum between 9 and 13 years and diminishes with age. The term "instinctive" is poorly applied because there is no

hereditary instinct for skiing in human beings.

Note. The label "instinctive" is usually applied to those skiers who are extremely gifted and have been skiing from a very young age.

2. The "instinctive" skier and the "reflexive" skier have a very limited mental vision of the movements they perform.

A fairly complete mental vision, on the other hand, exists in the constructed skier but this conscious mental vision does not necessarily correspond with the reality of the image of the movement. It often corresponds more closely to the descriptions or demonstrations of the instructor. We see, therefore, the importance of the instructor using language that is clear, concise and realistic; that is to say language that corresponds precisely with what the student is actually doing.

— *The "partially constructed" skier, or at least the skier made partially "conscious" of the nature of his movements, more readily succeeds in correcting his movements and in assimilating others.*

— *The instinctive skier can correct himself only through a search for an improvement in his effectiveness.* (For example: a racer trying to suppress ski-snow contact errors or modify his line in a course).

3. The use of video, film or photography is an aid, but not a cure-all, for helping to create a mental image of a movement and improve its execution. In fact, it is a product of:

a) providing the subject with supplementary visual information,
b) an interpretation of this information,
c) the eventual decision to modify behavior and to attempt the creation of

a new initial motor image, an image which likewise risks having an artificial character, and to not resist the execution of previously acquired automatisms.

Note: The student will have a much better chance of correcting himself if the instructor guides him through steps a, b and c.

The interpretation of the information presented by such an image is always very helpful:
• to confirm or illuminate certain judgements or advice already given by the instructor,
• to permit the student to compare his behavior with that of better skiers in the same circumstance,
• to visually inventory, after a certain period of time, the progress which he has or has not made.

4. The process of imitation should be exploited but presents some dangers. In fact:

— The student, often subconsciously, imitates the most flamboyant aspect of a movement. For example: a useless or even harmful throwing of the arms (a student tends to be visually very sensitive to accelerating movements). Consequently, an instructor's demonstrations must be very sober and include only the essential movements.

— The student sees not only the movements of the instructor, but the gestures of the other students in a group lesson who preceed him. He quickly can forget the gestures made by the instructor.

Furthermore, outside of the lesson the student sees other skiers and this experience will effect the image which he retains.

— Clear and concise instructions should guide a student's attempts at imitation by directing him to the salient features of the movements and mechanisms involved.

TEACHING GROUP LESSONS

Group instruction poses two unique problems. One is technical: the movements proposed must be globally adapted to the nature of the students — children, athletic adults, unathletic adults... — and be suitable for all of the students of the group in spite of their diversity. The other problem is pedagogical: how to arrange the lesson so that all of the students of the group ski as much as possible, an indispensable condition for progress.

When there is a change of students or instructors, or when students are moved from one class to another, an additional problem is encountered: how to assure a homogeneity and continuity in the instruction under such conditions ?

This third difficulty supports the implementation of a standardized instruction method yet this method must take into account the already mentioned diversity of the students and the need for keeping as many of the students moving as possible.

Another consideration that must be taken into account while designing the contents and presentation of any program of instruction is the quality of the instructors who will use it, both their technical mastery and their teaching ability. The more proficient the instructors, the more the instruction program can be general and flexible to allow maximum initiative of the individual instructors to better exploit their personal qualities.

The elements set forth in this book are applicable to several instruction programs adapted to various types of clientele and instructors.

I propose one of them to you that is perhaps best adapted to young people and fairly athletic adults (12 to 35 years old) and to instructors who have a sound knowledge of this book.

Up until level 4, the program covers the needs of a "classical" instruction that is desirable for most groups. Besides preparing for the latest developments in technique, this program is compatible with those promoted in most national ski school teaching systems.

Levels 5 and 6 integrate the latest technical developments and give them special importance because they are of concern to many good skiers who essentially want to modernize their technique.

A few considerations regarding this table.

This table is inspired by the work of the technical ski commission of the professors of physical education and athletics of the Grenoble Academy.

Practical and pedagogical considerations

— *Evaluation of slopes:*
The steepness of a slope, to use the same terminology as in ski lift construction, is the ratio of the vertical drop to the length. Depending on the condition of the snow, slopes of 3% to 7% won't allow speeds of over 7 to 12 miles per hour. Slopes are generally classified as: Flat = 5 to 10%; Medium = 10 to 20%; Steep = 20 to 50%; and Very steep = 50 to 100%.
— *Organization of the instruction:*
Using lifts of 50-300 yards length for levels 1 and 2 or 200-700 yards long for other levels, the instructor can position himself at the middle, at the bottom or at the top of the slope while his students continue to circulate.

Alternatively, the instructor can divide the run into 50-100 yard sections to be skied by the students but without systematic corrections after each section.

— If the class includes non-dynamic, intermediate and dynamic students, the instructor can propose different manuevers to each group or start all students with the same exercises and then progress the more dynamic students rapidly to other exercises. These exercises should be very similar and able to be made on the same terrain.
— Depending on the snow conditions, or the terrain, certain adaptations to the progression will likely have to be made. For example, don't try to study "carving" on soft snow.

Technical considerations

— The positions and the movements proposed are the same as those described in the first part of this book. Only in this way is it possible for the student to move in an orderly manner from level I to level VI.
— The classes are defined by the level which the skier wishes to attain taking into account the level he has already attained and not by his having knowledge of specific exercises.
— "Dynamic" students are students with daring who have the athletic potential to ski forcefully. Success in making a natural hockey stop starting straight down the slope after only a few attempts identifies these students to the instructor.
— Non-dynamic students are not necessarily less gifted. Their more gentle approach often predisposes them to a smooth gliding which better allows them to cultivate their balance and ultimately they may assimilate gliding skills better than the dynamic skiers.
— Practical experience and experimentation with every aspect of this progression has shown that level V and above is only applicable to those students who have been trained according to the preceeding levels. Good and even very good skiers who have not followed this progression should momentarily return to level IV.
— The movements proposed at each level are numbered to indicate the level, the type of student, then the skill category (No. 1 = straight running or schussing; No. 2 = serpents and wedeln; No. 3 = turns; No. 4 = braking and utilitarian movements for difficult terrain). For example, IIB1 denotes level II, average students, exercises of the schuss family.

A SUGGESTED PROGRAM FOR TEACHING GROUP LESSONS OF ADOLESCENTS AND YOUNG ADULTS

Objectives	Technical Elements to be Acquired	Slopes to be used	Non-dynamic students	Intermediate students	Dynamic students
LEVEL I The skier wants to: • Ski on very flat slopes • Stop himself	• Balance • Soft control of the skis • Slowing and stopping	Very flat slopes Flat slopes	IA1. Straight run at low speed. IA2. Long serpent turns in gliding wedge. IA3. Long turns in a 3-step stem. IA4. Braking with a downhill stem in a traverse.	IB1. Straight run at a slightly higher speed. IB2. Long turns in a gliding stem then return to parallel skis. IB3. Id. IA3 then at a higher speed with earlier return to parallel skis. IB4. Brake and stop with downhill stem then foot-steering in a traverse.	IC1. Straight run at higher speed. IC2. Long gliding turns with parallel skis. IC3. Long turns after a lateral spreading of the skis. Higher speeds than IB3. Turns not very round. IC4. Use "braquage" to stop from a straight run.
LEVEL II • Ski on flat slopes • Turn on intermediate slopes	• Control turns with flat skis • Pivoting with flat skis • Pivoting on the edges and braking	Flat slope Intermediate slopes; smooth or bumpy	IIA1. Schuss then stop with downhill stem brake. IIA2. Turns in a gliding stem with alternating pivoting of one ski. IIIA3. Long 2-step stem turns (see IB3). Controlled sliding. IIA4. Uphill stem turn then foot-steered braking. Possibly IA4 then IIA4.	IIB1. Same as IIA1 but with slightly higher speed. IIB2. Gliding turns with a synchronized pivoting of the skis. IIB3. Turns with spreading of the skis and controlled led by pivoting. IIB4. Choice between IIC4 and IIA4.	IIC1. Same as IIA1 but with higher speed. IIC2. Gliding parallel ski turns with linked pivoting. IIC3. Parallel ski turns in a wide stance with pivoting and controlled sliding. IIC4. Hop turn with foot-steering stop (standing start).
LEVEL III • Ski on intermediate slopes • Turn on steep slopes	• Refine flat ski control • Rhythmic pivoting (1st wedeln) • Brake then turn reflex	Intermediate and varied Flat then intermediate slopes Intermediate slopes; smooth or bumpy Steep slopes; smooth, bumpy or deep snow	IIIA1. Straight run in big bumps. IIIA2. First wedeln with rhythmic opening of the skis and braking sideslip. IIIA3. Turns with spreading of the skis and pivoting and controlled sliding. IIIA4. Braking stem then braking turns down the fall line with pole plant.	IIIB1. Id. IIIA1 at higher speed. IIIB2. First wedeln with desynchronized pivoting and braking. Discovery of recoil. IIIB3. Wide stance parallel turns by change of support foot and pivoting. IIIB4. Id. IIIA4 but brief check with a stem or parallel skis.	IIIC1. Id. IIIA1 at higher speed. IIIC2. First parallel ski wedeln with braking and recoil. IIIC3. Id. IIIB3 in a narrower stance with controlled sliding. IIIC4. Brief parallel ski check then hop turn with a pole plant.

LEVEL / Goal	Sub-goals	Conditions			
LEVEL IV • Become a good skier	• The flexion-avalement	Intermediate with bumps	IVa1. Straight runs and traverses over bumps with passive flexion-avalement.	IVB1. Id. IVA1 at somewhat higher speed.	IVC1. Id. IVA1 at higher speed with "braquage" stop.
	• Discover carved control	Intermediate smooth	IVA2. Gliding wedeln with desynchronized pivoting.	IVB2. Parallel ski wedeln with braking and recoil. Pole plant.	IVC2. Id. IVB2 with sliding control between the platforms.
	• Counter-turn platform snow	Intermediate or flat hard	IVA3. Carved, straight turns started by spreading or stemming.	IVB3. Carved turns at high speed started by spreading the skis.	IVC3. Id. IVB3 at higher speed with tail-pressure carving.
	• Gliding wedeln with platform platform	Steep slopes; smooth, bumpy or deep snow	IVA4. Braking counter-turn with pole plant then braking or sliding turn.	IVB4. Counter-turn in wide stance with platform and pole plant.	IVC4. Platform in narrow stance with pole plant. Check wedeln in a wide stance.
LEVEL V • Become a very good skier	• Carving control	Intermediate with bumps	VA1. Id. IVA1 but quicker.	VB1. Id. IVB1 but quicker and with braquage stop.	VC1. Id. IVC1 but quicker with active flexion-avalement.
	• The pivoting wind-up		VA2. Flat ski wedeln with forward thrust of the feet.	VB2. Wedeln with platform and flat ski control.	VC2. Wedeln with carved platforms by forward thrust of the feet (S).
	• The forward thrust of the feet		VA3. Gliding counter-turn with forward thrust of the feet (S).	VB3. Carved counter-turn or sliding with forward thrust of the feet (S).	VC3. Carved counter-turn with forward thrust of the feet (S) then carved control.
	• Passive avalement	Steep with bumps or deep snow	VA4. 'S' turn with passive avalement (bumps or deep snow).	VB4. 'S' turn with platform and passive avalement (bumps or deep snow).	VC4. Short 'S' turns with lateral projection from one ski to the other.
LEVEL VI • Become a complete skier	• Eliminate technical gaps	Intermediate • smooth or bumpy	VIA1. Schuss with active flexion-avalement. VIA2. Surf wedeln with carved platforms and controlled carving.	VIB1. Id. VIA1 and VIC1. VIB2. Id. VIC2.	VIC1. Refine flat ski sliding. VIC2. Surf wedeln with flat skis and with flexion-avalement to absorb the bumps.
	• Optimal snow	• soft or hard snow	VIA3. 'S' turns with carved platforms and control. With or without extension.	VIB3. Id. VIA3 and VIC3.	VIC3. Flat ski 'S' turns with flexion-avalement to absorb pressure. (Especially over bumps).
	• Maximum security	Steep slopes with bumps or deep snow	VIA4. Turns and wedeln with active avalement. Short 'S' turns with lateral projection.	VIB4. Id. VIA4.	VIC4. Turns and wedeln with active avalement.
		Very steep	VIA5. Check wedeln.	VIB5. Id. VIC5 or VIA5.	VIC5. Check wedeln with carving.

— The creation of a logical series of movements is accomplished through the same kinds of movements (eg. schusses, wedeln, etc.).

Nevertheless, the movements acquired in one family can intervene to aid the acquisition of other types of movements. For example, checks and platforms at the beginning of turns prepare for wedeln with platforms.

— The use of set courses is recom-mended as early as level I (use slalom gates or, at levels I and II, the ski poles of the students which also ser-ves to help them to relax their arms and shoulders).

— An introduction to competition can be made at level III.

— Genuine training for competition can begin at level V.

— At level V, it is advisable to prepare the skier for three types of skiing which can add interest:

• "expressionist" skiing (cultivation of the art of good skiing).

• competitive skiing.

• "all terrain", "all snow" skiing.

An orientation to "artistic" skiing (ballet, aerials, freestyle) can be made at level IV but must then be the object of a specialized training.

AN INVENTORY OF TECHNICAL ELEMENTS

This inventory does not pretend to be a scientific study of the movements and behaviors of a skier, but simply to enumerate the technical elements which every skier must acquire, either consciously or subconsciously, in order to become a complete skier. The objective of this inventory is essentially pedagogical.

A later chapter is devoted to biomechanical analyses. It perhaps can partially satisfy the scientific curiosity of those readers particularly interested in technique. Nevertheless, it isn't indispensable to an understanding of the inventory presented here. In sport, as in art, many things are felt or hypothesized. It isn't always evident that by trying to analyze them more, one will understand them better.

The pedagogical inventory which follows will be much too "serious" for many instructors who have already developed an understanding of what is essential in modern ski technique through my discussions in the earlier parts of this book. Nevertheless, it constitutes a com-plimentary step that is almost indispensable for ski professionals who want to dissect the potential behavior of their students or athletes to the finest detail and also for those who want to be able to sense the inevitable evolution of ski technique.

It also can be the starting point for other inquiries.

Method of classification

Three great families:
1. Elements permitting the maintenan-ce of balance.
2. Elements permitting the evolution of flat ski manuevers:
• smooth sliding of the skis
• flat ski pivoting
• linked pivoting (flat ski leg action).
3. Elements permitting the evolution of edged ski manuevers:
• carving
• pivoting on the edges
• counter-turns with platforms
• wedeln with platforms.

Compound elements: These elemen-ts can be acquired as a whole and generally constitute movements.

They can also be acquired incom-pletely, lacking one or more element units. In this case, the same element is usually lacking in all of the student's compound elements already acquired.

Elements acquired by "reflex"
The majority of these are balancing mechanisms.

The fact that these elements can not be learned in a voluntary manner, or even consciously, doesn't mean that we can avoid mentioning them because the instructor can program and control their acquisition by using specific situations to develop them.

Elements not mentioned: In order to streamline our inventory, we will not mention elements which are, in fact, technical errors. Some elements frequently used, particularly for the maintenance of balance, are not men-tioned apart from the compound elements which they are a part of.

This list is not definitive: First of all because exceptionally gifted skiers, starting from today's fundamentals, will invent new elements. Also, because our analysis, begun only 7 years ago, can not pretend to be per-fect. Our research continues in this area.

The vocabulary used has been ex-plained in the preceeding pages or will be explained in the following chapter.

ELEMENTS PERMITTING THE MAINTENANCE OF BALANCE

All of these elements are acquired subconsciously. Mastering them permits maximal relaxation of the legs and feet. When they are lacking, the skier is forced to compensate by blocking the leg and foot.

1. The integration of the ski equipment and the body

a) a total lack of heel lift in all flexion and extension movements.
b) an ability to move the foot, leg and thigh in the vertical and fore-aft plane and through the main axis of the ski.
c) the unusual use of movements which simultaneously mobilize the segments of the two lower limbs in two parallel planes.
d) a capability of finding supplementary support from the ground by planting the ski pole.

2. An acceptance of sliding (always limited to the terminal velocity) by overcoming the inhibitions and defense reflexes born from the sensation of sliding, the perception of acceleration and deceleration and the perception of speed.

3. Adoption of a state of ''muscular awareness'' in a more or less flexed position facilitates balancing mechanisms.

4. Fore-aft balance while sliding on smooth terrain consists of an ability for fine readjustment in the fore-aft balance (211-212-220).

The inability to find support to the front and to the back makes this kind of balance while sliding totally different from normal balance reflexes.

A compound element consisting of:
a) sensitivity in the feet to vertical thrusts from the ground toward the front or the rear.
b) distribution of bending facilitates the fore-aft balancing mechanisms.
c) relative muscular relaxation allowing mobility of the joints as directed by the balancing mechanisms.

5. Fore-aft balance over terrain changes. Maintenance of perpendicularity to the slope (211) (435).

A compound element consisting of:
a) An acceptance of the acceleration of the forward movement of the upper body during the change to a new perpendicularity.

b) an acceptance of the resultant unweighting.
c) a reflexive adjstment to the new perpendicularity.

6. Fore-aft balance in compressions (maintaining perpendicularity) (432).

A compound element consisting of:
a) resisting the fear of the compression which results in muscular blockage and a premature backweighting.
b) supple and progressive adjustment of flexion to maintain perpendicularity in spite of the muscular contractions necessary to resist the compression.

7. Fore-aft balance while passing over bumps (maintaining perpendicularity) (424-427-433)

On big bumps, in addition to the elements cited above, we find:
a) ample bending of the hips, knees and ankles without forward or backward displacement of the pressure exerted by the feet on the skis (note the importance of boots with sufficiently soft cuffs and also the rigidity of many of the plastic boots used today).
b) when the shape of the terrain (eg. moguls) produces an upward vertical thrust of the feet, an inhibition of the reflex reaction to push against this thrust and, instead, the execution of a passive flexion movement to absorb the thrust.
c) a relaxation of muscles to anticipate the passive flexion in (b). This relaxation is often associated with an active ''retraction'' of the legs underneath the body (relaxation of the extensor muscles plus a contraction of the flexors = a physiological unity).
d) flexion producing a forward displacement of the feet relative to the mass of the body (passive flexion avalement) while ascending the upper side of a bump and an extension with a backward displacement of the feet to descend the back-side of the bump. This is an adaptation of the technical element described in (a).
e) An anticipation by lifting the feet and displacing them to the front at the instant before the skis contact the side of the bump (active flexion avalement).

Fore-aft balance during turns.

(maintaining perpendicularity to the slope at each instant of the turn) (234-

437).
A compound element in which we find elements 5 and 6.:
a) accepting what we call the ''dive down the slope'' at the beginning of a turn (very similar to 5).
b) Maintaining fore-aft balance straight down the fall line in the middle of the turn.
c) Maintaining perpendicularity to the slope at the end of the turn (very similar to 6). An acceleration of the movement of the feet relative to the movement of the upper body during the compression tends to accentuate the displacement started in (a).

9. Lateral balance while schussing

A compound element including:
a) A redistribution of pressure on each of the two skis to neutralize any beginning of a loss of balance laterally.
b) A lateral readjustment of pressure over each foot such that the ski remains flat against the surface of the snow.
c) Mobility of body segments in the lateral plane (shoulders and arms in particular).

10. Fore-aft and lateral balance while jumping (217)

A compound element including:
a) A neutralization of all unbalancing impulses during take-off.
b) A forward banking movement which continues in the air to allow a balanced landing (perpendicularity to the slope).
c) An adjustment of balance in the air to neutralize the initial unbalancing impulses and to assure a balanced landing (in both fore-aft and lateral planes).

11. Balance at the beginning of sideslips

The skier leans in an oblique direction:
a) down the slope (maintaining perpendicularity to the slope in the new direction of travel).
b) to the rear relative to the new direction of travel to counteract the increasing braking forces. *Note:* for a very gliding sideslip it is element (a) which is perceived by the skier. For a braking sideslip, it is (b). Element (a) requires that the beginner overcome a genuine inhibition or fear of the slope.

12. Lateral balance during straight sideslipping involves a position often referred to as "vissage" or "twisting-angulation" but currently known as "balanced angulation".

This compound element includes elements of 4 and 9 but also:
a) An acceptance of a position with the chest and head turned in the direction of sliding while the feet and legs are oriented along the axis of the skis.
b) Balancing the frictional forces by increasing the weighting of the downhill ski and leaning slightly backward (opposite the direction of movement).
c) A mobility of the upper body in the lateral plane to compensate for the rigidity of the lower body necessary to maintain the angle of edge-set during sideslips with weighting of the edges.
Note 1: The technical elements permitting control of the lateral sliding of the skis are classified under flat ski sliding turns.
Note 2: The lateral banking movements which are produced during braking or sideslips or sideslipped stops are classified as braking elements or platforms.

Note 3: The "balanced-angulation" position during sideslips is produced by element (12a).

13. Lateral balance during sideslipped turns.
This compound element includes all of the elements of (12) but also:
— In addition to the leaning of the body to balance frictional forces and maintain perpendicularity to the slope, a lateral leaning of the body to balance centrifugal force.
Note: a "mechanical" analysis of the problems posed by the maintenance of balance is presented later.

ELEMENTS PERMITTING THE FLAT SLIDING OF THE SKIS

Skiing with the skis flat on the snow.

14. When skiing in a schuss, or with only slight skidding on the edges, the adapted reflex responses of each of the feet which bring the skis back to their original position every time they deviate from their path (supple skiing) implies elements (3) (4) and (9). Refer to 100.

15. The placement of the ski flat on the snow in a sliding stem is adjusted by displacement of the knee.
Note: We can already mention the "outside positioning" of the knee which will be referred to again in (16c).

16. Adjustments to keep the skis flat on the snow during sideslipping movements with the skis parallel (flat skis signifies only a very slight angle of edge-set).
A compound element consisting of:
a) Sensitivity to the friction between the skis and the snow created by the angle of edge-set (even when this friction is minimal) and by the groove in the base of the skis (and ultimately by the characteristics of the base itself).
b) adjustment of the positioning of the skis flat on the snow by lateral movements of the feet and ankles inside the ski boots (refers to the necessity of the foot not being blocked inside the boot) (514).
c) Adjustment of the positioning of the skis flat on the snow by lateral displacements of the knees (an "outside" positioning or displacement of the knees refers to a displacement of the knees down the fall line while in a traverse and to the outside during a turn. A "return" of the knees is a displacement in the opposite direction.)
d) An adjustment of the positioning of the skis flat on the snow by a lateral displacement of the hips relative to the center of mass. (A displacement of the hips to the outside or an angulation of the hips with the knees displaced to the outside is defined as the "surf" position) (511)

17. Adjustment of the "flat ski carved directional effect". (130)
A compound element consisting of elements (13) and (16) and eventually (19), (22), (23) and (26).
Note: A very fine adjustment or regulation of this sliding directional effect is generally referred to as a "flat ski piloting" of the turn.

Pivoting flat skis (sideslipping and turns)

18. An inclination or leaning of the body down the fall line during the initiation of turns down flat or intermediate slopes facilitates placing the skis flat on the snow at the beginning of the turn (231).
Note 1: This element is in addition to (16).
Note 2: This inclination of the body is only momentary to transiently place the skis flat on the snow at the beginning of the turn. If protracted, it will eventually place the skis on their outside edges.

Passive pivoting of flat skis (130)
19. A passive pivoting of the skis (and the feet) by forward-weighting, a relaxation of the ankles laterally and a lateral inclination to the inside can initiate a curved sideslipping or a turn down the fall line.
A compound element occuring in 2 phases:
a) an inclination of the body to the front and the inside plus a release of the edges causes the skis to sideslip and pivot around the forebody or tips of the skis.
b) an accelerating of the pivoting as the body is returned to a balanced position.
Note: Since this pivoting action is the result of a biting of the edge in the forebody of the skis, it can not be made when the skis are perfectly flat. On the contrary, if the skis are perfectly flat on the snow, something that is very difficult to obtain, forward weighting will increase and cause the tips to sideslip faster (21).

20. Passive pivoting of the skis by forward weighting and a pivoting of the entire body to the inside. This pivoting or "rotation" of the body facilitates the pivoting of the skis (522-a).

21. At the beginning of a turn, a passive pivoting of the tips of the skis down the fall line is produced by shifting the weight to a forward position and relaxing the ankles. (the pivoting is produced by a more pronounced slipping of the weighted tips of the skis down the fall line than the tails of the skis).

22. A passive pivoting of the skis (and the feet) under the knees in a curved sideslipping turn down the fall line results from relaxing the ankles and a lateral leaning of the body to the inside of the turn. The weighted tails of the skis sideslip laterally.

A compound element occuring in two phases:
a) A banking of the body in an oblique direction to the rear and to the inside and a releasing of the edges initiates a passive pivoting of the skis (a pivoting produced by the lateral sideslipping of the weighted tails of the skis being more pronounced than the sideslipping of the tips).
b) This is generally followed by a braking and a weighting of the edges which stops the pivoting (127) except in the case of (23).
Note: Only the initiation of this movement can be made with flat skis.

23. Balancing on the "center of pivoting of the skis", a point on the ski slightly behind the center which permits sideslipping without pivoting or, more precisely, without active pivoting (135).
Note: While sideslipping with the weight balanced over the "straight running center of the skis" there is a slight pivoting of the skis of the type mentioned in (19).

Active pivoting

24. Active pivoting of the feet (and the skis) under the knees with the skis placed in a flat stem and while weighting the center of pivoting of the skis can involve muscular action of:
a) An active pivoting of only one foot with the skis in a flat, gliding stem. This involves a displacement of the knee and a pivoting of the foot (511-c).
b) An active pivoting of both feet with the skis flat and placed in a wedge position (gliding wedge).
c) A sequential pivoting of one foot then the other in the same direction and with the skis placed flat on the snow.
d) Pivoting of one foot, then the other and then both feet simultaneously while in a wide stance (these last two mechanisms are often referred to as "desynchronized" pivoting of the two skis).

25. Simultaneous active pivoting of the feet (and flat skis) under the knees in a very flexed position and generally

in a wide stance (534).

A compound element implicating (23) and;
a) A synchronized pivoting of both feet under the ankles and the lower legs under the femurs. This pivoting movement is called "surf vissage".
b) Eventually a mild lateral pressure against the snow exerted by the forebody of the inside ski (551) in a pivoting started from a straight run. This pivoting, called "steering", is generally more dynamic than (a) and is not made with flat skis. Refer to (69) and (70).

26. Active pivoting of the lower limbs under the chest, ankles and feet in the lateral plane (flat ski "vissage" or an unwinding of flat ski "vissage") and generally in a narrow stance (530).

A compound element including:
a) A pivoting of the femurs under the pelvis,
b) or a pivoting of the pelvis under the lower back,
c) or a combination of (a) and (b).
d) A pronounced counter-rotation of the shoulders.
e) Or, the opposite of (d), a blocking of the counter-rotation of the shoulders aided by a pole plant (78).
Note: (26) can be associated with (25-a) or with (19-a), a forward-weighted passive pivoting. In this latter case, the pivoting is not made with the skis completely flat. The edging of the tips of the skis creates a center of pivoting that is moved forward.

27. An active pivoting of the feet under the knees by "vissage" and a lateral displacement of the knees to keep the skis flat on the snow ("surf pivoting") in a very flexed position and a narrow stance.

This pivoting is made exactly the same as in a wide stance (25-a) (535).

The lateral positioning of the knees permits the centrifugal forces to be balanced while leaving the skis flat. (535-d).

28. An active pivoting of the lower limbs and flat skis under the chest at the start of a turn down the fall line by a recoil or unwinding from "vissage" and a rotating hip projection. (Generally in a narrow stance and in deep snow) (522-d).

A compound element including elements of (26) linked to a rotating hip projection.

29. An active pivoting of the feet (and flat skis) at the start of a turn down the

fall line created by a rotation of the entire body (ususally in a narrow stance) ("thrown rotation" 520).
Note: (29) is usually associated with (19).

30. An active pivoting of the feet and flat skis by "avalement" at the beginning of a turn down the fall line in deep snow or soft snow on a bump.

This compound element is generally learned and made as a global movement. Nevertheless, it can be dissected into the following elements:
a) an unweighting and forward thrust of the skis by a quick "jackknife" type flexing movement followed by extension at the beginning of the turn.
b) During the unweighting (26), the skis are pivoted by an unwinding of the "vissage" that results from (a) occuring with the torso twisted down the fall-line (anticipation). This pivoting is around a center of pivoting that has been displaced to the rear.
c) A pole plant made at the moment of flexion improves balance and can stabilize or decelerate the pivoting of the upper body during the recoil or unwinding from "vissage".
d) During teh final extension, an active pivoting effort can be used with either flat or edged skis to prolong the recoil from "vissage".

31. *A change of support foot* creates a lateral thrust which tends to accentuate the pivoting of the outside ski at the beginning of the turn or wedeln. This is in addition to one of the passive mechanisms (19) thru (22) or active mechanisms (24) thru (29) already mentioned.
Note 1: The effect of changing the support foot is minimal in a narrow stance and greatest in a wide stance.
Note 2: This element includes the lateral spreading of the uphill ski with a slight lateral displacement of the mass of the body at the beginning of the turn but not the lateral throwing of the body mass which a platform on the edges requires (82).

32. An active pivoting of the skis at the end of the turn by thrusting laterally against either both skis or only the outside ski is facilitated by relaxed feet and a recoil of the legs.
Note: The recoil produced by the extension of the legs against the mass of the body produces a pivoting of the skis which is an amplification of (31). It also can be associated with (22) (back-weighting) or with (19) (forward weighting). Only the initiation of this pivoting can be made with flat skis.

33. An unweighting produced by extension in combination with one of the elements (24), (26), (27), (28), (29) or (30) produces a pivoting.
Note: This movement consists of an extension from flat skis. Platforms on edged skis are analyzed later.

34. Progressive edge sets following an unweighting by extension can be used to facilitate the passive pivoting of the skis mentioned in (19), (20) and (22).
Note: This element is frequently combined with a change of support foot (31). The resulting compound element is improperly termed a "weight change" by many national teaching systems including the "French National Ski School Method".

35. Using the thrust which follows an unweighting produced by flexion to accentuate an active pivoting (25) or passive pivoting (19), (20), (22) facilitates the edge release.
Note: Flexion contains two usable elements: at the beginning of the flexion an unweighting and at the end of the flexion a downward thrust.

36. A stabilizing pole plant at the moment that the edges are changed and the skis begin to pivot.
Note: This moment is delayed relative to an actual platform (78).

37. The gradual and prolonged weighting of the skis during an "absorbed-flexion" facilitates the initiation of the skis into an active or passive flexion and reduces ski-snow friction.

38. A forward weighted passive pivoting (19) can be associated with one of the following active pivotings: (24) stems, (26) vissage, (29) rotation, (32) leg recoil.
Note: The combination of (19) with one of the elements mentioned above generally results in such a coherent movement that we have considered them as constituting individual technical elements. Skiers who use them are incapable of using them without using active pivoting mechanisms with forward weighting.

39. Backweighted passive pivoting (22) can be combined with an active pivoting, such as: (24) stems, (25) surf pivoting in a wide stance, (26) vissage, (27) surf pivoting, or (28) hip projection.
Note: Idem 38.

LINKED FLAT SKI PIVOTING (leg action).

40. Rhythmically linked, desynchronized, active pivoting of both feet and with flat skis down the fall line (24 a, c, d *flat ski stem wedeln*)
Note: The rhythm, or more precisely the rhythm of the linking of these movements, is what constitutes the essence of this element.

41. The rhythmical linking down the fall line of an active pivoting of both feet in a wide or narrow stance by successive wind-up movements (linking of (25), (26) or (27)).
Note: Idem 40.

42. Sliding turns and counter turns in a wide stance with flat skis.
A compound element including one new element:
— Linking an active or passive pivoting of the skis up the hill (generally 25) by wind-up movements (409-410) to a pivoting down the fall line.
One generally also finds:
— A change of support foot(31) at the beginning of a second pivoting movement.
— A pole plant to improve balance (36) and facilitate the unwinding of the pivoting.

43. Counter-turns with flat skis in a narrow stance.
Similar to (42) without changing support foot provided there is constant and equal pressure on both feet.

44. Counter-turn with flat skis and a forward thrust of the feet (the 'S' turn).
A compound element including elements of (42) and (43) and also:
a) A slight forward thrust of the feet by extension of the calves under the thighs during the pivoting up the hill.
b) a prolonging of the counter-turn up the hill by planting the pole and tensing the muscles which will start the skis pivoting down the fall line.
c) a pivoting of the skis down the fall line around a center of pivoting that is relatively far back and a control of balance during the slight braking which results as the skis are pivoted into the fall line (427-543).

45. A flat ski counter-turn (or 's' turn) with *"passive avalement"*. Used in particular over bumps or in deep snow.
A compound element including

elements of (44) and also:
a) A folding of the thighs under the torso and a forward thrust of the feet during a sliding curve up the hill to absorb the compression (427-543).
b) An extension as the skis pivot down the fall line which helps the reestablishment of proper fore-aft balance.

46. During the counter-turn described in (44) and (45), the body leans down the fall line and to the inside of the next turn which is started by displacing the skis up the hill relative to the mass of the body. The result is a double pivoting (268).
Note: In (44) and (45), element (46) can replace element (18) (inclination of the mass of the body to the inside of the turn).

47. A rhythmic change of support foot added to the movements of flexion and extension with the feet and ankles relaxed.
A compound element including (31) and possibly including (32), (33), (34) and (35). Its essence is contained in its rhythm.

ELEMENTS UTILIZING EDGE SETS

HOLDING THE SKI ON EDGE

48. Solid edging of the ski is accomplished by: 1). blocking articulations of the foot and ankle in the lateral plane, 2). exerting pressure against the side of the boot (addresses the importance of lateral stiffness in ski boots and proper fit against the foot and calf).
Note: The pressure that is applied to the edge of the skis is often produced by exerting pressure against the shank of the boot both laterally and to the front or laterally and to the rear. This results in pressure being applied no longer to the holding center of the ski (52-127) but in front of or behind the center of the ski.

49. Blocking the thigh under the pelvis into an "angulated-edgeset" position.
Note 1: This position resembles "angulated sideslipping" (12) but involves a more pronounced knee angulation and a blocking of the lower limb in the lateral plane.
Note 2: This stiffening of the lower limb appears to imply a slight retroversion or backward tilting of the pelvis.

50. Placing the weight over the "holding center of the ski", a position that is located behind the pivoting center of the ski when flat. This results in what is referred to as *"tail pressure"*.
A compound element consisting of:
a) a precise static placement of this pressure on the ski.
b) retaining this placement of pressure during flexion movements.
c) retaining this placement of pressure during flexion-avalement when riding over bumps (note also the intervention of the principle of maintaining perpendicularity to the slope (211)).

51. Almost all of the weight is placed on the downhill ski in a traverse and the outside ski in a turn to increase the pressure on the edge of the skis and to facilitate balance.

52. The angle of pivoting of the ski and the amount of pressure applied to the edge are controlled to obtain either a braking sideslip or a carving action.

CARVING

53. The angle of edge-set is precisely adjusted to the degree of holding necessary and to the radius of the turn.

54. The angle of edge-set is regulated as a function of the terrain and turning radius by lateral movement of the outside knee (*"inward knee drive"* or more commonly, *"knee angulation"*).

55. Balance is adjusted laterally by movements of the torso and arms over the hip, or more precisely the head of the femur (12-c) and by adjusting the distribution of weight on the inside ski.
Note: The incapability of modifying the degree of sideslipping to maintain balance requires refined balance adjusting movements of the upper body mass.

56. Regulation of the turn radius by pivoting.
A compound element consisting of:
a) the thigh pivoting under the pelvis with lateral movements of the knee blocked.
b) slight pivoting of the calf under the thigh (tibia under femur) in addition to (a).
Note: The relative inability of the foot, ankle and knee to flex laterally forbids the adjustment of pivoting at this level (560).

57. Pronounced flexion movements in an angulated position without altering the angle of edge-set or the fore-aft distribution of pressure on the skis during a compression.
Note: It is easy to maintain angulation during flexion but difficult during extension.

58. Supple flexion with angulation and slight tail-pressure to establish a progressive and effective carving of the outside ski at the beginning of a turn.
Note 1: When started in an upright position, where lateral displacement of the knee is more difficult to obtain than lateral displacement of the hip, this movement is very different than when started in an already flexed position.

Note 2: The essence of this movement is the fact that the progressive application of pressure to the skis facilitates carving.

59. Dominant or total weighting of the inside ski while turning. (*"cramponnage"* or *"carving on the inside ski"*) (565).
Note: This movement is easier for skiers with bowed legs and is easiest to perform at the end of the turn. It is opposed to element (48).
A compound element containing two phases:
a) an anticipation of the banking of the body forward and to the inside of the turn.
b) then a shift of weight to the inside ski.

EDGE CHECKS

60. Progressive braking by opening a stem and applying pressure to the edges.
A compound element consisting of:
a) a pivoting of the lower limbs under the pelvis that is very different from (24-a) because the knees move to the inside essentially producing a pivoting of the hip.
Lateral blocking of the knee, ankle and foot (49), (50) and (51).
b) displacement of the pressure exerted on the ski back to a point situated between the "flat ski center of pivoting" and the "holding center of the ski".
c) banking of the body backward to compensate for the braking.
d) twisting of the body down the fall line to face the new direction of travel.
e) supple absorption of the compression by the support leg.

61. The stem check to give a powerful and quick braking while traversing.
This compound element includes elements of (60) and:
a) pivoting one foot and ski and placing it forward in the direction of travel.
b) precise application of pressure to the holding center of the stemmed ski in order to stabilize its pivoting. Same as (51-a).
c) Accentuation of the knee angulation produced by the pivoting of the lower limb under the pelvis in order to increase the angle of edge-set.

d) a reverse of the banking movement described in (a) at the end of the braking to return to a balanced position over the skis.

62. Checking by opening a *wedge*. The two lower limbs make movement (60) or (61).

A compound element including elements of (60) or (61) except for (60-d). Also:

In the case of an extensive braking, the action of the hip muscles becomes a special technical element: a "blocking" of the hips.

63. Progressive braking sideslip with parallel skis.

This compound element is sub-divided into:
— A pronounced weighting of the downhill ski to improve stability (12-b).
— A slight active or passive pivoting of the skis up the slope (25), (26) or (27).
— A blocking of the feet and lower limbs in the lateral plane (49), (50) and (51).
a) The pivoting of the skis necessitates pronounced knee angulation to increase the angle of edge-set.
b) The feet are displaced forward to simultaneously create backweighting and a backward banking of the body which stabilizes the braking.

64. Progressive braking with a forward weighted sideslip. One finds elements of (19-a-b) but with a minimum or no releasing of the edges;
a) The passive pivoting of the skis around their holding center, which in this case is positioned to the front, is very quick.
b) The compression produced by the forward weighting accentuates the holding of the skis.
Note: Often a scissoring of the feet, which facilitates a return to a stable position, is the third element of this mechanism (68).

65. Powerful braking in a sideslip.

This compound element includes elements of (63) but also:

Elements of (69) if there is a rapid pivoting of the skis in a wide stance.

Elements of (74) if there is pivoting in a narrow stance.
— The essence of this compound element resides in the linking of (69) or (74) and the anticipated placement of both feet forward in the direction of travel to permit a balanced braking.

66. The *braking directional effect* produced by positioning one or both skis across the direction of sliding.
Note: The frictional forces at the contact between the skis and the snow tend to create a curved movement. The skier maintains his balance over the skis during this movement.

67. Adjustment of the braking directional effect of the skis.

A compound element including elements of (63) or (64) or (65).

The essence of this mechanism resides in the three-way adjustment of:
— The pivoting of the skis relative to the direction of travel (63-b).
— The angle of edge-set controlled by the inward movement of the knee (63-b).
— The fore-aft placement of the pressure applied to the ski (located between the flat ski center of pivoting and the holding center of the skis (60-b)).

68. Adjustment of the braking directional effect of the skis by fore-aft "scissoring" of the two feet.

PIVOTING ON THE EDGES

69. Starting from a straight run down the fall line in a wide stance, a quick and simultaneous pivoting of the lower limbs and edged skis ("hockey stop" (550)). A compound element, the individual elements of which can all be acquired simultaneously in the global maneuver:
a) The decision to act must be made without hesitation and with total committment (an impossibility for some individuals).
b) The initial active phase of the movement involves a lateral pushing of the skis against the snow. The skis are banked onto edge from the beginning of the movement.
— A passive pivoting phase is linked to the braking (65).

70. A simultaneous pivoting of the lower limbs (and edged skis) with a change of support foot in a wide stance at the beginning of a turn.

A compound element including elements of (69) and also:
a) an even more difficult decision to act than in (69).
b) The initiation of the pivoting is similar to both (69) and (74) because the lateral pressure of the skis against the snow is only obtainable once the skis have begun to pivot and the

edges have been changed.
— A change of support foot with or without a displacement of the mass of the body (31) always accompanies the start of the pivoting.
— A desynchronized pivoting (71) is easier to initiate.
Note: the "uphill stem then steering" manuever that is often used in difficult snow conditions employs (70) with a lateral displacement of the mass of the body.

71. A *desynchronized pivoting* of the lower limbs under the pelvis and of edged skis at the beginning of the turn is a compound element including:
— An opening of an uphill stem and pivoting (60-a).
— A change of support foot (31).
— A pivoting of the downhill leg and ski to bring the skis parallel.
— Eventually a simultaneous pivoting of both lower limbs through (70) or (74).

72. Using flexion to thrust against the skis in (69) and (71) to assist their release and start their pivoting.
Note: This element is similar to (35) and is generally associated with a change of support foot (31).

73. Juxtaposition of the pivoting of the skis noted in (69), (70), (71) or (74) with an extension of the outside leg (or occasionally of both legs) to accentuate the braking and pivoting of the skis in a turn initiated in a flexed position or with flexion (72). This element is similar to (32).

74. Initiating a turn in a narrow or semi-wide stance by simultaneously pivoting the unweighted lower limbs and skis under the chest (*"vissage"* (530)).

A compound element including elements of (26-a-b-c-d-f) but without a relaxing of the feet and ankles in the lateral plane which makes an unweighting of the skis by extension (33) or flexion (35) almost obligatory.
Note 1: The displacement of the skis automatically produces the edge change.
Note 2: A change of support foot (31), even if only slightly effective in a narrow stance, can help to start the skis into a pivot (*"vissage with peddling"*).
Note 3: The mechanisms which are often referred to as a "recoil" or "unwinding" of vissage resemble vissage completely provided a platform and wind-up movements aren't used.

Note 4: As in (26), (75) and (77), a pole plant facilitates the vissage.

COUNTER-TURNS WITH PLATFOR-MS.

75. Initiating a turn with a braking counter-turn, a platform, then a dynamic recoil of the feet into the turn.

A compound element including elements of the downhill stem check (61), or parallel skis check (65) and also:

a) A psychological element: the brief check which preceeds the turn allows the attention to be focused on the turn initiation which follows.

b) A distinctive wind-up rhythm groups all of the mechanisms involved in the turn initiation. This rhythm is created by the inertia of the upper body which produces a very brief and intense thrust on the edges, a tensing of the muscles and a recoil that is simultaneously vertical and lateral.

c) A sudden increase in the angle of edge-set produced by a dynamic angulation of the outside knee or of both knees in a hip angulated position.

— The uphill banking of the body mass during the braking is reversed and directed toward the fall line. Idem (61-c), (262).

Note 1: The recoil is generally associated with a change of support foot (31).

Note 2: When this manuever is executed with significant braking it is often referred to as a "counter-turn with platform" or more simply a "turn with platform". When there is essentially no braking but a significant biting of the edges and recoil, the platform is referred to as an "edge-set" which generally implies a utilization of (76) and (77).

76. A "rebound" type of a flexion-extension wind-up movement added to elements of (75) to enhance the vertical component of the recoil.

Note 1: The briefness of the extension phase determines how closely the unweighting follows the platform.

Note 2: If the skier is launched into the air, the banking of the body down the fall line noted in (75) is made around the center of mass while airborn which produces a lateral displacement of the skis up the hill.

77. A pivoting wind-up movement added to elements of (75) and (76) to

add a pivoting component to the recoil.

Vissage involves a wind-up: a relaxed, pivoting "wind-up" of the upper body down the fall line and an active or passive pivoting of the skis up the hill. This recoil or return movement is produced by the elasticity of the antagonist muscles which decelerate this wind-up movement and create a double pivoting in the opposite direction.

Note 1: The upper body is prevented from pivoting in the opposite direction by a pole plant (78).

Note 2: The recoil is quick and follows immediately in turns made with a platform and rebound. It can be prolonged and delayed in 'S' counter-turns (79), (80) and (81).

78. A pole plant made during a platform to assist in (74), (75), and (76) and also to stabilize the upper body during vissage or the recoil from vissage (26), (74) and (77).

79. A counter-turn with platform and a forward thrust of the feet *(an 'S' counter-turn with platform).*

A compound element including all of the elements of a counter-turn with platform but also:

a) A forward thrust of the feet along the axis of the skis during the platform.

b) A utilization of this forward thrust of the feet combined with a pivoting of the skis up the hill and their placement on edge to obtain a curved movement up the hill (amplification of the directional effect).

— When the platform is modest, the movement is similar to that made with flat skis (44): a planting of the downhill pole, a passive pivoting of the chest down the hill line as the skis climb up the hill (44-b) followed by the skis pivoting back down the fall line around the back-weighted pivoting center (44-c).

c) When the platform is very pronounced, it is followed by a large extension of the skier's body.

Note: This extension tends to neutralize the backweighting produced by the forward thrust of the feet.

80. Counter-turns and carved turns ('S' turns) with a forward thrust of the feet and a change of support foot.

A compound element including elements of (79-a-b) and also:

a) A pronounced angulation of the downhill knee during the forward

thrust of the foot to permit a carving up the hill of the weighted downhill ski.

b) A second special element seems to be a recoil from pivoting and a movement intermediate between a change of support foot (31) and a lateral projection (82) following the uphill carving movement. The skier's weight is shifted from the downhill ski (with tail-pressure and knee angulation) and placed on the uphill ski, which becomes the outside ski of the following turn, with tail-pressure and knee angulation.

81. A counter-turn with platform and active avalement.

Used over bumps at high speed and in deep snow.

A compound element which includes elements of turns with flat ski avalement (30) but first:

a) The platform with forward thrust of the feet and counter-turn is made with an extension of the body in the trough that seperates two bumps. This extension is linked with the flexion of the avalement followed by another extension.

b) In deep snow, accentuating the backweighting during the platform with forward foot thrust packs the snow under the skier and creates a bump over which the skier then pivots his skis.

Note: The extension-flexion-extension movement, in both bumpy terrain and in deep snow, is centered in the lower body. The center of mass of the skier remains more or less at the same level.

82. A carved platform over one ski in a wide stance and low, flexed position *(the "surf" platform).*

A compound element including:

a) A platform somewhat resembling (83-c) but with a pivoting and thrust of the foot along the axis of the ski producing a carved support.

b) A change of support foot followed by a pivoting and forward thrust of the uphill ski (either carved or with flat skis).

83. A platform on the downhill ski followed by a lateral projection to the other ski.

This compound element always includes elements (a) and (b) which follow. It can include other elements depending on the form of the movement.

a) The body begins to lean up the hill and then is thrust upward in a direction perpendicular to the downhill ski.

b) The uphill foot is then displaced up the hill. This displacement is more rapid than that of the upper body resulting in a banking of the body down the fall line.

c) For minimal or no lateral displacement of the mass of the body, the platform can be made simply by an inward movement of the downhill leg and with virtually no extension. This movement can be executed in a very flexed position (''surf'' edge-set).

d) For a large lateral displacement of the body mass, the edge-set is made with pronounced hip angulation and with a powerful extension of the support leg. The uphill ski is thrust rapidly up the hill to produce a banking of the body down the fall line while still airborn. This movement is generally referred to as ''lateral projection''.

Note 1: In long turns, the uphill ski is pivoted passively. In short turns it is pivoted actively.

Note 2: The ''surf platform'' compound element (82) uses mechanisms very similar to (83).

84. A distinctive rhythm is used to link the extension of lateral projection with the flexion under compression which occurs at the end of the

preceeding turn.

The essential feature of this technical element is the ability of the skier to delay the linking of the extension to the flexion as a function of the skier's needs (particularly in competition). Linking by a systematic wind-up movement is not necessary.

WEDELN WITH PLATFORMS

85. The ability to link the wind-up movements of platforms in a rhythmic manner down the fall line (platform wedeln or rebound wedeln). These platforms can be (75), (76), (77), (79), (80), (81) or (83).

86. The 2-step rhythm of a braking wedeln. Braking sideslips between successive platforms (75).

Note 1: The extreme limit of this movement is the check wedeln performed in two steps: 1) a platform with pivoting recoil, 2) a braking sideslip with pivoting of the skis and a ''braking directional effect''.

Note 2: A lack of a good rhythm generally causes the skier to confuse the flexion under compression at the end of the turn (which is relatively slow) with the flexion of the platform (which must be very lively). The result is a wedeln with ''pumping''.

87. The 2-step rhythm of a flat ski wedeln with platforms. Sliding sideslips are executed between platforms (77) or (79) with pole plants (ie. the ''classic'' or ''Austrian'' wedeln).

Note: Each element of this wedeln consists of two steps: 1) a platform with recoil at a lively tempo, 2) pivoting sideslip with flat skis in a slow, relaxed tempo.

88. The 2-step rhythm of a carved wedeln. Carving is applied between the carved platforms of (80) or (83). (refer to (48) and (55)).

Note: A carved platform on both feet can be followed by carving on one ski or a carved platform on one ski can be followed by carving on the other. The change of rhythm of the carved platform is more a function of the ''roundness'' of the turn made by the skis than the vertical thrust.

89. Wedeln with carving of the outside ski by change of support foot (the ''peddled'' wedeln).

90. Wedeln by linking turns on the inside ski (linking of 59). This movement differs from compound element (59) in that the platform on the inside ski is made from the beginning of the turn.

Assorted technical elements.

Accelerations

90. Skating projection
A compound element consisting of:
The inclination and thrust of lateral projection.
a) followed by completing the turn with banking to the inside,
b) the projected ski is placed in a divergent position and the skier transfers to this ski.

91. Accelerating pole plants. One or two poles.
The pole is planted obliquely to the rear. The thrust of the arms must be greater than the speed of movement.

Jumped turns

92. Turns by pivoted jumps.
These can consist of one of the two following elements or (a) then (b).

a) a pivoted jump with rotation or ''projection circulaire''.
b) a jump with anticipation and then recoil from vissage.
A pole plant (78) stabilizes the body and the recoil from vissage in (b).

Hydroplaning and hyperback-weighting

93. A ''hydroplaning'' of the skis at high speed and on very light powder snow.
A compound element including:
a) An equal distribution of weight over both skis in a narrow stance.
b) Sliding with a minimum of braking
c) The discovery of a new flat ski center of pivoting in a back-weighted position.
Note 1: Tilting the tips of the skis upward relative to the snow surface while hydroplaning gives an im-

pression of extreme back-weighting which is incorrect.
Note 2: The pivoting of the skis seems to correspond simultaneously to a lateral slipping of the tails (22) and a ''windshield wiper'' pivoting (94). This pivoting is stopped by increasing the angle of edging.

94. Pivoting with extreme back-weighting in deep but dense snow and on steep slopes.
A compound element including element (93-a) and:
a) Backweighting is accentuated by leaning against the backs of the boots to make the tips of the skis rise out of the snow. The skis are then pivoted around a center of pivoting that is now situated behind the boots using a lateral displacement of the knees and feet in the same direction (''windshield wiper pivoting'').

b) This extreme backweighting can be produced by actually banking the upper body backwards.

c) The pole plant which accompanies this movement is made very far back. This permits stability during the backward banking of the body and aids the windshield wiper pivoting.

Note 1: The result of a moderate pivoting of this type is usually a "surf" type flat ski sideslipping.

Note 2: A dynamic pivoting can lead directly to a traverse in the opposite direction.

Note 3: This element is often confused with the 'S' counter-turn with passive avalement (45) or with avalement (30). The only common element is the forward thrust of the feet (543-c).

Tactical use of bumps

95. The rational exploitation of bumps demands a certain number of tactical behaviors:

a) Taking advantage of the tops of the bumps to pivot the skis.

b) Using the backs of the bumps (provided they aren't too steep) to brake by sideslipping or by extension (32-73) or to extend after an 'S' counter-turn (45-b).

c) On the contrary, bank against the sides of the bumps during the turns to minimize sideslipping and, consequently, loss of speed.

d) Use the front or flat summit of bumps to make a braking counter-turn, platform or 'S' counter-turn.

e) Ski with flat skis at the bottom of the troughs and with serpent between the bumps.

f) Use the rhythm imposed by a succession of bumps to accelerate the rhythm of a wedeln.

TECHNICAL ANALYSES

In this chapter I will attempt to present a few topics for those of my readers who are particularly interested in technical problems. Unfortunately, I'm not able to develop the supporting arguments behind certain new technical concepts presented in this book in a complete manner anymore than I was able to present the pedagogical experiences and the first statistical studies, that I completed with by students and collaborators, in the section "Pedagogical Documents". I therefore must excuse myself in advance to those with a scientific bent for the somewhat superficial nature of the analyses which follow and for any misunderstandings which may result.

I would also like to remind you that the object of my studies is technological and not purely scientific. I will adopt a non-scientific hypothesis more readily if it is based on practical observations or sensations that have been clearly perceived by specialists on snow or, furthermore, if it gives more coherence to a collection of indisputable practical phenomena. As an example, I can cite the hypothesis of the existence of centers of pivoting or of holding that are strictly defined along the length of the ski. Or, the involvement of a specific muscle group. These are observed facts which, nevertheless, would be extremely difficult to prove in a scientific manner. I therefore must ask for the greatest indulgence on the part of my readers.

Some readers may be surprised by the total absence of a bibliography in this chapter. First, I would like to point out that this book is a "popular" work. Furthermore, the diversity of the problems approached would have required me to refer to a great number of works and articles treating a variety of sports while my references to works treating skiing would have been very meager. This is why I prefer to devote these supplementary pages to as global a study as possible of the problems posed by skiing and continue to hope that perhaps this study may encourage specialists to research some of the problems discussed here so that skiing may evolve to the level already attained by numerous other sports.

A NEW CONCEPT OF SKI TECHNIQUE

1. The behavior of the skis on the snow

In the past, one usually spoke of the gestures of a skier. These have been described from an external standpoint using assorted biomechanical analyses to discuss the mechanics of the joint and muscle physiology involved.

I believe that I was the first author to attach less importance to the exterior form of a movement than to the perception that the subject has of the movement while executing it.

This requires a kind of an "interior" vision of the movement.

This analysis "from the interior" has led me to place considerable importance on the functioning of the machine which the skier drives: his skis. The race car driver can not draw more out of his car than it can give: be it acceleration, braking, road holding ability... He operates his car in such a way as to bring out the maximum but the characteristics of the car and its behavior on the track to a very great extent condition his own behavior. It is very much the same with skiing yet until the present we have paid far too little attention to the behavior of the skis themselves.

This is why I will first analyze the behavior of the skis on the snow as a function of their placement (flat, on the edges, more or less pivoted...) and of the placement of the pressures exerted on them by the foot of the skier and without ignoring the critical role played by the ski boots in transmitting these pressures.

2. The essential element of ski technique: maintaining balance.

The audacious beginner who launches himself fearlessly and without any instruction down the slopes and with the only objective of not falling will develop balance reflexes and skills that will make him far more effective on his skis than those students who have laboriously learned the movements of an artificial technique but who, because of a lack of mileage on skis, have not been able to resolve the problems of maintaining balance.

Even if the balancing mechanisms of skiing can not be perceived and, consequently, can not be consciously developed by the skier, it is essential to try to understand them so that we can avoid movements which seem to work in opposition to them and try to better understand the solid foundations of certain new movements.

It is interesting to note that the evolution of racing techniques seems to be more and more in the direction of balance reflex mechanisms.

At the same time, the general concept that the evolution of ski design and engineering is influenced by racing techniques leads one to conclude that more and more of the modern skis permit turns, wedeln and bumps to be skied simply by exercising these same balancing reflexes.

This is why before I address the movements of skiing, and after having studied the behavior of modern skis on snow, I will analyze the complex leaning movements that are indispensable to maintaining balance while sideslipping as well as in straight running, turning, and wedeln.

3. The "behavior" and the movements of a skier must be differentiated.

The skier is not a robot. One can not pretend to program him with thousands of responses to given situations. He must first perceive primordial sensations. He must also understand the emotional and psychic factors which play an essential role in his success or failure.

4. The analyses of the movements of skiing.

These will be presented briefly with special emphasis on new movements.

SKI-SNOW INTERACTIONS
THE BEHAVIOR OF THE SKIS ON THE SNOW

The analyses which follow pay little attention to the sensations of his skis that the skier perceives. As I have mentioned before, human senses are only of a differentiating or contrasting nature. Furthermore, the same sensations can be interpreted quite differently by different skiers. Nevertheless, I devote a special section at the end of this chapter to the perceptions that a skier has of the behavior of his skis.

100. Straight running with the skis flat on the snow.

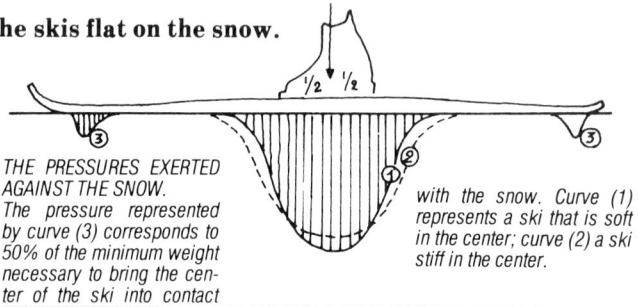

101. The skis exert a thrust perpendicular to the surface of the snow that is proportional to the weight of the skier plus the skis. The average thrust per square centimeter is a function of the surface area of contact.

102. The distribution of pressure exerted against the snow over the length of the ski is a function of the ski's stiffness and camber:
a) the force necessary to flatten the camber is transmitted to the snow equally by the two extremities of the ski;
b) the softer the central part of the ski is, the more localized under the foot will be the pressure exerted by the weight of the skier against the snow.

103. The friction produced by the packing of the snow under the ski as it slides forward seems to be a function of:
a) The pressure exerted at the first point of contact (the impact exerted by the tip of the ski depends on how far it sinks into the snow).
b) The progressiveness of the increase in pressure exerted between the first point of contact and the point where the pressure is maximum.
c) The existence or non-existence of a zone where the pressure exerted by the ski against the snow is excessive.

There must, therefore, be a compromise between (b) and (c).

A soft tip and shovel of the ski will reduce the impacts which are produced in the tip area. But an excessive softness will risk vertical oscillations or "flapping" of the tips (109). An excessively soft ski, therefore, accentuates the shocks transmitted to the feet of the skier and consequently to the center of the skis against bumps.

THE PRESSURES EXERTED AGAINST THE SNOW.
The pressure represented by curve (3) corresponds to 50% of the minimum weight necessary to bring the center of the ski into contact with the snow. Curve (1) represents a ski that is soft in the center; curve (2) a ski stiff in the center.

slight push

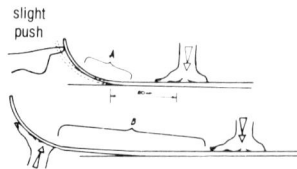

Two zones of flexing (a and b) in the front half of the ski must be considered.

104. A constant pressure exerted on a ski seems to produce less braking than a series of alternating weak and strong thrusts.

By the same token, a constant and equal weighting of each of the two skis produces less braking than a continual transfer of weight from one ski to the other.

105. Slight variations in the placement of pressure over the length of the skis by the skier don't seem to significantly effect their sliding in a straight run. These variations in pressure distribution seem to have a more pronounced effect on the straight running directional effect of the skis (117).

The manufacturers determine, through repeated tests on snow, the location of the central point of the ski. This point is marked on the skis and permits the bindings to be located in such a way that the sole of the boot coincides with the center of the ski.

The positioning of the foot along the length of the ski is more critical for the control of turns than for straight running. It more or less corresponds to the point of application of forces exerted by the skier on the skis. Yet today, young skiers and racers seem to habitually apply pressure to the ski ½ to 1½ inches behind this point.

106. The braking produced at the contact between the skis and the snow is a function of the coefficient of friction. The coefficient of friction defines the relationship between the force of friction and the component of the skier's weight that is perpendicular to the surface of the snow (for example, a coefficient of friction of .03 or 3% that is typical of polyethylene ski bases represents 3 pounds of friction for every 100 pounds of skier and skis or a force of friction that is more or less equal to the component of gravity that is in the direction of travel of a skier in a straight run on a slope of 3%).

This coefficient of friction is a function of the nature of the materials which are in contact. On one side, the snow: the shape of the crystals (or more precisely the shape and form of the irregularities of the surface of the

258

snow), the hardness of the crystals, water content... On the other side, the base of the ski: the plastic running surface (the physical-chemical nature of this surface, the shape and form of any irregularities and the alignment of these irregularities) and the surface of the edges (size and shape of any irregularities or scratches, alignment...).

The presence of wax can modify the nature of this contact. The characteristics of the wax and of the surface of the wax can be the same as the plastic surface or only partially the same if the wax is scraped just to the level of the ridges of the base irregularities.

The condition of the surface of the base, even at the microscopic level, seems to have a considerable effect on sliding. Consequently the importance of any modifications of the state of the surface, which has been microplaned at the factory, by successive impregnations of wax or by repeated use of solvents for removing wax. Furthermore, the deleterious effect of any indentations or scratches accidentally made in the base with a metal scraper.

107. The unique characteristics of snow make the friction of the skis sliding over the snow correspond neither to the rules of friction between two solid surfaces nor to those of a solid surface sliding over a liquid sur-

face.

It is generally acknowledged that at the microscopic level, small droplets of water are formed at the points of contact between the ridges of the skis base and the surface of the snow and that these water droplets serve as lubricants.

These micro-droplets must be formed by the relative warming produced by friction and by the property of ice that causes it to be transformed into water when compressed (the specific weight of water is less than that of ice). This characteristic of snow explains the difficulty of trying to manufacture an artificial skiing surface which slides as well as snow.

Sliding becomes poorer when there is an increased production of water between the snow and the base. The droplets of water then become a film of water which has a braking effect.

Sliding is also poor on very cold snow (-15° to -30°C.) where the snow crystals are very sharp and very hard. Evidently, because micro-droplets of water are no longer formed, the snow can only be slightly more slippery than sand and this creates very difficult waxing conditions. On these very cold snows, the charges of static electricity that are produced by the friction of the skis sliding over the snow appear to play a role in reducing the sliding.

108. The particular characteristics of ski wax are:

— **Hardness**. The hardness of the wax must be just a little less than the hardness of the crystals on the surface of the snow. Wax manufacturers produce ranges of waxes with different hardness and these are indicated by different colors.

—**Hydrophobicity** (the capacity to repel water). Most manufacturers seem to have adopted yellow coloring for their most hydrophobic wax.

—**Plasticity**. This characteristic of wax allows it to cover the irregularities in the base of the ski so that they are less abrasive. Any additional materials which make the waxes adhere better to the base or make it more resistant to abrasion are always less "slippery" than the fundamental components of the wax.

Manufacturers often speak of "secret" additives which can be added to their wax formulas much as one adds doses of additives to automobile oils. Waxing has always had a hint of alchemy...

109. The mechanical construction of the ski can influence the vibrations of bending and torsion at high speeds. This "flapping" of the skis (low frequency vibrations of bending) plays an important role in their sliding. It seems to be essential to dampen these vibrations but not to dampen them too much.

110. The flat ski sliding directional effect in a straight run.

111. The length of skis makes them slide best along their main axis.

112. The pressure transferred to the front and back extremities of the ski by its camber (102-a) accentuates this effect (111).

113. On snow that is soft enough for the skis to leave a track, the central groove of the base, or more precisely the two lateral sides of this groove, create platforms against the snow which enhance the ski's stability.

114. The very fine grooves that are engraved in the surface of the plastic base, or etched in a layer of wax, produce the same effect as the central groove, particularly on snow with very sharp and hard crystals or very hard

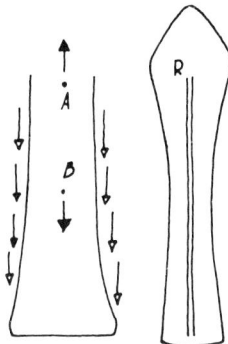

STRAIGHT RUNNING DIRECTIONAL EFFECT.

A = center of pressure of the skier plus skis. B = center of application of

and broken crystals that have been packed by the wind.

Note: The grooves that are etched into the ski by a belt sander can make the ski unsteerable in certain snow conditions because it "tracks" too well.

115. The curved edges and the progressive widening of the ski creates a slight "snowplow" effect (the back half of the ski flares approximately 1 centimeter from the center to the tail). The braking that this snowplow effect creates makes it behave as a rudder to stabilize the direction of sliding except on extremely hard snows with a very smooth texture (ie. frozen water).

frictional forces from the "snowplow" effect.

116. The curved directional effects which are produced by the arc of both sides of the ski (sidecut) neutralize themselves when the skis is perfectly flat. This is no longer the case as soon as the ski is tipped slightly onto edge, particularly if the edges are railed because of excessive wear of the base.

117. A slight forward or backward displacement of the pressure that the skier applies against the skis over their length effects the straight running directional effect.
a) A backward displacement of this pressure seems to increase the "rudder" effect of the tail mentioned in (115) but also diminishes the directional effect of the forebody of the ski which then tends to "float" laterally.
b) A forward displacement of pressure will increase the directional effect of the tip of the ski but will also increase the risk of catching an edge. If one ski is tipped slightly onto edge, it will immediately diverge from the direction of travel. Likewise, the "rudder" effect of the tail is reduced.

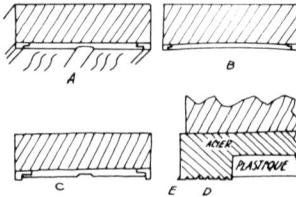

ELEMENTS WHICH CAN HAMPER A "SUPPLE" STRAIGHT RUN SLIDING OF THE FLAT SKI SLIDING DIRECTIONAL EFFECT.
A, grooves or scratches running across the base or edges of the ski. B, a concave base with protruding edges. C, railed edges resulting from excessive base wear. D, deep grooves or scratches. E, a "burr" resulting from improper filing of the edges.

A specific point intermediate between (a) and (b) can be defined the "center of pressure for flat ski straight running".
Note: Physiological considerations (421) require that the binding be placed on the ski such that the center of the foot is adjacent to the center of pressure of the ski as just defined.

118. During slight lateral displacements (a pivoting or tipping of one ski) in a straight run, all of the elements which may produce a flat ski curved directional effect (138) will result in slight braking. This braking seems to be at a minimum when the base is perfectly plane and smooth laterally.

119. Holding the ski firmly in place by the foot will control the displacements of the ski mentioned in (118) but the resulting play of the edges against the snow will generally create more braking than (118).
Consequently the importance of what we have termed the "supple control" of the skis.

120. The carved sliding of the skis.

121. When banked onto edge, the ski imprints a track into the snow.
This track can be more or less distinct depending on:
a) The hardness of the snow. It must be soft enough that the edges will bite into it yet firm enough that it won't crumble under the pressure. The ski can also leave a track by pressing against the fine irregularities of the surface of a very hard snow.
b) The effectiveness of the "tool" which slices through the snow: the edge of the ski. This tool acts somewhat like the blade of a knife; it should be hard and well sharpened.
c) The manner in which the edges work: the angle of attack, speed and pressure exerted on them.
Note: The angle between the base of the ski and the snow surface is called the **"angle of edge-set"**.

122. A ski tipped onto edge but not weighted contacts the snow only at the two extremities. The arc of the edge of the ski, or side-cut, doesn't allow it to contact the snow over its entire length if it isn't flexed into a

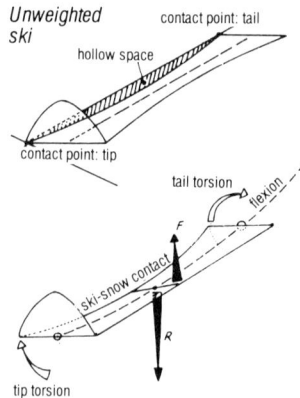

FLEXION AND TORSION OF A SKI PLACED ON EDGE.
The ski is held on edge by the force F exerted by the skier on the lever system represented above. A is the fulcrum, R the skier's weight and F the force applied by the abductor muscles of the foot.

reverse camber. When weighted, it establishes an arc of contact. The tip and tail of the ski are twisted during this flexing. The form of this arc of contact depends simultaneously on:
a) The lateral arc or side-cut of the ski (since this arc isn't uniform over the entire length of the ski, one normally refers to the arc of the tip, center and tail of the ski).
b) The flexibility of the ski and the distribution of this flexibility over the length of the ski.
c) The torsional flexibility of the tip and tail of the ski (and the distribution of this flexibility).

123. A curve scribed by the ski will be perfectly carved if if follows precisely the arc made by the edge in contact with the snow. In reality, however, there is always a degree of sideslipping which results in a bank or ledge of packed snow over which the ski slides. One refers to this as a "carved directional effect".
Note 1: The difficulty of precisely drawing the same carved arc with both skis at the same time is one

reason why carved turns are made with the weight carried on one ski (usually the outside ski but occasionally the inside ski). Another reason is the better holding available by weighting only one ski.
Note 2: A traverse in a straight line can not be perfectly carved.

124. A line which permits a perfectly carved turn implies the creation of a groove in the snow which makes a solid platform perpendicular to the thrust exerted by the skier against the ski.

125. In a carved turn, the momentum of the skier is "deflected" much like that of a train against the rails in a turn.

126. The mechanical work required to make this track, even in a perfectly carved turn, implies a certain amount of braking. This braking can be very slight in certain snow conditions and relatively great in others (for example, a very dense, well packed snow with a high water content results in a great deal of braking during a carved turn).

127. Carving seems to be most easily attained when the axis of the pressure exerted by the skier on the skis passes through the ankle and is applied to a point on the ski that is

MEASURING TORSION
*The ski twists around the pressure point **A**. For a given moment (**P** x **l**) there will result an angle of torsion (**X**). This angle of torsion ranges from 3° to 4° for metal skis and from 5° to 8° for fiberglass skis.*

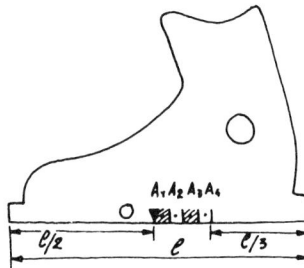

*The arrow engraved on the boot (identified by 0 in the diagram above) indicates the mid-length of the sole. Zone **A1** is the pressure center for straight running (101). **A2** is the center of flat ski pivoting (135). **A3** is the pressure zone for braking sideslipping (157) and **A4** the pressure zone which permits maximum holding of the edges (127).*

relatively far back in relation to the two points defined earlier (the center of pressure for flat ski straight running (117) and the flat ski center of pivoting (135)). I propose that we define this point the *"center of maximum holding"*.

128. The mechanical and dimensional characteristics of the ski which facilitate carving are: 1) the ski width (a narrower ski requires less muscular effort to hold it on edge); 2) the shape of the side-cut (the more extreme or "radical" the side-cut, the more the ski tends to scribe a carved turn); 3) a good balance between flexion and torsion (taking into account the skier's weight and customary skiing speed); 4) a proper compromise in the elastic dampening of flexion and torsion; 5) the proper distribution of all of these elements between the tip and tail of the ski.
   Since all of these elements combine to define the character of the ski, it is extremely difficult for the skier to attribute a perceived behavior of the ski on the snow to any one of these elements. By the same token, advertising claims made by the manufacturers regarding one or another of these elements doesn't necessarily imply an improvement in performance. The ski is a "cocktail" of elements and must be appreciated as such...

130. The flat ski sideslipping of the skis. Passive pivoting. The curved flat ski directional effect.

131. During flat ski sideslipping, the carrying surface of the ski is at a maximum. Sinking of the ski into the snow is, therefore, at a minimum (contrary to 121).

132. Flat ski sideslipping always increases the danger of catching the outside edge. The skier can reduce this risk by applying slightly more pressure to the inside edge of the ski. This results in a slight deformation of the snow surface or a very slight "edge-set".

133. In reality, flat ski sideslipping is not made with the skis perfectly flat. It therefore to some extent shares the same characteristics as sideslipping on the edges.

134. A flat ski sideslipping executed

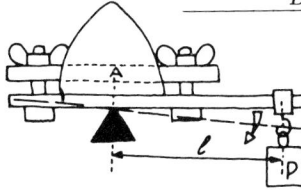

The edge of the groove opposite the direction of lateral sliding plays an important role in the flat ski directional effect.

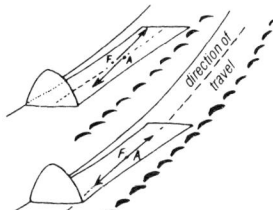

*If **A**, the point of application of pressure exerted by the skier, and **F**, the point of application of frictional forces, are not overwhelmed, they will combine to cause the ski to pivot around itself.*

with the skier's weight applied to the same position on the ski where it is during flat ski straight running will result in a passive pivoting of the ski with the ski turning up the hill or to the inside of the turn.
   One can conclude that this passive pivoting is the result of increased forces of friction at a point ahead of the pivoting center of the ski.

135. The passive pivoting of the ski vanishes as soon as the skier moves the point of application of pressure slightly to the rear. I specify "slightly" because a more pronounced displacement will produce a different effect.
   It is in this precise position where the skier encounters the least resistance from the ski for making an active pivoting of the ski up the hill

and forward ("active" implies the use of muscular action).

I propose that we call this point the *"flat ski center of pivoting"*.

136. The process of turning a ski from a straight run down the slope to a flat ski sideslipping requires a three-way displacement of the ski in the plane of the slope.
a) it moves forward
b) it pivots around itself (134)
c) it transforms its initial momentum into a curved movement in a direction very near its longitudinal axis. This is what we call the "flat ski curved directional effect" or more shortly the "flat ski directional effect".
Note: As we mentioned in (133), since the ski is actually never placed perfectly flat on the snow, this movement involves frictional forces but these are trivial compared to the frictional forces produced by a braking directional effect (150).

137. This directional effect can only be analyzed mechanically by considering the forces of the ski-snow contact which progressively modify the direction of travel just as the front tires of an automobile do during a slightly skidded turn.

The forces arising from the ski-snow contact are referred to mechanically as centripetal forces.

138. Which forces create this directional effect and where are they applied ?
a) The small forces exerted against the inner side of the base of the ski which is weighted more than the outside of the ski (132). The shape of the arc of this edge tends to provoke a curved displacement but this effect is very small.
b) The inside edge of the central groove of the ski pressing against a ridge of snow produced by packing tends to create a sliding of the ski along its longitudinal axis. The resultant sliding of the ski is in an oblique direction between the longitudinal axis of the ski and that of the initial movement.
Note 1: This inside edge of the central groove is less sharp than the edge of the ski but its angle of attack to the snow is much more favorable (the angle of attack of the edge of the ski is only a few degrees).
Note 2: The action of (b) can be clearly demonstrated by filling the central groove of the ski with wax or

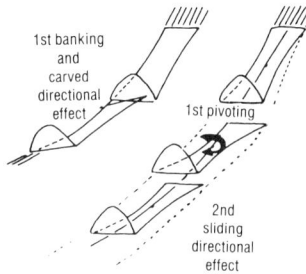

1st banking and carved directional effect

1st pivoting

2nd sliding directional effect

by eliminating the groove under the foot such as on ballet skis.
c) The longitudinal grooves mentioned in (114) appear to have the same effect.
Note: A laterally concave base or edges sticking out above the base (railed) create an effect too brutal to favor the flat ski directional effect which is, above all else, a sideslipping manuever. A perfect laterally planed base allows the optimal flat ski directional effect.

139. The very small increases in pressure exerted on the inside edge of the base can produce holding forces in the tip directed toward the inside, because of its greater width, relative to the direction of sliding.
Note: this is a uniquely sensitive mechanism when going from a

straight run to initiating a flat ski directional effect.

140. This directional effect increases as a function of the angle of pivoting of the skis only to a point from which there seems to be a very clear increase in braking without a corresponding increase in the directional effect.

141. The forces producing this directional effect will have little influence on major directional forces in the opposite direction.
a) gravity (or more precisely the component of gravity in the plane of the slope) as it draws the skier down the fall line during a turn up the hill or the end of a turn down the fall line.
b) gravity on slopes of a certain pitch.
c) these directional forces can not be used to drive turns with significant centrifugal forces (eg. turns with short radii for a given speed or a turn with speeds too great for a given radius).

142. The flat ski directional effect is particularly effective at the beginning of turns where it acts in the same direction as gravity.

There is a genuine directional effect of the skis only when the resultant arc at the beginning of the turn is rounder than the simple trajectory that would result if the skier merely allowed gravity to progressively effect the direction of travel of the skis.

At the initiation of turns down the fall line, even on steep slopes, the skis are momentarily placed flat against the snow because of the anticipated inclination to the inside of the turn.

143. The flat ski curved directional effect seems to be more effective when the skier has more or less equal pressure on both skis. The passage to a weighting of one ski generally is accompanied by an increase in the angle of edge-set.

144. The characteristics of the ski which facilitate active flat ski pivoting are different from those which facilitate the flat ski curved directional effect. Soft skis, which carry much of the weight directly under the foot, facilitate active flat ski pivoting. A ski that distributes weight more evenly over its length (traditional and some "intermediate" skis) are more sensitive to the flat ski curved directional effect.

150. Braking while sideslipping on the edges. Passive pivoting. The braking directional effect.

151. A sideslipping with weighting of the edges, or a braking sideslipping, implies simultaneously:
a) A significant pivoting of the skis across the direction of travel (more than 10° or 15° depending on the snow conditions). This is customarily referred to as the "angle of pivoting of the skis". A lesser pivoting, with the skis banked onto edge, tends to produce a carving.
b) A significant angle of edge-set (121).

152. The carrying surface of the ski during this kind of sideslipping depends only on the consistency of the snow. If the ski doesn't sink into the snow at all, the carrying surface is theoretically limited to the edge of the ski. In reality, however, there is always some sinking in and the carrying surface diminishes as the angle of edge-set increases.
Note: The surface of the edge can essentially be the carrying surface.

153. In a braking sideslip, one can consider the edges to be a tool working against the snow.
This tool is somewhat like a scraper. To be effective on ice, it must be hard and well sharpened. It must "attack" the snow with a favorable angle of edge-set. Equally, the angle of pivoting must be significant relative to the direction of travel. If not, the "scraping" braking action becomes a "carved" action (161).

154. The flexion and torsion produced on the ski during edging (122) results in a certain distribution of pressure along the entire length of the ski and, consequently, a characteristic holding quality. The holding ability of the front and tail halves of the ski should be equal if the skier is to feel balanced during a braking sideslip.
A ski that is too stiff in flexion or in torsion will place too much pressure on the extremities of the ski and vice versa. The tip and tail of the ski will then successively bite the snow and then release, a phenomenon that is called "chattering".
To distinguish between the holding of the ski on the snow during a braking sideslip and the holding which allows carving, we often refer to the first kind of holding as "biting"

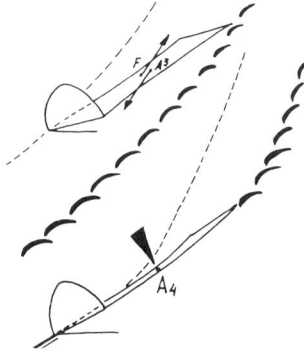

In a braking sidelip, the combination of elements cited on page 261 tend to accentuate the pivoting of the ski. The skier's foot resists this pivoting.
*Increasing the angle of edge-set and moving the skier's weight from point **A** to point **A4** (the center of maximum holding) can stop the pivoting and produce a carved effect.*

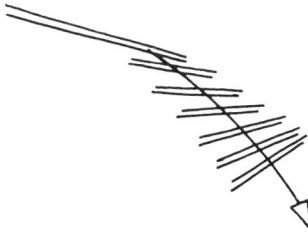

On a steep slope, gravity can oppose the braking directional effect and even result in a direction of travel in the opposite direction.

and the second as "carving".

155. A braking sideslip made with the skier's weight applied to the pressure center of straight run sliding produces a passive pivoting of the ski around itself uphill during a sideslip or to the inside during a turn.
As with flat ski pivoting (134), One can conclude that this is due to a combination of braking forces applied to the front of the ski.

156. The flexing of the ski, when placed on edge, increases its tendency to pivot.
The side-cut of the front half of the ski tends to increase the angle between the arc scribed by the tip of the

ski and the direction of travel while the side-cut of the tail of the ski tends to decrease this angle. As a result, braking is increased in the tip of the ski and decreased in the tail. Adjustment of the angle of edge-set therefore allows the skier to control the rate of pivoting.

157. The tendency of the ski to pivot is reduced if the point of application of pressure on the ski by the skier is displaced toward the tail. The tendency to pivot is at a minimum when the skier's weight is placed on the point that we have previously defined the "center of maximum holding of the ski" (127).

158. The amount of pivoting often reaches a limit when the degree of movement in the joints of the lower limbs involved in pivoting reach a limit (511). The skis and the skier become "blocked" and passive pivoting ceases.
A skier will often voluntarily block his skis once they have pivoted a sufficient amount but the systematic blocking of the skier over his skis from the very beginning of a pivoting movement is a fault that is often the result of forward weighting or initiating a turn by rotation (circular projection).

159. A directional effect that tends to progressively orient the direction of the displacement of the skis up the hill accompanies the braking. It results from a combination of longitudinal displacement and pivoting and is called the "braking directional effect". Mechanically, it can be interpreted in the same way as the flat ski directional effect (137).

160. The forces that create the braking directional effect are essentially exerted on the contact between the inside of the base and the snow and particularly the edge of the ski:
a) The side of the base tends to create a sliding of the ski along its major axis.
b) The arc created by the contact of the edge of the ski and the snow following flexion and torsion of the ski tends to produce a sliding of the ski along this arc (156).
In both cases, the direction of travel

263

changes.

Note: I don't believe that the greater width of the ski in the tip than in the tail is involved in the carved or braking directional effect other than during the passage from the flat ski position of straight running to a position with weighting of an edged ski (139). This opinion is disputed.

161. The braking directional effect can become a carved directional effect by:

a) A reduction of the angle of pivoting.

b) A backward displacement of pressure toward the center of maximum holding but without passing the center of maximum holding.

c) A rapid acceleration of forward sliding in combination with (b).

Note 1: b and c correspond to a carved platform by forward foot thrust.

Note 2: The edge of the ski becomes more of a "slicing" tool than a "scraping" tool much as a wood scraper does if it is moved laterally across the wood. The same phenomenon occurs if the bindings are mounted too far back on the skis. The ski holds too well and goes straight instead of pivoting.

162. On steep slopes, gravity can work against the braking directional effect.

a) An attempt to make a braking counter-turn up the hill starting from a traverse on a steep slope with hard snow can quickly result in a curved trajectory down the fall line. The directional effect is not longer sufficient to overcome the component of gravity which pulls the skier down the slope.

b) The same thing can happen at the end of a turn. In certain cases, the very skilled skier or racer can use a carved directional effect when a braking directional effect is no longer effective.

170. Changing edges, the angle of edge-set and turns down the fall line.

171. At the start of every turn down the fall line, the skis are tipped from a position where the uphill edges are weighted to a position where they lie flat on the snow and eventually to a position where the inside edges are weighted. This process is called a change of edges.

The instant when the skis rest flat on the snow is the moment most favorable for pivoting them into the turn.

172. The tipping of the edges can be progressive during an edge change.

a) It can lead to the use of a curved directional effect which can be prolonged until the phase when the skis slide straight down the fall line.

b) It can correspond to the passage from one carving turn to another.

For example: counter-turns.

173. The tipping of the skis can be rapid by quickly and simultaneously displacing the skis laterally and pivoting them.

a) either a harsh displacement with significant ski-snow friction;

b) or displacing unweighted skis after a platform.

174. Passing from the type of directional effect used in a traverse to another type is made by shifting the weight from one point on the length of the ski to another. This results in a momentary acceleration or deceleration of the skis relative to the movement of the skier's body mass.

a) The skis can be pushed slightly

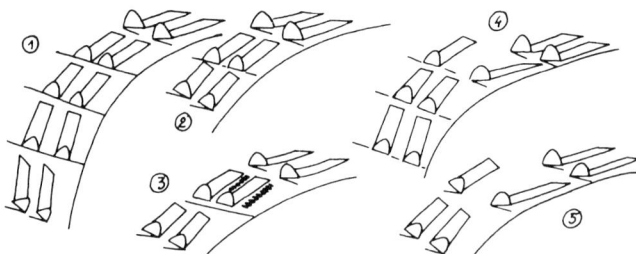

Different kinds of edge changes: (1) very progressive with flat ski directional effect, (2) progressive, (3) with a hop, (4) with opening or spreading flat skis, (5) with opening or spreading edged skis.

forward to go from a traverse on soft snow to a flat ski directional effect. This results in a backward displacement of the center of pressure on the ski.

b) A similar but more pronounced forward push of the skis results in a braking directional effect.

c) The skis can be pushed backward to go from a carved traverse with tail-pressure to a flat ski directional effect. This results in a forward displacement of the center of pressure on the ski.

d) The skis can be pushed backward to give a forward weighted directional effect.

Note 1: A forward displacement of the skis during the edge-change seems to facilitate the change. A backward displacement of the skis, however, seems to hinder the change of edges.

Note 2: Depending on the amplitude, the forward thrust of the skis can have two goals. A small thrust favors the

start of flat ski pivoting or a very slight edge-set. A more pronounced forward thrust favors holding of the tails. These two effects can be produced sequentially.

175. Don't confuse the fore-aft adjustment of pressure on the ski with a forward or backward leaning of the body which may be the result of an effort to maintain balance during a sudden transition to a steeper slope or a sudden deceleration of the skis.

a) These banking movements of the upper body mass can be made without effecting the distribution of pressure over the length of the ski.

b) The upper body can be banked away from the center of pressure on the ski, for example while going from a platform with forward weighting to a braking sideslip.

The efficiency of such a banking movement becomes doubtful. Instead, a banking of the body in the same direction as the center of pressure on the ski seems better adapted to the mechanics of skiing, such as during the transition from a slightly back-weighted platform to a braking sideslip.

176. A lateral displacement of the skis to the outside of the turn aids the initiation of the turn.
a) A passive lateral displacement by banking the body following the edge change.
b) An active lateral displacement after the edge change by angulation or extension of the outside leg or both.
c) A passive lateral displacement before the edge change by using an 'S' counter-turn.
d) Idem but active: increasing the directional effect of the skis by a forward thrust of the feet.
Note 1: a and b, because of (134) and (155), are accompanied by a passive pivoting in the direction of the turn.
Note 2: c and d correspond to a counter pivoting movement which, of course, implies that the subsequent pivoting of the skis into the turn must be greater.

177. The effort to make the skis hold must be increased from the beginning through the end of a turn down the fall line.
The ski experiences a lateral thrust which increases throughout the turn and can be explained in the following manner:
a) Until the fall line is crossed, the centripetal forces which create the turn act in the same direction as gravity. They are small and don't require a large angle of edge-set. After crossing the fall line, the centripetal

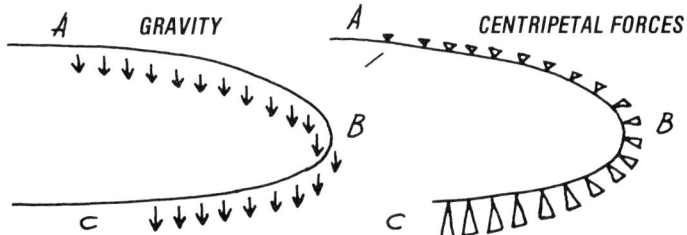

A **GRAVITY**

*From **A** to **B**, gravity acts in the same direction as centripetal force to help create the turn. The flat ski directional effect is usually sufficient to start the turn. From **B** to **C**, gravity works*

A **CENTRIPETAL FORCES**

against centripetal force and a directional effect using the edges of the skis must be used to complete the turn.

forces act against gravity and the holding of the edges must be better and the angle of edge-set greater.
b) Until crossing the fall line, the increasing pitch of the slope tends to unweight the skis, but as the turn progresses to a lesser pitch the skier is compressed onto his skis and the resulting overloading tends to make the skis sideslip.
Note 1: It also happens that the skier progresses from a high stance at the beginning of the turn to a low position toward the end of the turn and this vertical fall increases the overloading mentioned above.
Note 2: In certain circumstances, the overloading can improve carving on the outside ski (certain slalom and giant slalom techniques in fact utilize the loading resulting from braking the vertical fall of the body mass mentioned in note 1). A turn with a constantly diminishing radius can be used in this regard.

178. Angles of edge-set, turn momentum and turn shape.
a) The angle of edge-set automatically increases during the turn. Consider a

turn down the fall line scribing a half circle with a constant centrifugal force (ie. the speed and turn radius are constant) and a lateral inclination of 30 degrees from vertical of the skier's body on a slope of 15°. In the traverse at the the beginning of the turn, the skier leans 15° to flatten the skis, then 15° more (total of 30°). The angle of edge-set is now 15°.
As the skier slides straight down the fall line, the angle of edge-set is 30°.
At the end of the turn, the 15° pitch of the slope adds to the 30° banking of the skier's body to result in an edge-set angle of 45°.
b) Becuase of the increasing angle of edge-set, the edges of the skis often hold better at the end of a turn of constant radius than at the beginning.
c) A consistent holding of the edges allows the earlier part of a turn to be made with a shorter radius (177 a,b) (178 a,b).
Note: (178c) corresponds to turns made close to the limits of holding such as round turns on very hard snow. This type of turn is the opposite of the turn mentioned in (177, Note 2).

180. Biting of the edges during edge-sets.

181. Carved platforms are brief and short carved arcs while the skis are under significant compression. They last only several tenths of a second.
a) This overloading of the skis is partially due to the fact that the platform is made against the skier's forward momentum.
b) At the level of the skis, this compression can be dissected into two forces:
—One which acts perpendicular to the edges and maintains the holding of the

skis.
—Another which acts over the length of the skis and tends to accelerate their forward sliding (see page 183). It's this effect which characterizes carved platforms.
c) The overloading of the skis can also result from the sudden braking of a flexion movement (438) or a "recoil" of the legs (extension).
Note: The compression of the skis described here occurs with both carved and braking platforms.

182. Braking platforms are ubiquitous. They are intense and short checks made by the skis during which they undergo significant overloading. These checks brake the sliding of the skis in their initial direction of travel and cause the upper body to fall forward.
Note: The analyses made in 181a, b and c apply equally here.

183. During all platforms, the skis tend to produce a braking curved directional effect which makes them slide up the hill and forward, thereby reducing the braking.

As the skier leans backward in the fore-aft plane, the angle between the axis of the skier's body and the major axis of the skis increases. The skis then tend to slide forward along their major axis underneath the skier and braking is reduced.
a) to neutralize this forward "escape" of the skis, and therefore to brake more effectively, the skier should use a complex banking movement (261, 272).
b) This forward "escape" of the skis is often the first step toward the discovery of the voluntary forward thrust of the feet which is a technique used by many very good skiers (425 to 427).

184. Very brief braking platforms are called edge-sets. Even if the skis are pivoted within a matter of several tenths of a second, the intense compression of the skis which makes the edges bite doesn't last more than one

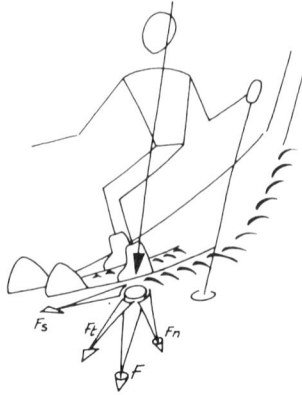

*One can dissect the thrust **F** exerted by the skier on the snow during an edge-set into three components: **Fn** acting perpendicular to the surface of the snow creates holding; **Ft** acting tangentially thrusts the ski in the direction of travel. **Fs**, resulting from the directional effect produced by the ski, tends to accelerate the sliding of the ski along its major axis.*

or two tenths of a second. The edges of the skis act neither as a scraper (153) nor as a knife (121) but somewhat more like a center punch.

A "Carved edge-set" is a brief and intense weighting of the edges made with a forward thrust of the feet.

185. The elasticity of the torsion and bending of the skis during platforms made in ruts (or in mogulled terrain) enhances the vertical recoil of the skier's body. On flat terrain, this recoil is negligible (a few pounds on flat snow but tens of pounds in ruts). Any elasticity from the snow is added to that of the skis and also appears to be negligible.

The skier's perception of the behavior of his skis.

186. For flat ski sliding:
a) In straight running, the skis can be felt to be: 1) either too directed or insufficiently directed (the terms stable, floating or wandering are often used to describe the behavior of the skis); 2) damped or nervous (soft or too reactive); 3) easy (permissive or soft) or erratic; 4) stable or unstable on bumpy terrain; 5) slippery or slow (either because they butt in the tips or because the bases are non-slippery)...
b) In controlling flat ski turns: Idem (a, 1-5), and also: 6) the ability to hold the arc of the turn (turn by themselves); 7) pivot excessively or insufficiently in the turn; 8) too little or too much responsiveness to pivoting efforts (either don't hold the turn or "lead" the turn too much); 9) are easy (or too easy) or difficult to pivot from a straight run at low or normal speed...

187. For carved sliding: 1) the edges bite too well or not well enough; 2)

they don't permit the turning radius to be corrected; 3) they carve well in the tip, the tail (with tail-pressure) or with balanced weighting over the length of the ski; 4) they carve only long turns; 5) they carve poorly in bumpy terrain; 6) they carve poorly in traverses; 7) they are difficult to start carving from a straight run or an edge-change; 8) they require pivoting, compression or unweighting.

188. For braking sideslips: 1). the skis are well balanced or not well balanced, they hold too well in the tip, in the tail or under the foot; 2) they hold too much or not enough; 3) they are graters or damped; 4) they have too great a tendency to carve (are too directed); 5) they tend to ricochet laterally, to chatter...
189. Platforms:
—Classic platforms, Idem 188 1-5, and also: 6) too damped or too nervous (maximum holding is difficult to obtain or, on the contrary, is excessive and unpredictable); the recoil

is excessive or insufficient...
—Carved platforms: 1) the edges bite the snow too much or not enough; 2) they tend to favor either carved sliding or carved braking; 3) they require substantial weighting or little weighting; 4) they either do or don't require a forward foot thrust with substantial tail-pressure...
Note: These are the only objective judgements that the skier can make regarding his skis. From the moment that he states, for example, "My skis are too soft in the tails" or "too stiff torsionally", he makes a very hazardous opinion. In fact, the sum of the mechanical properties which result in the overall personality of the ski, or only some of its aspects, is extraordinarily complex and these properties are always narrowly linked and dependent on each other.

The skier should appreciate his skis as one appreciates a good cocktail; without bothering about what went into the mixture.

THE ROLE OF THE BOOTS IN TRANSMITTING PRESSURE TO THE SKIS

The ski boots play an essential role in skiing. Their mechanical characteristics simultaneously effect the behavior of the skis on the snow and the behavior of the skier on the skis.

These characteristics can not be adapted perfectly to the morphological peculiarities of the skier, to his stance and his "style" of skiing. Therefore, I propose several possible corrections to improve this adaptation.

191. The thickness of the sole of the boots has an effect on the action of the foot.

a) A thinner boot sole allows the foot to better sense lateral movements that tip the ski onto edge (pronation or supination of the foot). This allows a better control of these movements and therefore better control of the arc of turns.

b) Differences in sole height between the front and heel of the boot influence the distribution of pressure exerted on the front and heel of the foot. A raised heel will tend to place more pressure on the tail of the ski.

c) The difference in sole thickness mentioned in b will to some extent modify the amount of flexion used by the skier.

Corrections: The heel of the foot can be raised either by wedges inside the boot and under the heel that are 5 to 10 millimeters thick (these wedges are sold by orthopedists) or by having a shoemaker place a lift under the feel of the boot.

In the lateral plane.

192. The distribution of pressure on the inside or outside edge of the ski when resting flat on the snow.

a) Excessive pressure on the inside edge resulting from flat feet.

Correction: Use an orthopedic sole that is laterally oblique to raise the inside edge of the foot inside the boot.

b) Excessive pressure on the inside edge due to *talus valgus* over the *calcaneus* (the ankle bone is tilted to the outside over the heel bone).

Correction: Place a laterally oblique wedge under the heel to straighten the ankle.

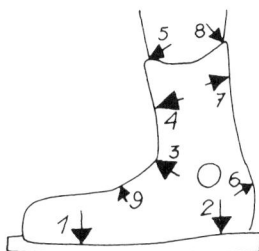

FORE-AFT PRESSURE OF THE FOOT AND LEG AGAINST THE BOOT.
Vertical: 1) on the ball of the foot, 2) on the heel.
Forward: 3) against the instep, 4) against the tongue, 5) against the upper edge of the shell, 6) occasionally backward against the heel pocket, 7) against the back of the shell, 8) against the upper edge of the shell, 9) occasionally the arch of the foot in contact with the lower part of the boot.

LATERAL PRESSURE OF THE FOOT AND LEG AGAINST THE BOOT.
Inside: 1) vertical pressure, 2) side of the foot below the ankle, 3) ankle bone, 4) above the ankle bone, 5) leg against the upper edge of the shank.
Outside: 6) vertical pressure, 7) ankle bone, 8) lower leg, 9) leg against the upper edge of the shank.

c) Excessive pressure on the inside or outside edges in spite of a normal foot and a boot that is well fitted to the contour of the leg because the knee stands to the inside or outside of the vertical plane of the foot (valgus or varus).

Corrections: A correction of this anomaly must be made by correcting the skier's technique. The knees must be maintained in their correct position through a constant effort on the part of the skier. The skier must be careful, however, that this effort doesn't result in the problem mentioned in (195).

193. The role of the boot in maintaining pressure on the edges.

Muscle action allows the foot and ankle joints to be blocked laterally and the weight of the skier to be applied to the edges of the skis. The boot aids this muscular blocking of the foot and ankle in the lateral plane and to some extent assures that the ski will be held perpendicular to the lower leg in spite of the forces which will tend to tip the ski flat.

a) A boot that is soft laterally won't help the skier to find sufficient articular rigidity in the lateral plane, particularly in the joint under the ankle bone (articulation of the ankle and heel bones).

b) A boot that doesn't fit the sides of the foot snugly will give under the vertical pressure of the skier's weight in spite of a blocking of the foot by muscular effort. This can result in a decrease in the angle of edging.

Corrections: Strips of leather or flexible but hard plastic can be glued to the outside shanks of the liner in places where contact between the foot of the leg and the shell isn't being made. These strips of plastic or leather can also be glued to the walls of the shell.

c) A boot that doesn't fit snugly under the ankle bone doesn't allow pressure from this critical area of the foot to be transmitted to the boot and often results in increased pressure of the inside of the leg against the shank of the boot which doesn't allow as fine an adjustment of pressure during the control of the arcs of turns.

Corrections: Use strips of leather or plastic as in (b) but place them in the open spaces beneath the ankle bone.

194. A boot that is too tight makes lateral play of the foot inside the boot impossible.

a) The slight contraction and relaxation of lateral fixing muscles in the foot allow a very fine and constant adjustment of the angle of edging that is necessary for the precise control of a carved turn or flat ski sliding.

If these fine adjustments are impossible at this level, they will be made, but with much less finesse, by lateral movements of the knee.

b) A slight amount of lateral play of the foot in the boot also seems to be necessary for what we have called the "soft control of the skis" during flat ski sliding.

Corrections: Don't buckle the boots so tight. Use thinner socks. Find liners with softer padding. Remove the inner soles.

195. Abnormal lateral pressure between the leg and the shank of the boot can hamper the flat placement of the skis.

The lower third of the tibia always bowes more or less to the outside. A positioning of the knees to the inside (valgus) or outside (varus) of a vertical line from the foot will diminish or increase this lateral inclination of the lower leg to the outside. The shank of the skier's boot must be canted so that it follows the contour of the skier's lower leg. Otherwise, the skier may experience one of the following anomalies:

a) The skier habitually presses against the outside shank of the boots.

This results in too much pressure on the outside edges of the skis and the skier often experiences a sharp and radiating pain at the point of contact between the leg and the boot.

Corrections:

1st case: The skier always walks on the outside of his feet (the soles of his street shoes wear on the outside). Wedges must be mounted between the skis and the bindings or the skis

*HEEL LIFTS
Dotted lines = position before wedging.*

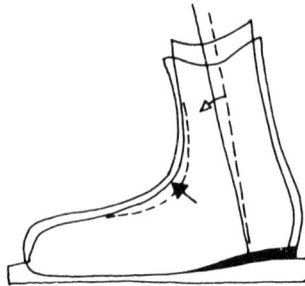

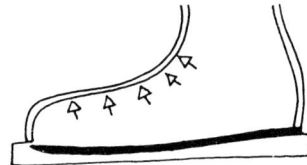

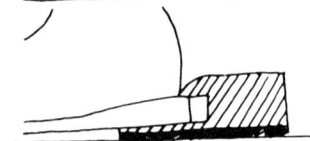

WEDGING TO MODIFY FORWARD LEAN.

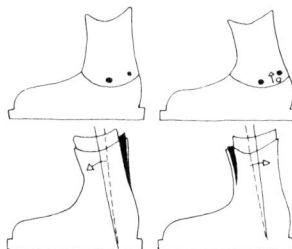

and the boot to lift the inside edge of the boot. These wedges can raise the inside of the boot from 1 to 4 millimeters.

2nd case: The feet stand flat in the boots (the soles of the individuals street shoes are worn evenly). The solution is then to modify the shells of the boots so that the lateral canting of the cuff of the boot follows the contour of the lower leg. This can sometimes be done by blocking the soles of the boots (for example by the bindings of the skis), heating the shells with a powerful hot air gun or by soaking them in water at 120° to 140° F. and then bending them into place with a lever.

b) The skier presses against the inside shank of the boots.

This results in excessive pressure on the inside edges of the skis and the skier often experiences pain at the point of contact between his leg and the shell of the boot which can develop into tendonitis. This pain hinders proper weighting of the edges.

1st case: If the skier is flat-footed (191a) or has valgus talus over the calcaneus (191b), a wedge placed inside the boot as proposed in (191a) and (191b) occasionally can upright the tibia sufficiently to eliminate the excessive pressure against the inside of the shank of the boot.

2nd case: If the skier weights his feet normally, the shank or cuff of the boot must be modified as in (195a, 2nd case) but to the inside.

196. Some boot shells may twist which results in lateral bending and a reduction in the angle of edging.

Because of their construction, some types of plastic shells will twist during leg pivoting movements without pivoting the sole of the boot and the ski and as they twist they bend laterally.

Corrections: If the boot is of the "floating cuff" design, where the cuff is joined to the shell only at one point in the back of the boot, the remedy consists of riveting the cuff to the shell on the sides of the boot adjacent to the ankle bones to make the boot more rigid.

Note: A lack of rigidity in certain materials used in making boot shells can result in a deformation or twisting of the boot where it contacts the bindings during particularly harsh edgesets. The angle of edge-set no longer follows the banking of the boot.

197. Altering the forward lean of the boot to adjust the distribution of fore-aft pressure on the ski.

Adjusting the forward lean of the boot so that it corresponds to the amount of ankle lean normally used by the skier presents three advantages:
a) It will allow a slight amount of play during flexion and extension movements even when the boot is very stiff.
b) It allows the skier to more quickly and easily find his optimal amount of flexion and a balanced weighting. We can call this a "reference position".
c) It avoids the overloading of the tips of the skis that usually occurs with a boot that is too straight or the overloading of the tails that occurs with boots with excessive forward lean even though this imbalanced distribution of pressure on the skis may not be perceptible to the skier who has adjusted his gestures to compensate (300).
Corrections:
a) If the shell is in two parts locked together by rivets, remove the rivets redrill the holes and re-rivet the shells in the correct position.
b) If the hinging of the cuff is not locked, allow for more forward flexing, when necessary, by rasping the bottom of the lower buckle strap of the cuff where it contacts the bottom of the boot.
c) If the forward flexing of the boot must be reduced, it is sometimes possible to rivet the cuff and the shell where they butt together in the back of the boot.
198. The boot should flex progressively during flexion and extension movements and during the transmission of pressure to the tip and tail of the ski.
a) A shell that is too stiff and fits snugly against the back and front of the leg will transmit every flexion and extension movement into a harsh weighting of the tip or tail of the ski. These excessively stiff and unforgiving boots are often the cause of hairline fractures or "bruises" of the shin.
Correction: Soften the back and front of the shell either by shaving the shell with a rasp of by cutting grooves into the shell 3 to 5 millimeters long every 3 to 5 millimeters with a hacksaw or trim the top of the shell in the front and back to lower it and then soften it using the techniques just described.
b) If the shell is too stiff but allows a

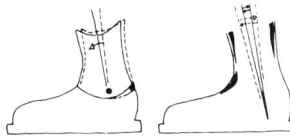

LATERAL WEDGING
Dotted lines = position before wedging.

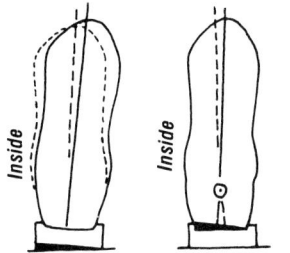

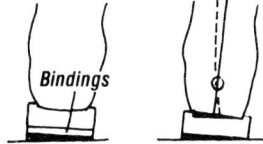

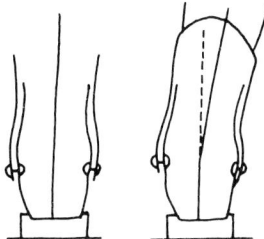

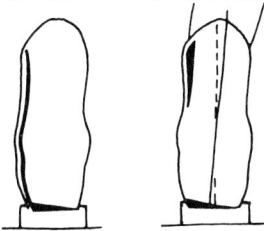

little bit of "play" between the leg and the boot, every forward and backward movement of the skier results in an erratic transmission of pressure to the ski.
Correction: Glue layers of leather or hard, flexible plastic against the shell of the boot to take up the vacant space . If necessary, make the same corrections as described in (a).
c) If, on the contrary, the boot is too flexible, a flexion or forward weighting movement can result in a sudden and erratic transmission of pressure to the tip of the skis once the limit of hinging of the boot has been reached.
Correction: If the boot has a two-piece shell with a hinge that isn't locked, try locking the hinging action by adding a rivet to each side of the boot behind the joint.
d) A boot that is flexible to the rear won't allow a skier to recover from a loss of balance to the rear.
Corrections: It's not always possible to correct this situation.
1st case: Occasionally it's possible to block the backward flexing of the boot by riveting as in (c), but more than two rivets are usually required because the forces involved are so great.
2nd case: Straightening of the shaft of the boot can often be suppressed by inserting a wedge in the opening between the cuff and shell of the boot in back. These wedges should be very hard and as wide as possible.
e) A deformation of the plastic of the shell can brake an extension or flexion movement. This usually results in an elastic recoil which can aid in rapid recoveries of balance.
f) On the contrary, this braking can be the result of the friction of parts of the shell rubbing against each other in which case the braking is damped and without recoil.
g) If the instep of the ankle doesn't press perfectly against the instep of the boot, forward flexing movements can be accompanied by a lifting of the heel inside the boot. This results in too much free play at the beginning of every flexion movement followed by a harsh butting against the shell of the boot with sudden forward weighting and occasionally irritation of the instep of the foot and at the point of contact between the leg and the shell of the boot.
Correction: Raise the heel with a 4, 8 or even 12 millimeter thick wedge between the sole of the shell and the liner.

199. Forward and lateral or backward and lateral pressure during edge-sets.
a) The difficulty of making the skis hold on the snow by a strictly lateral pressure against the boots causes many skiers to press simultaneously laterally and forward on their boots (ankles flexed and forward weighting) or laterally and backward (ankles straight and back-weighting).
b) A forward and lateral pressure is the most common because of the necessity of making the edges bite in the bottom of a turn when the body is compressed into flexion. However, the biting of the edges is poor, particularly with modern skis which are no longer designed for forward weighting techniques.

This forward weighting often results in a scissoring and weighting of both skis with an extreme flexing of the downhill ankle.
c) Starting from a position with straight ankles (the "modern" position (423-424)), the skier has a greater tendency to use strictly a lateral pressure.
d) A forward thrust of the feet relative to the body mass allows weighting of the center of maximum holding of the skis (127) - often described as "tail-pressure" - and leads to the use of a lateral and backward pressure if the boot is relatively straight. This seems to be a very effective way of making the outside ski carve at the end of a turn.

Some downhill specialists seem to ski with constant pressure against the backs of their boots to improve sliding. By trial and error, these racers often place a wedge behind the shank of their boots to give them the necessary backward support.

MAINTAINING BALANCE

Staying in a balanced, upright position poses a complex set of problems for man. This corresponds, in fact, to a vertical stacking of unstable body segments which implies a constant series of recoveries to remain in balance. It's the finesse of these recoveries, and not their suppression by muscular blockage, which defines the quality of balance.

The problems of staying in balance that the skier faces are of the same order but much more acute due to the constant imposition of exterior forces. I propose that staying in balance for a skier should not imply any blocking of the muscles but aim toward a state of minimal muscular contraction, particularly in the feet.

In addition to other things, movement on skis presents man with entirely new problems which I will analyze briefly in this chapter. The difficulties that the skier encounters in maintaining his balance have led to the use of exterior supports, particularly against the shanks of the boots once they became sufficiently stiff. This is an error that is even worse than excessive muscular contraction because it results in a disturbance of the balance mechanisms which the skier is likely unaware of.

200. To clarify a few concepts.

201. The axis of the skier's body.
This axis is a straight line which joins the skier's center of mass to the center of the skier's base of support on the ground.

202. The "fore-aft" plane of the skier and banking of the body to the front or rear.
a) The fore-aft plane is the plane through which the axis of the skier's body moves in the direction of travel.

b) Foreward and backward banking movements are pivoting movements in the fore-aft plane around the center of mass (209, 211, 213).

203. Differentiation between the direction of movement and the direction of the skis.
In straight running and straight sideslipping, the fore-aft plane is vertical. In sideslipping, the major axis of the skis, as well as the plane of the flexion of the ankles, knees and eventually the hips, are no longer situated in this plane. The skis, knees and hips are said to pivot to the inside and one refers to their angle of pivoting.

204. Fore-aft plane and centrifugal force.
In a turn or curved sideslip, the axis of the skier's body, and therefore the fore-aft plane, are inclined in the direction of the center of pivoting to

270

balance centrifugal force (202).

At each instant, the fore-aft plane is tangential to the arc of the turn.

205. The lateral plane of the skier.

The lateral plane is the plane passing through the axis of the skier's body and perpendicular to the direction of travel.

206. Braking forces and plane of inclination.

Braking forces are provoked by the forward movement of the skier and are exerted in a direction opposite to this forward movement. The axis of the skier's body is inclined in the fore-aft plane described above to balance these braking forces in straight running as well as in sideslipping.

207. Centripetal forces, centrifugal force and the plane of inclination.

Turns are made because of the generation of centripetal forces at the ski-snow contact which act toward the center of the turn. This results in the generation of centrifugal forces which operate in the opposite direction. To balance centrifugal force, the axis of the skier's body is inclined to the inside of the turn in the lateral plane which passes through the center of the turn.

208. Braking forces + centrifugal force = oblique inclination.

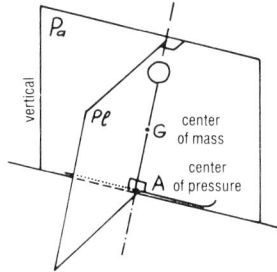

IN A TRAVERSE.
GA: the axis of the skier's body. Pa: the fore-aft plane. Pl: the lateral plane perpendicular to Pa.

The axis of the body is inclined obliquely between the fore-aft and lateral planes. We define this inclination in terms of its fore-aft and lateral components.

209. The distinction between "banking" and "inclination".

Banking is a pivoting movement around the center of mass (for example in straight running where there is no forward or backward weighting or in the air).

Inclination is a pivoting of the body around a platform on the ground (for example an inclination up the hill or down the fall line in a traverse). There can be no inclination in the fore-aft plane, only banking.

Note: We make a distinction between

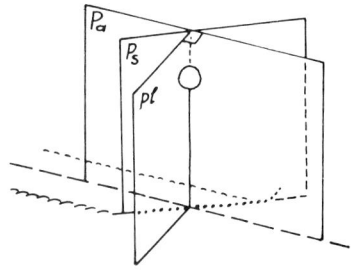

IN A STRAIGHT SIDESLIP
Ps: the plane of the skis.

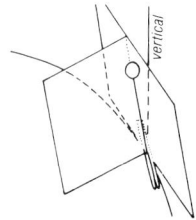

IN A TURN
Pa is tangent to the arc of the turn and inclined to the inside of the turn relative to the vertical.

passive banking, where the motor force is gravity, and active banking which is produced by muscular contraction (213).

210. Balance as a function of the slope.

211. The rule of perpendicularity to the slope.

a) Initial hypothesis: ski-snow forces of friction and air friction are negligible.

It's possible to conceive that if the force exerted by the legs of the skier against the snow is not oriented perpendicular to the snow surface but obliquely backward, the skis will be pushed back and the body will bank forward, and vice versa. Therefore, pressure must be directed perpendicular to the plane of the slope.

Blocking ankle flexion can put the skier in a forward weighted position. the skier's downward thrust will still be exerted perpendicular to the plane of the slope, but at a point under the balls of the feet or even in front of the feet. Such a blocking of ankle movement will prevent normal skiing manuevers. In fact, a slight forward or backward displacement of pressure is

customary in typical skiing movements (424).

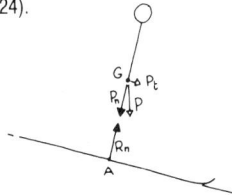

The effect of gravity (P) on the center of mass of the skier (G) has two components: Pn, perpendicular to the slope, which is resisted by the skier by contracting the extensor muscles of the legs, and Pt, in the plane of the slope, which creates acceleration down the slope.
Rn denotes the support of the ground which acts against Pn at the center of pressure (A).

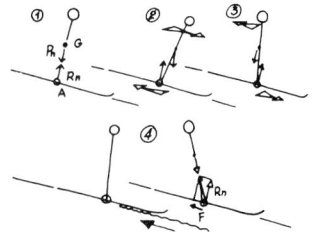

1) balanced condition, ankles supple: Pn and Rn are in the same axis. 2) Forward banking around G. 3) backward banking. 4) Balancing of a braking force (F) by backward inclination.

b) If there is significant air resistance at high speeds.

The pressure of the air is generally exerted against the center of mass. Consequently, in both upright and low positions air resistance doesn't create a balance disturbing pivoting of the body.

c) If there is significant friction between the skis and the snow.

Ski-snow friction will cause the body to bank forward. Therefore, to avoid blocking the ankles in an effort to maintain balance, the body should be banked backward.

212. Balance during accelerations and decelerations.

a) Positive acceleration is the result of gravity, or more precisely the component of gravity which is exerted in the plane of the slope (P sin d where d is the angle of the slope).

All of the elements of the skier/skis unit undergo the same acceleration (remember: if we discount air resistance, all objects fall with an acceleration of 32 feet/second²). Therefore, acceleration on a uniform slope will not upset balance. What makes us believe that acceleration disturbs our balance over a drop-off is, in reality, the requirement to reestablish perpendicularity to the slope (211).

b) Deceleration can only be the result of air friction (211b) or ski-snow friction (211c), but in no case to a decrease in pitch of a slope (the principle of conservation of momentum remains valid even on a flat).

213. Passive and active banking (fore-aft plane).

a) *Passive banking using gravity.*

—By relaxing certain extensor muscles, the skier can pivot around his ankles with his feet moving backward and his upper body banking forward.

—Or around the knees: feet forward, upper body backward.

—Gravity is the motor force of these movements. The center of mass is lowered. Halting this banking movement implies that the inertia of the movement is overcome by muscular action and a platform against either the front or the back of the foot.

—The speed of these passive banking movements depends on the degree of relaxation of the extensor muscles which are at their origin. A total relaxation results in maximum speed.

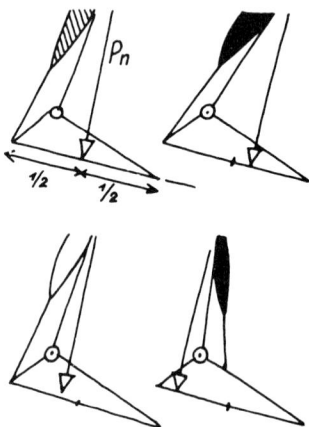

Schematic representation of the foot and tibia and the extensor muscles and articulation of the ankle. (1) In and upright standing and skiing position, Pn is situated at the center of the foot. Muscle tension is normal. (2) Pn is in front of the center of the foot: tension of the extensor muscles is excessive and articulations of the ankle are less flexible. (3) Pn is applied behind the center of the foot but infront of the ankle joint. The very relaxed extensor muscles can't insure the maintenance of proper balance. (4) If Pn is located behind the ankle joint, the flexor muscles are tensed and the joint again loses flexibility.

(1) Example of passive banking with a lowering of the center of mass.
(2) Example of active banking.

b) *Active banking.*

—Using muscular action, and without gravity, the skier can adjust the center of pressure and the center of mass.

—Stopping this banking movement implies only one muscular action. For example, a forward thrust of the feet with forward movement of the upper body and backward movement of the hips (the center of mass doesn't move) is stopped without inertia and without pressing against the back of the foot.

—These banking movements involve pivoting of body segments around the knees, the hips and the lower back.

—All active banking movements imply the displacement of two body masses in opposite directions. The amplitude of the displacements of these two masses is inversely proportional to their inertia or, more precisely, to their "moment of inertia" (moment of inertia is equal to the product of the mass and the square of the distance of this mass from the center of pivoting).

—Active banking can be accompanied by a raising or lowering of the center of mass (see the analyses of the so-called "vertical" movements of a skier (430)).

c) The speed of active and passive banking movements.

—Since the motor force of passive banking is gravity, these movements can not be accelerated beyond a certain limit.

—Since active banking movements are powered by muscular contraction, they can be slow, quick or extremely quick. For example, the forward displacement of the feet during a sudden and harsh impact against a bump or the forward movement of the feet before a platform on the edges.

—In passive banking, the skier can accelerate the movement somewhat if the moment of inertia of the displaced masses is diminished by flexion and vice versa.

Note: It is possible to make banking movements using muscular action which, nevertheless, should be classified as passive banking since they are effected by inertia. For example, straightening from an extreme back-weighted position by pressing against the backs of the boots.

214. Passive banking can assure the maintenance of balance over drop-offs and compressions.

By maintaining perpendicularity to the slope by banking forward when the slope increases (a drop-off) or banking backward when the slope decreases (transitions).

a) Over progressive drop-offs or compressions, a gradual readjustment can be made by passive banking (213a).

b) The sudden passive banking (passive flexion of the knees and backward banking of the body) in a sharp compression generates an inertia which is very difficult to overcome and presents a danger of falling over backward.

c) Over a sharp drop-off, a quick , passive forward banking (passive flexion of the ankles and forward body) is easy. It invovles an inertia which is easy to neutralize with an active backward banking movement (forward movement of the feet) (216a).

Note: A passive banking movement over a drop-off is made with a lowering of the center of mass and tends to accentuate, for a brief instant, and then neutralize the unweighting produced by the terrain (432).

215. Passive forward banking and the thrust of the ground before taking air at a drop-off.

—A skier frequently uses the thrust exerted by a small bump to facilitate his becoming airborn at a drop-off. If a passive forward banking has already been started when the skier experiences the perpendicular thrust exerted by the ground, a significant banking is produced.

—If this thrust is unexpected (for example a pre-jump that is made too early), it can result in an irrecoverable loss of balance.

216. Active banking movements can assure the maintenance of balance over compressions and drop-offs.

a) Compressions: an active backward banking (forward thrust of the feet by straightening the knees and bending hips) assures the maintenance of perpendicularity without involving the skier's inertia.

The perpendicular pressure exerted by the ground against the feet because of the decreasing slope reduces the amount of muscular action necessary to produce the flexion movements which produce this banking.

b) Drop-offs: One kind of active forward banking consists of a backward movement of the feet by straightening the calves under the thighs. Even though the ankles flex during this

PROGRESSIVE PASSIVE BANKING
A, at a drop-off,
B, in a compression.

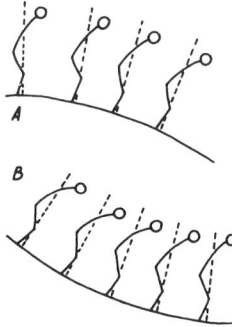

RAPID PASSIVE BANKING
A, at a drop-off without taking air. (1) Flexion begun by relaxing the calves.
B, with aerial flight.
C, in a compression. (1) Flexion begun by relaxing the thighs and buttocks.

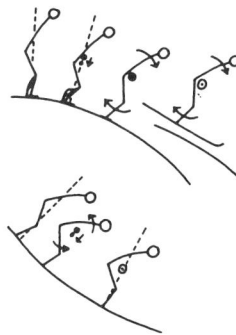

ACTIVE BANKING
A, by actively folding the calves under the thighs over a drop-off.
B, by actively folding the thighs under the chest in a compression.

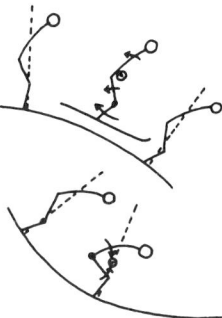

movement, there is no passive banking around the ankles. This banking does not invovle inertia.

c) Drop-off: A second type of active forward banking (backward movement of the feet) involves an extension of the upper legs under the hip. The feet and the upper body are displaced backward relative to the center of mass. This kind of banking is particularly effective when started in a very low position (for example on the top of a bump or following avalement).

217. Balancing in the air.

a) If a banking around the center of mass is begun during take-off, it will continue through the flight. There can be no change in the amount of angular movement while in the air. This implies a conservation of the angular momentun which is a function of the mass that is pivoting, the speed of rotation, and the distance which seperates these masses from the center of pivoting.

b) Acceleration of the banking movement. By rotating the arms opposite the direction of banking, an angular momentum equal in magnitude but opposite in direction to the rotation of the arms will be translated to the body.

c) Decelerating the banking movement. By rotating the arms in the same direction as the banking movement, an angular momentum equal in magnitude but opposite in direction to that of the arms will be translated to the body, thereby reducing the velocity of banking.

d) Neutralization of the passive forward banking movement on landing.

An active backward banking (a forward movement of the feet) will neutralize a passive forward banking started during take-off over a transition or bump.

218. Every turn down the fall line consists of several variations in slope. Fore-aft balance.

a). In the initial traverse, the skier's trajectory corresponds to a relatively flat slope. But as he begins to turn down the fall line, the slope becomes progressively steeper. During this phase of the turn he experiences:

—An increase in vclocity (this is not an unbalancing phenomenon (212) but an anxiety producing phenomenon);

—A need to bank his body forward in order to maintain perpendicularity to the slope (211).

b) Turning out of the fall line and into a traverse corresponds to a passage from a steep to a relatively flat slope. The skier experiences:
—A necessity to bank backward (by displacing the feet forward) in order to maintain perpendicularity to the slope;
—Idem to counter-balance the stronger braking forces in this phase of the turn.
c) The backward banking as the skier crosses the fall line neutralizes the inertia of the forward passive banking movement begun in the first part of the turn.
Note: Fore-aft balance only poses difficult problems during short radius turns down the fall line.

219 Balance at the beginning of turns down the fall line with no centrifugal force.
a) If a skier releases his edges in a traverse, the component of gravity acting in the plane of the slope will gradually modify his trajectory until he is sliding straight down the fall line. Provided the skier never edges his

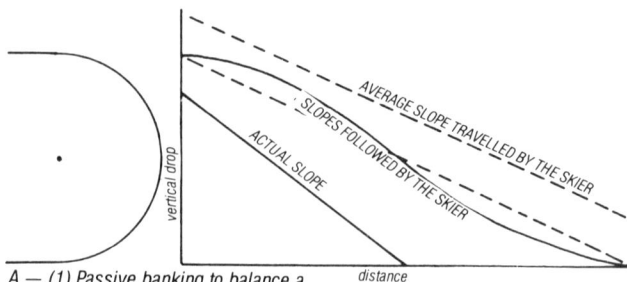

A — (1) Passive banking to balance a braking. (2) The passive banking creates an unbalancing at the end of the braking.

B — Banking by active flexion. (2) Reverse banking by "deploiement".

skis, there can be no centripetal force at the ski-snow contact, therefore no centrifugal force.
b) Throughout this drifting turn down the fall line, the fore-aft plane of the skier is a vertical plane tangent to the arc of the trajectory. In this plane, the axis of the skier's body remains perpendicular to his direction of travel.

Perpendicularity to the slope is maintained as in (211).
c) Upon reaching the fall line, however, the turn can not be continued without creating centripetal force and, therefore, without centrifugal force.

220. Balance and braking forces.

221. Passive banking to maintain balance while braking in a straight run.
a) Possible areas of articulation:
—Knees: flexing the knees over the calves;
—Hips and lower back: extension of the torso over the thighs.
b) During a very progressive braking: a gradual, passive, backward banking.
c) During a harsher braking: a quicker, passive banking. The inertia of the banking movement itself can create balance problems.
d) Once the braking stops, the feet fly forward and it becomes impossible to readjust balance by passive banking, particularly if the braking is very brief. (Inertia noted in c).

222. Active banking to assure balance while braking in a straight run.
a) Possible areas of articulation:
—Knees: straightening the calf under the thigh displaces the feet forward;
—Hips: folding the thighs under the

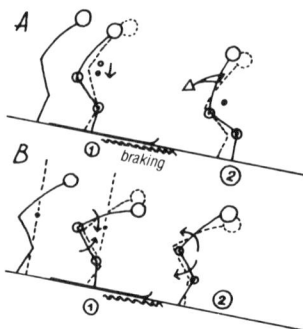

ADJUSTING BALANCE TO A BRAKING
A: by passive banking, with loss of balance once the braking subsides. B: by active banking during and after the braking.

upper body displaces the feet forward;
—Lower back: extending the upper body backward displaces the feet forward.
The simultaneous flexion of the hips and lower back is often grouped together as one movement and spoken of as a flexion of the thighs under the torso.
b) This banking can be either progressive or quick and doesn't involve inertia.
c) This banking is generally accompanied by a lowering of the body mass. Checking this drop of the body mass results in a thrust of the legs against the snow which in turn increases the frictional forces between the skis and the snow.

223. Fore-aft balance during traversing sideslips.
a) Braking forces which make balance while sideslipping difficult are exerted opposite the direction of movement in what we call the fore-aft plane. The

274

mechanical problems involved are of the same nature as during straight running: the axis of the skier is banked backward, in the fore-aft plane, to balance this braking (206 and 211c). The positioning of the skis, the feet and the lower limbs slightly across this plane introduces new elements.

b) The downhill foot is placed ahead of the uphill foot relative to the direction of travel. A dominant weighting of this foot seems to improve balance (this is a balance reflex which seems to be instinctive).

c) By controlling the biting of the edges, the skier can adjust the braking of his lower body and, consequently, control forward and backward banking movements.

Note: This explains why timid skiers prefer to sideslip rather than slide straight ahead. They feel more secure by eliminating any possibility of a sudden braking of the skis.

d) The active or passive banking movements cited in 213, 221 and 222 are less effective because the planes of flexion of the ankle, knee and, to a certain extent, the hip no longer coincide exactly with the fore-aft plane.

In the classic angulation position, with the head and chest facing the direction of travel, the essential hinge of passive or active banking movements is situated in the pelvis (hips and lower back). One often refers to an adjustment of balance by "banking in angulation". Placing the head to face the direction of travel is essential for the best possible functioning of the balancing organs of the inner ear.

224. Balance during straight sideslips.

Only the head, and eventually the shoulders, can be twisted to face the direction of travel. The problems of balance mentioned in 223d are increased.

225. Fore-aft balance at the beginning of a straight sideslip.

a) When a sideslip is started without braking, the body is inclined to a position perpendicular to the direction

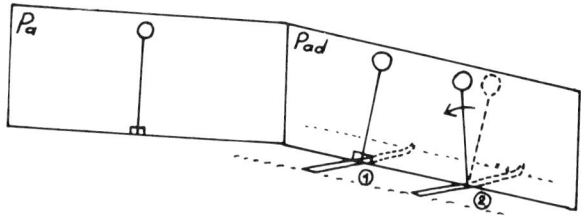

Pa: Fore-aft plane in a traverse (vertical). *Pad:* Fore-aft plane during sideslipping (vertical).

(1) Theoretical case: no braking, balancing as a function of the slope. *(2)* Balancing during braking.

to be followed. This inclination is made both forward and down the fall line by mobilizing the chest in the direction of travel.

b) When a straight sideslip is initiated, braking forces appear and there is a backward inclination in the new vertical plane of travel.

c) If significant braking forces are generated from the beginning of a sideslip — for example if there is excessive pivoting of the skis — the combination of (a) and (b) can give the image of an inclination made backward and uphill relative to the starting position.

Balance seems to be easier in (c) where the skier has a greater feeling of security.

226. Fore-aft balance at the beginning of a braking turn up the hill.

We have already seen that in a turn up the hill with no braking, the body must be banked obliquely backward

to adjust for the decrease in slope (218b).

If this turn is accompanied with braking, the backward component of the banking will be more pronounced.

227. Fore-aft balance at the beginning of a braking turn down the fall line.

We have seen (218) that maintaining perpendicularity to the slope implies a forward banking in the fore-aft plane at the beginning of a turn which becomes noticeable only in short radius turns.

If a braking is produced at this instant, for example by excessive pivoting of the skis, a backward banking must be initiated in the same plane.

These two banking movements are in opposite directions. Their resultant will be to the rear if there is significant braking; forward if the slope is steep, the radius of the turn short and the braking slight.

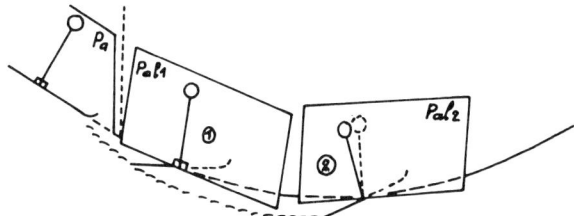

Pa: Fore-aft plane in a traverse. *Pal1* and *Pal2:* Fore-aft plane during a turn. *(1)* Theoretical case: no braking

(balancing as a function of centrifugal force and the slope). (2) Balancing during braking.

230. Lateral balance and centripetal forces.

231. Lateral inclination at the beginning of an arced sideslip and turn down the fall line with centrifugal for-

ce.

We have seen that the objective of a lateral inclination to the inside of turns

is to balance the centrifugal force which is generated by the centripetal forces which create the turn (207).

At the beginning of sideslips that curve up the hill and turns down the fall line where centrifugal force is generated immediately, the inclination must be anticipated.

This can be executed:

a) By a simple global inclination of the body in the lateral plane around the support made by the edges of the skis on the snow (with the skis already pivoted and the edges weighted for a turn down the fall lin; this inclination is slow (251c)).

b) By a passive global banking of the body in the lateral plane. With the skis kept flat on the snow, they sideslip laterally to the outside while the body banks to the inside. This banking is possible only after the skis have been flattened by a passive inclination (a) or by an active banking (b).

c) By inclination followed by a passive banking resembling (a) and (b) but with the hinge in the pelvis (banking in angulation).

d) By a banking similar to that in (c) but active (generally following a platform which unweights the skis to start a turn down the fall line); ie. a lateral slipping of the skis by angulation.

Note 1: The passive banking mentioned in (a), (b) and (c) involves an inertia which must be braked before the desired angle of inclination is attained. This isn't the case in (d).

Note 2: The lateral inclination results in a divergence of the trajectories of the center of mass and the skis. It's necessary, of course, that by pivoting and the directional effect of the skis, the skis begin to make an arc which results in a turn, centrifugal force, and balancing of the forces of the turn by the skier.

232. Lateral inclination at the beginning of turns by hopping the skis.

—The skis are hopped and displaced sideways and pivoted.

—We won't discuss the details of the

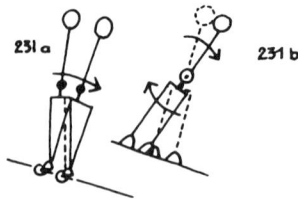

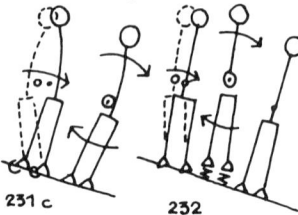

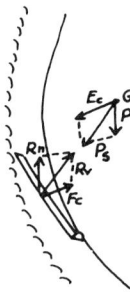

231 a 231 b

231 c 232

BALANCE REQUIREMENTS IN TURNS.
Fc: *centripetal force which creates the turn.*
Rn: *the reactionary force from the ground perpendicular to the plane of the snow.* **Rv:** *resultant of Fc and Rn.*
P: *gravity.* **Ec:** *centrifugal force.* **Ps:** *resultant of P and Ec.*

banking which may preceed and accompany a lateral hop. They are very similar to those which we will analyze during our discussion of counter-turns with platforms and unweighting in the air.

Note: A pivoting hop to bring the skis into the fall line is accompanied by a

curved trajectory of the center of mass down the fall line. This implies an inclination of the body to the inside of the turn to balance the braking forces produced upon landing. It also implies a forward banking of the body to maintain perpendicularity to the slope.

233. lateral inclination by a change of support foot. (This mechanism is the same as that studied in the chapter on edge change (253)).

234. Lateral balance during turns with significant centrifugal force.

The inclination of the body can be adapted to balance centrifugal force by:

a) shifting the weight from a dominant weighting of one ski to a dominant weighting of the other (for example by shifting weight to the inside ski if the skier begins to fall to the inside).

b) modifying the radius of the turn by using the directional effect of the skis (ie. by "piloting" the skis to either accentuate or diminish the centripetal forces) or allowing the skis to sideslip momentarily by releasing the edges or by active or passive lateral banking.

c) flexion or extension, which permits the radius of the arc described by the center of mass to be momentarily increased or decreased without effecting the curve described by the skis.

d) increasing the braking forces and converting the inclination to the inside of the turn to a backward banking.

Note: It is imprecise to speak of a lateral adjustment of balance during a turn by pressing against the inertia of the center of mass of the body to displace the ski-snow support toward the center of the turn. It is the ski-snow support, in fact, which directs the center of mass along the curved trajectory of the turn. It's therefore absurd to speak of a transfer to the inside ski to diminish the radius of the turn.

240. The combination of banking movements at the beginning of the turn.

241. The combination of banking movements at the beginning of turns up the hill (or counter-turns).

a) A backward banking to balance the decrease in slope:

—Significant if the slope is steep and the radius of the turn is short;

b) Banking backward to balance braking:

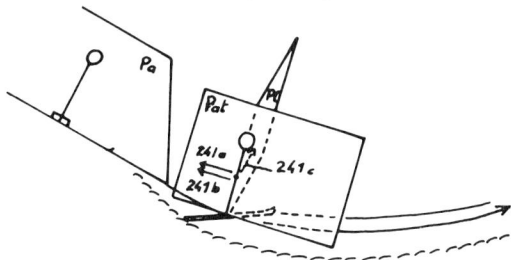

—Signiticant if the skier crosses suddenly from a snow surface where the skis slide well to a snow surface that grabs the skis;

c) Inclination to the inside of the turn to balance centrifugal force:

—Significant if the speed is great and the radius of the turn is short.

Note: If (a) and (b) overlap, the backward component of the banking is the dominant element.

242. The combination of banking movements at the beginning of turns down the fall line.

a) A forward banking due to the increase in slope:

—This is particularly noticeable if the slope is steep and if the radius at the beginning of the turn is short, a rare situation.

b) A backward banking if there is a sudden and pronounced braking of the skis.

c) An inclination to the inside of the turn to balance the centrifugal force

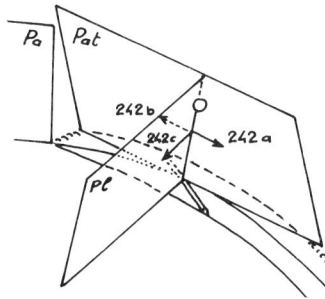

THE CHANGE OF EDGES.

(Passage from a weighting of the uphill edges to a weighting of flat skis, and finally a dominant weighting of the inside edges of the turn).

generated by the turn and produce a change of edges (the inclination to the inside of the turn produces a progressive change from a weighting of the uphill edges to a weighting of flat skis and eventually to a dominant weighting of the inside edges of the turn).

Note 1: (a) and (b) neutralize each other. The lateral inclination becomes the dominant element.

Note 2: The forward banking mentioned in (a) can be increased if the skier wishes to use a forward weighted position to pivot the skis around their tips. The braking that results from this pivoting will tend to accentuate the forward weighting of the skis if the skier doesn't adjust by reestablishing his banking backward. The forward weighting is the dominant component.

Note 3: Skiers who are afraid to slide directly down the fall line try to increase braking from the beginning of the turn. Back-weighting then becomes the dominant component.

243. The combination of banking movements at the beginning of turns preceeded by counter-turns or during linked turns.

We will discuss this topic after we have had an opportunity to discuss platforms (268).

250. Balance at the moment of edge change during turns down the fall line.

251. A "minimum" turn produced simply by inclining the body to the inside of the turn.

a) A global inclination of the body can produce a turn if it simultaneously results in:

—a flattening of the skis on the snow;

—a displacement of the skis both laterally to the outside of the turn and with just enough pivoting to produce sufficient centrifugal force to balance the lateral inclination of the body.

b) This somewhat theoretical turn implies a perfect adjustment of the slope, velocity, rate of lateral inclination and the centripetal forces created by the skis.

c) The duration of passive inclinations as a function of starting position.

(Refer to the accompanying table).

252. Adjustment of the change of edges and lateral inclination.

a) A global inclination of the body down the fall line will place the skis flat on the snow and allow them to be slipped up the hill with a passive or active pivoting provided the body has been inclined to perpendicular to the slope in the lateral plane and only on very flat slopes.

b) On steeper slopes, the inclination of the body requires too much time.

c) Furthermore, the inertia of an inclination of the body down the fall line on steep slopes becomes too great to

TABLE OF CALCULATED ANGLES OF INCLINATION

	20 km/h	40 km/h	60 km/h	80 km/h	100 km/h
5 m	32°				
10 m	17°	51°			
20 m	9°	32°	54°		
40 m	4°	17°	34°	51°	
60 m	3°	11°	25°	39°	50°

TURN RADII

TABLE OF TIMES REQUIRED TO GO FROM A GIVEN INITIAL ANGLE OF INCLINATION TO A GIVEN FINAL ANGLE OF INCLINATION BY SIMPLE BANKING.

INITIAL INCLINATION

	4°	6°	8°	10°
10°	0,50sec	0,42sec	0,25sec	
20°	0,73sec	0,67sec	0,55sec	0,46sec
30°	0,87sec	0,82sec	0,70sec	0,62sec
40°	0,95sec	0,91sec	0,81sec	0,73sec

FINAL INCLINATION

on steep slopes becomes too great to be overcome.

253. Changing support foot, inclination and edge change.

a) A transfer of weight from a dominant (or total) weighting of the downhill ski to a dominant (or total) weighting of the uphill ski can result in an inclination sufficient to allow a change of edges and balance the centrifugal forces generated by the turn. This movement results in no inertia to be overcome.

b) A spreading of the uphill ski into a stem combined with a change of support foot resolves, among others, the problems of quickly balancing centrifugal force.

c) A parallel spreading of the uphill ski implies a pivoting effort to rapidly produce centrifugal force to balance the inclination.

254. Angulation, inclination and edge change.

a) Passive angulation (displacement of the hip to the inside of the turn) produced by muscular relaxation allows the skis to be placed flat on the snow and transforms the lateral inclination into a global inclination of the body.

b) This early flattening of the skis and lateral inclination causes the skis to be slipped uphill with passive pivoting. The uphill slipping of the skis is accelerated when the angulation is accompanied by a flexion (a flexion resulting from compression (438)).

255. Pivoting of the skis and braking, inclination and edge change.

A significant, pivoting, muscular effort (or less significant when made with unweighted skis) permits a rapid displacement of the skis:
—pivoting into the turn,
—laterally to the outside of the turn being started,
—forward to balance braking.

This three-fold movement results in a change of edges.

256. Platforms, banking and edge changes.
a) Balance during platforms is analyzed in (260).
b) The edge change can be executed

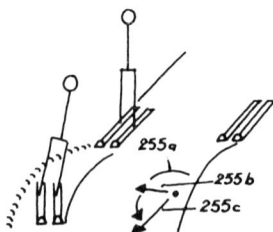

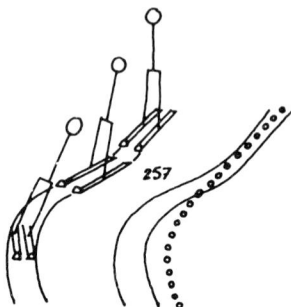

in the air during a complex, passive, banking movement (265).

257. The pivoting of the skis during a counter-turn simplifies the edge change.

Since the skis are pivoted obliquely up the hill relative to the body mass, the skier's body banks over his skis. This results in an automatic transfer of weight from the uphill edges to the downhill edges.
Note: The pressure applied to the skis by the feet is displaced forward (269).

258. The pole plant to aid balance during the edge change.

By supporting himself with a lateral planting of the downhill pole, the skier can decelerate his inclination and accelerate the lateral slipping of his skis (251a) once they have been placed flat on the snow.

260. Balance and platforms at the beginning of turns.

261. Fore-aft balance during a side-slipped stop with no change in the direction of travel.

There is successively:
a) A generally active backward banking (a forward movement of the feet) to balance the braking.
b) An accentuation of the braking by a backward banking (a) followed by a forward banking.
c) The banking movement described in (b) decelerates as the skier slows down. This banking is slowed, among other things, by gravity as the center of mass is elevated. The banking reaches 0 velocity when the the the axis of the body is vertical.

Maintaining balance during this movement is very difficult and usually requires a forward pole plant.
Note: Braking is accentuated in (b) by the greater edge angle as the skier is banked backward in the plane of movement. It's interesting to note, however, the tendency that the skis have to "escape" from under the body by sliding along their major axis. The backward banking mentioned above corresponds, in fact, to an increase in the angle between the axis of the skier's body and his skis. The thrust exerted by the skier on his skis, therefore, tends to make them slide forward along their major axis. This can be neutralized by:

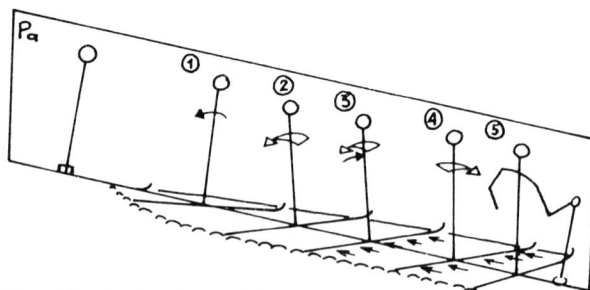

(1) Banking backward to anticipate the braking; (2) the banking continues; (3) accentuation of the braking slows the banking; then, (4) banking

—a muscular blocking of the ankles,
—an increased pivoting of the skis,
—by backweighting of the feet relative to the mass of the body (a generally automatic and therefore involuntary response).

262. Balance during braking followed by a banking into the turn without changing the direction of travel.
a) Idem 261a.
b) Idem 261b and c except that the banking is continued beyond perpendicular to the direction of travel. This banking is generally quicker than that produced at the beginning of a turn without a platform.
c) Braking of the forward banking

in the opposite direction; (5) the skier stops as he returns to vertical and balances with a pole plant.

movement.

The skis are displaced laterally and pivoted to start the turn at the moment of edge change. The skis should be displaced forward relative to the center of mass to decelerate the passive forward banking of the body mentioned in b. This forward displacement of the skis can only be produced by an active banking (forward movement of the feet).
d) Another alternative: use a forward weighted position to control the turn (242, note 2).
Note 1: Idem (261, note 1).
Note 2: Even if the forward banking (b) is used only to maintain perpendicularity to the slope (for example in

a short turn on a steep slope), it remains necessary to slow this banking movement; the braking is simply delayed. In the case of a turn that is hopped into the fall line, forward banking is subconsciously made during the jump and must be slowed and reversed toward the end of the turn.

Note 3: The active banking mentioned in (c) resembles that cited in (217d) (balance is readjusted upon landing following an aerial flight with forward banking).

263. Balance during braking, with the trajectory deflected down the fall line, followed by banking into the turn.

The direction of travel arcs down the fall line (233) during the banking movements mentioned in (242a) and (242b). At slow speeds on steep slopes, these banking movements occur in the lateral plane relative to the initial direction of travel.

264. Lateral balance during braking and banking into turns with centrifugal force.

When a skier moves to perpendicular over his base of support by banking forward, he must begin a lateral banking to the inside of the turn (for example a passive banking started by shifting the weight from the downhill to the uphill ski or banking as mentioned in (261) or an active banking by braquage or vissage).

265. Balance during a platform with rebound and banking into the turn.

a) The banking described in (242) is slowed by a significant biting of the edges. Because of the harsh braking of the lower body, the banking is immediately reversed and the skier can be launched into the air with a passive forward banking while in the air (even without specific muscle effort).

b) As in (242) and (243), this forward passive banking must be accompanied by:

—A lateral banking to balance the centrifugal force generated by the turn (244);

—An active backward banking (a forward movement of the feet) to neutralize the inertia of the passive forward banking cited in (a).

Note: The backward banking (a) doesn't just balance the braking produced. It also allows the skier to center his weight further back over the

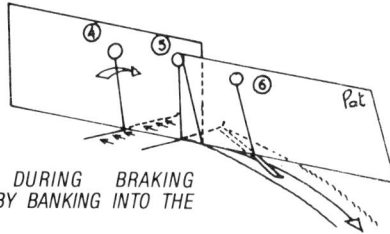

BALANCE DURING BRAKING FOLLOWED BY BANKING INTO THE TURN (262).
(1) - (4), Same as preceeding diagram; (5) in the Pa plane between the forward banking to anticipate the change of slope or backward to an- ticipate the braking; (6) inclination in the lateral plane to balance centrifugal force.

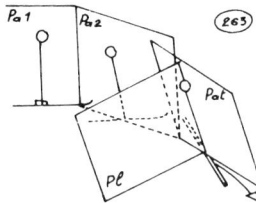

Pa1: *fore-aft plane in a traverse.* **Pa2**: *during a straight, braking sideslip.* **Pat**: *plane tangent to the arc of the turn.* **Pl**: *lateral plane.*

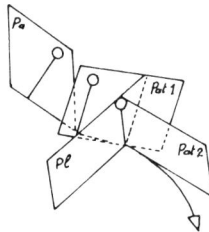

Pat 1: *plane tangent to the arc of the counter-turn.* **Pat 2**: *plane tangent to the arc of the turn down the fall line.*

"holding center of the ski" ("tail-pressure").

266. Balance during a carved counter-turn and banking into the turn.

Hypothesis: The counter-turn is assumed to be perfectly carved and, therefore, doesn't create braking in the fore-aft plane. It's therefore simple to maintain perpendicularity to the slope during the counter-turn and turn (217).

a) At the beginning of the carved counter-turn up the hill, there is an uphill lateral inclination to balance centrifugal force.

b) The centrifugal force becomes great enough to slow the lateral inclination cited in (a) and reverse it to a lateral inclination down the fall line.

c) Once the skier's body becomes perpendicular to the slope, the skis should start into the turn. Theoretically, tipping the skis onto edge will suffice to initiate a carved turn. In reality, a slight change of support foot or a slight pivoting is made at this instant.

Note: Maintaining perpendicularity to the slope, except for counter-turns or very round carved turns (very rare), is made by progressive balancing without genuine fore-aft banking movements.

267. Balance during a braking counter-turn which results in a curved movement up the hill.

This situation involves backward banking of the braking counter-turn (241a, b and c). It also involves the lateral inclinations of carved counter-turns (266a and b). A lateral inclination down the fall line created by the centrifugal force of the counter-turn replaces the lateral banking which the skier must make in the other cases.

268. Balance during a flat ski counter-turn.

The skis can be made to slide up the hill without banking the upper body uphill or even during a banking down the fall line. If a pivoting down the fall line quickly follows, the displacement of the skis up the hill can be considered a lateral displacement relative to the turn being initiated. The necessary lateral inclination is then accelerated.

Note: This mechanism is included in compound elements 266 and 267. It is an integral part of the banking process.

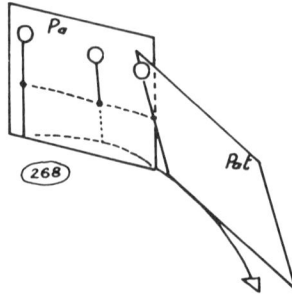

269. A pole plant to assist balance at the instant of the platform.

A pole plant simultaneously "secures" the platform, controls the speed of the banking down the fall line and, if the platform results in a lifting of the skis or a rapid change of edges, facilitates balance at this critical moment (258).

Note: The pole plant can also play an important role in fore-aft pivoting mechanisms (531b,d,e).

270. A combination of banking movements before, during and after a platform made with a lifting of the skis.

271. In the fore-aft plane.
a) A backward banking which includes braking and applies pressure to the tails of the skis is converted into a forward banking.
b) When the skis are lifted, the forward banking continues and accelerates around the center of mass.

272. In the lateral plane.
a) A lateral inclination to the inside of the arc of the counter-turn is converted into a lateral inclination in the opposite direction (toward the center of the turn down the fall line).
b) When the skis are lifted, this banking continues around the center of mass. It gives an image of a lateral displacement of the skis to the outside of the turn being started.
c) This lateral displacement can be accelerated by active lateral banking during the time the skis are in the air (the angulated position of the platform is reversed to an angulation in the opposite direction upon landing).
d) The movement of the skis along their major axis mentioned in (273b) corresponds partially to a lateral banking.

273. In the plane of the skis.
It is interesting to examine the problems posed in this plane which, in reality, originate in the two planes mentioned above.
a) The skier begins a forward banking during the platform to prevent his skis from sliding forward out from under him by displacing his feet backward.
If this banking has been neutralized, nothing happens during

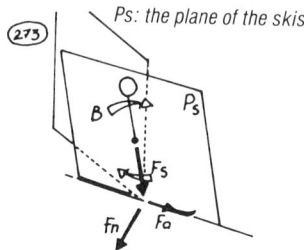
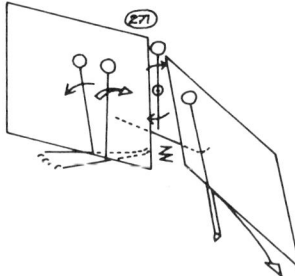
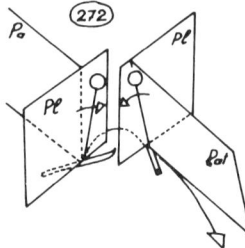

Ps: the plane of the skis

the time that the skis are suspended in the air.
b) If the banking has only been partially neutralized, it causes the skis to move along their major axis.
A forward displacement of the skis neutralizes the forward banking mentioned in (271b).
An uphill displacement of the skis aids the lateral banking mentioned in (273).

274. A forward thrust of the feet and balancing during counter-turns and turns.
a) We have discussed in (273b) the tendency that the skis have to slide forward along their major axis during a platform. The passive banking which they start in part in the fore-aft plane.
b) This banking can then neutralize the forward banking mentioned in (271a) and thereby permit a perfectly balanced initiation of the turn in the fore-aft plane.

Note: This forward displacement of the feet is not generally perceived as a passive movement — even when it is — because the skier has developed the habit of doing something which, in reality, doesn't occur.

Fs: thrust exerted by the skier on his skis, dissectable into Fn (the thrust exerted perpendicular to the surface of the snow) and Fa (the thrust exerted along the major axis of the skis).
B: banking initiated by the skier in the plane of the skis to neutralize Fa.

THE BEHAVIOR OF THE SKIER ON HIS SKIS

Even if it were possible to take a robot built with a human morphology and program it with all of the motor mechanisms of balance and all of the motor mechanisms required to slow down, to turn and to wedeln, it would still be impossible to fabricate a skier.

In the first place, this robot must be given the capability to gather information about the snow conditions, the terrain, and the speed and be able to constantly monitor it's position in space and sense any beginning of a fall. Then, it must have the capacity to interpret this information and make appropriate action decisions. Still, this robot wouldn't duplicate the human being if it didn't experience the conscious fear which can paralyze, the subconscious anxiety which handicaps, or occasionally the state of euphoria which makes everything seem easy and sometimes allows inspiration and the creation of new movements.

It's these different aspects of human behavior, which have already been discussed to a greater or lesser extent in the chapter on Teaching, which will be examined briefly here.

300. The sensations perceived by the skier.

With regard to position and movement.

301. The human being is only capable of perceiving sensations of change. A sensation which he is accustomed to will likely not even be noticed, only a variation of this sensation will be perceived. For example, a skier who habitually skis with forward weighting will no longer be aware of it; likewise a skier who skis with constant backweighting. But if a skier who always skis in a forward weighted position suddenly assumes a position that is only slightly backweighted, he will immediately be aware of it and judge it to be excessive. Another example is the skier who always presses against the front of his boots. He soon reaches the point where he is no longer aware that he does this and I have even seen skiers deny it despite having genuine wounds on the front of their shins from constant chaffing against the boots.

302. Even sensations of change, when resulting from the execution of habitual movements, are generally no longer perceived. For example, exiting turns with forward weighting or initiating turns with hyper-backweighting.

303. The essential sensations that must be perceived with regard to position and movements are:
a) pressure of the feet against the boots — and in particular against the soles of the boots — for balance.
b) Sensations of limb movements and muscle tension for adjustment of balance and control of movements.
c) Sensations originating in the inner ear (acceleration and movements in all planes).
Note: Some skiers, who habitually look at their skis, use visual information to monitor the action of their legs. We regard this an error because it overrides feedback from the feet and legs. The skis become merely extensions of the feet of good skiers and we can then speak of an integration of the skis into the body of the skier. The skier no longer perceives his movements relative to the displacements of his skis, but perceives the movements of an autonomous skier/skis unit relative to his environment.

With regard to the environment and velocity.

304. Skier's essentially perceive their environment through their eyes and their feet. Initially they use their vision to examine the terrain, the consistency of the snow and their velocity. They subsequently use the kinesthetic feedback from their feet to correct their initial interpretations. Some skiers rely primarily on visual information and are very handicapped when they have to ski in fog and usually are poor gliders. Others use the kinesthetic feedback from the ski-snow contact. The "visual" skiers can sometimes learn to become "kinesthetic" skiers through sheer will, but this requires a total reeducation.

305. Sensations emanating from the ski-snow contact can be violent (eg. hard snow or bumpy terrain) or very soft (eg. powder or packed powder snow). Some skiers are only capable of feeling the first but skiers who are "good gliders" can perfectly sense the latter.

Some violent sensations can disturb the skier who is not accustomed to them: very hard and bumpy snow, icy slopes which echo under the impact of the skis. Auditory senses can intervene in these kinds of situations to have a stimulatory or inhibitory effect.

306. Because of their mechanical characteristics (design and materials), the skis and boots can either dampen or amplify the sensations emanating from the ski-snow contact. Some skiers use equipment that compounds their weaknesses by dissipating the ski-snow sensations.

The interpretation of sensations — the control of actions.

307. An ability to interpret speed is essential to the skier. By itself, it is of little value, but in combination with an evaluation of the snow and terrain to be negotiated, it has a pronounced effect on the skier's behavior.

308. Anticipation of movements is indispensable to the skier.

Anticipation presupposes an accurate visual perception of the terrain, an accurate perception of the speed and technical proficiency because the skier must simultaneously calculate his action as a function of the distance to an obstacle, his speed and the time duration of the different phases of movements which will be made.

Undoubtedly it is this tendency to anticipate movements which makes intermediate skiers transfer their attention away from the kinesthetic sensations of the ski-snow contact to focus on visual sensations and body movements. (This often results in the skier using a stance that is too narrow and excessive unweighting...).

The very good skier anticipates his movements but corrects them as a function of the ski-snow contact. This is why he never appears to be out of control. On the other hand, many skiers who are too dynamic or too hurried are at a disadvantage. They need to learn to "listen" to their skis and moderate their actions.

Note: A journalist once wrote, "A ski champion has a very quick eye and is very mobile, but slow in moving".

310. The intervention of emotional factors.

311. The sensation of sliding, which in fact is a suppression of sensations of support in the fore-aft plane, sometimes produces anxiety.
a) It can result in a global tightening of the muscles and inhibit balance reflex muscle actions.
b) It causes some skiers to habitually use braking (ie. a snowplow or sideslipping).

312. The sensation of sliding is often pleasurable, even intoxicating. This is evidenced by the attraction of such sliding sports as ice skating, roller skating, skate boarding, etc...

313. Sensations of acceleration or deceleration occasionally produce anxiety in beginning skiers. A constant speed doesn't give a perceptible sensation of change (one perceives, for example, only the start and the slowing down of an elevator). It's therefore advisable to have the beginning skier make long runs at slow speeds to educate his balance reflexes rather than short runs with many starts and stops.

The acceleration that is created by the increase in slope at the beginning of a turn is anxiety producing. The intermediate skier neutralizes this acceleration by braking, thereby "refusing the fall line".

314. The sensation of acceleration can be intoxicating for some skiers, making it easier for them to keep their balance over drop-offs.

The acceleration produced by the slope — or more precisely by gravity and without muscle effort — is exhilarating, like the acceleration of a powerful car. This seems to be one of the fundamental attractions of skiing.

315. The perception of speed that is judged to be dangerous is anxiety producing. This perception is first visual and secondarily the kinesthetic sensation of the friction of the skis on the snow (particularly on hard snow). It can be 6 miles per hour for the beginner, 60 miles per hour for the good skier, or 120 miles per hour for the speed trial competitor...

316. The sensation of weightlessness over drop-offs can be anxiety producing... or invigorating.

If anxiety producing, it results in a tensing of the muscles and an extension backward (in a futile effort to retain support) which is contrary to the proper balance mechanisms of passive forward banking (214).

If invigorating, it encourages the skier to seek out moguls and jumps.

317. The suppression of certain habitual sensations can produce anxiety or merely be moderately disturbing.
—Anxiety producing in the case of a suppression of visual information in fog.
—Disturbing when it means a reduction in the amount of visual information necessary to adapt movements to the terrain in poor visibility of "white out".
—A change of boots will result in different pressure sensations in the feet which can be at least disturbing if not anxiety producing.

318. A fear of the slope, somewhat related to a "fear of heights" is at the origin of numerous technical faults (including an inclination up the hill and an excessively rapid pivoting of the body during a turn down the fall line).

319. A fear of falling can also produce anxiety. It can be an underlying factor that has a pronounced effect on the skier's behavior without his even being aware of it.

320. In competition, emotional factors can have a significant influence on the skier long before, immediately before and during the competition.

Personal temperament and technical behavior.

321. An incisive, aggressive behavior seems to be a positive factor in the execution of certain gestures; such as carving, platforms, rebound and braquage. On the other hand, it perhaps can have a negative influence on gliding and flat ski directional effects.

322. A mild temperament is more suitable for learning flat ski sliding movements. Consequently the distinction that we've made in group instruction for dynamic and non-dynamic skiers.

323. A sense of harmony seems to be a positive factor in the execution of skiing movements.

324. Imagination and creativity play a positive role in acquiring a more varied technique but can often detract from the moderation which facilitates balancing mechanisms.

Environmental factors.

325. A fear of failure or a fear of appearing ridiculous can halt all progress; particularly in a group situation.

326. A group atmosphere can be either positive or negative.

327. The nature of the relationship between the instructor and the student can have either a positive or a negative effect.

328. The presence of a family member can have a positive or a negative effect.

329. For all skiers, the sight of the snow (or more precisely a winter scenery) and a long slope, the sensation of being able to slide and ac-celerate without effort, produces a special emotional reaction. This emotional state can assume very diverse forms among different individuals and to a great extent will influence their behavior on the snow. A general euphoria can be a positive learning factor but can also lead to accidents.

The general atmosphere of the ski resort can put the skier at ease or make him uncomfortable. A timid, begining skier will be handicapped, for example, in a ski area with predominantly expert terrain and frequented by a very athletic clientele.

Weather conditions can also play a considerable role.

330. The intervention of psychological factors.

331. Motivation has a profound influence on the skier (We could just as easily have classified motivation among the emotional rather than psychological factors).

Motivation can assume very diverse forms among skiers and can lead to very different skiing "styles". The attraction of a new and changing environment, a form of poetry that comes from the snow just as it does from the sea: a relaxed skiing in perfect communion with the elements. The taste of an aesthetic physical activity where the body can express itself fully: classic slope skiing becomes, in fact, a genuine sport of expression. A desire to dominate the elements or taste risk: skiing on difficult slopes. A desire to surpass oneself: a broadening of one's technique, systematic training. Sharpening aggressiveness, challenging a friend, or tasting competition or extreme skiing. The passion for speed; a taste for violent — I could almost say visceral — sensations which speed can give: downhill racing, speed trials. A passion for unrestrained corporal expression: freestyle skiing...

332. The level of attention directed to the slope and the control of the movements made by the skier is an important factor in the skier's effectiveness.

a) Attention to the slope and the interpretation of the terrain and snow must be distinguished from the attention to the movements made by the skier and occasionally even to the attempt to apply movements to the present situation. These two concepts are often contradictory, particularly among skiers who have been "constructed" by traditional teaching methods. Consequently, the importance of a teaching system that is based on using terrain appropriate to the movements being taught and experiencing a great deal of "free" skiing on varied terrain between ski lessons.

b) A skier's movements should be a sophisticated response made in a reflexive manner to the situation as analyzed. It shouldn't be an invariate, compound movement, but a combination of specific elements with each one addressing an aspect of the problem being confronted. For example, a turn is executed with a specific form of unweighting, pivoting, weight distribution between the two skis, and fore-aft displacement of the skis. By viewing the skier's response in this manner, it becomes easier to understand the meaning of the term "strategy" as applied to skiing by sports psychologists.

c) In skiing, perhaps moreso than in many other sports, the "strategy" selected by the skier confronting an obstacle (eg. crossing a bump or making a turn) is immediately answered: by a fall or the beginning of a fall or, on the other hand, by the perfect execution of the movement. By directing his attention simultaneously to the elements of the movements and their results, the skier accumulates experience which ultimately allows him to adopt better, more appropriate strategies.

The ability to define these better adapted strategies is more a function of the skier's attention to detail, to his capacity for deduction, to his possession of a rich "technical repertoire" than to a simple quantitative increase in experience.

333. The ability to consciously substitute a new behavior for a subconscious habitual behavior is an important factor for progress and an ability that is unequally distributed among individuals. This substitution can be made:

a) With regard to one, specific aspect of a movement; for example to accentuate the precision of the platforms at the beginning of turns or wedeln.

b) In a more global manner dealing with the entirety of a movement or of a skier's behavior; for example to "be more precise" in the case cited above.

340. Instinctive or innate behavior.

We can use the terms instinctive or innate in the same way here as we do in discussing a young infant making his first steps or standing up without falling.

341. The displacement of pressure exerted against the ground by moving the feet forward during an active forward banking (213) is very similar to the forward displacement of the feet while walking or running or while jumping forward with both feet.
The essential difference is that instead of first tilting the body forward and then moving the foot (or feet) forward, both movements occur simultaneously.

342. Lateral balance by distributing the weight between the feet is unaffected.

343. Balancing by moving segments of the upper body laterally (ie. arms, shoulders, head) is unaffected.

344. Keeping the body facing the direction of travel and, as much as possible, in the horizontal plane during rapidly linked curved movements seems to be instinctive (eg. in running, cycling, skiing).

345. Stabilizing the head at a certain angle during long curved movements seems to be equally instinctive. This undoubtedly allows a finer perception of changes in inclination relative to this reference position (eg. in skiing, cycling...) in order to adjust the arc of the turn more precisely.

350. Behavior related to particular body morphologies.

We have already discussed the influence of particular morphological characteristics in skiing, such as flat feet, bowlegs, knock knees, excessive curvature of the lower leg, antiversion or retroversion of the hip and an excessively straight or hollow back (pages 97 and 98) (191-199).
These morphological characteristics can have a considerable influence on a skier's behavior by making specific movements easy or difficult and give the skier a unique personal style and distinguishable silhouette.

360. The skier's perception of his own behavior.

I'm not concerned here with the simple perception of sensations, but with the global image that a skier has of his motor behavior.

361. The skier tends to think of his habitual behavior as "normal". He perceives every modification as being "abnormal". Even ski technicians don't escape this phenomenon, but ignore it.

362. A skier doesn't necessarily make the movements he thinks he makes or visualizes himself making. This is the primary value or film or video, since it provides the skier with a true and accurate image of his motor behavior, but this realistic appraisal can often be very depressing for the skier.

363. Skier's tend to place particular importance on technical details recently learned which greatly improve their effectiveness. These details, however, can represent only a tiny fraction of the entire global motor behavior that the skier has already mastered.

364. A skier's conscious experience seems to be inversely proportional to the ease with which he has learned his technique.
This explains why some exceptionally gifted skiers, even champions, have greater difficulty assimilating new movements than less gifted skiers. Since they have less experience in learning motor skills, they know less about how to learn.

For this reason, these gifted skiers are often less prepared than others to become instructors or coaches, since they aren't as intellectually aware of the problems confronting their students. This assumes, of course, that the less gifted skiers who have become the better coaches and instructors have, nevertheless, succeeded in mastering all of the technical elements.

365. The instructor or coach must not neglect dealing with the totality of his student's or racer's behavior; not just the technical behavior but, as we have seen, also the psychological and emotional behavior.

THE MECHANICS OF SKIING MOVEMENTS

400. Several bio-mechanical considerations.

The skier's movements

Biomechanics is the study of the mechanics of movement and uses every investigative technique available. These methods are evidently richer than those available to the instructor or coach working on the snow. Biomechanics can, therefore, assist the instructor and coach, but can't replace them.

Eventually, because of the use of computers, biomechanics will allow a synthetic reconstruction of all of the movements of a skier or the analysis of skiing technique from catalogued, observed input.

Our goal here will be far more elementary: to use several biomechanical principles to give a better understanding of the motor behavior of skiing.

Several biomechanical concepts have already been discussed in the chapters dealing with ski-snow effects and maintaining balance.

401. Two forces are at the origin of all movements made by man: gravity and the mechanical force generated by muscular contraction. All movements that use gravity to produce the movement of body segments must then use muscular force to moderate this movement (407).

Gravity tends to produce, or accentuate, a flexing of all articulations in the fore-aft plane of a standing man. The muscles which operate against these flexions are called "extensor" muscles.

402. A third factor plays an essential role in skiing movements and, more precisely, in those involving the skier/skis unit: the effect of inertia, which is a function of the skier's velocity.
Note: This effect dictates that any modification of the trajectory of the center of mass is impossible without the intervention of forces at the ski-snow contact. These forces become greater as the speed increases and are generally produced by changes in the terrain or a voluntary displacement of the skis.

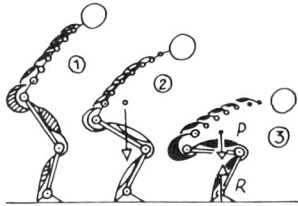

1) The extensor muscles are semi-tensed to resist the pull of gravity. 2) Relaxing these muscles produces flexion. 3) Their contraction slows the flexion. This is the muscle force that produces the reaction from the ground.

Because of his speed as he crosses a bump where he pivots his skis, the skier experiences a compression which he responds to by muscular contraction.

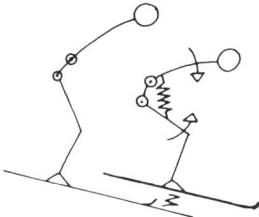

Example of a double displacement of body segments provoked by muscle contraction (flexion-avalement).

403. A muscular contraction always shortens the distance between its two extremities, thereby moving the two body segments to which it is attached in opposite directions. The speed of movement depends on the inertia of the two segments being moved, the distance seperating the point of insertion and the point of pivoting, and the force of the contraction. A muscular contraction can not create a limb displacement if the opposing force is too great. Nevertheless, we can speak of muscular effort even if it results in no movement; for example, a pivoting effort.

In skiing, exterior forces (see ski-snow effects) can provoke a pivoting or lateral displacement of the skis resulting in displacements of limbs without muscular action (sometimes even with moderating muscular action operating in the opposite direction). One then refers to *passive* displacements of the limbs or skis.

404. Pivoting movements of the limbs in man are called articulations. Every articulation can be mobilized in one or several planes, but not in others. For the legs and the torso, for example, there are movements:
—In the fore-aft plane of flexion or extension (the latter are always oriented against the action of gravity in the standing position). These movements are controlled, at each joint, by groups of muscles called "flexors" and "extensors".
—In the lateral plane of abduction (movements away from the axis of the body) and adduction (movements toward the axis of the body). These movements are controlled by muscle groups called "abductors" and "adductors".
—In the horizontal plane, of internal and external rotation controlled by muscle groups called "internal rotators" and "external rotators" (and for certain articulations *pronation* and *supination*). In a simpler context we refer to the pivoting of a given segment "over" or "under" another segment, eventually taking into account which segment is serving as a fulcrum.

The majority of articulations allow complex movements by combining the displacements described above. The fact that these movements become complex to describe doesn't imply that they are more difficult to perform. In fact, most muscles have several functions (extensor, rotator and abductor, for example, in the foot or hip). A single muscle can, therefore, produce a movement which we can analyze in three planes.

Note: Don't confuse the center of pivoting of an articulation and the center of pivoting of the skier/skis unit in space (415).

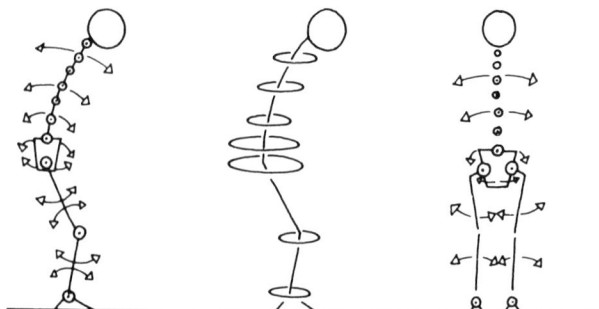

Fore-aft plane: movements of flexion and extension.

Horizontal plane: movements of rotation.

Lateral plane: movements of adduction and abduction.

405. Any movement around a joint generally also involves a number of neighboring articulations:
—Either to amplify the movement,
—Or to moderate the movement (for example in balancing reactions)
—Or to solidify the segments displaced by the movement or allow a solid platform from the ground.

A muscle contraction that produces a localized limb displacement can, therefore, involve the contraction of a number of muscles in different articulations.

406. The analysis of limb displacements (with the help of photosequences or movie film taken from different angles) and muscular activation (by electromyography) isn't yet at a stage where it can permit a precise analysis of the movements of skiing. Mechanical analyses are essentially used to test hypotheses.

By corollary, every analysis of complex movements retains a degree of uncertainty.

407. When a muscular contraction creates a limb displacement that isn't immediately slowed by an exterior force, the movement tends to continue by itself to the limit of motion permitted by the joint.

A defensive mechanism automatically decelerates this displacement with a contraction of the antagonist muscle group before the limit of the range of motion is reached.

408. One characteristic of muscular contraction is that a muscle that has already been pre-stretched contracts more powerfully.

409. Any contraction of a muscle or group of muscles produces a limb displacement which stretches a muscle or group of muscles which act in the opposite direction and are called antagonists. This explains why it is easier to link movements in opposite directions than to execute isolated movements (for example wedeln or counter-turns, even when performed in a slow rhythm).

Not only is the muscle contraction facilitated by this pre-stretching of the muscles, but the first movement permits a more precise selection of the muscles to be recruited for the second movement.

410. We refer to the rapid linking of two movements in opposite directions as "wind-up - release" movements. For example, flexion-extension producing a rebound, or "anticipation-deangulation" causing the skis to pivot into the turn. There is already a contraction of the muscles in these movements which will produce the recoil movement, before the wind-up movement is completed, to brake and reverse it.

During typical wind-up - recoil movements, the moment of maximum muscle tension occurs at the end of the wind-up movement and at the beginning of the recoil movement. Teh recoil

410. The rapid linking of two movements in opposite directions is often referred to as a "wind-up - recoil" movement. For example, flexion-extension producing a rebound or "anticipation-deangulation" resulting in the skis beginning to pivot into a turn. There is already a contraction of the muscles in these movements which will produce the recoil movement to brake and reverse the wind-up movement before it hase been completed.

During typical wind-up - recoil movements, the moment of maximum muscle tension is situated at the end of the wind-up movement and at the beginning of the recoil movement. For example, the thrust of a rebound by flexion-extension is maximum at the end of the flexion and at the beginning of the extension.

Wind-up - recoil movements are linked according to a distinctive rhythm, which is reminiscent of the rebound of a rubber ball. The elastic qualities of the muscle are, in fact, utilized.

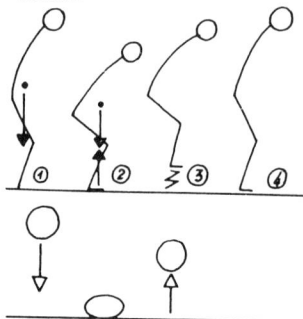

EXAMPLE OF A WIND-UP - RECOIL MOVEMENT.
(1) The wind-up movement is a flexion (comparable to the fall of a ball). (2) The muscles which slow the flexion store the energy for the rebound, just as the elastic deformation of a ball. (3) and (4), the rebound can be made in an upright or folded position.

The wind-up movement permits a recruitment of muscles to be used in the recoil that is even finer than in (409). These muscles can be contacted faster and with greater intensity resulting in a maximal initial acceleration of the recoil movement. The active phase of the recoil movement can become imperceptible, for example a vertical rebound with visible extension while the feet are in contact with the ground. The extension which follows is a passive recoil movement.

411. Most muscle contractions in skiing are made not to displace limbs but to hold them within their plane of movement. For example, the lateral blocking of the feet, ankles, knees and hips to hold the skis on edge.

This kind of action implies the use of isometric contractions which neither shorten nor lengthen the muscle. Isometric contractions are very different from normal contractions with fiber shortening (the forces involved are often greater and the physical-chemical processes that take place are somewhat different). Isometric contractions are more similar to contractions which include an active braking of stretching.

A skier's physical training should take this characteristic behavior of the muscles during skiing maneuvers into account without, nevertheless, neglecting the necessity of conserving the capability of "fine" contractions which are so indispensable to balancing mechanisms. Fortunately, different muscles appear to be involved in these two kinds of function.

412. The majority of muscle contractions in skiing are used to resist the effects of gravity and, therefore, to slow flexions and accompanying movements.

These contractions, as mentioned in (411), are known as "eccentric" movements. They imply somewhat the same kind of muscle qualities as the isometric contractions which block articulations but also require the capacity to act in a very short period of time (see 413) and the ability to operate over a broad range of movement. The muscles which are best adapted to this kind of action are soft and very long, fleshy fibers as opposed the the muscles involved in isometric contractions which tend to be short and hard. The current ski champions tend to have a

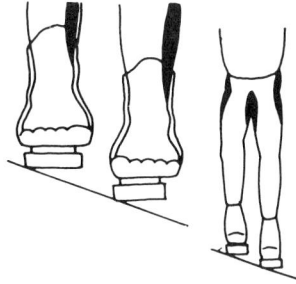

Isometric contraction of the lateral fixator muscles of the feet, ankles and hips hold the skis on edge.

predominance of muscles of this type.

It's well established that muscle includes both "fast twitch" (ie. white) fibers and "slow twitch" (ie. red) fibers that participate equally in static efforts. An analysis of the proportion of muscle types in the best skiers would, of course, be of very great interest.

A high proportion of fast twitch fibers in the muscle is generally associated with the high degree of explosive power demonstrated by the greatest ski champions as they project from one ski to the other.

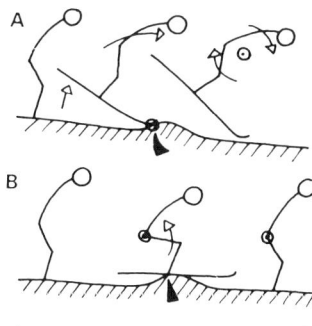

*The effects of a sudden shock from a bump on a stiff skier (**A**) and a supple skier (**B**).*

413. Muscle power (power is the quantity of work done in a unit of time) gives the skier the quality of "suppleness" by allowing him to ski without blocking muscle groups. In straight running over bumpy terrain or turning, for example, the deceleration of flexion movements which result from compression will be greater if the muscles are more powerful.

Greater power will allow linked flexion movements to be made at a faster rhythm. A lack of sufficient muscle power can force the skier to block his muscles by isometric contraction which will result in harsh contact between the skis and the snow and excessive skidding and braking.

Note: Force and power are two different characteristics. Power can be estimated by the distance that can be jumped vertically with both feet, whereas force can be measured in a maximal contraction on a dynamometer. But the power required in skiing is characteristically a braking power. I believe this to be a critical distinction. Physical training for skiing could most certainly be improved if physiological studies were undertaken of the power requirements of skiing much as recent studies of the endurance requirements which have led to important discoveries.

Movements of the skier/skis unit in space.

414. Because of the velocity of the skier/skis unit in the direction of travel, every exterior force exerted on it can produce:

a) A global displacement of the entire skier/skis unit by a sudden impulse, such as a bump or a sudden edge-set, if it is too rigid.

b) Limb displacements within the unit. For example, colliding with a bump can result in a passive flexion-avalement, or a compression or sudden decrease in slope can result in a braking flexion. Pressures as high as 660 pounds (a thrust roughly equivalent to that exerted against the ground by an internationally elite high jumper) have been measured.

Note: The limb displacements mentioned in (b) are often assumed to be produced by gravity. In reality, they can be much quicker due to the speed of the subject. An example would be a flexion edge-set with the skis placed ahead of the body in the direction of travel.

287

415. All movements of the skier/skis unit are made in space around the center of mass, regardless of anyh involvement of centers of pivoting.

Even movements in the fore-aft plane during straight running obey this rule as a result of the free sliding of the skis.

416. When a global movement of the skier/skis unit is started in space, isolated movements within the global movement can be analyzed individually unless they involve braking, a platform, or a carved platform introduced because of an exterior force.

417. All of the global movements of the skier/skis unit, in addition to any movements arising from the inertia of the skier's momentum, must be analyzed in the fore-aft plane (202).

418. Centrifugal force is only a manifestation of the inertia of the skier's momentum. Proper placement of the skis creates "centripetal" forces against the snow surface which constantly modify the direction of travel of the skier/skis unit. Within this unit, the demands of balance necessitate lateral inclination.

419. Gravity is the driving force of the movement of a skier. It operates in two components: one perpendicular to the surface of the snow (211), the other tangent to the slope. On a uniform slope, the component of

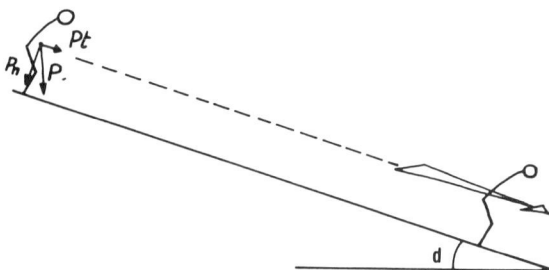

On a uniform slope and snow, the component of gravity tangent to the slope **Pt** *(where* Pt = *P*sind *and* d *represents the angle of the slope) creates a uniform acceleration. At slow speeds, one can compute the speeds attained and the distances travelled from the equations* V = gt *and* L = ½gt².

The resistance of the air is computed from the equation R = QSV², *where Q can be measured in a wind tunnel.*

gravity tangent to the slope will produce a uniformly accelerated movement if we eliminate the resistance of the air and the friction between the skis and the snow.

In a traverse, gravity can only produce an acceleration if the skis are placed on edge to create forces which prohibit any other displacement of the skis than movement forward along the direction of the edges. If these forces are eliminated, the effect of gravity will produce a trajectory arcing down the fall line.

Conclusion

I believe that in order to understand the movements of skiing, it is indispensable that we study them relative to the entirety of the forces which operate on the skier and the problems that are posed by the need to maintain balance. With regard to analyzing movements, it is more useful to keep in mind the few principles of muscle mechanics which were discussed above than to have a thorough knowledge of muscle nomenclature, anatomy, the actions of each, the planes of mobilization, and the amplitude of each articulation. I tackle these subjects only to support a few new technical concepts.

420.The movements of the skier in the fore-aft plane. The "modern" flexion. The forward thrust of the feet.

Movements in the fore-aft plane (active or passive banking movements) have been studied in the chapter "The Maintenance of Balance".

—During straight runs over drop-offs and compressions, over bumps and in the air (211 - 217).
—During sideslipping and edge checks (221-225, 261, 262).
—During turns and counter-turns (226, 227, 241, 242, 262, 263-271).

421. The localization of pressure in the middle of the foot (see diagram page 273).
a) In a resting, upright position, the human being centers his weight halfway along the length of the foot.
b) Precise measurements have revealed that modern, good skiers weight the same point while skiing. Consequently, the bindings are mounted on the skis in such as way that the center of the boot rests over the center of the ski as defined by the manufacturer.

On the other hand, similar measurements of virtuoso racers demonstrate conclusively that they position their weight an average of 2 centimeters behind the center of the boot.

Note: 20 years ago, a prominent ski manufacturer remarked that the best skiers of that time weighted the front two fifths of the boot, or a point approximately 3½ centimeters ahead of the center of the boot. This observation reflects the forward weighting techniques that were commonplace in that particular era.

c) Boots which displace this pressure point significantly during slight flexion or extension movements of the ankle are too stiff to allow the skier to ski "with finesse" (198).

d) It's by weighting the center of the foot that the extensor muscles of the calf are best able to decelerate flexions without lateral blocking and remain ready to react (some extensor muscles are also lateral fixators (514)). Weighting the center of the foot consequently provides optimal stability while schussing.

e) A backward displacement of weight is generally accompanied by reduced ankle flexion which facilitates relaxing the rotators and lateral fixators of the foot. This relaxation enhances the ability of the skis to "float" as described in (117-a) and their flat ski pivoting (130). Furthermore, a slight backweighting improves the sliding of the skis.

f) A forward displacement of weight is usually accompanied by increased ankle flexion which increases the lateral fixation of the foot. This improves the straight running directional effect of the ski in a schuss but also increases the risk of catching an edge and the braking mentioned in (117-b). It also hinders the flat placement of the skis while sideslipping.

For optimal maneuverability of the skis, the center of pressure of the foot on the ski should be located over the straight running center of pressure.

422. Don't confuse backward banking and backweighting.

a) A skier can make all of the necessary banking movements to adjust for drop-offs, decelerations and turns without altering the center of pressure applied to the ski.

b) It's also possible, of course, to shift the weight forward or backward on the ski by banking the body in the fore-aft plane. An active, backward banking before an edge-set, for example, displaces pressure backward to the "holding center of the skis". This is a banking with displacement of weight whereas the banking described in (a) is a banking to maintain balance.

These two kinds of banking movements can be passive — produced essentially by gravity — or active — produced by muscle action (213).

423. The "modern" position.

Relative to the typical skiing stance of 10 years ago, which was the result of a long tradition of turning by for-

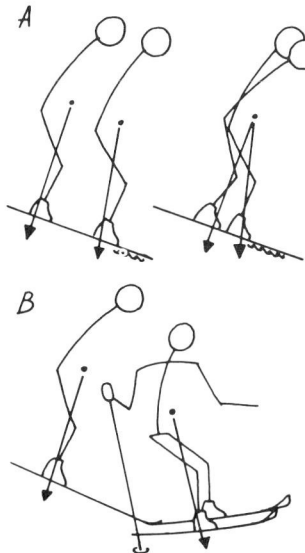

A, Banking for balance without displacement of the fore-aft distribution of weight.
B, Banking for balance with displacement of weight to obtain better ski performance.

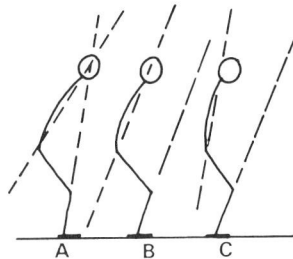

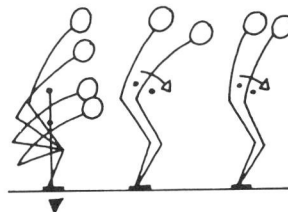

A, Modern stance; b, traditional French stance; C, traditional Austrian Ski Technique stance.
In A, flexion is possible without forward weighting and is easier to make with backweighting. In B and C, flexion is easier to make with forward weighting.

ward weighting, the modern stance is characterized by:
• A less pronounced bending of the ankles;
• A somewhat more pronounced forward tilting of the torso over the thighs. The axis of the lower legs is inclined less forward than the axis of the upper body, whether the skier is in an upright, flexed, or very low stance. These two axes were relatively parallel in the classic Allais-Gignoux French Ski Technique and the axis of the lower legs was inclined further forward than the axis of the torso in the official Austrian Ski Technique and the French Christiania Leger Technique.

Note: The skier can move his skis further forward and backward under his center of mass in the modern position than in the traditional French and Austrian Ski Technique stances described above.

424. The "modern" balanced flexion.

a) Modern flexion movements make minimal use of ankle bending and greater use of knee and hip flexing. This is as true for a voluntary flexion producing an unweighting without forward of backward weighting as it is for an involuntary, balanced flexion produced by the upward thrust from passing over a bump on an otherwise uniform slope. In this latter situation, the skier feels his knees rise in front of his body rather than underneath his body.

b) A balanced "modern" flexion is most easily started from a "modern" position (421).

c) In a modern flexion, the skier doesn't reach the limit of articulation of the ankle joint as soon as in a "traditional" flexion.

Furthermore, the "modern" flexion results in a greater amplitude of flexion before the limit of articulation of the ankle is reached.

Note: This phenomenon has resulted in the use of boots somewhat softer than those used only a few years ago, even in elite competition.

425. A forward displacement of the feet is most easily made in a modern position and should proceed:
a) The impact of the skis against bumps (215, 216-d);
b) edge checks (222) or platforms (242) (245).

426. Modern flexion, apparent back-weighting and extension.

A quick "modern" flexion over a bump (passive flexion avalement) or which lifts the skis off the snow (active flexion avalement) can momentarily give the impression of a back-weighting by forward thrust of the feet, but the extension which follows, as the skis are in the air, brings the feet back under the center of mass.

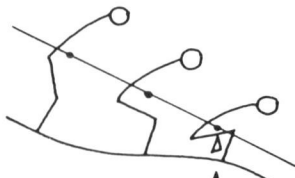

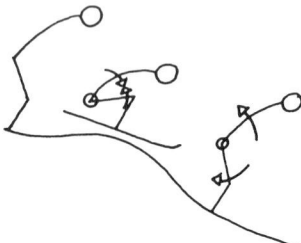

427. Various types of modern flexion with forward foot thrust.

a) Passive flexion avalement over transitions in the terrain. If the lower legs are relatively perpendicular to the snow surface, a relaxing of the thigh, buttock and lower back muscles can produce a flexion with increasing ankle bend. The feet and knees are simultaneously displaced forward (passive backward banking (213)). This is the most prevalent type of flexion, even in downhill racing.

b) If the lower leg moves behind perpendicular to the ground at the beginning of a passive flexion-avalement, the thrust of the ground simultaneously creates a passive forward displacement of the feet. This type of flexion is encountered only at intermediate speed over very sharp bumps.

c) Active flexion avalement. Muscle action is used to bend the torso forward over the thighs and displace the knees and feet forward resulting in the

Flexion with backweighting during an edge-set.
Passive flexion-avalement.
Active flexion-avalement followed by an extension and return to a balanced stance.

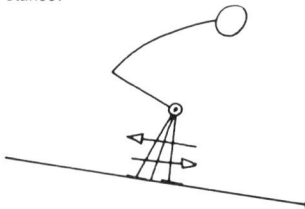

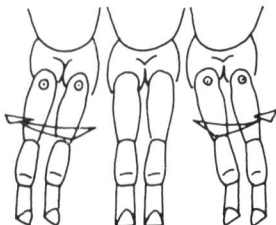

same kind of movement as described in (a) but produced by muscle effort. This kind of flexion is used during a "pre-jump" in downhill racing where the skis are lifted off the snow before arriving at the edge of a drop-off so that the racer flies closer to the slope.

This movement can be augmented by an active forward thrust of the feet, a gesture that is used by very good skiers when crossing sharp bumps at high speed.

428. The very low "surf flexion".

In the low surf position, the thighs are nearly parallel to the slope. This represents an extreme version of the "modern" position. The essential characteristics of this position are:

a) The feet can be easily displaced forward or backward.

b) Pivoting of the femur around its axis no longer produces a pivoting of the feet as it does in a higher stance. Instead, there is a pivoting of the tibia under the femur and inside the foot (ie. the calcaneum under the talus). The ski remains flat during this pivoting.

Note: (a) and (b) permit flat ski surf techniques.

c) A pivoting of the femur around its axis creates a lateral banking of the leg under the femur and can place the ski on edge without pivoting it.

Note: (a) and (c) allow "carved surf techniques" or the "surf technique with edge-set".

430. The "vertical" movements of the skier. Unweighting and compression.

431. Vertical flexion and extension.

In reality, these movements are made:

a) along an axis perpendicular to the direction of travel, provided there is no braking (211).

b) When there is a global, backward inclination of the body because of braking, or a banking of the body in the lateral plane to balance centrifugal force while turning, the flexion and ex-

tension movements are made along an axis which extends from the center of mass to the center of pressure on the skis.

Note: The skier is, of course, unaware of the direction in which he makes flexion and extension movements. The axis of movement is determined by the positioning of the feet such that the weight is properly distributed over the front and back of the feet.

432. Compressions in terrain transitions.

Mechanical Considerations

a) We can assume that the pressure that a skier exerts against his skis in a compression corresponds to the centripetal forces created to transform a straight run in the fore-aft plane into a curved sideslip. It's possible to calculate the force of compression which arises from the centrifugal force as a function of the velocity of the skier and the radius of the turn ($F = mv^2/r$). This force, which is added to the body weight, can be as high as 100 kilograms for a good athlete at 40 kilometers per hour over an arc of 9 meter radius, or 80 kilometers per hour over a 36 meter radius, or 120 kilometers per hour over an 80 meter radius.

b) If a skier makes a prolonged and deep flexion in a harsh compression, his center of mass makes an arc with a much greater radius. Therefore, the force of the compression is less.

Anatomical considerations
c) The most important of the muscle masses which are recruited to resist the forces of compression are: the muscles of the calves, the muscles in the front of the thigh (quadriceps), and the muscles of the buttocks and lower back (lumbar muscles).

d) There will simultaneously be a lateral blocking of the ankle since some extensor muscles are also lateral fixators.

e) There is also a lateral fixation of the knee during brutal compressions because of the symmetrical action of the hamstrings even though these muscles are flexors.

f) There is simultaneously a braking and a fixing action of the hips. The force that can be generated in the hips is more than doubled if there is braking with both legs than if there is braking on only one leg. Consequently the difficulty of resisting the forces of compression in an angulated position with the weight supported on only one foot. See (433).

g) The muscle force available in the lower back is greatest if the pelvis is slightly retroverted. This, perhaps, is one of the reasons for the position used by modern downhillers. Another reason might be a better distribution of mass mobilized in the opposite direction during active banking movements (213) resulting from the displacement of the hinges of flexion.

433. Compressions while crossing bumps.
a) The problems posed by crossing bumps are virtually the same as for a sudden flattening of the slope. Both situations create a sudden upward deflection of the trajectory of the skier's center of mass.

b) If, over a bump, however, the skier can use a deep flexion to avoid any change in the trajectory of his center

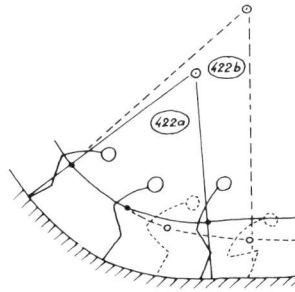

of mass, there will be no compression. Consequently, the importance of using flexion or passive flexion-avalement to "absorb" bumps and the rapid extension movements once the bumps have been crossed.

c) If a platform is made between two bumps, and if this platform is slightly delayed so that it is made against the side of the second bump, the forces of compression will be concentrated in the platform and can become too harsh.

434. Compressions during the second half of turns down the fall line.
Refer to (218) with regard to maintaining perpendicularity to the slope at the end of the turn.

Mechanical considerations
a) The steeper the slope, the shorter the radius of the turn, or the higher the speed, the greater the compression will be.

b) If a skier unweights during the first

part of a turn, and if he reweights his skis after crossing the fall line, the compression that results will be added to the compression generated in the second half of the turn.

Anatomical considerations
c) The compression at the end of the turn occurs at the moment when the angle of edge-set is maximum (178), which then requires a significant lateral fixing or blocking of the ankles.

d) The same is true for the knees. The platform at the end of the turn is essentially made on the outside leg and, consequently, the blocking of the hamstring muscles mentioned in (432-e) is more pronounced.

e) The same comment can be made for the action of the outside hip. This explains why young girls, particularly if they have a wide pelvis, have a difficult time remaining on the outside ski at the end of turns and, therefore, tend to assume a blocked position square over their skis.

435. Unweighting over a drop-off.
a) While sliding down a uniform slope, the skier resists the component of gravity which pulls him into the slope by exerting an equal force against the ground. When the slope suddenly increases in pitch (ie. a drop-off), the skier's center of mass assumes a trajectory that resembles that of a projectile, arcing downward under the influence of both gravity and any force in the opposite direction that the skier continues to exert against the ground. If the drop-off is acute, the skier won't

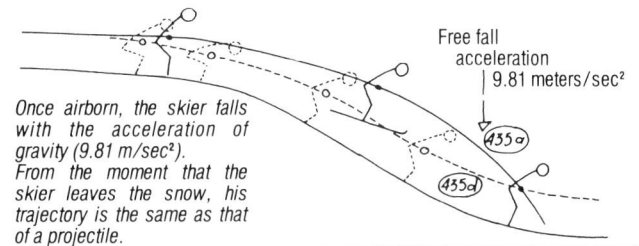

Free fall
acceleration
9.81 meters/sec²

Once airborn, the skier falls with the acceleration of gravity (9.81 m/sec²).
From the moment that the skier leaves the snow, his trajectory is the same as that of a projectile.

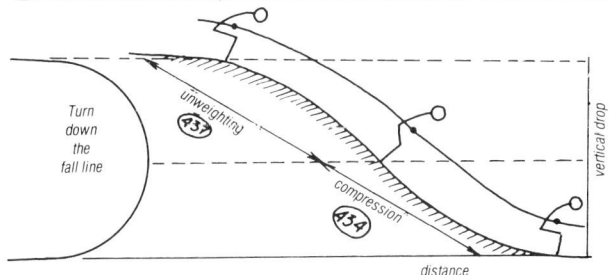

Turn down the fall line

unweighting

compression

vertical drop

distance

be able to maintain contact with the ground, even by extension, and he will become airborn. If the drop-off is less pronounced, the skier can adjust the pressure he exerts against the ground, but in any event it will be less than the pressure he exerted against the ground before the drop-off. Consequently, there is unweighting of the skis.

b) When the trajectory of the center of mass ceases to curve downward, there will be no compression provided it remains tangent to the slope. This is the ideal landing following a flight.

c) If, on the other hand, the trajectory begins to arc upward, there will be compression. This will always be the case for a landing on a flat, and explains why skiers always tend to extend their legs at the end of a flight to regain contact with the ground.

d) Both the aerial flight and the unweighting it produces when crossing a sharp drop-off (a) can be reduced by an anticipated flexion by the skier, either a passive flexion or a flexion preceeded by a pre-jump. This allows the center of mass to follow a trajectory which partially neutralizes the transition. By properly timing the pre-jump or flexion, a trajectory can be selected such that the landing is made tangent to the slope (b).

436. Unweighting after crossing bumps.

The problems posed by crossing bumps are essentially the same as those posed by skiing over drop-offs.

a) Even at intermediate speeds, an anticipated flexion seems to be necessary so that the bump doesn't launch the skier into the air.

b) When a series of bumps must be traversed, the extension that the skier makes after crossing the crest of each bump must be quick so that he is able to flex sufficiently to cross the next bump. Nevertheless, this extension must be passive so that it can adapt immediately to the terrain.

c) Linking these passive extension movements with active flexion is one of the greatest problems of skiing fast through bumpy terrain. It's essentially a problem of finding the proper rhythm.

d) When a bump launches a skier into the air, there can be a passive flexion during the flight because of the greater upward acceleration of the legs during take-off.

This upward thrust of the legs evolves from a passive flexion to more

of an active flexion or upward "retraction" of the feet (438).

437. Automatic unweighting at the beginning of short radius turns.

In a mechanical sense, the problem posed here is essentially the opposite of that posed by the compression at the end of turns.

a) I say essentially, because if there is total unweighting there can be no generation of centripetal force to produce the turn and the turn becomes merely a progressive dive down the fall line (419).

This is the case in slalom. Often an unweighting made after a platform at the beginning of a turn is added to the unweighting from the dive down the fall line, particularly in bumpy terrain or rutted slaloms.

During this unweighting, as during the unweighting produced by a bump, the skier quickly extends to prepare for the flexion and braking of the compression which will follow.

Note: This kind of extension is made against the mass of the body and, therefore, is different from most extension movements with pressure against the surface of the snow.

b) An extension made during an unweighting at the beginning of a turn, and which accompanies an inward inclination of the body, will result in a quicker application of pressure against the snow to generate the centripetal forces that will make the turn rounder.

c) This extension is generally associated with the start of hip angulation and a pivoting of the outside foot. It's important to start hip angulation at this moment. It can then be increased during the following compression phase, but if it is started too late, or is insufficient, the compression tends to nullify it resulting in a less effective holding of the edges and a weighting of both skis. This is a particularly common error among women in racing.

438. Unweighting and compression be flexion.

Mechanical concepts

a) If a skier relaxes his muscles and ceases to resist gravity, his center of mass begins a uniformly accelerated downward movement for a total (or nearly total) unweighting. The duration of the unweighting, for a given amplitude of flexion, can be calculated from the acceleration produced by gravity (9.81

meters/sec²).

b) If the skier then slows or stops this downward flexion, he must exert a force against gravity. The greater this force, the briefer will be the following compression. This resistance to the flexion is continued until the downward movement of the center of mass stops. The skier must then stand up again, but he can use the muscle tension utilized to resist the flexion to do this (see wind-up movements (410)).

c) We have been able to observe that a flexion of a given amplitude which results in a total unweighting of the feet produces an unweighting during half of the flexion and a compression during the other half. If we assume a constant braking action by the muscles, we can calculate that for a flexion that displaces the center of mass 0.30 meters, which is approximately maximum, the total unweighting lasts approximately 0.17 seconds and the compression phase another 0.17 seconds. The compression (and consequently the vertical resultant of the muscle force which opposes it) can then be considered to be equal to gravity if we assume it to be constant. The force of the compression is added to the weight of the skier. If the skier weights 70 kilograms, and is unweighted to 0 kilograms during the 0.17 second unweighting phase, he will weigh 140 kilograms during the 0.17 seconds of compression before returning to 70 kilograms.

For a 50% unweighting during a flexion of the same amplitude, the duration of the unweighting phase increases to 0.25 seconds. However, since an intermediate unweighting is generally followed by a less pronoun-

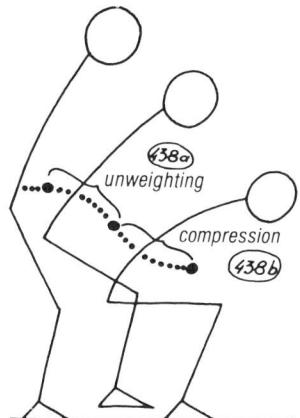

438a
unweighting

compression
438b

ced deceleration of the fall of the center of mass, the duration and amplitude of the compression phase are reduced and will remain on the same order of magnitude as before.

At 36 kilometers per hour, the unweighting occurs during a forward displacement of 1 to 2 meters; at 18 kilometers per hour (a speed typical of many recreational skiers), over a forward movment of 0.5 to 1 meters, a distance which is generally overestimated.

d) The unweighting then compression mechanism during a platform is more complex.

There is always unweighting by flexion to facilitate the banking which displaces the skis: 1) into a pivoting; and 2) forward relative to the direction of travel. The following compression is also used.

The unweighting corresponds more or less to that described above. If the banking is fairly significant, it can result in a lowering of the center of mass despite an extension of the legs.

When the skis eventually hold the snow, there will be a three-fold compression because of:

—the inertia of the skier's momentum,
—a deceleration of the dive down the fall line as the edges begin to bite the snow (260),
—and the deceleration of the vertical fall of the center of mass by flexion.

The briefer the platform, the more the skier will use the first source of compression, which can exceed 200 kilograms. It's this thrust against the skis which allows the edges to bite an icy slope.

Nevertheless, without sufficient vertical compression, there can be no lateral holding of the turn.

Anatomical and technical concepts
e) A total unweighting by flexion implies not only a total relaxing of the extensor muscles, but also the involvement of flexor muscles which "retract" the legs and feet upward toward the center of mass.

If this "retraction" is predominantly a folding of the calves under the thighs, it will result in forward weighting (eg. the *"ruade"* of the old French Ski Technique). If it is a folding of the thighs up in front of the upper body, it will result in backweighting (active flexion-avalement). In order to be performed without altering the fore-aft weight distribution, it must be a simultaneous retraction of the calves under the thighs and the thighs under

and in front of the chest.
f) Flexion by both passive and active flexion-avalement produces an unweighting by flexion combined with a backweighting by a forward displacement of the feet.

439. Compression and unweighting by extension.

Mechanical concepts
a) A skier in a slightly flexed stance resists the downward pull of gravity by using the extensor muscles of the legs to exert a constant thrust against the ground that is equivalent to the skier's body weight. If the skier exerts a greater pressure against the ground, the result will be an upward acceleration of the center of mass. When this thrust ceases, the upward displacement of the center of mass will continue until it is slowed and eventually reversed by gravity. During this deceleration, the skier is unweighted and, if the upward velocity of the center of mass produced by the thrust against the ground is sufficient (velocity = acceleration × time), the skier can be thrown into the air.

b) If the skier becomes airborn, the amplitude of the vertical displacement of the center of mass allows the duration of the unweighting to be calculated (for a uniformly decelerated movement under the effect of gravity, $D = \frac{1}{2}gt^2$).

c) If the center of mass continues to be displaced after contact with the snow is lost, the skis will be unweighted from the point of take-off until the center of mass ceases to drop after landing.

d) The compression which follows can be equal in duration and intensity to the compression at the beginning of the extension (a). On the other hand, the compression can be less intense if the deceleration of the drop of the center of mass is prolonged, but the amplitude of the flexion which decelerates the fall of the center of mass will be greater.

e) A vertical thrust equivalent to the weight of the skier (or as great as twice the weight of the skier) exerted during a vertical lifting of the center of mass by 15 centimeters can create an unweighting phase in the air of 0.17 seconds as the center of mass continues to rise after contact with the ground is lost followed by another 0.17 seconds of unweighting as the center of mass falls to its original position. The resulting compression will be as great as twice the skier's body weight and last 0.17 seconds or, be half as much and last twice as long if the amplitude of flexion is doubled to 30 centimeters.

f) The thrusts exerted against the skis by extension can only be made along an axis that is perpendicular to the surface of contact between the skis and the snow (211).

A slight thrust backward or forward at the end of an extension can create a passive forward banking (Christiania leger) or a passive backward banking (forward thrust of the feet) (213).

Anatomical and technical concepts

g) When a skier is launched into the air in a position with slight leg flexion, there is involvement of the flexor

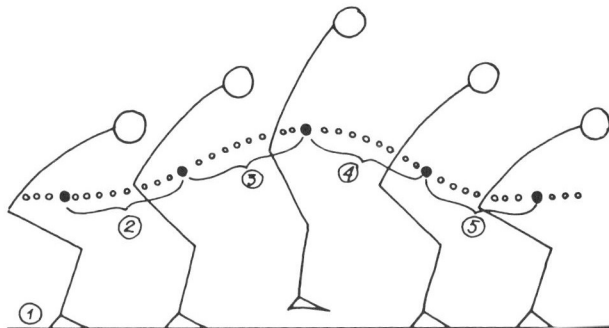

UNWEIGHTING BY EXTENSION THEN FLEXION.

(1) Low starting position. (2) Extension: a compression phase. (3) Upward flight of the center of mass: an unweighting phase. (4) Downward fall of the center of mass: an unweighting phase. (5) Decelerated flexion: a compression phase.

muscles as in (438-e).
h) The generally greater acceleration

imparted to the upper body during take-off explains why the body has a

tendency to extend passively during the flight.

500. Muscle mechanisms which pivot the skis.

These mechanisms are in addition to the passive pivoting of the skis produced by the friction between the skis and the snow (134, 135, 155 and 156).

First we will examine the anatomical and physiological possibilities for pivoting and then the

various families of pivoting mechanisms which are used in skiing.

510. Centers of pivoting and muscle rotator groups.

511. The hips
a) The spherical head of the femur and its socket in the pelvis acts like a ball and socket joint. Its range of pivoting, however, is limited by the ligaments and muscles.
b) Amplitude of pivoting: 30° to the inside, 60° to the outside. This variation in degree of rotation sometimes explains the "divergence" of the inside ski at the end of very round turns made in positions with very pronounced vissage-angulation.
c) For the same reason, angulation, which is an abduction of the outside hip, limits the range of pivoting of the hip to the inside.
This also explains why very "tight-jointed" racers with bowlegs have such a difficult time slowing down using a downhill stem or wedge.
Note: Skiers who are very bowlegged should always ski with an internal rotation of the hips to correctly position their knees so that they can flex in the fore-aft plane.
d) In the "surf" position, with the thighs virtually parallel to the ground, a pivoting of the femur around its axis no longer produces a pivoting of the feet. Instead, it causes the lower leg to bank laterally under the knee, displaces the foot laterally, and tilts the ski onto edge.
e) The rotator muscles of the hip are extremely powerful. They also act as lateral fixators of the hip and in skiing are used for both of these functions (pivoting and holding the ski on edge in angulation).

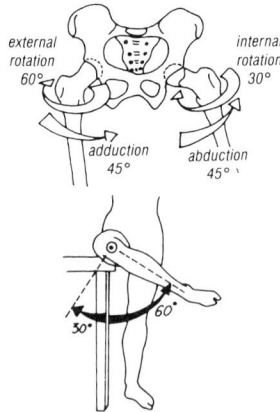

external rotation 60°

internal rotation 30°

adduction 45°

abduction 45°

60°

50°

512. Articulations of the lower back.
a) A pivoting of the 5th lumbar vertebra over the sacrum (which forms the dorsal side of the pelvic girdle) is usually associated with a pivoting of the 5th lumbar vertebra under the 4th, of the 4th under the 3rd, etc....
b) The amount of pivoting used varies greatly among individuals. In some skiers, pivoting of the lower back totally replaces pivoting of the hips, in which case the pelvis remains "square to the skis"... Among very good skiers, pivoting of the lower back is always associated with pivoting of the hips and increases when the hips have been pivoted to their limits.

c) The muscles that perform this rotation are very powerful.

513. The knee
a) The tibia can pivot passively approximately 30° under the femur to the inside and 40° to the outside when the knee is flexed 90°. This rotation is negligible when the knee is straight and the amplitude of pivoting, with the knee flexed, is less when controlled by muscle action.
b) In the flexed knee skiing stance, this pivoting is obtained by the action of the quadriceps, which fix the angle of flexion of the knee, and the hamhamstrings and internal and external rotators (The top ski champions have extraordinary development of these muscle groups).
c) The rotator muscles also act as lateral fixators to transmit the pivoting of the hip or to hold the skis on edge.

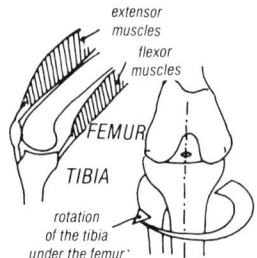

extensor muscles

flexor muscles

FEMUR

TIBIA

rotation of the tibia under the femur

Note: Insufficient muscle strength can make the "seated" stance and "surf" leg action potentially damaging for the knee joint.

514. The foot

a) Articulation of the tibial-tarsal (ankle) joint doesn't allow pivoting movements. However, there are two possibilities for pivoting within the bony assemblage of the foot. First, around the axis of the tibia (adduction and abduction of the foot) and also rotation of the foot around its axis (pronation and supination). Pronation of the outside foot, for example, corresponds to a banking of the ski onto edge and supination results in a flattening of the ski.

These two types of pivoting are associated in such a way that a pivoting of the outside foot in a turn will keep the skis flat despite a slight lateral inclination of the tibia. Likewise, pivoting of the inside foot through the turn results in a flattening of the inside ski because of both mechanisms acting in the opposite direction.

b) A pivoting of the foot in skiing is generally associated with a pivoting of the knee (513).

c) The muscles which provoke this pivoting have limited power. They are fairly effective if the skis are flat and inefficient if the skis are held on edge because they then act as lateral fixators.

d) When these muscle groups act as lateral fixators, they produce a slight pivoting of the feet to the outside. If the skis are in contact with the snow, the feet don't pivot. Instead, the knees "angulate" to the inside of the turn or up the hill in a traverse.

e) These pivoting movements of the feet create slight fore and aft displacements of the ankle in the boots, consequently the necessity of fitting boots so that they won't block the foot (194).

515. Vertebral articulations

a) The back can be pivoted in the same direction as the feet, hips and lower back; for example in a global rotation. The back can also rotate in the opposite direction to enhance the counter-rotation of vissage.

b) Tall skiers, in particular, can split the rotation of the back, with part of the back pivoted as in (a) to enhance the counter-rotation of vissage, yet

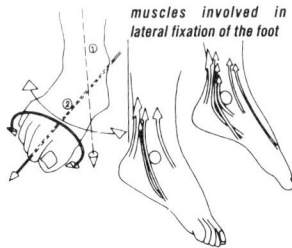

muscles involved in lateral fixation of the foot

(1) and (2) represent the two axes of pivoting mentioned in (514-a), (3) the lateral fixation of the ankle through muscle action.

with the shoulders and head twisted in the opposite direction to face the skis (ie. vissage without displacement of the shoulders).

c) Pivoting the shoulders in the horizontal plane can enhance the pivoting inertia of the spinal column. During vissage, for example, this can increase the counter-rotation of the upper body. On the other hand, it can compensate for pivoting of the lower back; for example to keep the shoulders square to the skis despite vissage or even hip rotation.

516. Pivoting of the hip and lower back and hip angulation.

a) A skier who uses leg action in a slightly flexed stance to pivot his skis appears to be in a position of "hip angulation" when seen from along the axis of the skis (ie. the hip appears to be flexed laterally).

The same is true if the skier pivots his torso to face down the fall line (anticipation) without pivoting his skis.

b) The skier can combine these two gestures with angulation by accentuating the abduction of the outside hip joint and the adduction of the inside hip joint and by readjusting balance by displacing the upper body laterally to the outside.

In both (a) and (b), the tibia, femur and foot remain in the same plane and their ability to flex in this plane is not disturbed.

517. Knee angulation: pivoting of the hips and feet in opposite directions.

If the legs are pivoted in a flexed position, and if the skis, held against the snow, pivot less than the lower legs, the foot and hip will pivot in opposite directions. This pivoting of the foot becomes automatically associated with the edge-set, as we have seen in (514-a). The resulting double pivoting is called *knee angulation.*

The femur, tibia, foot and ski are no longer in the same plane. Every flexion, therefore, produces a significant and dangerous straining of the lateral ligaments of the knee.

518. Pivoting of the feet with displacement of the knees to the outside, pivoting of the upper leg and lateral banking of the lower leg: see surf pivoting (534 and 535).

519. Pivoting of the hips and lower back and hip projection.

a) A global rotation of the body down the fall line which isn't followed by the skis gives the appearance, when viewed from along the axis of the skis, of a displacement of the hips to the outside of the turn. This silhouette can result either from the body being thrown into rotation (522-c) or into anticipation rapidly followed by deangulation (531-c) or a combination of these movements.

b) Hip projection can be accentuated even more by the action of the hips and lower back in the lateral plane (see hip angulation (516-b)), particularly in deep snow (522-d).

295

520. Initiating turns by rotation.

521. The wind-up then transmission of the recoil to the skis.

a) 1st phase: Part of the body is rotated, thereby generating a force in the opposite direction which is applied against the ground and requires that the skis be held firmly in place. The energy expended by the rotator muscles in producing this movement is stored in their antagonists and is a function of the body mass that has been rotated, the speed of rotation and the distance between the rotated body masses and the center of pivoting (the effect of rotating an outstretched arm can be considerable despite its relatively small mass). In the old French Allais-Gignoux Ski Technique (1937), only the upper body was rotated. In the Christiania Leger Technique (1957), virtually the entire body was rotated.

2nd phase, pivoting of the skis: The part of the body that has been rotated is attached to the lower limbs (and eventually the skis) by muscles that are antagonists to those which started the rotation. These muscles progressively decelerate the rotation and can then smoothly reverse the rotation to vissage. Many technicians have mistakenly dissociated vissage techniques and rotation techniques when, in reality, they are perfectly compatible

522. Forms of rotation used today.

a) *Minimal form:* A simple rotation by a symmetrical relaxing of the extensor muscles associated with an inclination forward and to the inside of the turn can add a mild motor effect to the passive pivoting of the skis ("Christiania leger" or "circular projection" of the French National Ski School).

b) *Maximal form:* A rapid rotation of all limbs down the fall line preceeded by a preparatory rotation up the hill to make a hopped turn.

c) *Thrown anticipation:* A global pivoting of the body down the fall line from a slightly flexed position followed by a platform with pole plant and a slightly prolonged, global pivoting down the fall line during the unweighting.

d) *"Hip projection" in deep snow.*

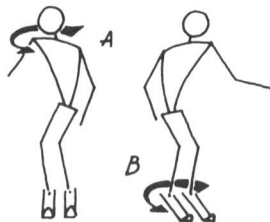

A, wind-up of rotation. B, transfer to the skis.

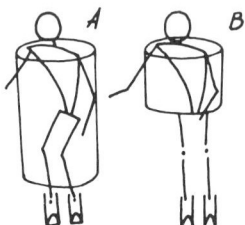

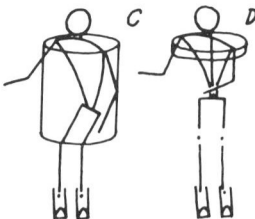

The body mass thrown into rotation can be maximal (in A, the entire body less the feet) or minimal (in D, only the arms are rotated) or involve only the torso (b). A rotation of the torso and pelvis (c) is often referred to as "hip projection".

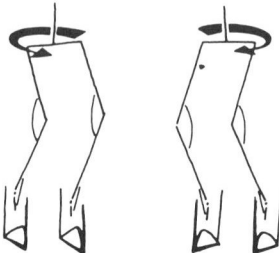

Rotation facilitates the change of edges as the ankles are increasingly flexed.

Similar to (c) but with an accentuated displacement of the hip to the outside of the turn (519-b) which allows the skis to be kept flat despite the obligatory global inclination of the body to the inside.

523. Thrown rotation, edge change and unweighting.

a) The edge change that is produced at the start of a turn where the entire body is thrown into rotation is facilitated by a flexing of the ankles in a stance that is as upright as possible in the other joints (the lower leg is inclined laterally following the pivoting).

b) The edge change is linked to a passive inclination of the body to the inside of the turn.

c) It's easiest to set the platform during the first phase with a vertical thrust of the legs.

The relatively slow rhythm of this manuever dictates that the associated vertical thrust will be slow, thereby giving the flexion and extension of Christiania Leger its characteristically slow rhythm.

d) The relationship between the counter-turn and thrown rotation is more a function of the vertical support of the platform than the pivoting mechanism.

524. Thrown rotation and wedeln.

a) On hard or well packed snow, the inertia of the rotation movement and the difficulty in quickly regaining pressure on the edges makes the linking of short turns into a wedeln rhythm difficult.

Note: Since the rotation is generally associated with forward weighting, the inertia of these two movements is added and a rapid wedeln is made even more difficult.

b) On the contrary, hip projection in deep snow (522-d) is very effective. It allows the skis to be kept flat and uses the inertia of the rotation movement to push the skis laterally through the snow. Deangulation is immediately linked to this rotation followed by another anticipation. The relatively slow starting rhythm of a thrown rotation is also beneficial for turns in deep snow.

530. Initiating turns by "vissage".

531. The "action-reaction" mechanism.

a) *Principle:* The skis and lower body are pivoted by rotator muscles which attach to the upper body. The upper body is pivoted in the opposite direction resulting in counter-rotation.

b) *Amplitude of rotation and counter-rotation:*

—The amplitude of these two movements is inversely proportional to the inertia of the two displaced body segments or, more precisely, the inertia of momentum (the product of the mass and its distance to the axis of pivoting).

—The inertia of the lower body mass includes the skis and, by way of simplification, can include the ski-snow friction.

—The inertia of the upper body mass includes the torso, arms and, for simplification, any force eventually exerted on a planted ski pole.

—The inertia of any previous pivoting movement of the upper body down the fall line (thrown anticipation or a passive pivoting of the chest supported by a pole plant) is added that mentioned above.

c) *positions of the body at the start and finish of the movement:*

—Vissage can start with the body square to the skis,

—Or start from an anticipated position and return to a normal position. This is a *"vissage recoil"*.

—Or start in an anticipated position and return to a position with the body twisted in the opposite direction.

—If the anticipation and vissage recoil are made dynamically, it is referred to as a *"Vissage wind-up"*.

—If the upper body is stabilized by a pole plant during vissage, the movement can be made around a more or less fixed point which becomes the primary support. This is true for both the vissage recoil and the wind-up.

—An anticipation that is sufficiently prolonged to become a rotation of the upper body into the turn is referred to as a thrown anticipation or thrown rotation with vissage recoil.

—If the skis are prevented from pivoting by being held on their uphill edges, vissage can be very pronoun-

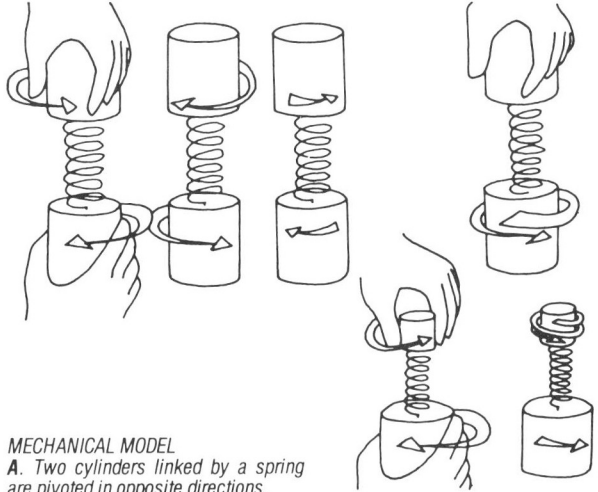

MECHANICAL MODEL
A. *Two cylinders linked by a spring are pivoted in opposite directions.*
B. *When released, the two cylinders pivot back until eventually stopped by the spring.*
C. *The spring, wound up during B, starts a recoil.*
D. *If only one cylinder is released,* it will pivot twice as fast as in B.
E & F. *If one of the cylinders is twice as heavy as the other, it will pivot only half as far.*

ced in the upper body and have no effect on the lower body (eg. falls in slalom with exaggerated vissage).

d) *Speed and force of movement.*

Since vissage is activated by muscular effort, it can be instantaneous (2 to 3 tenths of a second for the wind-up, 1 to 2 tenths for the recoil) or prolonged. The degree of pivoting produced is limited by:

—The inertia of the upper body.

—The amount of support available from the pole plant.

e) *Wind-up vissage over a platform with pole plant.*

—Vissage with a pivoting of the skis up the hill (counter-turn) and a twisting of the chest down the fall line (anticipation) leading to an edge-set with a pole plant permits (because of the support available from the pole plant) a tensing of the rotator muscles which slow this movement followed by a recoil of the lower body pivoting in the opposite direction during the unweighted phase. There is a platform followed by a recoil of the skis.

The pole plant serves: 1) to accelerate the anticipation of the torso;

2) to delay or prevent an unwinding of the upper body in the opposite direction. For these two reasons, a more significant pivoting of the lower body is created. The support lasts 1 to 3 tenths of a second.

The recoil of the skis is particularly noticable and effective if it is made while the skis are unweighted. An unweighting by rebound is necessary because even the compression of a simple initiation by extension can neutralize the vissage recoil.

f) *Wind-up vissage and counter-turns:*

The vissage wind-up causes the sksi to pivot up the hill and this effect can be in addition to any passive pivoting.

—A counter-turn with a platform can conclude this pivoting and initiate a pivoting down the fall line.

—Even if a platform isn't used, the recoil of the vissage will halt the uphill pivoting and start the skis pivoting down the fall line.

—When the counter-turn uses the directional effect of the skis more than the braking produced by their pivoting, refer to (g).

g) *Slow motion wind-up vissage.*

The slow motion wind-up vissage is made either without a platform or during a prolonged platform (particularly true for an 'S' counter-turn or a turn with passive avalement or a turn with "windshield wiper" pivoting).

—The wind-up phase is a pivoting of the upper body down the fall line provoked by a forward thrust of the skis and the support of a solid pole plant. The rotator muscles are stretched.

—The return is not so much a recoil as it is a muscular response to the stretching produced during the wind-up phase. The contraction generally has 2 objectives: 1) to slow or reverse the movement which tends to increase the distance between the mass of the body and the support of the skis on the snow for balance; 2) to pivot the skis, which will then permit them to aid in the rebalancing.

Note: The pole plant is indispensable to the backweighting of the upper body and is also used to assure balance during the pivoting.

532. Vissaage angulation of the hips.

a) The center of pivoting resides essentially in the hips. Pivoting of the lower back is only of secondary importance. The pelvis doesn't pivot with the thighs.

b) We have seen that vissage of the hips can appear to be angulation (516-a).

c) Angulation can accompany vissage at the beginning of turns down the fall line. It adds an outward lateral thrust to the pivoting exerted on the skis. This lateral thrust facilitates a flat ski edge change of a lateral displacement of the skis in the air at the beginning of the turn (lateral banking (273-c)).

d) Vissage uses powerful muscle groups in the hips. In all sports, movements that require a great deal of power start in the pelvis and are then diffused upward or downward.

e) Vissage hip angulation typically provokes a global pivoting of the lower body, with lateral blocking of the knees and ankles.

f) The change in inclination of the lower legs eventually combined with (b) promotes the change of edges, especially in a position with very pronounced ankle flexion.

g) A lateral relaxing of the ankles permits a flat ski displacement which can be combined with the vissage of

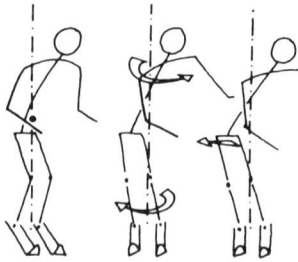

Because the upper body is flexed over the lower body, vissage looks like angulation. An actual angulation can be combined with vissage.

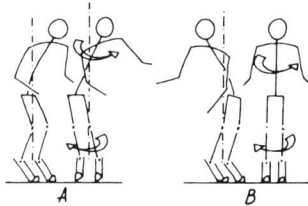

A: Vissage wind-up. B: Vissage recoil. C: Complete vissage. D: Complete vissage with the upper body supported by a pole plant.

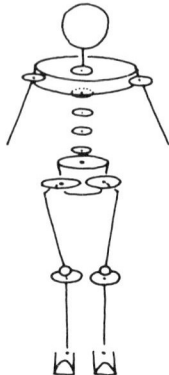

THE DIFFERENT LEVELS WHERE VISSAGE CAN BE EFFECTED.

the hips but requires a voluntary effort. It is most easily obtained in a position with the ankles slightly flexed (the "modern" position).

533. Different forms of vissage angulation of the hips.
Progressive vissage at the beginning of "controlled" turns.

a) A wind-up vissage with change of support foot is used if the turn that follows is to be carved. This can be accomplished with an extension and spreading of the uphill ski if a very progressive weight change is desired. Or, a flexion in a wide or semi-wide stance can be used if immediate holding of the outside ski is needed.

b) Vissage recoil with both skis weighted can be used if the turn is to be controlled with flat skis. This generally implies anticipation then extension and a progressive vissage recoil during the following unweighting and in a narrow stance.

c) The same mechanism can be used in deep snow following a "thrown" anticipation (or "thrown rotation" or "hip projection"). The rotation is generally combined with an extension in a backweighted position in a narrow stance.

Rapid forms

d) Using vissage without pole plant for short, round and quick turns (for example in slalom on easy or moderate slopes). The pole plant acts as a balancing aid. Generally the turns are started with flexion and controlled by the edges of the skis. The chest is bent forward and the arms are outstretched to prevent any significant counter-rotation of the chest.

e) Wind-up vissage with edge-sets and pole plants is used to prevent the chest from pivoting (for braked turns such as check wedeln or slalom on steep slopes) or to prevent sideslipping and allow the next turn to be started earlier. Vissage angulation is the technique that best uses the wind-up mechanism and is necessary for good wedeln.

In a narrow or wide stance.

f) Many skiers can more easily execute vissage angulation of the hips in a narrow stance. This explains why many skiers abandon wide stances and foot steering mechanisms.

—The pivoting mechanism in a narrow stance tends to be situated both in the hips and the spinal column and the hips pivot with the skis more often than in a wide stance.

—Having both feet weighted equally and positioned close to the center of pivoting on the snow seems to give the pelvis and legs a certain unity.

The counter rotation of the upper body then tends to be more significant.

—This "unity" of the pelvis and legs seems to lend a certain elegance and efficiency to skiing in deep snow but is inconsistent with the lateral balance adjustment capability and rapid pivoting that are necessary to handle all terrain and competition situations.

g) Vissage-angulation in a wide stance seems as if it should be made more in the legs, but appears to be made more in the hips.

—The lateral distance between the pivoting axes of each of the legs and the vertical axis of pivoting of the torso seems to account for the lesser counter rotation reaction of the upper body and the scissoring of the feet.

—Vissage in a wide stance permits better edging by knee angulation following the pivoting of the outside leg into the turn (517). This is often used in competition.

—Vissage in a wide stance is often combined with a change of support foot (See "steering of the outside foot" (556)).

h) *Delayed vissage-recoil.*

A delayed vissage-recoil is used in 'S' counter-turns, turns with passive avalement, and turns with "windshield wiper pivoting" (531-g).

534. vissage-angulation of the knee and foot: "flat ski surfing".

a) The two centers of pivoting are the knee and foot. The skier must assume a very low position with the knees flexed (428). The upper body mass, in this instance, is taken to include both the torso and the thighs. Thus, the mass that is displaces is smaller which results in faster displacements of the feet and skis and a lesser reaction of the upper body.

b) For anatomical reasons (514-a), the pivoting that is produced is made with flat skis, even if the lower legs and the axis of the body are inclined slightly to the inside of the turn to balance centrifugal force.

c) Like vissage-angulation of the hips, surf vissage-angulation is very easily made with wind-up movements (eg. counter-turns, wedeln).

535. Different forms of flat ski surf pivoting.

a) Turns in a wide stance with flat

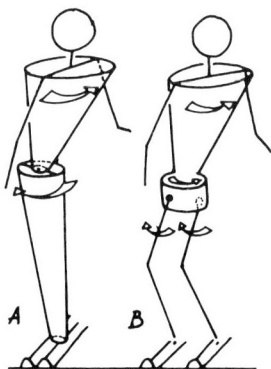

A. In a narrow stance, with the feet blocked against each other, the center of pivoting is located almost exclusively in the lower back.

B. In a wide stance, vissage in each of the two hip joints is independent.

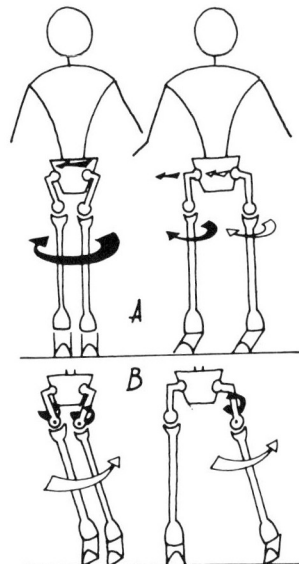

SURF POSITION.

A. Pivoting of the tibia under the femur in a wide stance, just as in a narrow stance, results in only a slight lateral displacement of the pelvis.

B. Pivoting of the femur around its axis doesn't result in a pivoting of the tibia, but a lateral displacement of the foot as the tibia "swings" underneath the femur.

skis, and particularly flat ski surf wedeln or easy slalom turns on soft snow with linked wind-up movements. Because both feet are spread laterally away from the pivoting axis of the upper body, counter-rotation of the upper body is substantially reduced and can even be eliminated entirely, even though this phenomenon is difficult to explain in mechanical terms. This kind of pivoting can accompany a change of support foot.

b) In a narrow stance with flat ski turns, but particularly in wedeln by linked wind-up movements. The counter-pivoting of the upper body is somewhat more pronounced but remains minimal even without a pole plant provided the chest is banked forward and the arms are extended.

c) In deep snow: a narrow stance and forward thrust of the feet during turns or wedeln. The pivoting produces a braking. Therefore, the feet are pushed forward just before the pivoting. This is followed by a combination of braking and a slight vertical platform from a backweighted position then an anticipation into the next turn.

d) Flat skis and carved tail-pressure in counter-turns or wedeln. A slight forward thrust of the feet during flat ski surf pivoting results in tail-pressure. A carved directional effect then allows the skier to reestablish his balance and start into the next turn.

Amplification of surf pivoting by passive lateral displacement of the knees.

—When seen from along the axis of the skis, a simple pivoting of the feet makes the knees appear to move to the outside of the turn.

—This outward displacement of the knees can be far more pronounced if the skier lets his knees follow the movement of the skis along their axis after they have been pivoted as described above during a wedeln. The thighs are displaced laterally in front of the body in a passive manner until the pivoting in the opposite direction is begun. This is the case in certain very round surf wedeln or counter-turns.

e) *Amplification of surf pivoting by active lateral displacement of the knees.*

The lateral displacement of the knees can also be active which corresponds to a voluntary acceleration of the sliding of the skis.

There is a simultaneous forward thrust of the feet.
—This active displacement of the knees can be combined with a platform made by a mild flexion-extension (eg. surf wedeln with platform in deep snow).
—The active lateral displacement of the knees, if combined with a banking of the skis onto edge, is no longer a flat ski surf pivoting, but the following pivoting can be a flat ski surf pivoting (eg. surf wedeln or surf counter-turn with carved platform).

536. Surf carving vissage-angulation.

a) The pivoting mechanism is the same as in flat ski surf pivoting (534-a) but a pivoting of the femurs around their axes provokes a lateral displacement of the tibias under the knees and a banking of the skis onto edge. Since there is no lateral fixation of the foot, the pivoting is located exclusively in the knees and is of a very small amplitude.

b) The carved pivoting immediately generates centrifugal force which is compensated for by a lateral inclination produced by the lateral displacement of the skis.

c) A simple pivoting of the femur around its axis can produce a lateral displacement of the skis with little or no pivoting of the feet (eg. long, easy turns at high speed).

537. Different forms of surf carving.

a) *"Surf carving on one ski in a wide stance"*. A carved pivoting of one ski gives the appearance of an inward push of the knee. The centrifugal force generated instantaneously results in a balancing over this ski and a carved directional effect. The other ski can then be displaced laterally and sometimes is placed down in a slightly convergent position to produce a carving effect in the opposite direction (eg. carved surf wedeln with a change of support foot such as is often used in easy slalom gates).

Before each carving, the outside ski is pushed forward (forward thrust of the foot) to center the weight over the holding center of the ski and improve balance at the beginning of the turn.

b) *Surf with carved platforms on one ski*. A brief flexion-extension movement (of a rebound type) is combined with the carving. The forward placement of the outside foot just before the platform is even more

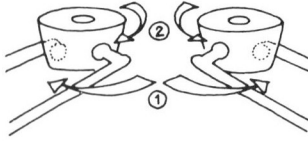

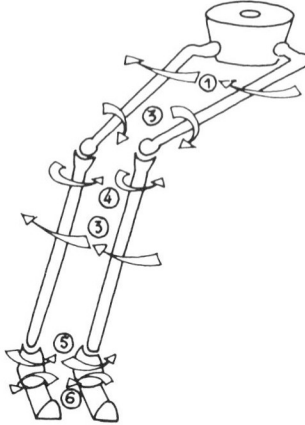

pronounced than in (a).

c) *Carved surf in a narrow stance*. This movement is essentially the same as that described in (b) except that both legs are pushed forward before the platform and both skis can be weighted (both skis are weighted in particular by skiers with bowed legs or tibias, or skiers who use excessive inclination to the inside of the turn).

d) *Surf in an upright stance*. The absolutely latest development in slalom technique appears to be a surf type leg action made in a semi-flexed stance, with the feet extended very far forward and the lower back characteristically round (retroversion of the pelvis).

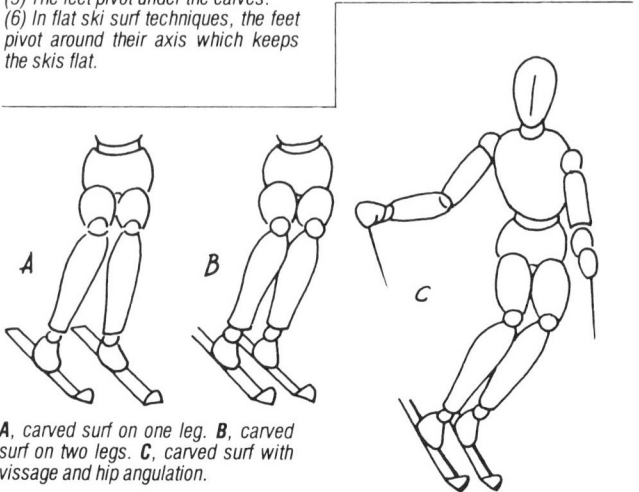

THE 6 ARTICULATIONS OF THE SURF TECHNIQUE IN A VERY LOW STANCE.
(1) As seen from above, the knees are displaced in an arc around the axis of the body. When viewed from the front, their displacement appears to be lateral (abduction-adduction).
(2) The hips accompany the pivoting of the knees in (1).
(3) A pivoting of the femurs around their axes produces a lateral banking of the tibias.
(4) The tibias pivot under the femurs.
(5) The feet pivot under the calves.
(6) In flat ski surf techniques, the feet pivot around their axis which keeps the skis flat.

A, carved surf on one leg. B, carved surf on two legs. C, carved surf with vissage and hip angulation.

540. Initiating turns by avalement.

541. Mechanism
a) The movement which I christened "avalement" in my new book *"How To Ski The New French Way"* (1967) consists of 3 elements:
—A rapid flexion localized in the hips and lower back (the legs are lifted up in front of the chest) which unweights the skis;
—A forward displacement which results from the movement above and sometimes also by a forward extension of the lower legs;
—A vissage-recoil with a general "surf" pivoting of the feet. This vissage-recoil results either from a previous anticipation or an anticipation that is created following a pole plant and the forward displacement of the skier during the first moments of the turn.
b) Avalement is automatically followed by an extension which also consists of three elements:
—A delay of the pivoting ("surf" vissage),
—An extension which brings the feet back under the center of mass (active banking (426)),
—A prolonged banking movement begun just before the avalement (passive banking), particularly when the avalement turn is made over a bump or drop-off, or during a short turn on a steep slope (maintaining perpendicularity to the slope (216b, 217, 218).

542. Possible uses of the complete avalement movement.
a) To turn over a bump without slamming into the front of it.
b) To negotiate very rutted slalom courses (mechanically the same as (a)).
c) To ski deep powder:
—The flexion and forward thrust of the feet make the skis float to the surface;
—The recoil from vissage made in a surf position pivots the skis on the surface of the snow;
—The extension which follows permits contact with the snow to be regained more aggressively.
d) Avalement during the compression of the short traverses between round, short radius turns linked down the fall line corresponds to an avalement of an imaginary bump which simulates the slope followed by the skier's feet (218).

ELEMENTS CONSTITUTING AVALEMENT.
(1) and (1 bis), flexing the legs/pelvis to create a jackknife movement with unweighting or even a lifting of the skis. (2) and (2 bis), unwinding of vissage. (3), eventually an extension of the legs forward under the thighs. (4), eventually a surf pivoting of the feet and lower legs under the thighs.
An extension with a return of the feet backward under the body is an automatic reaction to the "unwinding" of avalement.

543. Using the elements of avalement during various movements.
a) A flexion with a forward displacement of the feet is called *"active flexion-avalement"*. The same flexion, but passive, is called *"passive flexion-avalement"* because of its resemblance to active flexion-avalement but without the muscle driven avalement mechanism.
b) The linking of "passive flexion-avalement" and a pivoting of the skis by vissage has, for the same reason, been called "passive avalement" or "braquage avalement" in the official French Ski Technique.
c) The "forward thrust of the feet" without flexion, or even during a platform, comes from avalement but has become an individualized technical element.
d) The "windshield wiper pivoting" of the skis by flexion, backweighting and forward thrust of the feet before pivoting in a backweighted position is also derived from avalement but is characterized by a genuine backward banking of the upper body and an obligatory braking after the skis have been pivoted to reestablish balance.
e) The forward thrust of the outside foot following an extension or lateral projection is also related to avalement.
Note: The movement adopted by some national teaching methods that uses a flexing of the legs then a pivoting of the skis by leg extension is not a genuine derivative of avalement.

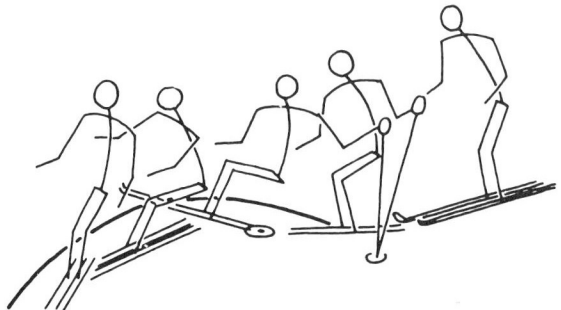

SLOW AVALEMENT AND WINDSHIELD WIPER PIVOTING.
A, 1st phase: backward banking with pole plant and anticipation.
B, 2nd phase: avalement (see above)
with pivoting around the pole plant on the tails of the skis.
C, 3rd phase: Extension of the legs with pressure against the snow to reestablish balance.

550. Initiating turns by braquage.

551. The two phases of braquage.

The foot steered "hockey stop" started from a straight run is an elementary gesture that can be mastered by 30 to 50% of all athletic beginners after only half a day of skiing. This movement is, however, very difficult to analyze.

Even though the foot steering movement may be very brief, one must distinguish 2 successive phases.

a) Starting in a straight run with pressure exerted against the inside edge of the tip of the inside ski and the inside edge of the tail of the outside ski, the skier applies a quick, almost brutal, muscle action to pivot both skis. The skis pivot quickly across the fall line.

—The muscle force used to produce this initial movement is substantial. You can convince yourself of this by trying to hold a subjects boots in place when he attepts to pivot them by braquage in a wide stance.

—There is a simultaneous pivoting action of the hips, knees and feet.

b) As soon as the movement is started, two things seem to occur simultaneously:

—The pivoting is amplified by friction between the skis and the snow (passive pivoting (155)). The skier pivots with the skis.

—By balancing reflexes that are perhaps instinctive, the skier shifts most of his weight to the downhill ski to avoid banking down the fall line. The support foot is then subconsciously pushed along the direction of travel which seens to neutralize any tendency of the skis to start scissoring (a).

Furthermore, the braking of the outside ski diminishes the spreading of the skis started in (a).

Note: I have not mentioned a counter-rotation of the upper body in (a) because it is extremely limited in practice. This is one of the essential features of braquage.

552. Braquage and edge change.

Braquage involves a simultaneous pivoting of both legs under the pelvis. It seems to be easier to execute with pronounced ankle flexion.

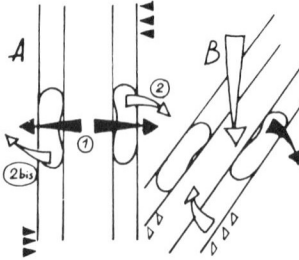

BRAQUAGE MECHANISM.
A*. Initial impulse. (1) a lateral thrust is exerted on both skis. (2) and (2 bis), a pivoting movement is generated from both hips with the knees and feet held rigid to transmit the movement to the skis. (1) and (2) are linked by a lateral and forward thrust of the inside foot and the heel of the outside foot.*
B*. Continuation of pivoting. The pivoting is continued essentially in a passive manner by the forces of friction between the downhill ski and the snow. The thrust on the heel of the outside foot mentioned in (a) is prolonged and the outside ski is pushed forward as a balance reflex.*

In this position, the pivoting of the leg provokes an immediate lateral inclination of the tibia and a banking of the ski onto edge.

a) When initiated from a straught run down the fall line, the edges of the skis find the necessary support (551-a). This makes braquage easier to perform.

b) When initiated from a traverse, even on flat slopes, the proper distribution of pressure on the edges necessary to pivot the skis by braquage is difficult to find because the knees must be displaced so much further.

553. Braquage, change of support foot and linked braquage.

In the hockey stop, there is an automatic shift of weight from both feet to the outside foot. If several braquage movements are linked, there is a shift of weight from one foot to the other with each turn. Linked braquage appears to involve more a successive change of support foot than a wind-up foot steering movement.

A. The initial impulse of braquage mobilizes only the lower body with little or no perceptible reaction from the upper body.
B. During the following passive pivoting phase, the entire body follows the pivoting of the skis. Balancing reflexes cause the skier to angulate.

554. Braquage and vissage.

During the passive pivoting phase (541-b), the skier can use vissage to accelerate the pivoting. There is then a linking:
—of the initial impulse of braquage,
—to a continuation by vissage.

Depending on the technical refinement of the skier, the role of the braquage can decrease and that of the vissage increase until the braquage disappears.

555. Braquage flexion and extension.

a) A flexion can assist braquage during the compression phase which decelerates it. During unweighting, however, the support from the ground isn't clearly felt and, therefore, beginners have a more difficult time trying to learn to execute the initial impulse of braquage.

b) When braquage is linked in a

Braquage automatically creates an edge change.

rhythmic manner to form a rudimentary wedeln, the pivoting of the skis gradually starts to take place at the uppermost point of the extension while the skis are unweighted

resulting in a progressive evolution of braquage into vissage as in (554).

556. Braquage of one leg.

a) According to our analysis of the braquage mechanism, there can be no such thing as a braquage of one leg.

When a skier progressively evolves a linked braquage down the fall line to a linked pivoting with lifting of one ski (often improperly referred to as a "braquage of one leg"), two things can happen:

b) There can be an extension of the support leg with a passive pivoting of the ski (there is a holding of the tip of the ski and a lateral thrust of the center of the ski). This is accentuated by a stiffening of the support foot and forward weighting.

c) There can be a vissage of the support leg and an active pivoting of the ski by a progressive change from the braquage foot steering mechanism to a vissage (554). Mechanisms (b) and (c) can be overlapped.

560. Controlling the pivoting in turns. "Piloting".

561. Controlled turns and piloted turns.

We have studied the passive pivoting of the skis (134 and 155), the flat ski curved directional effects (136), braking sideslipping (159) and carving (123).

We have also studied the balancing mechanisms used during turns and other curved movements (207 and 231).

a) A turn is called "controlled" when the skier makes maximum use of the flat or carved directional effects of the skis. This control implies a constant regulation of the angle of edge-set and the fore-aft distribution of pressure which moderate the directional effect.

b) We reserve the term "piloting" of the turn for supplementary adjustments by actively controlling the pivoting of the skis which permit the skier to make precisely the turn which he wants to make.

562. Adjusting the pivoting of the skis.

These adjustments are made in three ways:
a) Braking or accelerating the passive pivoting of the skis by blocking the lower body and feet.
b) Active pivoting can be added to passive pivoting.

c) Slight active counter-pivoting efforts can be used to decelerate passive pivoting.

563. The mechanisms of flat ski adjustments.

These are very fine and very quick adjustments that are localized as close to the skis as possible.
a) Pivoting and counter-pivoting exclusively by movements of the feet (514).
b) Pivoting and counter-pivoting by movements of the tibia under the femur (513). "Flat ski surf" adjustments.

564. Controlled carving on the edges.

a) Idem above. Edge-set and pivoting are always more or less associated in the feet.
b) The same is true in the knee. The adjustment of knee angulation can simultaneously effect the angle of edge-set and pivoting.
c) Fine adjustments require double movements of both the foot and knee. This implies a little bit of movement of the foot in the boot (514-e). If the boot fits too snuggly, the piloting of the skis will be without finesse. In this case, one senses a greater effectiveness from lateral movements of

the knee and the skier can be led to believe that piloting is improved.

The surf position, with greater independence of the pivoting actions of the foot and hip, allows better piloting of the skis.

565. Piloting while weighting both skis, the inside ski, or the outside ski.

a) With flat skis, piloting seems to be facilitated if both skis are weighted.
b) In carving, piloting is more effective with the weight on the outside ski for two reasons:
—Balance is improved (there is a balance reserve to the inside).
—The mobility of the outside foot is greater.

When weighting the outside edge of the inside ski, the bony structures of the tibial-tarsal articulations and of the tarsus transmit pressure more directly but also harsher and less easily adjusted. But when the inside edge of the outside ski is weighted, the arch and the articular mobility of the foot permit a finer regulation.

Note: When the skis were unable to hold on very hard snow and steep slopes, the top racers used to control their turns by weighting their inside skis at the end of the turn. This is no longer true today.